CLAY AND GLAZES FOR THE POTTER

Clay and Glazes for the Potter

Daniel Rhodes

Revised and expanded by Robin Hopper

Third Edition

Published by

krause publications
700 E. State St.
Iola, WI 54990-0001
Telephone 715-445-2214
www.krause.com

Please call or write for our free catalog. Our toll-free number to place an order or obtain a free catalog is 800-258-0929 or please use our regular business telephone 715-445-2214 for editorial comment and further information.

Library of Congress Catalog Number: 00-104633

ISBN: 0-87341-863-8

Printed in the United States of America

Front cover photos (clockwise):
- Giant Head, Leros, stoneware, 1988. Photo by Jeff Guido. Courtesy of the Estate of Daniel Rhodes.
- Japan, Stem Bowl, stoneware ca. 1810. H: 14.5cm. Courtesy of the Art Gallery of Greater Victoria, Fred and Isabel Pollard Collection. 62.116. Photo by Janet Dwyer.
- Japan, Nabeshima plate, ca.1803, porcelain with overglaze enamels. Courtesy of the Art Gallery of Greater Victoria, Fred and Isabel Pollard Collection. 66.71. Photo by Janet Dwyer.
- Persia, Wine Ewer. 9th-10th century A.D., earthenware. Courtesy of the Art Gallery of Greater Victoria, Fred and Isabel Pollard Collection. Photo by Janet Dwyer.
- Mexico, Seated female figure. Earthenware, burnished, Jalisco, Mexico ca.1200 A.D. Courtesy of the Art Gallery of Greater Victoria Photo by Janet Dwyer.
- U.S.A. Vase, Jacques Sicard, 1902-1907, earthenware with resist brushwork and reduced luster decoration, Weller Pottery, Ohio. Private Collection. Photo by Janet Dwyer.

Frontispiece photo:
Robin Hopper, Trifoot Plate, Southwest Series, 1987, porcelain with white terra sigillata and bronze/black pigment, fired at cone 9 oxidation, chrome red glaze applied by brush and trailer and refired to cone 06 in oxidation. Photo by Trevor Mills.

Back cover photos (top row, left to right):
- Judi Dyelle, Canada, Large Ball Form, hand-built stoneware and molochite, sprinkled ash on top, reduction fired to cone 9, 16″ x 15″.
- Steve Heinemann, Canada, Apparition, 1999, cast earthenware, multiple firings, 25″ x 19″ x 11″. Photo by Andrew Leyerle.
- Steven Forbes de Soule, U.S.A., Triangulated Vessel #3, thrown and altered bowl with layered copper and silver glazes and underglazes, raku-fired, 14″ x 13″.
(bottom row, left to right)
- Walter Ostrom, U.S.A., Fish Vase, majolica, thrown and altered, 11″ high.
- Yih Wen Kuo, U.S.A., Dance with Me, 33″ x 22″ x 10″.

If not knowing something

holds you back from achieving

what you want to achieve,

you owe it to yourself

to learn that something!

To all the family, friends, and students who loved and worked with Dan Rhodes

To my wife, Judi Dyelle, for her help, tolerance, editing, and computer skills in preparing this manuscript

To Daniel Rhodes, who pointed the way through his work, teaching, and writings

To Dan's wife, Marybeth Coulter, and the Rhodes family for entrusting me with the responsibility of this edition

To potters and ceramic artists everywhere who continue both in traditions of the past, the personal expressions of today, and the development of the future in this challenging but wonderful and unlimited art

CONTENTS

Author's Preface to the First Edition - 1957

My purpose in writing this book has been to present in as clear and understandable a form as possible the important facts about ceramic materials and their use in pottery.

The ceramic medium has a rich potential. It is so various and adaptable that each culture and each succeeding generation finds in it a new means of expression. As a medium, it is capable of great beauty of form, color, and texture, and its expressions are unique not only for variety but for permanence and utility as well. To make full use of the medium, the ceramist or potter not only needs skill, imagination, and artistic vision; he also needs to have a sound knowledge of the technical side of the craft. This knowledge has not been easy to come by, and many of those seriously engaged in pottery have learned through endless experimentation and discouraging failures. It is hoped that the present work will enable the creative worker to go more directly to his goal in pottery, and that it will enable him to experiment intelligently and with a minimum of lost effort. While technical information must not be considered as an end in itself, it is a necessary prerequisite to a free and creative choice of means in ceramics.

None of the subjects included are dealt with exhaustively, and I have tried not to overwhelm the reader with details. The information given is presented in as practical a form as possible, and no more technical data or chemical theory is given than has been thought necessary to clarify the subject.

I wish to acknowledge here my debt to my colleagues at the State University of New York, College of Ceramics at Alfred University, and particularly to Dr. S.R. Scholes, Sr., for his thoughtful editing of the manuscript.

- Daniel Rhodes
Alfred, N.Y., 1957

AUTHOR'S PREFACE TO THE SECOND EDITION - 1973

In this revised edition I have added new material on a number of topics including raku, salt glazing, the use of fibers and fiberglass in clay, fuming with metallic salts, and overglaze processes. I have expanded the text in many places, both for clarity and to include useful information which has come to my attention since the book was first written, and I have revised certain passages to bring them more in line with my present thinking. The basic form of the book has been retained, and I have resisted the temptation to add more details, feeling that an overly detailed exposition of a subject can hamper rather than aid understanding.

While the forms of ceramic art may change suddenly and drastically, materials and methods change very slowly, and potters today are using, for the most part, techniques that have been common for centuries. If no other book on pottery making existed, *Arte del Vasaio*, written in Italy in 1559 by Cipriano Piccolpasso would do quite well as a handbook. This earliest of books on pottery techniques tells how to dig clay, how to build a wheel and kiln, and how to throw, trim, make handles, glaze, and decorate. Although the basic elements of the craft are relatively unchanging, new colors, new textures, and new reactions do occur constantly in the ceramic laboratory. This results from an almost infinite number of variables in material combinations, application, firing, and refiring. Thus ceramics, even after thousands of years of development, remains endlessly fascinating and a field of activity in which a variety of creative insights can find expression.

In the period since this book first appeared, studio potters have been concentrating on stoneware, and there has been much interest in reduction firing and more recently in salt glazing. The exploitation of these basic methods was a healthy trend, and the quality of individually made pottery has improved greatly. Traditions and standards that originated with early Chinese and Japanese pottery were absorbed and adapted to fit our particular aesthetic needs. In some mysterious way this Oriental influence supported the freedom and energy which clay working gained from abstract expressionist tendencies in art.

During the past few years many ceramists have begun to make greater use of the brighter colors and the varied surfaces that can be obtained at lower firing temperatures. It is good that a more complete range of possibilities is being made use of and that the pre-eminence of stoneware as the preferred medium of the studio potter is being challenged. Many potters are finding that making earthenware may involve more complex procedures than stoneware. In the case of earthenware, exacting control of formulation and firing is necessary and unless slips, glazes, and overglaze colors are skillfully applied, the results can be disastrous. The use of low-fire bodies and glazes may call for more, not less, technical knowledge and craftsmanship.

The selection and documentation of the illustrations for this edition was a collaborative effort of my wife Lillyan and myself. She also assisted in every other phase of the revision. The illustrations are not intended as a complete survey of ceramic possibilities. Rather they are a selection of pieces to which we respond and which we feel are stimulating and worthy of study.

I wish to thank Michael Kan of the Brooklyn Museum, Pat Oyama Clarke, Elisenda Sala, Norman Bielowitz, and Jean Biagini for their assistance.

- Daniel Rhodes
Alfred, N.Y., 1972

Daniel Rhodes
Born ~ Iowa, 1911, died ~ Nevada, 1989

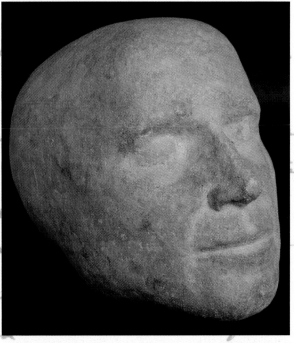

Daniel Rhodes, Giant Head, Leros, stoneware, 1988. Photo by Jeff Guido. Courtesy of the Estate of Daniel Rhodes.

Daniel Rhodes, Artia, Goddess of Abundance, Strength, and Harvest, large head, wood-fired stoneware, 19″ high x 17″ wide, 1989. Photo by Gary Huibregtse.

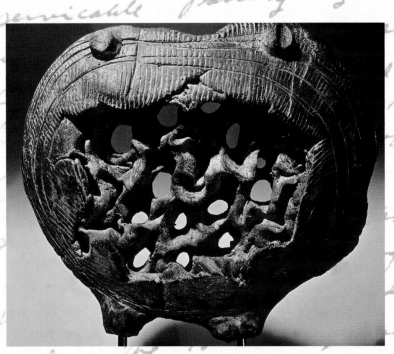

Daniel Rhodes, Abstract Head, stoneware, 1955.

The handwritten script behind these images, and on the cover, is taken from pages of the original manuscript.

Daniel Rhodes, Lidded Jar, stoneware, 1956.
Illustrated opposite page 160 in the first edition of
Clay and Glazes for the Potter, 1957.

Daniel Rhodes, Vase Form Lamp, stoneware, 1960.
Courtesy of the Schein-Joseph International
Museum of Ceramic Art, 1992.76. Photo by Brian
Oglesbee.

Daniel Rhodes,
Bowl, stoneware,
1956.

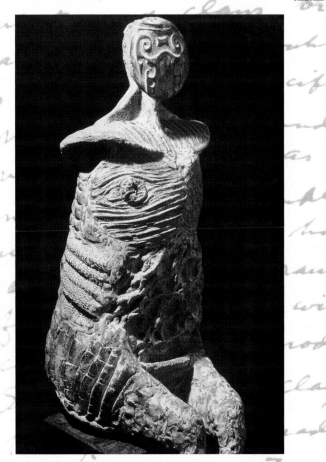

Daniel Rhodes, Figurative Sculpture, stoneware, 1956.

Daniel Rhodes, Bulbous Vase with Sgraffito, 1956. Illustrated opposite page 161 in the first edition of *Clay and Glazes for the Potter*, 1957.

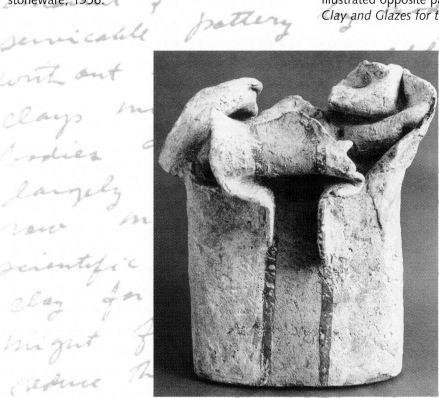

Daniel Rhodes, Sculptural Vessel, stoneware with fiberglass, 1972. Illustrated opposite page 109 in the second edition of *Clay and Glazes for the Potter*, 1973.

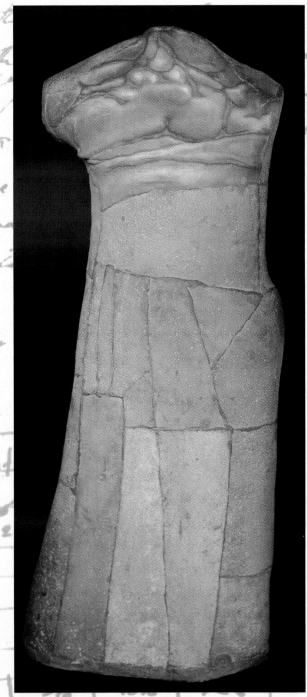

Daniel Rhodes, Xiuhtechtli, Aztec Fire Lord who resides at the heart of the earth, large torso, wood-fired stoneware, 14˝ tall x 19˝ wide, 1989.
Photo by Gary Huibregtse.

Daniel Rhodes, Seishi Basatu, the Bodishatva who proceeds with vigor, small torso, wood-fired stoneware, 34˝ tall x 20˝ wide, 1989.
Photo by Gary Huibregtse.

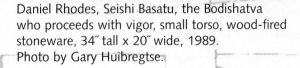

Daniel and Marybeth Coulter Rhodes, California, 1988.

Editor's Preface to the Third Edition - 2000

Daniel Rhodes died in 1989, before he could write a third edition of what has become the most widely used text in the ceramics field. It has been the major source for ceramics study since its first publication in 1957, helping and influencing potters and ceramic artists worldwide for generations.

As a student in England during the late 1950s, where the technology of ceramics was little understood or encouraged in art schools, *Clay and Glazes for the Potter* seemed to me to be a revelation that filled the technical void students were generally experiencing. It made possible a much more thorough investigation of this amazingly challenging medium, which is a complex blend of art and science. Without a balance of the two, little true understanding or value is likely to occur.

It has been nearly fifty years since the first edition and nearly thirty since the second edition were published. It has often been said that the field of ceramics has changed more since the end of the Second World War than in the previous five thousand, a period of only fifty-five years. Even during the last thirty years we have seen many new introductions of technology that I feel sure Dan would have included if he had been here to write this new edition.

Ceramic processes are apt to change as the pendulum swings between low fire and high fire and over the life span of this book we have seen the huge developments in the contemporary exploration of earthenware, stoneware, porcelain, raku, paperclay, majolica, soda firing, salt firing, wood firing, computerized firing in studio-sized kilns, and carbon monoxide metering devices for reduc-tion control - a vast and widely variable group of processes that opens up possibilities for ceramic expression undreamed of forty-five years ago. Materials that have been around and depended on for decades have gone and new ones taken their place. Other developments that continue to affect the knowledge and lives of ceramic artists include problem solving through computer software programs that take most of the work out of glaze and body development, health hazards from materials, and an increased awareness of color palette and surface considerations to name the most important.

Looked at from afar, the ceramic medium seems static and unchanging. Nothing could be further from the truth. Enhanced technical understanding is what has given rise to this incredible and exciting new growth in a continuum of one of mankind's earliest creative avenues of expression.

My task in preparing this new edition has been to bring the book up to date with the changes that have taken place in approaches, materials, and technology, and to make the book as relevant to the next generation as it has been for the past two. Where possible, I have tried to simplify a mysteriously complex medium, which many felt was beyond their understanding, and to approach the medium in a friendly and not overly academic or scientific way. I have tried to tread lightly on the original and revised texts, changing only those areas that were felt needed change. A medium that has been based on human needs for survival on the one hand - the simple fired clay object - combined with the needs of space research on the other, must necessarily be complex. The wonderful thing for the potter - and this book is designed for the potter, not the ceramic researcher - is that he or she can approach the medium on whatever level seems comfortable. For the artist, the approach can be extremely flexible and variable. For the ceramic scientist, it must be consistent.

The principles of clay and glaze development laid out here are essentially those that have been in use for millennia. They have been combined with the latest developments to aid the potter in his understanding and use of this medium. It is my hope that this new edition will serve to prepare the potter for future work in clay without restriction by lack of technical understanding.

Illustrations

The images used for illustration in this book are of my own selection. With full color throughout, I have been privileged to be able to select widely. However, I have Dan to thank for much of the direction here, as I have gone over much of the same ground he covered and handled many of the same pots. I have selected images of historical objects shown in the earlier editions by visiting the museums and looking at the objects firsthand. I have also used work by many of the artists illustrated in the earlier editions.

The images fall roughly into six sections or categories. First is a short photo selection of Daniel Rhodes' work. Second are historical objects to show a wealth of ceramic expression throughout time. Third is a group of objects by some of Dan's contemporaries, colleagues, mentors, students, and fellow educators. Fourth are artists working in low-fire processes including slipware, raku, majolica, and overglaze enamel or china painting. Fifth are artists

working in the mid-range area of low-temperature stoneware and porcelain. Sixth are artists working in high fire using stoneware, porcelain, salt, soda, and wood firing.

I am greatly indebted to all of the artists who have volunteered illustration material and am sorry that I couldn't have used more. To the various museums' staff for their help, especially Dr. Margaret Carney and Susan Kowalczyk of the Schein-Joseph International Museum of Ceramics, Alfred, N.Y., Tara Coram at the Freer Gallery of Art in Washington, D.C., and the staff of the Art Gallery of Greater Victoria, Victoria, British Columbia, Canada.

I would particularly like to thank the following artists and teachers for their assistance, wisdom, advice, and condolences in shaping some of the new directions in this edition: Val Cushing, Richard Burkett, Tony Hansen, Ron Roy, Phyllis Blair Clark, Peter Pinnell, Rosette Gault, Gordon Hutchens, Louis Katz, Walter Ostrom, David Pendell, Robert "Irish" Flynn, Randy Johnston, John Neely, Linda Sikora, John Gill, Dr. William Cardy, Rick Hirsch, Nils Lou, Rick Malmgren, Joe Molinaro, Angela Fina, Julie Brooke, Chris Gustin, Lana Wilson, John Williams, and the irrepressible Jim Robinson. Thanks also to my secretarial assistant, Morgan Saddington, for keeping me organized - a difficult and often futile task!

To all of the potters and ceramic artists who have benefited from Daniel Rhodes' writings in the past, and to those who will continue to benefit from his insights well into the future, my very best wishes as you go on your journey of discovery in this medium.

- Robin Hopper
Victoria, British Columbia, Canada
June 2000

WARNING: THE CONTENTS OF THIS BOOK COULD BE HAZARDOUS TO YOUR HEALTH

Since the earlier editions of this book, there has been a much greater concern for all things to do with health and the environment - from air, soil, sound, and water pollution to concerns in our own homes, workplaces, and studios.

Potential health problems in the ceramic industry, of which we are a small part, are generally well known and, in the main, have been known for decades, if not hundreds of years. Most potters of my generation and older have been aware but not overly concerned with these problems as they represent a small part of the ceramic process. Most of the working potters that I have known of the generation previous to my own have generally lived well into their seventies, eighties, and nineties. There have even been a few that made it past the one hundred year mark, still working! Most of the time they worked without masks but took other elementary precautions in the workplace.

As we start the 21st century, the environment of the whole planet is in a fragile state and health problems seem to be far more prevalent than ever before. It is in your own interest to take elementary precautions for your own health in working in this wonderful and creative medium. It used to be said that "what you don't know can't hurt you." Well, it can, so become informed about the materials and tools that you work with! Wear masks when necessary and use rubber gloves in handling some materials.

This is not the place to do a thorough exposé of health hazards as there are other books and references available, often written by medical doctors, that give thorough explanations. Three such books are *Artist Beware!* by Dr. Michael McCann, published in 1979 by Watson-Guptill, *Keeping Claywork Safe and Legal* by Monona Rossol, published in cooperation with the National Council for Education in the Ceramic Arts, NCECA, 1996, and *The Artist's Complete Health and Safety Guide*, published in 1996 by the same author.

The hazards of the pottery studio generally fall into the following categories: molds, dusts, some glaze materials, heavy metals, toxic fumes, caustic materials, and playing with fire. Unlike the addiction that heavy smokers have to cigarettes and other addictive problems of today's society, it is very easy for the potter to keep himself, or herself, out of harm's way. Wearing masks is one of them. Problems linked to the potter's product may be to do with the materials being used, such as lead or barium, or to glazes with built-in defects for functional pottery, such as shivering, where slivers of fired glaze can flake off edges of objects and into the food or drink. Other glaze defects may be unsightly but are seldom a health hazard. There is plenty of awareness and information available, and if working with materials which may be hazardous, it is only commonsense to read the labels and take the necessary care.

The only addiction a potter should have is to the development of his work in an amazingly diverse medium without parallel for personal expression. An understanding of potential problems helps in the realization of the work in hand.

Throughout the previous editions of this book Mr. Rhodes included much that referred to the use of lead in glazes. At that time in North America, lead was not perceived to be the problem that is perceived today. In this edition I have eliminated some references to lead, particularly in all the usable glaze formulas in Appendix 8. However, I have retained most references to the use of lead. Historically, lead has been one of the most important sources of low-temperature glaze flux for at least 4,000 years. Many of the colors and surfaces that we associate with ceramic historical development can only be made with the use of lead. Removing lead as a primary glaze material also removes a large percentage of the potential ceramic spectrum, particularly the red, orange, yellow colors and many shades of green. Currently available ceramic stains will not adequately cover this range of color.

Unquestionably, lead in any form, including frits, is a potential problem material for functional food-safe products. However, its use in glazes for purely decorative purposes such as tiles, murals, sculpture, and other artwork which cannot be used for storing food or liquids should be hazard free. Lead products, including lead frits, should **only** be used by very experienced glaze makers and artists who are well informed about its poten-

tial problems. The same goes for glazes which use cadmium, selenium or uranium coloration.

Unfortunately, in almost every public library in North America one can find books that contain formulas for potentially toxic lead glazes. If you don't know how to use them without a shadow of doubt, and if you are planning on making functional pottery, do **not** use lead-based glazes under any circumstances. The jury is still out on the use of barium in food-safe glazes, so until there is positive definite proof about its leaching ability, barium is recommended for use only on nonfunctional surfaces.

In the chapters relating to glaze calculation I have also retained lead as an ingredient of the glaze as it makes the concept of the Unity Molecular Formula (UMF) easier to understand, lead being the only simple flux that can totally fill the unity requirement of the RO Column. I do not suggest making up the glazes in these calculations for use on pots, they remain in the text only as examples of the process.

The degree of scare-mongering about materials that has been recorded in the last few years has, I feel, been excessive. Being aware and informed are the best protection. Using masks for ceramic material dusts and gloves for sensitive skins, along with protective clothing when firing kilns, is just commonsense.

Introduction

Clay is a deceptively simple material. It is cheap and abundant. Often it may be found in the earth already softened with moisture and ready to be worked. It keeps forever and improves with age. Unfired clay objects may be crumbled, mixed again with water, and made into something else. As a material it is soft, pliant, plastic, impressionable, without grain or direction. It can be modeled, pounded, flattened, rolled, pinched, coiled, pressed, thrown on the wheel, cast into molds, scored, shredded, pierced, stamped, extruded, cut, or spun. Small and delicate objects may be made with it, or massive architectural forms. Clay shapes may resemble the looseness of a crumpled dishrag or may have the precision of electronic machines. In color, objects made from clay may be dazzling white, creamy, red, orange, yellow, grey, brown, black, or textured with spots, streaks, speckles, flashings, and tintings. They may be smooth and ivory-like, or rough, sandy, gritty, or harsh. Fired clay can have a translucence approaching that of glass or a density like that of the hardest stone.

All these possibilities are to be found in the craft of ceramics. Clay, formless in the earth, is laden with potential. It responds to shaping, to drying, to firing, to blending and combining, to texturing, to smoothing. A given lump of clay may become a roof tile, a brick, a votive sculpture or effigy, a water jug, a child's toy, or a venerated tea bowl or vase in a museum case admired by thousands. The knowledge of ways to make things from clay and to fire them brought about a significant advance in man's standard of living. Bricks, tiles, drain and water pipes, dishes, bowls, cooking pots, storage vessels, and sarcophagi have helped to make life easier and more pleasant, and have lent dignity to burial.

But many difficulties arise in shaping and in firing clay. Every child or adult addressing himself to the problem of making something out of clay has the same initial response: this is *easy*. It is easy, but clay has its own subtle ways of resistance to mishandling. Clay does not have the obdurate hardness of stone, the temperamental stringiness of wood, or the hard-to-join quality of metal, but it has a fragility and changeableness which require coddling. One set of problems arises from the inevitable shrinkage of clay as it dries. Firing, with its further shrinkage and almost total transformation of the material from one form to another, brings still more difficulties that must be anticipated and mastered. Thus even the most primitive clay-working procedures have been directed by craftsmanship of a delicate sort; each brick, tile, or pot has been nursed into existence with some care. Clay working admits of spontaneous, rapid, intuitive methods but does not tolerate carelessness.

Countless generations of potters have bequeathed to us an art or craft of great complexity and beauty. In many cultures pottery making was one of the household arts. In the art of clay working there is a place for feminine as well as masculine sensibilities. Merely to handle a raw, dried pot properly and to get it into the kiln requires some feeling of tenderness toward it.

Like most crafts, ceramics is based on a relatively few principles. A large number of variables may arise, ranging from differences in the composition of the materials to the vagaries of the fire. The work of chemists and earth scientists has, of course, brought a great deal of order and understanding to a craft which once was practiced entirely by rule-of-thumb methods. But the practical answers to the potter's technical problems still have to do more with craft than with science, with the patient application of "shop" knowledge rather than with the microscope or the test tube. What the potter needs in order to get the ceramic process under some measure of control is an understanding of the principles that govern the behavior of his raw materials. He needs to know, among other things, why clay shrinks, why some clays shrink more than others, why pots sometimes crack during the cooling of the kiln, and how to blend and fire his materials to obtain certain desired colors and textures.

Clay is one of the few materials that has little or no apparent value of its own in a raw state, yet can be made into valuable objects. The value is put there by the potter. Clay itself is relatively amorphous and the forms the potter makes are entirely of his invention and draw little from the inherent form of the clay. Of course, clay imposes certain limitations of shape. Pyroplastic deformation from warping due to excessively high temperatures or the non-use of architectural principles in the structural concepts of objects, or forms which are too attenuated are not suitable to clay because of the brittle nature of the fired material, and forms that are too extreme may collapse in the wet state before they can be finished. But within these limitations the potter is free to express his vision, and the forms of objects which have been made from clay have been characterized by tremendous variety and freedom.

Pottery, at least to those who make it, seems to have a value which is quite beyond the sum of its usefulness and beauty. There is in pottery a thread of connection with the earliest traditions of civilization and culture. Pottery forms, even simple ones like cups or plates, still symbolize for us, in a particularly direct way, some of the most fundamental of human activities. Many ordinary pots, including those with no special claim to distinction, seem to share something in common with the greatest examples of a craft which has been the vehicle for fantasy, humor, symbolism, and sculptural invention as well as for the more mundane practical needs of the kitchen and barnyard.

Ceramics may be defined as the art of making permanent objects of usefulness and/or beauty by the heat treatment of earthy raw materials. The field of ceramics includes, besides pottery, glass, brick, tile, and other structural clay products, refractories, laboratory porcelains, sanitary wares of all sorts, dielectric porcelains, insulators and other elements used in electronic devices, cements, plaster, lime, and vitreous enamels on metal. The industries that mine and quarry ceramic materials, fabricate and distribute ceramic products, as a whole, form an important segment of industry. Rarely does the taking of ceramic material from the earth upset the ecological balance of nature, and used or discarded ceramic objects sink unobtrusively back into the earth and cause no pollution. Ceramics, one of the first useful arts to be developed by man, continues to be an essential activity.

PART I

CLAY

1 GEOLOGIC ORIGINS OF CLAY

1. The Nature of the Earth's Crust

In order to understand clay as a raw material it is necessary to consider its geologic origins. Clay is the product of the geologic weathering of the surface of the earth. Since this weathering process is continuous and goes on everywhere, clay is an extremely common and abundant material in nature. It is, in fact, a nuisance to the farmer, miner, and road builder. Clay should not be thought of as something that is rare, unusual, or valuable in itself, but rather as an important part of the earthy material that makes up the surface of the planet.

Clay is still being produced by natural forces and no doubt more clay is being formed daily than man is able to use up in ceramics and other forms of common usage. We think of the surface of the earth as being permanent and unchanging, but this is only because we have the opportunity of observing it over such a relatively limited period of time. Actually, the earth has undergone continuous change, through freezing, geothermal activity, and condensation. Vast areas of the continents have been alternately mountainous or covered by inland seas. The climate of various localities has varied from arctic to tropical. The familiar surface features of the earth as we know it - mountains, plains, rivers, valleys, lakes, deserts, and oceans - represent the cumulative effect of geologic forces over millions of years.

In remote geologic time the earth was a mass of molten material, and the crust of the earth, as we know it, is a relatively thin, solidified layer covering a still very hot interior. When the surface of the earth was still molten, the heavier material, such as the metals, tended to sink to deeper levels. This settling process tended to make the surface layers of molten material fairly uniform in composition. Gradually, as the earth cooled off, the upper layer, or crust, solidified. Rocks that are formed by the cooling of molten matter are called igneous rocks.

The composition of the original blanket or crust of igneous rock that covered the earth must have been quite uniform all over the surface of the globe. The variety that characterizes the surface now is mainly the result of later changes. Below a depth of a few thousand feet the earth is composed largely of a basalt layer more than one hundred miles thick. Below that, we are uncertain as to the exact nature of the earth, except that it is known to be heavier than the crust, extremely hot, and dense, due to the pressure of overlying material. Probably iron and nickel predominate in the earth's core.

The average percentage composition of all the igneous rocks of the earth, down to a depth of about ten miles, is approximately as follows:

Silica (SiO)	59.14
Alumina (Al_2O_3)	15.34
Iron ($Fe_2O_3 + FeO$)	6.88
Calcium (CaO)	5.08
Sodium (Na_2O)	3.84
Magnesium (MgO)	3.49
Potassium (K_2O)	3.13
Water (H_2O)	1.15
Titanium (TiO_2)	1.05
	99.10
All others	.90
Total	100.00

An interesting feature of this analysis is that a very few oxides make up the great bulk of the material at the surface of the earth. Silica and alumina make up about 75% of the crust of the earth, and, as we shall see, these two oxides are the essential elements of clay.

As the surface of the earth cooled into a solid, various minerals were formed. A mineral may be defined as a natural earthy substance having a definite chemical composition. During the cooling, which caused the crystallization of minerals from the molten mass, various conditions caused different minerals to form. Local variations in the composition of the molten material, different conditions of pressure, and different rates of cooling gave rise to numerous minerals. As would be expected from the great preponderance of certain oxides in the molten mass, the mineral composition of the crust of the earth is quite simple. The following list gives the approximate percentage of the various minerals that make up the crust of the earth:

Feldspar	59.5
Ferro-magnesian group	16.8
Quartz	12.0
Biotite	3.8
Titanium minerals	1.5
All others	6.4
Total	100.0

2. Forces of Geologic Change

About two billion years ago the forces of geologic change began to act upon the recently cooled igneous rocks. An interaction began between the gaseous atmosphere surrounding the earth and the surface of the earth, which affected both. As the earth cooled, the moisture in the atmosphere, which had until then existed only as vapor, began to condense, and a torrential rain began that must have lasted millions of years. This rain filled in the basins of the oceans and had a profound effect upon the surface of the earth at relatively higher elevations.

Water has been by far the most important agent of geologic change. It has, first of all, literally dissolved incalculable quantities of rock. One tends to think of rock as insoluble, unaffected by water, but over a period of millions of years water has washed away mountains. The presence of salt in the sea - and there are an estimated 1,500 billion tons of it - gives evidence of the dissolving action

of rain water on the earth, which has gradually leached out soluble matter from the rocks and carried it off to the sea where it remains in a solution of ever-increasing concentration.

In addition to its chemical action as a solvent, water, which carries mineral particles, has a mechanical effect of abrasion upon rocks. The abrasive effect of rainfall and the grinding of rocks in streams and glaciers readies the rocks for chemical disintegration by breaking them into smaller and smaller pieces. This attrition, so unnoticeable in any particular instance, in the aggregate is a mighty force.

Water also splits rocks by seeping into cracks and expanding when it freezes. The effect of water upon rock is to break it into ever smaller pieces and at the same time to dissolve from it all that is soluble.

Plants contribute also to this process by the action of their roots, which gain foothold in cracks and in growing tend to split the rocks into smaller units. Other significant forces of geologic change, which are of lesser importance, however, than water, are the abrasive effects of glaciers and of wind-borne particles.

The original rocks of the earth, then, though seemingly hard and eternal, have in fact been profoundly altered over the whole surface of the earth. This process, called weathering and erosion, accounts for the varied and fascinating character of the landscape. Mountains, formed by the upward thrust of rock as the surface of the earth cooled, contracted, and heaved up, have been torn down by erosion and deposited as silt in oceans and lakes. There these stratified layers of material have been altered by heat and pressure into new or metamorphic rock, then again thrust upward into new ridges and mountains, only to be again worn down and redeposited.

A characteristic product of this grinding maw of geology is clay. It is an end product of the weathering of rocks. As mountains and hills are worn away by water, the resulting debris, ground ever finer by the action of water, is finally laid down quietly in still estuaries or deltas, sorted out as it settles in the water to various particle sizes. Later these beds of disintegrated rock, from which most soluble matter has been removed, may, by gradual geologic upheaval, be elevated to dry land, where they await the potter's spade.

2 THE CHEMICAL COMPOSITION OF CLAY

1. Typical Composition of Clays

As might be expected, the usual chemical composition of clay is quite similar to the average composition of the surface of the earth as a whole. Compare, for example, an analysis of a common red clay with the approximate percentages of oxides on the surface of the earth as a whole:

	Earth as a whole	Common red clay
SiO_2	59.14	57.02
Al_2O_3	15.34	19.15
Fe_2O_3	6.88	6.70
MgO	3.49	3.08
CaO	5.08	4.26
Na_2O	3.84	2.38
K_2O	3.13	2.03
H_2O	1.15	3.45
TiO_2	1.05	.91

Note particularly in these two analyses that the silica and alumina contents are very similar and account for the bulk of the material, and that iron is present in almost identical amounts.

Clays more pure in composition than the specimen listed above are apt to contain a great deal less iron and relatively more alumina, as shown by analysis in the following table of a North Carolina kaolin, but nevertheless the similarity of even this relatively pure clay to the typical composition of the earth's crust as a whole is noteworthy.

	North Carolina kaolin
SiO_2	46.18
Al_2O_3	38.38
Fe_2O_3	.57
MgO	.42
K_2O	
Na_2O	1.22
H_2O	13.28

Clay, then, might be thought of as being almost a representative sample of the crust of the earth after it has been disintegrated and pulverized to very fine particle size by the action of erosion.

Clay differs from the average of all rocks more in its physical state than in its chemical makeup. Actually, clays vary rather widely in chemical composition. The more pure, light-burning clays, such as kaolin and ball clay, have a relatively high percentage of alumina and a low percentage of iron and other impurities. Since clay is made up predominantly of alumina and silica, all other oxides present may be considered impurities.

The composition of clay varies, depending on the source of the parent rock. In different localities the igneous rock that gives rise eventually to clay may differ widely, some of it being more or less free of iron, some containing much quartz, and some being loaded with iron oxide. Sometimes the debris from the erosion of a very wide area will be brought together by some river system and deposited as clay in a delta or estuary. Such a clay will be a representative sample of the disintegration of the rocks of many localities.

Chemical analyses of clay indicate considerable water. This is chemically combined water, which is the result of the hydrating process, or hydrolysis, by which clay was formed.

2. The Molecular Composition of Clay

As a mineral, clay is said to have the following formula:

$$Al_2O_3 \cdot 2SiO_2 \cdot 2H_2O$$

In this formula the relative amounts of the oxides present are stated as a molecular ratio rather than by percentage weight. In clay, one molecule of Al_2O_3 (alumina) is associated with two molecules of SiO_2 (silica), and two molecules of H_2O (water). This formula, which is typical, overlooks the complex array of "impurities" always present in actual samplings. Kaolinite is the mineralogical name that has been given to this pure clay substance.

3. The Origin of Clay from Feldspar

In tracing the chemical parentage of clay, we must look more closely at the feldspar family of minerals, which are, as we have seen, our most abundant minerals, and which, therefore, enter importantly into the formation of any clay. Feldspars contain alumina (AL_2O_3) and silica (SiO_2) combined with one or more other oxides of an alkaline nature. Commonly occurring feldspars are illustrated in the following formulas:

Orthoclase	$K_2O \cdot Al_2O_3 \cdot 6SiO_2$
Albite	$Na_2O \cdot Al_2O_3 \cdot 6SiO_2$
Anorthite	$CaO \cdot Al_2O_3 \cdot 2SiO_2$

These are typical, or generalized, formulas. In the case of actual specimens of rock it would be probable that two or more alkalies would be present in any feldspar and that there would be some impurities such as iron. Furthermore, the ratio of the molecules would seldom be exactly one to one to six, as indicated above. More likely, the ratio would vary somewhat from this general proportion.

When feldspar is disintegrated by geologic weathering, the alkali part, namely the soda, potash, or lime, being relatively soluble, is carried off by water. This leaves the alumina and silica. Part of the silica also is split off by chemical combinations. The remaining alumina and silica, after long exposure to moisture, then become hydrated, or chemically combined with water. Stated as a chemical equation, the whole process, which may take millions of years to effect and which cannot be duplicated in the laboratory, is as shown at the bottom of the page.

This sketch of the kaolinization of feldspar tells nothing of the physical properties of clay but accounts only for its chemical composition. It is obvious that clay, a material that is the end product of a long process of erosion and change, is an extremely inert material chemically. All the natural changes that can take place in clay have done so, with the possible exception of the formation from it of shale or slate by heat and pressure, but the formation of these metamorphic rocks requires rather special conditions. The melting point, or temperature at which clay fuses, tends to be high. Even common surface clays fuse at temperatures above 1000°C. The reason for this, which will be explained in more detail later, is that all the more fusible alkali compounds have been removed, leaving only the very refractory oxides of alumina and silica, together with smaller amounts of iron or other minerals.

Chemical Equation of Feldspar Disintegrated by Geologic Weathering

$$K_2O \cdot Al_2O_3 \cdot 6SiO_2 + xH_2O \longrightarrow Al_2O_3 \cdot 2SiO_2 \cdot 2H_2O + K_2O(SiO_2) + SiO_2$$

Feldspar   a clay mineral   in solution   in solution or in the clay

Pre-20th Century

Iranian, Jar, decorated with three horned animals between geometric designs, pottery, unglazed. Provenance: Tepe Sialk (III,7). Prehistoric period, ca. 3400 B.C. H: 20-7/8" D: 19-1/8". Courtesy of the Metropolitan Museum of Art, purchase Joseph Pulitzer Bequest, 1959. 59.52. ©1982 The Metropolitan Museum of Art.

China, unknown Chinese Han Vessel. Courtesy of the Schein-Joseph International Museum of Ceramic Art, Alfred University, 1992.19. Photo by Brian Oglesbee. D.C. S1998.163.

Greek, Vase, Neck Amphora with cover. 6th century B.C., ca. 540 B.C. Procession in a Chariot. Side A: A man and woman in a chariot, accompanied by woman and kithara player. Attributed to Exekias as potter and painter. Terracotta. H: 18-1/2" with lid 22". Courtesy of the Metropolitan Museum of Art, Rogers Fund, 1917, and Gift of J.D. Beazley, 1927. 17.230.14ab, 27.16. ©1999 The Metropolitan Museum of Art.

Peru: Central Coast, Chancay, Whistling Vessel with Figure of Man, late intermediate period A.D. 1000-1400. 11-1/2" x 7-5/8" x 3-7/8" (29.2cm x 19.4cm x 9.8cm). Courtesy of the Brooklyn Museum of Art, Gift of the Ernest Erickson Foundation, Inc. 86.224.140.

Iran, burnished earthenware ewer, 1000-800 B.C. Courtesy of the Freer and Sackler Galleries of Art, Smithsonian Institution, Washington, D.C. S1998.163.

China, Neolithic Jar, Gansu Province. Courtesy of the Freer and Sackler Galleries of Art, Smithsonian Institution, Washington, D.C. F1975.13.

Mesopotamia, Asia, Model Cart, Early Dynastic 11-111A, terracotta, length 30.5cm. Courtesy of the Brooklyn Museum of Art. Purchased with funds given by Shelby White. 87.77.

Hippo, Provenance not known, Middle Kingdom, Late Dynasty 12-13 (ca. 1878-1627B.C.), faience, blue glazed and painted. Courtesy of the Brooklyn Museum of Art, Charles Edwin Wilbour Fund. 35.1276.

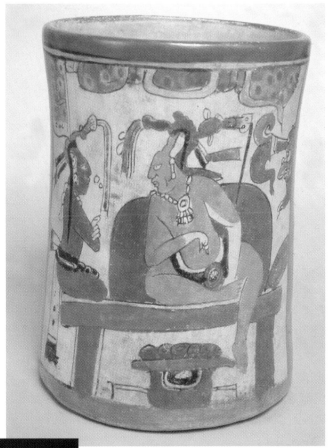

Maya/Guatemala, 700 A.D. Two-panel vase with presentation theme, 8-1/8" x 6". Courtesy of the Denver Art Museum, Gift of M. Larry Ottis, 1984.604.

Japan, Stem Bowl, stoneware ca. 1810. H: 14.5cm. Courtesy of the Art Gallery of Greater Victoria, Fred and Isabel Pollard Collection. 62.116.

Iranian, Cup, decorated with band of gazelles. Composite body, underglaze frit-painted. So-called silhouette ware. Maximum diameter 5-5/8″. 12th century A.D.. Courtesy of the Metropolitan Museum of Art, Purchase Joseph Pulitzer Bequest, 1967. 67.104. ©1982 The Metropolitan Museum of Art.

China, Banshan Burial Jar,
circa 2600-2300 B.C.,
earthenware. Courtesy of the
Brooklyn Museum of Art.
Gift of Gary Smith. 86.189.3.

China, Tang Dynasty, Winepot. Courtesy
of the Freer and Sackler Galleries of Art,
Smithsonian Institution, Washington,
D.C. F1917.404.

Mexico, Seated female figure, earthenware, burnished, Jalisco, Mexico ca.1200 A.D. Courtesy of the Art Gallery of Greater Victoria.

Egyptian, Figurine of the Goddess Isis, 26th dynasty, upper part of blue faience. Courtesy of the Brooklyn Museum of Art, Charles Edwin Wilbour Fund. 37.332E.

Ecuador, Standing Couple, 100 B.C., 15-5/8" x 11-1/2" x 5-1/2". Courtesy of the Denver Art Museum, museum purchase, 1987 Collectors' Choice Benefit, 1987.72.

Japan, Kofun era, Haniwa Horse, 4th century. Terracotta hollow-built horse with mane, cylindrical legs, bridle, bells, and saddle, hand-built earthenware, 27-5/8" x 25-1/2" x 10". Courtesy of the Denver Art Museum, Museum Exchange and Purchase, 1961.3.

Iran, Gazelle Rhyton. Courtesy of the Freer and Sackler Galleries of Art, Smithsonian Institution, Washington, D.C. S1987.31.

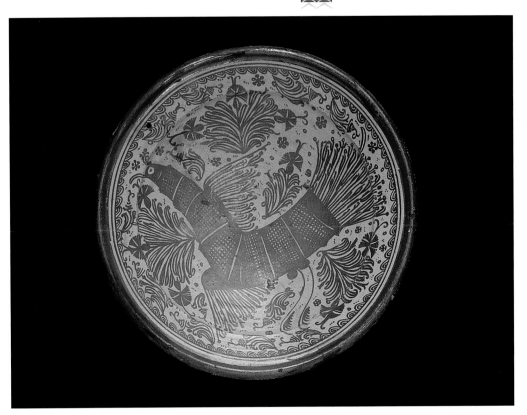

Luster bowl, bird motif. Earthenware with painted and reduced luster over cream glaze. Spanish-Hispano-Moresque 17th century A.D. Courtesy of the Art Gallery of Greater Victoria, Canada. Gift of J.J. Mero. Photo by Janet Dwyer.

China, Yuan Dynasty, Jün Ware flower pot. Courtesy of the Freer and Sackler Galleries of Art, Smithsonian Institution, Washington, D.C. F1929.7a&b.

Pre-Columbian, Mexico, Turtle Effigy. Courtesy of the Schein-Joseph International Museum of Ceramic Art, Alfred University. 1987.91. Photo by Brian Oglesbee.

Iran, Bird Form Vessel. Courtesy of the Freer and Sackler Galleries of Art, Smithsonian Institution, Washington, D.C. S1987.949.

Peru, Chancay, Zoomorphic jar. Courtesy of the Schein-Joseph International Museum of Ceramic Art, Alfred University. 1987.3. Photo by Brian Oglesbee.

Charles Harder, U.S.A., Vase, 1933. Glazed earthenware. Courtesy of the Schein-Joseph International Museum of Ceramic Art, Alfred University, 1993.56. Photo by Brian Oglesbee.

Peru, North Coast Style, Stirrup Vessel with Ducks, A.D. 1000-1500. 9-3/4" x 6-1/2" (24.8cm x 16.5cm). Courtesy of the Brooklyn Museum of Art. Gift of the Ernest Erickson Foundation, Inc. 86.224.173.

Peru, North Coast, Moché, Stirrup Vessel, A.D. 450-550, ceramic, slip. H: 11-3/4"
(28.9cm). Courtesy of the Brooklyn Museum of Art, Gift from the Eugene Schaefer
Collection 36.328.

China, Han Dynasty, lead glazed jar, earthenware. Courtesy of the Freer and Sackler Galleries of Art, Smithsonian Institution, Washington, D.C. F1905.87.

Costa Rica, Tripod Jar, 500 – 1000 A.D. A realistic crocodile is depicted on each tripod leg. The tall jar was slipped in red over a buff surface with applied adornos. 23" x 16" x 16". Courtesy of the Denver Art Museum, Gift of Jan and Frederick Mayer, 1993.489.

Korea, Unified Silla Period, covered jar with fern frond handle. Courtesy of the Freer and Sackler Galleries of Art, Smithsonian Institution, Washington, D.C. F1916.422.

Khmer, Cambodia, Elephant shaped vessel. Courtesy of the Freer and Sackler Galleries of Art, Smithsonian Institution, Washington, D.C. S1996.124.

Japan, Tamba Ware, large storage jar. Courtesy of the Freer and Sackler Galleries of Art, Smithsonian Institution, Washington, D.C. F1966.28.

China, Song Dynasty, Vase with temmoku glaze and iron brushwork. Courtesy of the Freer and Sackler Galleries of Art, Smithsonian Institution, Washington, D.C. F1917.192a&b.

China, Yuan Dynasty, Tzu Chou jar with engraved pattern. Courtesy of the Freer and Sackler Galleries of Art, Smithsonian Institution, Washington, D.C. F1911.340.

China, Qing Dynasty, Copper red vase. Courtesy of the Freer and Sackler Galleries of Art, Smithsonian Institution, Washington, D.C. F1942.19.

Persia, Wine Ewer. 9th-10th century, earthenware. Courtesy of the Art Gallery of Greater Victoria, Fred and Isabel Pollard Collection.

Japan, Edo Period, Teabowl, Koetsu. Courtesy of the Freer and Sackler Galleries of Art, Smithsonian Institution, Washington, D.C. F1897.38.

Iran, Bowl Depicting a Cheetah, late 10th-early 11th century, ceramic, engobe, slip, glaze. Courtesy of the Brooklyn Museum of Art, Frederic Loeser Fund. 73.165.

Iran, Deep Bowl, Samanid, 819-1005 A.D. Courtesy of the Freer and Sackler Galleries of Art, Smithsonian Institution, Washington, D.C. F1957.24.

Korea, Celadon Ewer and Cover, (918-1392), first half of 12th century. Porcelaneous grey clay body covered with translucent "kingfisher blue" feldspathic glaze, with carved and inlaid design of lotus petals forming leaf sprays. H: 9-7/8" (25.1cm) W: 9-1/2" (24.1cm). Courtesy of the Brooklyn Museum of Art, Gift of Mrs. Darwin R. James III. 56.138.1 a&b.

Japan, Oribe tray with handle. Courtesy of the Freer and Sackler Galleries of Art, Smithsonian Institution, Washington, D.C. F1960.30.

Japan, Momoyama Period, Shino ware water pot. Courtesy of the Freer and Sackler Galleries of Art, Smithsonian Institution, Washington, D.C. F1967.16.

Korea, Bowl, unknown Korean Yi bowl. Courtesy of the Schein-Joseph International Museum of Ceramic Art, Alfred University, 1960.14. Photo by Brian Oglesbee.

Mexico, Water Jar (Tai Lai), Zuni Pueblo, Zuni, late 19th-early 20th century. Pottery, slip. 12-1/4" x 15" (30.8cm x 38.1cm). Courtesy of the Brooklyn Museum of Art, Museum Expedition 1904, Museum Collection Fund. 04.297.5249.

Japan, Edo Period, Kutani dish, 17th Century. Courtesy of the Freer and Sackler Galleries of Art, Smithsonian Institution, Washington, D.C. F1968.13.

Japan, Edo Period, Arita, seven sun plate. Courtesy of the Freer and Sackler Galleries of Art, Smithsonian Institution, Washington, D.C. F1963.9.

Panama, Coclé, 500-700 A.D. Polychrome plate, red and black four-toed footprints encircling upper face. Courtesy of the Denver Art Museum, Gift of Mr. and Mrs. I.J. Shore, 1991.1270.

Japan, Nabeshima plate, ca.1803, porcelain with overglaze enamels. Courtesy of the Art Gallery of Greater Victoria, Fred and Isabel Pollard Collection. 66.71.

Japan, Banko Ware, 1910-1930, Teapot with motif of sea creatures. Intended gift of Carol Peckham Potter. Courtesy of the Art Gallery of Greater Victoria.

U.S.A., Pie Plate, Maker: David Spinner 1758-1811, Bucks County, Pennsylvania, circa 1800. Ceramics. Courtesy of the Brooklyn Museum of Art, Gift of Mrs. Huldah Cail Lorimer in Memory of George Burford Lorimer. 56.5.8.

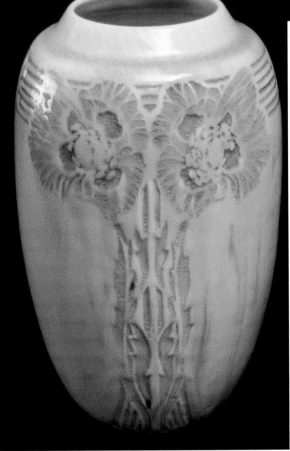

U.S.A., Poppy Vase, Adelaide Alsop Robineau, 1910, porcelain. Courtesy of the Everson Museum of Art, PC 16.4.3. Photograph © Courtney Frisse.

U.S.A., Vase, Jacques Sicard, 1902-1907, earthenware with resist and reduced luster decoration, Weller Pottery. Private Collection.

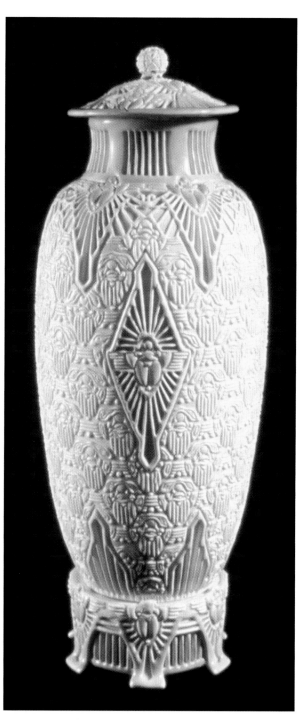

U.S.A., Scarab Vase, Adelaide Alsop Robineau, 1865-1929, c. 1910, porcelain. Courtesy of the Everson Museum of Art, PC 30.4.78a,b,c. Photograph © Courtney Frisse.

3 THE PHYSICAL NATURE OF CLAY

1. Particle Size and Shape

The physical nature of clay is more obscure, and our knowledge of it less exact than its chemical composition. The chemical composition of a clay can be readily determined by routine analysis. The size and shape of the particles in clay and the factors that account for its plasticity can be known only through microscopic study and other types of analysis.

Clay was formerly thought to be more or less colloidal, or glue-like, in its physical makeup, but later studies seem to indicate that the extremely small size of the grains of clay account for most of its physical properties. Many clays have been found to have a substantial percentage of particles below one micron in diameter. (A micron is a unit of length, one thousandth part of a millimeter.) These small particles may be thought of as single crystals of clay. Examination under the electron microscope has revealed that these clay particles are plate-shaped, elongated in two dimensions, and thin in the other dimension. Clay, because of the shape of its particles and their extremely small size, has a very large surface area per unit of volume.

It has been estimated that the particles in one cubic millimeter of kaolin number more than three and a half million. This is for a relatively coarse-grained clay. A finer-grained clay such as a ball clay would have a great many more individual particles per unit of volume.

The extremely fine particle size of clay can be accounted for by the processes of weathering, chemical change and disintegration, grinding during water transportation, and the sorting out that occurs during sedimentation in quiet water. In any clay, however, in addition to the very fine particle size of the bulk of the material, there will be some fragments of larger size. These may be bits of unaltered feldspar or quartz, or other minerals that have become associated with the clay during transportation or sedimentation. In some clays, such as most kaolins, there is so much coarse material of this sort that it must be removed from the clay by washing. In other clays there is relatively little coarse material.

Clay usually contains some organic matter in addition to the inorganic minerals present. Although the organic matter burns out and disappears in firing, its presence has an important effect on the physical behavior of the material before firing. Clay is frequently formed in situations where organic matter becomes associated with it. For example, clay may be formed in quiet estuaries where vegetation may be prevalent. This organic matter leaves a residue of carbon in the clay. Sedimentary layers of clay and coal are, in fact, frequently found one on top of the other. Carbonaceous matter in clay may also be caused by bacterial action in the damp clay itself.

As found in nature, clay may be very densely compacted and may look like a rocky material. If such clay is exposed to atmospheric moisture in the form of rain, snow, ice, or condensation, however, it quickly slakes into a soft crumbly mass.

2. Plasticity

Clay, when wet with the proper amount of water, will tend to hold any shape that is given to it. This property is known as plasticity, and it is one of the principal virtues of the material. Among natural materials clay is unique in the degree of its plasticity. It is plasticity that makes possible the fabrication of the endlessly varied shapes of ceramic objects. Pinching, squeezing, or rolling a ball of clay, the potential that lies in the moist, pliable mass is instantly recognizable. A child's imagination is invariably excited by the discovery that clay can quickly be manipulated into almost any shape. No synthetic material has yet been devised that approaches clay in the ease with which it can be shaped.

The plasticity of clay has been much studied by scientists but the exact mechanism is still not completely understood. To some degree plasticity can be attributed to fineness of grain. The smallness of the particles, each one of which is wet with water and lubricated on the surface with moisture, tends to make the particles cling to one another and thus cause the whole mass to retain a given shape. The fact that wet sand can be modeled, which when dry has no plasticity at all, illustrates this principle. The finer the sand, the more successful will be the sand castle. The plate-like shape of clay particles also contributes to plasticity. Plastic clay might be likened to a deck of playing cards wet with water. Each card is saturated with water, and a film of water between surfaces makes the cards slip and slide on one another and also causes them to stick together. Similarly, clay particles slip upon one another when a force is applied, but then hold to their new position.

Chemical attraction between particles also contributes to plasticity. When an electrolyte is added to wet clay, the chemical affinity between particles is diminished and plasticity is drastically impaired. (See the following section on casting clays.)

The carbonaceous matter ordinarily present in clay also contributes to plasticity. Most common clays, which tend to have a significant amount of carbon in them, are rather plastic. The organic matter seems to act almost like a gum or glue in the behavior of the clay. While a small amount of organic matter in a clay may be helpful in developing plasticity, too much will make the clay excessively sticky, hard to work, and high in shrinkage.

Subtle differences in plasticity are hard to evaluate in any exact way. But a good idea of plasticity can be gained simply by pinching, rolling, or bending a small sample. The experienced thrower is perhaps the best judge of the plasticity of a clay, and shaping on the wheel might be thought of as the ultimate test for plasticity.

Clays vary a great deal in plasticity, depending on their geologic history. Some coarse clays, even though quite nonplastic, are useful for making bricks and other heavy clay products such as tile and drainage pipes. Other clays are too plastic and sticky to be used by themselves and must be blended with other less plastic clays to be useful. Many clays, however, are usable just as they come from the earth and may be modeled or thrown on the potter's wheel without any adjustments in composition.

The effect of aging on clay is discussed in a later section.

3. Primary Clays

Clays may be classified in various ways, depending on what properties are of interest to the classifier. They might be classifed according to their color as they exist in nature. Or the classification might center around the idea of use, or of geologic origin. The potter is interested in what the clay will do in the making and firing of pots, and he will look at clay from that standpoint. He is interested in the plasticity or workability of the clay and in its reactions during drying and firing. The division of clays into two broad groups, *primary clays* and *secondary clays*, helps to classify clays for the potter and helps him to understand and make use of the peculiar working and firing properties of various clays.

Primary clays, or residual clays, as they are sometimes called, are those clays that have been formed on the site of their parent rocks and have not been transported, either by water, wind, or glacier. Primary clays are unusual, since normally the products of weathering are carried off down slopes by water into creeks and rivers, and eventually to lakes or to seas. But in some instances clays are left on the spot where they were formed by the disintegration of feldspathic rock.

Rock beds are broken down into clay largely by the action of ground water seeping through the rock and thus gradually leaching out the more soluble components. In some cases the percolation of steam or of gases from below, geothermal activity, may have contributed to the formation of clay. In typical deposits of primary clay, much unaltered rock remains, and the clay is found in irregular pockets. Since the clay has not been waterborne, there has been no opportunity for the selective sorting out of the various particle sizes, and large and small grains of clay are found mixed together. Deposits of primary clay are apt to be coarse-grained and relatively nonplastic. There has been little opportunity for fine grinding and sorting.

Primary clays, when they have been cleared of rock fragments, tend to be relatively pure and free from contamination with nonclay minerals. The reason for this is that most primary clays originate from beds of more or less pure feldspar, a rock that is relatively easily broken down in geologic time by the action of water alone. Another obvious reason is that since the clay is not carried by streams, there is much less chance for admixtures from other localities to alter its composition. Potters value primary clays, then, for their purity, their whiteness, and their freedom from objectionable mineral or organic contamination. Most kaolins are primary clays.

4. Secondary Clays

Secondary clays are clays that have been transported from the site of the original parent rock. Although water is the most common agent of transportation, wind and glaciers may also carry clay. Secondary or transported clays are much more common than primary clays. In nature it is almost certain that eroded material will be carried to a new site.

Transportation by water has an important effect on clay. For one thing, the action of the water in streams tends to grind up the clay into smaller and smaller particle size. Then, when the water of the stream begins to slow down, some of the material it carries will settle out. The coarse particles naturally settle first, leaving the fine particles still suspended in the water. When quiet water is reached, as in a lake or sea, the remaining very fine particles of clay sink to the bottom, forming a layer or sediment. This process of sedimentation tends to separate the coarse from the fine.

Transported clays are ordinarily composed of material from a variety of sources. In any one stream, silts from numerous erosion sources are apt to be mixed together. This accounts for the more complex makeup of most secondary clays compared to pure kaolin. As would be expected, transported clays are apt to contain iron, quartz, mica, and other impurities. Carbonaceous matter, usually in the form of lignite, is also commonly found in secondary clays. Lignite, a form of coal, is formed with the clay as it is laid down by sedimentation in shallow marshes, lakes, or deltas where there is heavy vegetation.

Secondary clays vary widely in composition. Some are relatively pure and iron-free, such as the secondary kaolins, but these are quite rare. Ball clays are highly plastic secondary clays with little iron content. The great majority of secondary clays contain enough iron to make them fire to a buff, brown, or red color, and the maturing temperature is usually quite low. The clay may be found in small localized pockets, the sedimentation of one stream, or it may occur in vast deposits of millions of tons covering several square miles.

Glacial clays and aeolian or wind-deposited clays are also considered secondary clays. Clays that have been transported and deposited by glaciers are ordinarily rather impure and tend to be very uneven in particle size, since no sedimentation has occurred. Aeolian clays are more rare, but in some localities occur in rather surprisingly extensive deposits. They too tend to be quite impure.

Clay may be defined as an earthy mineral substance, composed largely of a hydrous silicate of alumina, which becomes plastic when wet and hard and rock-like when fired.

4 DRYING AND FIRING CLAY

1. The Process of Drying

Clay, until it is fired and made durable, is a material of little or no practical value. The adobe, or sun-dried brick, is an exception, but no one would maintain that an adobe brick as such was superior to a fired brick. We are interested in clay not so much for what it is in the natural state as for what it may become. By a happy coincidence, clay, which is so plastic and easily shaped, becomes a hard and permanent substance when fired to red heat or more.

The discovery that clay will become hard and durable when fired ranks as one of man's most important early finds. The domestic life of primitive man was immeasurably enriched by the possession of fired clay vessels for storing grain, carrying water, cooking, washing, holding food - to say nothing of the ceremonial and purely aesthetic uses to which clay objects were put. Any ancient civilization can be gauged by the quantity and the quality of the pottery it produced. Clay was no doubt first fired accidentally in a campfire, perhaps in the form of a mud-lined basket. Much early pottery was made in the shape and texture of baskets - a fact that strongly suggests the probability that pottery began as mud smeared on the inside of baskets to make them more water or rodent-proof, or to stop small seeds from falling through the basket mesh.

When plastic clay dries, it shrinks about 5%. Some very plastic clays may shrink as much as 8%. Although this shrinkage takes place rather slowly, it creates a problem in completing any object made of plastic clay. When dry clay is moistened, it takes up a surprising quantity of water. Each individual particle of clay holds chemically combined water like an absorbent pebble, and in between the particles, water creates a film. An average clay, to become plastic enough to model, will require about thirty-five parts of water, by weight, to each one hundred parts of clay. Any mass of plastic clay, therefore, is at least one quarter water.

The drying of clay proceeds at a rate controlled by the humidity of the surrounding atmosphere. When the humidity is 100%, nothing dries. But if the humidity of the surrounding air is less than 100%, water leaves the clay as a vapor, by evaporation. When the surface of the mass of clay is dried slightly, more water is drawn out from the interior of the mass by capillary attraction. Unless the mass of clay is very thick, drying will proceed quite evenly throughout. If this were not the case, it would be impossible to make objects from plastic clay, because cracks would develop on the dried surface.

The drying of clay is always accompanied by shrinkage. As the film of water between the particles of clay is drawn off by evaporation, the particles draw closer and closer together, thus taking up the space that had been occupied by the water. The cumulative effect of each particle drawing closer to its neighboring particle is the shrinkage of the entire mass. The amount of this drying shrinkage will depend upon the size of the clay particles and on the amount of water that separates them. Those clays having a very fine particle size will shrink more because of the presence of more water-filled interstices which close up. Conversely, more open clays, that is clays with larger particle size, will shrink less. Drying shrinkage is always related to the grain structure of a clay and, therefore, also to plasticity.

When the water has evaporated from between the clay particles and all the particles are in contact, drying shrinkage is complete. At this stage, which is called the leather-hard state, the clay particles themselves may still be damp and drying will not be complete until this moisture also leaves by evaporation. The drying of the clay particles themselves does not cause any further shrinkage.

The drying shrinkage of a clay may vary, depending on how the plate-like clay particles have been oriented in the forming process. The clay platelets tend to align themselves at right angles to the force applied to the clay. Linear shrinkage will be less in the direction parallel to the alignment of the platelets than it will be in the direction at right angles to them. Thus when a ball of clay is pounded or pressed to form a sheet or slab, the linear shrinkage across the slab will be less than that of a bar or roll made of the same clay. This variation in shrinkage, although measurable, seldom causes any practical difficulty.

If warping, cracking, or deformation are to be avoided, objects made of plastic clay must be dried slowly and evenly. If one part of a clay object dries more rapidly than another, the unequal shrinkage between the two portions may cause warping or cracking. This may happen, for example, when a clay pot is dried in the sun or in a place where a draft strikes one side. Another familiar example is the tile that curls upward when it dries; the face of the tile, which is exposed to the air, shrinks more rapidly than the back. In the case of objects made from very plastic clays, drying may be a serious problem, not only because of the excessive shrinkage, but because of the tendency of the clay to warp and crack. Handles, spouts, and other appendages may be difficult to attach without subsequent cracking.

Drying is greatly facilitated by the presence in the clay of any sort of nonplastic particles. Such particles tend to take up much less water than clay and are, therefore, more easily dried out. Nonplastic particles also furnish open pores or channels through which moisture can escape toward the surface. Clays that contain a large percentage of non-clay particles, especially if these particles are relatively large, are called "open" bodies. When objects are to be made having thick walls or sections, as in some sculptures or terracottas, open clay bodies are necessarily used. Grog is ordinarily used for this purpose. Grog is clay that has already been fired and then ground to more or less fine particle size. Such a material, of course, having already been dried and fired, undergoes no further shrinkage, and the addition of grog to a clay body will decrease the total shrinkage. Other materials that may also decrease shrinkage and promote rapid drying are silica, sand, and feldspar. When a very plastic clay is necessary, as in a clay designed for throwing, the nonplastics must be held to a minimum.

A piece of dried clay will contain more or less free water, as the surrounding atmosphere is, respectively, more or less humid. For this reason drying is actually completed in the kiln. When the temperature of the kiln reaches the boiling point of water, 100°C, all the uncombined water in the clay will have evaporated, and at that point the clay will be completely dry.

Dried clay bodies vary greatly in dry strength. An object made from ball clay, for example, may be six or seven times as strong as one made from Georgia kaolin. The property of dry strength is directly related to particle size, and thus to plasticity; the more plastic a clay is, the more strength it will develop in the dry state.

2. Early Stages of Firing - Drying and Water-smoking

Profound changes occur in clay during firing. A piece of fired clay is quite different both chemically and physically from raw clay. The material, which was once soft, easily disintegrated, plastic when wet, and without cohesion or strength, becomes, when fired, hard, rock-like, and impervious to water. Clay is actually a relatively indestructible material after it has been fired. Although a piece of pottery will break, its fragments will remain unchanged for thousands of years even when buried in damp soil or when immersed in water.

The first change that firing brings about in clay is a completion of drying. This final drying must be brought about slowly; otherwise the formation of steam within the body of the clay may cause it to burst. This is the familiar explosion in the amateur's kiln, which is usually caused by a too rapid advance of heat in the early stages of firing, by pockets of air in the clay, or by excessive or uneven thickness. No matter how dry a clay object may seem to be when it is put in the kiln, a considerable amount of water must still be driven off. In the case of large kilns filled with heavy clay products such as brick or tile, large quantities of water escape from the kiln, and sometimes blow-holes are provided in the top of the kiln to let off the water vapor. In smaller kilns the escaping moisture, though present, may not be noticeable. The danger of localized explosions resulting from steam forming in the object is greatly increased by heavy cross sections or thick-walled objects, and such objects must be fired with great care.

Humidity dryers are sometimes used to facilitate safe and rapid drying. The damp clay pieces are heated to nearly 100°C in an enclosure kept at a humidity of close to 100%. Although the clay pieces are heated, no drying occurs. Then the humidity is gradually reduced and the clay pieces, being hot throughout, dry rapidly.

Another version of humidity drying is the practice of "wet firing." Damp pots, even some taken directly from the wheel, are tightly packed into the kiln. The burners are turned on with the damper partially closed to prevent too much draft through the kiln. The temperature advances rapidly, but the humidity in the kiln rises and thus prevents the pots from breaking from the formation of steam. When the pots reach a temperature approaching 100°C, drying proceeds very rapidly and the firing may be continued on a normal schedule. Wet firing is not practical for pieces with thick walls. It is sometimes used in salt glazing. Wet pots, fresh from the wheel, are placed in the kiln and the firing commenced. They are next seen finished and glazed as they come from the completed firing.

The next change that occurs in the firing of clay occurs at about 350°C, at which point the chemically combined water in the clay begins to be driven off. This chemically combined water is not to be confused with pore water and water of plasticity, which escapes from the clay during drying. Chemically combined water is a part of the molecular structure of the clay and is unaffected by temperatures below about 350°C. It will be noted from the chemical formula of clay that there are two molecules of water to each two molecules of silica and each single molecule of alumina. Expressed as a percentage, this means that clay contains about 14% water by weight. When this chemically combined water leaves the clay, enough time must be allowed in firing to prevent the sudden evolution of steam and the possible breaking of the object.

Once a piece of clay has been fired to about 500°C, it will be completely dehydrated, and it will no longer slake or disintegrate in water. It will also have lost its plasticity. Although such a clay may be very friable, it may not be reclaimed and used again. An irreversible chemical change has taken place. This change, known as dehydration, is not accompanied by any shrinkage. If a kiln were to be opened after it had been fired to about 500°C, it would be noted that the ware was even more fragile than when it was put in the kiln and that no shrinkage had taken place.

3. Oxidation

Another important change that occurs in the clay during the early stages of firing is the oxidation or decomposition of all those components of the clay that are not already in oxide form. These would include such organic matter as carbon and the inorganic carbonates or sulfates. The oxidation of all these compounds is usually incomplete until the temperature has advanced to about 900°C. The familiar smell of a firing bisque kiln is that of sulfurs and carbons being burnt out. It is not particularly hazardous, just unpleasant.

All clays contain an appreciable amount of carbon, and firing has the effect of oxidizing or burning up this carbon. This process of oxidation requires that oxygen in the form of air be present in sufficient quantities in the kiln. Ordinarily oxidation proceeds without difficulty. However, if the firing is carried on too rapidly, or if insufficient air is present in the kiln because of improper adjustment of burners, some carbon may remain in the ware. This may cause blackening or, in the case of heavy clay products, blackening and bloating. Sometimes, when ware is tightly stacked together in the kiln, oxidation may be incomplete and a blackening or discoloration will be noticed. This is due to carbon still remaining in the fired piece.

Clay may contain small percentages of calcium carbonate or other impurities such as sulfates. As the firing advances, the dissociation point of these compounds is reached and the carbon or sulfur is driven off. These impurities are ordinarily present in such small quantities that no problem attends their oxidation.

4. Quartz Inversions

All clays contain an appreciable amount of quartz or silica. This quartz may be associated with the clay in nature as an accessory mineral, or it may be quartz that has been added to the clay as flint. Crystalline quartz has a number of different forms, depending upon the temperature. When the temperature advances, the crystals of quartz rearrange themselves into a slightly different order, and these rearrangements are accompanied by slight changes in volume. Thus, when 573°C is reached, quartz crystals undergo a change known as the change from alpha to beta quartz. This adjustment is marked by a slight (+2%) increase in volume, which is reversible; that is, upon cooling the quartz changes from beta to alpha quartz and resumes its original crystalline form and size. This change of volume in the quartz portion of a clay body, although rather slight, must be accomplished slowly to avoid damage to the ware. If one part of an object in the kiln is heated up faster than another, the unequal expansion in the piece may cause it to crack. Care must likewise be taken in cooling so that the contraction that occurs at 573°C may be passed safely. A large percentage of ware that comes from the kiln cracked is damaged by either too rapid heating or too rapid cooling at this critical temperature. Large objects particularly must be carefully fired at this temperature, especially if the kiln does not fire very evenly. Cracking that occurs during cooling is called dunting.

5. Vitrification

As the temperature of firing increases beyond red heat, other changes occur in the clay that are called vitrification. Vitrification is the hardening, tightening, and finally, the partial glassification of clay. Vitrification gives to fired clay its characteristic hard, durable, dense, and rock-like properties. It is accompanied by shrinkage in the clay. Vitrification proceeds gradually, at first causing the clay to be rather loosely compacted and then, with the advance of temperature, causing it to become increasingly hard, up to the point of melting and deformation. The same clay may be either very soft and chalk-like or very dense, hard, and impervious, depending upon the temperature at which it is fired.

In part, this hardening results from fusions or melting of some of the components of the clay, more particularly those minerals, such as iron oxide, which are considered impurities. All substances melt at some degree of temperature, and clay, being usually a rather complex aggregate of numerous oxides, tends to fuse gradually. As the heat of the kiln advances, the more fusible impurities of the clay may melt into small beads of glass. These liquid beads of melted material soak into the surrounding area, binding the particles together like a glue, and act like a solvent in promoting further fusion. If the firing is carried on to a sufficient degree of heat, clay fuses completely into a liquid, which, upon cooling, is a glass. In practice, of course, we stop far short of this, but in the case of porcelain manufacture, such a complete fusion is approached, and the similarity between porcelain and glass is apparent. Some common red clays that contain a high percentage of iron and other impurities have a relatively low melting point. The tendency of these clays to melt between the temperatures of cone 8 to 11 has been utilized in making slip glazes, or glazes that are made up largely of fusible clay.

The strength of fired clay is due not only to glassification but also to the formation of new crystalline growths within the clay body, particularly the growth of mullite crystals. Mullite, which is an aluminum silicate, is characterized by a long needle-like crystal. These mullite crystals tend to grow at higher temperatures and extend themselves into the glassy matrixes within the clay. Mullite laces the structure together, giving it cohesion and strength.

Clays vitrify at various temperatures, depending on their composition. A common red clay, for example, which is high in iron and other mineral impurities, may fire to hardness and density at about 1000°C and may melt to a liquid at about 1250°C. A pure kaolin body, on the other hand, may still be quite open and porous after having been fired to 1250°C and may not melt until temperatures in excess of 1800°C have been reached.

Further shrinkage occurs during vitrification. This shrinkage is due to the diminished size of the particles as they approach fusion and to the closer arrangement of particles in their glassy matrix. The firing shrinkage of a clay is usually about the same as the drying shrinkage. Total shrinkage of a fired piece of clay may be as high as 10%, and this shrinkage will vary according to the degree of vitrification. However, when a clay actually begins to melt, it usually goes through a boiling or bloating stage and, at that point, may swell or grow in size, much as a cake rises from the distension of entrapped bubbles of gas.

The art of firing clay consists of bringing about just enough fusion and hardness in the material to serve the purposes at hand, but not of overfiring to the point of melting or the deformation of the shape of the ware. The desired extent of heat treatment, involving both time and temperature, is called maturing.

The well-fired piece of clay, then, is characterized by hardness, great compressive strength, denseness and impermeability to liquids, resistance to abrasion, chemical inertness and insolubility, and a very large and easily controlled variety of color and texture reminiscent of the variety in the earthy materials of the landscape. The one fault of clay wares, brittleness, may be, from the potter's point of view, an advantage, since the fragile nature of the product has ensured a steady demand for it.

5 KINDS OF CLAY

Clay may be thought of as either *primary*, found at the source of the decomposing mother feldspathic rock, or *secondary*, transported by water in the form of rains, creeks, and rivers or by wind.

1. Kaolin

There are a great many different kinds of clay. The differing geologic conditions that have resulted in clay formation have produced clays of various chemical compositions and physical makeup. These differing clays may merge into one another from strata to strata and from locality to locality. From this wide variety, the ceramist distinguishes certain types that are similar in origin, composition, and usefulness.

One such clay, kaolin or china clay, though relatively scarce in nature, is of particular interest to the potter. It is indispensable in the making of pure white porcelain or china. Its scarcity is indicated by the fact that the presence of deposits of kaolin in Europe was largely unnoticed until early in the 18th century. Prior to that time kaolins in Europe were used for cosmetics and wig powder. Deposits of kaolin occur in Europe, England, and North America, as well as in Asia, but they are by no means as common as other types of clay.

In China, wares made from white clays were fashioned at least from the beginning of the Han Dynasty, 200 B.C., or earlier. The management of kiln temperatures up to about 1200°C and the manufacture of vitrified whiteware using kaolin as the chief clay, dates, in China, to at least as far back as A.D. 600. This pre-dates the manufacture of porcelain in Europe by more than a thousand years. In China, china clay or white burning kaolins are more commonly found than elsewhere; furthermore they are more plastic and workable than the white clays of other regions. Early Chinese potters at first made a soft white earthenware from kaolin. Gradually, over a period of development lasting several hundred years, they learned to reach higher temperatures in their kilns and to make the proper additions to their clays to achieve the hardness, whiteness, and translucency of true porcelain. This discovery of porcelain was a technical triumph in the development of ceramics.

Kaolins are primary clays and are formed by the weathering, on the site, of feldspar. They are coarse in particle size and are therefore nonplastic compared to most sedimentary clays. Kaolins are relatively free from mineral impurities such as iron.

As found in natural deposits, kaolins are usually located in pockets rather than in extensive stratified beds. The clay substance is usually mingled with rock fragments of feldspar and quartz. Before the clay can be used, these mineral fragments must be removed by some method of purification. Sometimes the clay is floated in a series of ponds or pools where the finer fractions of clay are separated from the coarser material. Hydraulic mining is sometimes used to recover kaolin. Powerful streams of water are played against the clay beds and the resultant mixture of clay and water is led by sluices to settling ponds. The smaller particle-sized fractions of clay recovered in this manner will have a maximum of plasticity and purity.

In chemical composition kaolins approach the formula of the mineral kaolinite. Kaolin is a highly refractory clay and has a melting point above

1800°C. Used by itself, kaolin is difficult to shape into objects because of its poor plasticity, and also, because of its refractoriness, it is difficult to mature by firing into a hard, dense object. In practice, therefore, kaolin is seldom used by itself; other materials are added to it to increase its workability and to lower the kiln temperature necessary to produce a hard, dense product. As would be expected, the shrinkage of kaolin is low because of its relatively coarse grain structure, and it has little dry strength.

Kaolins will vary rather widely in their whiteness and in their plasticity. There are some less contaminated or pure secondary or sedimentary kaolins, but these tend to be darker burning, although they may have good working properties. Some of the primary kaolins are much more plastic than others, as, for example, some of those found in Florida, which are widely used to lend plasticity to whiteware bodies. English china clay is a kaolin of unusual purity and is used where extreme whiteness in the finished ware is desired.

2. Ball Clays

Ball clays are somewhat the opposite of kaolin in their properties. They are higher in iron content, more fusible, much more plastic, and fine in particle size. Ball clays and kaolin are really complementary in character and are often combined in clay bodies to adjust the mixture toward a practical, workable clay. Ball clays are said to have been so named because of the practice in England of forming the damp clay in the mines into large balls which could be rolled up onto wagons for transport.

Ball clay is a secondary or transported type of clay found in stratified layers, often alternating with layers of coal and with other types of clay. It is highly plastic. Although not so pure as kaolin, ball clay is relatively free from iron and other mineral impurities and fires to a light grey or light buff color. It tightens into a dense structure when fired to about 1300°C. Different ball clays vary considerably in composition.

Ball clays are impossible to use by themselves in pottery making because of their excessive shrinkage, which may be as high as 20% when fired to maturity. They are usually used as an admixture to other clays to gain increased plasticity and workability. In manufacturing whitewares, ball clay is indispensable as an addition to the body to overcome the nonplastic properties of kaolin. However, if whiteness is desired, not more than about 15% of ball clay can be added to a clay body; more than this amount in a whiteware body results in a grey, off-white, or buff color. The presence of ball clay in a porcelain body decreases its translucence.

In the raw, ball clays are usually dark grey because of the presence of carbonaceous material. This carbon burns off in the firing and does not affect the final fired color of the clay. The more carbon a ball clay contains, the more plastic it is apt to be. Some ball clays, however, such as those from certain districts of Tennessee, contain little carbon and are quite white in their raw state. Ball clays from England, which are valued for their high plasticity and freedom from iron, often have a great deal of carbon in them, which gives to the raw clay its dark brown or almost black color. Ball clays that contain a large amount of carbon, particularly if this carbon is in the form of bits of lignite or coal, must be carefully screened before they are used.

Ball clays are useful in a great variety of ceramic products and are mined in large quantities from extensive deposits in Kentucky and Tennessee. Various producers market them under different trade names, but the name "ball clay" always indicates a light-burning clay of high plasticity.

3. Fire Clays

Fire clay is not so well defined a type of clay as either ball clay or kaolin. The term "fire clay" refers to refractoriness or resistance to heat, and clays that vary widely in other properties may be called fire clays if they are refractory. Some fire clays are very plastic and some lack plasticity, and the fired color may vary. Any clay which resists fusion or deformation up to about 1500°C may be called fire clay. Such refractoriness or resistance to heat means that the clay is relatively pure and free from iron, although most fire clays burn to a buff or brownish color, sometimes with darker splotches due to concentrations of iron-bearing minerals.

Fire clays are useful for a great variety of products, principally in the manufacture of fire brick and other refractory parts for kilns, furnaces, boilers, and melting pots. Industries such as steel, copper, and other metallurgical industries could not operate without fire brick furnaces in which high-temperature smelting is done.

Fire clays are also used as additions to stoneware bodies or to bodies for saggers and other kiln furniture where an increase in refractoriness is desired. In stoneware bodies fire clay may furnish a desirable roughness or "tooth" to the body and may also give texture to the body, because of the presence of dark iron spots. Fire clay is also useful in mudding-in kiln doors, making clay pats for pyrometric cones, and for wadding under kiln shelves and sagger lids.

In bodies for large terracotta pieces or sculptures, the open, coarse texture of some fire clays makes them an ideal addition.

4. Sagger Clays

Saggers are clay boxes in which ware is fired to protect it from direct heat and flame in the kiln. Sagger clay is a kind of clay which has been found suitable for the manufacture of such products. A sagger clay must be quite refractory and plastic enough to be shaped by modeling, and, when fired, it must form a dense, tough body resistant to thermal shock and the "fatigue" caused by repeated firing. Sagger clays vary quite widely from medium to high plasticity, and they ordinarily fire to a light grey-buff color. Sagger clays are frequently used as additions to stoneware, terracotta, or earthenware bodies.

5. Stoneware Clays

Stoneware clays are plastic clays that mature or become vitreous between 1200°C to 1300°C. Their fired color ranges from a very light grey or buff to a darker grey or brown. Stoneware clays are secondary, or sedimentary, clays. They vary widely in color, plasticity, and firing range, and there is no sharp distinction between what might be called a fire clay, a sagger clay, or a stoneware clay. The classification really hinges on the possible use of the clay in ceramics, rather than on the actual chemical or physical nature of the clay or its geologic origin. One clay, for instance, might be successfully used both as a fire clay in the making of bricks and refractories and as a stoneware clay

in the making of high-fired stoneware pottery. Many clays are quite suitable for making stoneware without any additions. Such clays may have just the right plasticity for wheel work and may have desirable drying and firing characteristics. The small country potteries of the last century, which produced utilitarian wares such as crocks, jugs, and churns, usually employed a single stoneware clay which was dug in the neighborhood and pugged ready for use without the addition of any other clay. Such a natural clay body may burn to very pleasing colors and textures and may take salt glazes, slip glazes, or high-fired stoneware glazes.

6. Earthenware Clays

Most of the usable clay found in nature might be called earthenware clay or common clay. These clays contain iron and other mineral impurities in sufficient quantity to cause the clay to become tight and hard-fired at about 950°C to 1100°C. In the raw, such clay is red, brown, greenish, blueish, or grey, as a result of the presence of iron oxide. Fired, the clay may vary in color from pink to buff to tan, red, brown, or black, depending on the clay and the condition of the firing. Most of the pottery the world over has been made of earthenware clay, and it is also the common raw material for brick, tile, drain tile, roof tile, and other heavy clay products.

Common red clay may be highly plastic, in fact, too plastic and too sticky to be used by itself. On the other hand, it may be quite nonplastic because of the presence of sand or other rocky fragments. The potter will look for a smooth plastic earthenware clay that he may modify by the addition of some sand or some nonplastic clay. The brick maker will look for an earthenware clay that is naturally coarse and contains considerable sand or other nonplastic fragments, and with such a clay he will be able to press, dry, and fire bricks without having them warp, crack, or shrink excessively.

Vast quantities of common red clay outcrop on the earth's surface. Much of it is unusable because it contains either fragments of calcite or soluble alkaline salts. There are, however, immense reserves of usable clay, naturally forming more quickly than they are being used.

7. Other Kinds of Clay

Adobe is a surface clay suitable for making adobe or sun-dried bricks. It is rather nonplastic and contains a high percentage of sand.

Flint clay is a refractory clay which has been compacted into a relatively hard, dense, rock-like mass.

Shale is a metamorphic rock formed by nature from sedimentary clay. It has very little plasticity unless it is finely pulverized and allowed to temper for a long while. Shale may be used as an addition to, or as the principal ingredient of, bricks and other heavy clay products.

Bentonite is a clay of volcanic origin. Its major constituent is the mineral montmorillonite. Although its chemical composition is like that of clay, its physical nature is different in that it contains more colloidal, or glue-like, matter. Bentonite is used to lend plasticity to clay bodies and as a floatative in glazes. A small percentage of bentonite added to a clay body may bring about a marked increase in plasticity. Bentonite cannot be used by itself because of its tendency to swell when wet and because of its stickiness and extremely high shrinkage.

Terracotta clay is a low-grade fire clay which may be used in the manufacture of large terracotta pieces. It has an open, coarse grain structure that permits rapid and even drying.

High-alumina clays, such as bauxite or diaspore, are clays that contain a high percentage of alumina. These clays may be highly refractory and are used as the raw material for the production of the metal aluminum.

Gumbo is a surface or soil clay that is very plastic and sticky and contains a considerable quantity of organic matter.

6 MINING AND PREPARING CLAY

The great majority of ceramic artists and potters in North America purchase their clay ready-made, so, to some, the next two chapters may seem redundant. However, in order to affect a more complete understanding of the medium, I feel that it is important to include this material. Moreover, without knowing what goes into a clay body, it is often extremely difficult to solve glaze problems emanating from the clay source. To add to this problem, albeit understandably, commercial suppliers of clay bodies will seldom give out the recipe or formula of ingredients that make up their clays. Therefore a general understanding of mining and preparing clays, along with the principles of developing clay bodies, is a great help towards troubleshooting.

1. Prospecting

Although the present work is obviously not the place for an exhaustive description of clay mining and prospecting, a few words on the subject may be of interest, especially to those who wish to make use of resources that lie close at hand. One of the valuable things about ceramics, particularly from the viewpoint of teaching, is that the raw materials are very common and can usually be found, processed, and used without recourse to outside suppliers or commercial processors. It would seem desirable, furthermore, that everyone who is seriously interested in ceramics should have the experience of finding, digging out, and using a native clay. Such an experience, although it may have no commercial implications, is bound to give the potter a broader viewpoint in dealing with his materials.

The occurrence of clay is so common that finding beds of it is quite easy in most localities. However, potters must know how to look. Clay is ordinarily covered over with loam and topsoil that conceal it. This is particularly true in areas of ample rainfall where the ground is normally completely covered with vegetation of one sort or another. In drier country the earth may be more exposed and clay may be found at the surface.

The most likely place to look is usually some spot where the earth has been cut through, revealing some of the underlying strata. Along creeks and rivers, or where highway or railroad grading has cut down into the earth, the layers of clay that so frequently underlie the topsoil can be found. Clay may be recognized by the irregular and rather crumbly surface produced in its exposed faces by the rain. Outcroppings of rock tend to hold their shape, whereas clay is very rapidly disintegrated and washed down by water.

If an outcropping is thought to be clay, closer inspection and a few simple field tests will quickly determine whether or not it is. If a small sample is mixed with a bit of water and it produces a plastic sticky mass, it is undoubtedly clay. If, on the other hand, the resulting mixture remains sandy and nonplastic, the material may be sandy loam or some mixture of sand and clay, with the former predominating.

Beds of clay may be revealed during the excavation for buildings or when land is being plowed or graded. Flood conditions may deepen or widen stream channels, revealing clay beds whose presence was not suspected before. If searching for clay, expert advice may be sought from local well drillers, who usually have a wealth of data on what kind of strata underlies a particular region, or a geologist may be consulted. State geologists can sometimes be of real help in locating good clay. For many regions of the country, extensive geological and mineral resource studies have been published which may indicate the presence of usable clay in various places.

When some clay has been located, the next step is to determine of what use it might be in ceramics. Many clays, if not most, are not suitable for any practical purpose. For example, a clay that is too highly contaminated with soluble alkalies is generally not worth digging. The presence of these soluble impurities can usually be detected by scum or white staining on the dried clay. If a small piece of clay is wet down to the plastic state and then allowed to dry out, the presence of a noticeable scum on the surface, or of discoloration, usually indicates the presence of undesirable alkalies.

Another impurity that disqualifies a clay for ceramic use is lime. Lime or bits of limestone cannot be tolerated in a clay because when lime is fired it is altered from calcium carbonate to calcium oxide. Calcium oxide is an unstable oxide in the atmosphere because it takes on water or hydrates. This hydration, which will occur slowly even in a small lump of limestone buried in a fired clay object, causes the lime to swell. The swelling exerts an irresistible pressure against the fired clay that surrounds the bit of lime and the piece will break or a flake of clay will break off, revealing the troublesome impurity. Bits of plaster of Paris in fired clay cause the same difficulty. This breaking or flaking off will occur within a few days or months after firing, depending on how porous the clay body is and on the humidity to which it is exposed. It is extremely difficult to extract lime from clay, especially if the lime is in small particles. If a clay contains lime, it is better to look for another one that doesn't. A simple test will reveal the presence of lime in clay. A sample of clay may be dropped into a beaker containing a 50% solution of hydrochloric acid. If lime is present, an effervescence or bubbling will be noted. To a limited degree vinegar will also detect the presence of lime. Small percentages of finely divided lime may not cause any difficulty in high-fired clay bodies. In this case the lime is taken into combination with other oxides in the clay during firing.

Even if a clay is not contaminated with either soluble alkalies or with lime, it may be difficult to use because of the presence of too much sand or other mineral fragments. Such granular material can be screened out of the clay, but it may be found that it is not worth the trouble, especially if another clay can be located which is freer of impurities.

The presence of too much organic matter may also disqualify a clay for use. Surface clays are sometimes so loaded with carbonaceous matter and decayed vegetation that they are unusable. If a clay is excessively sticky when wet it is probably impractical for this reason, especially if it is dark brown or black.

Clay in the natural state may be white, grey, tan, red, greenish, blueish, brown or brown-black. Color in the raw clay indicates the presence of either iron oxide or carbonaceous matter. The great majority of clays contain considerable iron, and any clay which, in the raw state is grey, brown, red, yellow, blueish, or greenish may be expected to fire to a red color. The variety of color in raw clay is due to the presence of iron in different forms. Iron, which is present as hematite, or red iron oxide, will produce a red color. Limonite will give a yellow color, while ferrous iron will produce greys, greens, and blacks. All these forms of iron become hematite upon firing and produce the familiar red, tan, or brown color of fired clay. Most surface clays contain from 2% to 5% of iron oxide, and for this reason they cannot ordinarily be fired to temperatures above about cone 1. Fusible red-firing clays may be used as a major ingredient in dark-colored glazes at temperatures above cone 4. If the iron content is below 2%, the clay may be usable as a stoneware or hard earthenware clay at temperatures in excess of cone 1.

If a clay in the raw state is white or very light in color, it may be assumed that it has little iron in it and that it will fire to a light color. Such white-burning clays are usually primary or residual clays and would be more apt to occur in pockets rather than in strata. White clays are almost always of a nonplastic kind and are frequently found intermingled with considerable sand or other mineral fragments.

The degree of plasticity of a clay can best be tested by using it for whatever process is intended. One simple test is to wet the clay into a plastic mass, then to make of it a small rope about the thickness of a pencil. If such a coil of clay can be bent into a ring of 1″ or less in diameter without showing cracks, the clay is reasonably plastic. If a small amount of clay is put into the mouth and does not grit on the teeth excessively, it can be assumed to be very fine-grained. It is recommended that this test be used with restraint!

Clay is mined commercially either in open-strip mining or in underground mining of seams or strata below the surface of the earth. In strip mining the clay is scraped, dug, or planed off by power machines. Terraces are maintained to give access to the clay. Kaolins are frequently mined hydraulically, streams of water under pressure being used to dislodge the clay from the deposit and to wash it into settling ponds.

If clay is to be dug for small-scale use, the bed or seam of clay must first be uncovered and all soil, sand, or rock shoveled back, so that it will not get into the clay. Then the clay is dug out with a small sharp spade. Even if only a relatively small amount of clay is needed, it is well to select, if possible, a source that is not likely to be soon exhausted. Also, it is well to try to dig at a place where the clay is uniform in color and texture over some considerable area, so that uniform results can be expected from various batches dug. Sometimes beds or strata of clay are tilted vertically, so that although only a fairly narrow seam of clay shows at the surface, a great deal of usable material lies below. Digging clay is hard work, particularly if the clay is damp.

The following tests are suggested to determine the usefulness of a clay. Some of these tests are described in the Appendices.

1. Test for soluble impurities.
2. Test for excess sand or other mineral fragments.
3. Test for the presence of lime.
4. Test for plasticity.
5. Test for water of plasticity and for dry shrinkage.
6. Test to determine the possible firing range of the material and its fired color by firing samples to various temperatures. Cones 08, 04, 1, 4, and 9 might be suitable intervals for the first tests.
7. Test for shrinkage and absorption on samples fired to various temperatures.
8. Deflocculation test.

The accumulated data from these tests, together with the experience gained from working samples of the clay in modeling and perhaps on the potter's wheel, should give an informed estimate of the value of the clay. Of course, clay that is good for one purpose may be worthless for another. For instance, clay that would be ideal for making common bricks would be quite unsuitable for wheel-thrown pottery. Most deposits of clay are of little or no commercial value. This is because of the abundance of the material and the cost of transporting common clay any distance from the place where it is mined. However, large commercial deposits of

kaolin and ball clays are very valuable.

In testing clay to determine whether or not it can be used, it is not usually necessary to make a chemical analysis. While such an analysis may be essential in determining and controlling the composition of commercial clay, the physical nature of the clay and its reaction to firing are much more important to the ceramist. Chemical analysis rarely gives any surprising data that could not have been guessed at by an experienced person who had actually worked with the material.

In most situations it is preferable, in the long run, to buy clay from suppliers rather than to dig it. The man-hours spent in digging, screening, and mixing clay by hand are usually not justified, even considering the relatively high cost of clay and freight. However, it is a very valuable learning experience that should be part of every potter's personal development.

2. Mixing Clay

No involved or complicated procedures are required in preparing clay for use. As a material it is essentially readied by nature and needs only to be mixed with the right amount of water and cleaned of foreign matter, such as sand, leaves, twigs, or rocks.

Where two or more materials are to be mixed together to form a clay body, or where the clay must be screened to remove impurities, it is best first to mix the clay with an excess of water. Water is put into a barrel, vat, bucket, or other container of a suitable size, and the clay is added to the water. Adding the clay to the water, rather than the water to the clay, ensures that each particle of clay gets thoroughly wet and does not ball up into a sticky mass of partly wet, partly dry clay, as would be the case if water were poured on dry clay. If a clay body is being made which contains both clay and nonplastic material such as silica, it is best to add the clay first, so that it can slake in a maximum amount of water. If the clay is in lump form, it will take some time and considerable stirring to break down and disperse the lumps, so it is better to break down the lumps into small pieces. Enough water should be used to produce a fluid slip about the consistency of thick cream.

Mechanical mixers for clay slips are of two types. The blunger is a mixing machine with paddles that revolve at slow speeds, keeping the slip under constant but not violent agitation. Sometimes two sets of revolving paddles are employed to increase the turbulence. The other type is the propeller mixer, which consists of a propeller not unlike that of a marine screw, which revolves at relatively high speed and agitates the slip violently in one area of the mixing vessel. Such a mixer works exactly like a large version of a kitchen blender, and is extremely rapid and efficient in making slip from clays that have no very large lumps in them. If the material to be mixed is lumpy, such as would be the case with clay dug out of the ground, the slower action of the blunger is preferred. The blunger will take very coarse and lumpy material and, by agitating it gently in the water over a period of time, will produce a thorough mixture.

For small batches clay may be mixed by hand with a paddle or stick. This goes faster than might be expected, but for larger volumes a machine is certainly desirable to do the work. An old washing machine may be used. The back-and-forth swishing action of a washing machine is quite efficient in mixing clay.

If the clay slip must be screened to remove granular impurities, this can be done after the fluid slip is thoroughly mixed and smooth. Two barrels or containers are convenient; the slip is poured from one barrel, through a screen, into the other barrel. Screens of various mesh sizes can be used. For most clays a screening through the 60-mesh screen will remove all objectionable matter. Porcelain bodies, or whiteware bodies which must be of great purity, may be screened through a 100-mesh screen or one even finer. Screening removes not only the sand and rock fragments in the clay but also the bits of lignite or carbon.

When the slip has been screened, some or all of the water must be removed. This is a troublesome problem, even when the best equipment is available. If plastic clay is desired, enough water must be removed from the clay to bring it to a stiff, plastic condition. If casting slip is to be made, it may be best to remove all the water, so that a carefully proportioned mix can be made for the deflocculated slip. One simple way to remove a good deal of the water from slip is by settling. If the slip is allowed to sit in the barrel for several days, the clay goes to the bottom and clear water will rise to

the top. The water may then be siphoned off, and the relatively heavier slip left in the barrel. This process, though effective, may take more time than is available. Plaster of Paris bats or drying vessels may be used to suck off the excess water. Plaster is very absorbent and draws the water rapidly from the slip. For small batches, this method works very well. The difficulty is that the drying bats soon become soaked with water. Also, putting the clay into and taking it out of the bats can be a rather messy job. Sometimes one large plaster vessel is used, which may be in the form of a square vat with sides about 2″ thick and held together with an iron or wooden frame. The slip is poured into this, and when the sides of the vat have become saturated with water, the water drips off, gradually stiffening the slip. Still another method of drying slip is to put it into stout canvas bags that are hung from the ceiling. As the water seeps through the canvas and drips out, the slip in the bag gradually becomes thicker. This is a rather awkward method, and the slip bags soon become unsightly. Without any machinery for pressing the water out of clay, the best method is undoubtedly to put the slip out into drying bats of plaster or of soft-fired clay. If these bats are in a position where the air can get to them, and where the temperature is fairly high, they work quite efficiently and can be rapidly re-dried between batches. If clay is allowed to settle until it is a heavy mud and is then put into the drying bats, it will take only a short while to stiffen to a plastic condition ready for use.

Water can be removed from slip with the filter press. This machine forces the clay under pressure into fabric-lined chambers which permit the water to be squeezed out but retain the clay. The slip is put into a pressure tank and forced into the press under fifty to one hundred pounds of pressure. The individual leaves of the press are not large, which permits the water to escape fairly rapidly. After no more water will squeeze from the clay, the pressure is released, and the leaves of the press are opened, revealing in each a cake of plastic clay. While the filter press works well enough for large batches of clay, it is not a very practical machine for making small batches, especially where various compositions are being made and where the press must be cleaned between batches. This is a tedious job.

If casting slip is to be made, it is common practice to continue to dry the plastic clay until it is bone-dry, and then to make the slip by adding just the right amount of water and electrolyte (see Casting Clays, Chapter 7) to the dry clay.

If the raw materials are in the right condition, it may be possible and desirable to mix the plastic clay or the slip directly, without going through the stage of making a fluid slip with an excess of water as described above. After all, the only purpose of such a step is to insure the thorough intermixture of the ingredients of the clay and to make possible the screening of the clay to remove impurities. If the clay and the other materials of the body are already free from impurities and are in the form of fine flour or dust, it may be better to skip the step of making a thin slip. Many clays are now furnished to the trade in air-floated form. Air-floated clay has been pulverized and bagged, after having gone through an air classifier that removes and returns for further grinding all particles above a certain size. Such material is in the form of a very fine dust and needs no further screening.

Where only air-floated clays and other finely pulverized materials are to be used in a clay body, they can be mixed directly in a mixer with just enough water added to give the desired degree of plasticity. A wet-pan or Simpson type mixer may be used for this purpose. These mixers employ wheels or mullers that revolve in a pan, pressing, turning, and mixing the plastic material. The mixing can be done quite rapidly on such a machine. Mixers designed for use in bakeries to mix bread dough have been found to work well for plastic clay. There is one difficulty, however: if different batches are to be made on the same mixer, a great deal of time is lost in cleaning the machine. If no machine is available for mixing, finely ground clays may be made up by hand. The dry ingredients are first sifted or shoveled together to intermingle the dry powders thoroughly. Then water is sprinkled on gradually, while the mass of clay is turned and mixed with a spade or hoe. Clay is a very sticky substance, and mixing it by this method is a good deal of work. When the desired degree of plasticity is reached, the clay is put into a container to temper, and after a day or two it may be wedged up for use. Methods of clay mixing that aim at arriving directly at plastic clay are successful only if the raw materials are already free from impurities and in a finely ground form.

If casting slip is to be made up directly from the raw materials, the water is weighed out and the deflocculant, dry clay, and nonplastic ingredients are added to the mix in that order, stirring all the while.

To illustrate the method of mixing a relatively refined clay body, the following steps are outlined for the preparation of porcelain slip:

1. The ball clay is mixed in a blunger or agitator with a great excess of water, then screened through a 200-mesh screen.
2. The resultant ball clay slip is then dried and pulverized to small lumps.
3. The water for the slip and the deflocculant are weighed out and put in a ball mill.
4. The ball clay and the kaolin are added to the water and the mixture is ground for several hours.
5. The nonplastic ingredients are added and the slip is further ground for about three hours.
6. Before casting, the slip is strained through a 30-mesh screen to make sure no lumps are present.

Ball milling a slip serves to pulverize all particles in the mix to a very finely ground state and to give a thorough intermingling of all the materials. In the case of porcelain and whiteware slips, milling helps to break up and disperse the particles of carbon or lignite usually present in the ball clay.

Magnetic filters are used when clay bodies of exceptional whiteness are desired. The slip is passed over a magnet which draws out particles of iron. This method is particularly effective in removing specks of tramp iron, which get into clay from machinery used during mining and processing.

3. Aging, Kneading, and De-airing Clay

To the uninitiated, the aging of clay must seem like one of those superstitious practices that make potting more than a manufacturing routine. But it is an undeniable fact that the workability of clay improves with age. The subtle quality of plasticity is hard to measure exactly, but every potter will agree that his clay gets better with age and sometimes dramatically so. How can this be, since clays are already inconceivably old, having lain in the earth for millions of years?

One reason for the development of plasticity in clay over a period of time is the more thorough wetting of the particles. Time is required for water to permeate each individual grain or particle of clay and to wet over the surface of each particle. Mixing the clay first as a fluid slip facilitates this wetting. It will be noted that clays made up from dry ground clay and just enough water to achieve plasticity take longer to reach a workable condition than does clay that is stiffened to the plastic state from a fluid slip.

But, after a few days of tempering, a clay body will be thoroughly wet, and any further development of plasticity must be accounted for by bacterial action. Damp clay, especially if it is kept in a warm place, is a good culture medium, and bacteria grow rapidly in it. These bacteria produce acid residues and form gels which undoubtedly affect the clay. Aging can be promoted by adding a bit of old clay to each new batch. Placing new clay in containers to which some old clay still clings, or using coverings of old cloths may help to start the clay "working." Potters sometimes add a bit of vinegar to clay, on the theory that some acidity is a step in the right direction, and in the past various organic additions have been made to clay batches. A small amount of starch added to a batch of clay seems to hasten the development of plasticity, perhaps by giving something for bacteria to feed on. Dissolving a small amount of soap in the water used to wet the clay is thought by some to aid plasticity.

After a period of about two weeks a change begins to come over the clay. It seems denser, oilier, more friendly to the touch. This mellowing and ripening of the clay is signaled by a rich musty perfume which seems to speak of the cool darkness of the bowels of the earth. The clay is ready.

It is doubtful if prolonged aging, beyond, say, a month or two has much beneficial effect. Potters dream of a storage pit or cellar full of tons of aged clay, but rarely do they get as far ahead as that. It is said that Chinese potters put down clay for their grandchildren and use that which was prepared by their grandfathers. But in all probability even the Chinese are not so well organized as that, and their pottery shops are probably chronically short of aged clay, just as ours are.

As is described in the next chapter on earthenware bodies, some clays that have in them materials that contain slightly soluble alkalies will thus suffer rather than benefit from aging because of deflocculation, even to the point where they cannot be used. Clays which contain a relatively high amount of nepheline syenite are likely to deflocculate extensively and become unworkable.

Storing clay in the relatively sterile environment of new plastic bags is not favorable to the aging process, but it is probably the most convenient way to keep clay. Any container with a lid is suitable for clay storage. For larger amounts of clay, a brick or concrete bin or pit is ideal.

For modeling, and particularly for throwing, clay must be kneaded or wedged to remove the pockets of air and to disperse lumps and make the clay smooth and homogeneous. The clay is rolled or kneaded by hand on a plank or plaster table, or is repeatedly cut and recombined, which has the effect of crushing out all pockets of air. These methods are age-old and have been used by potters everywhere.

Clay comes alive on the wedging board. The inert ball of clay seems to acquire a coiled spring of energy within, a resilience it did not possess before, a transmission of tone from potter to clay.

Wedging by repeatedly cutting and recombining a ball of clay will give the clay particles a thoroughly random orientation. On the other hand, spiral wedging, originally an oriental method, aligns the particles parallel to the surface of the ball, and if the ball is placed on the wheelhead in the proper position, the clay platelets will be already aligned in the general direction they will assume in the walls of the thrown piece. This is thought by some to facilitate throwing, and sometimes we need all the help we can get.

For large-scale production the pug mill performs the mixing and kneading operation. The pug mill is a machine which forces the clay through a chamber with a revolving screw, operating very much in the manner of a meat grinder. The old country potter of a hundred years ago used a crude forerunner of this device, powered by a mule. A further refinement is the de-airing pug mill. This machine holds the clay under a vacuum while it is being mixed and extruded, and thus effectively removes all air pockets and produces a smoothness and density that would be impossible by hand methods. But most potters find hand-wedged clay more responsive for wheel work.

PIECES FROM COLLEAGUES, CONTEMPORARIES, MENTORS, AND STUDENTS

Charles Fergus Binns, U.S.A., Vase, 1908. Glazed stoneware. Courtesy of the Schein-Joseph International Museum of Ceramic Art, Alfred University, 1908.1. Photo by Brian Oglesbee.

Gertrud and Otto Natzler, U.S.A., Large Bowl (H331), 1956. Earthenware, crater glaze, 14-1/8" x 18-5/8" x 18-5/8". Collection of American Craft Museum, New York. Gift of the Johnson Wax Co., from Objects: U.S.A., 1977. Donated to the American Craft Museum by the American Craft Council, 1990. Photo by Eva Heyd.

Wayne Higby, U.S.A., Entry Gate Creek, 1999, tile sculpture, earthenware, raku technique, 8" x 9" x 4-1/2". Collection of the Memorial Art Gallery, Rochester, NY. Photo by Brian Oglesbee.

Rudy Autio, U.S.A., Timepiece, 1994, 33" x 24-1/2" x 17". Photo by Chris Autio.

Viktor Schreckengorst, U.S.A., Keramos, 1938. Courtesy of the Everson Museum of Art, PC 42.472. Photograph © Courtney Frisse.

Glen Lukens, Death Valley Plate, 1941. Courtesy of the Everson Museum of Art, PC 63.32. Photograph © Courtney Frisse.

Harrison McIntosh, U.S.A., Bowl, 1990. Glazed porcelain. The Corsaw Collection, museum purchase by the Schein-Joseph International Museum of Ceramic Art, Alfred University, 1991.34. Photo by Brian Oglesbee.

Edwin and Mary Scheier, U.S.A., Platter, 1991. Glazed stoneware. The Corsaw Collection, courtesy of the Schein-Joseph International Museum of Ceramic Art, Alfred University, 1994.88. Photo by Brian Oglesbee.

Rosanjin Kitaoji, Japan, Bottle, 1954. Wood-fired stoneware. Gift of the artist, courtesy of the Schein-Joseph International Museum of Ceramic Art, Alfred University, 1954.2. Photo by Brian Oglesbee.

Theodore Randall, U.S.A., Light Box, 1980. Glazed stoneware. Courtesy of Lee Baldwin. Photo by Brian Oglesbee.

Otto Heino, U.S.A., Bottle, 1994. Wood fired. The Corsaw Collection, courtesy of the Schein-Joseph International Museum of Ceramic Art, Alfred University, 1994.91. Photo by Brian Oglesbee.

Lucy Lewis, U.S.A., Jar with fine line design, 1964. Unglazed earthenware. Gift of Ann and David Shaner, courtesy of the Schein-Joseph International Museum of Ceramic Art, Alfred University, 1998.83. Photo by Brian Oglesbee.

Ken Ferguson, U.S.A., Vessel with running hares. Wood-fired stoneware. The Corsaw Collection, courtesy of the Schein-Joseph International Museum of Ceramic Art, Alfred University, 1988.2. Photo by Brian Oglesbee.

Pablo Picasso, France, Owl Wine Jug, 1958. Courtesy of the Everson Museum of Art, PC 83.5.15. Photograph © Courtney Frisse.

Georges Jeanclos, Kamakura, c. 1997. Unglazed earthenware, 13-1/2" x 24" x 22".
Collection of Nanette L. Laitman, promised gift to American Craft Museum, New York.
Photo by Eva Heyd.

Beatrice Wood, Tea Set, c. 1947. Red clay, glaze, 9-1/4" x 10" x 10" (teapot). Collection American
Craft Museum, New York. Gift of W. Osborne Webb from the estate of Aileen Osborne Webb; donated
to the American Craft Museum by the American Craft Council, 1990. Photo by Eva Heyd.

T.S. Haile, U.K., Vase, 1943. Stoneware. Courtesy of the University of Michigan Museum of Art, transfer from the College of Architecture, 1979/2.17.

Peter Voulkos, U.S.A., Bowling Green, 1999, wood-fired stoneware stack, John Balistreri anagama kiln, Ohio, 43-3/4" x 26" x 25". Photo by Schopplein Studio.

Robert Turner, U.S.A., Ashanti, 1975, stoneware, sand blasted after firing, feldspathic glaze over iron slip, 12-3/4" x 9-1/4".

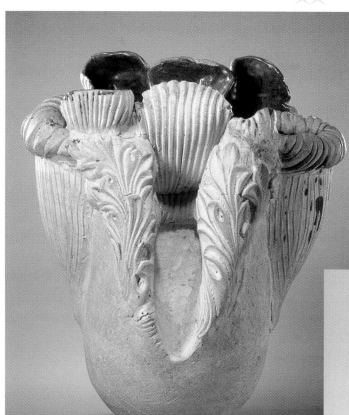

Frans Wildenhain, U.S.A., Deep Sculptured Bowl. Courtesy of the R.B. Johnston Collection. Photo by Geoff Tesch.

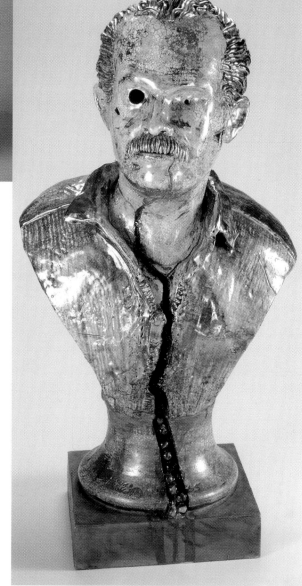

Robert Arneson, U.S.A., Self Portrait of the Artist Losing His Marbles, 1965. Earthenware, luster glaze, marbles, 31" x 17-1/2" x 9-1/2". Collection of American Craft Museum, New York. Gift of the Johnson Wax Co.; donated to the American Craft Museum by the American Craft Council, 1990. Photo by Eva Heyd.

Harding Black, U.S.A., Porcelain Bowl, 1984, wheel thrown, reduction
fired with flame glaze over iron slip, 2-1/2" x 7-1/2" x 7-1/2". Courtesy
of Baylor University. Photo by Paul McCoy.

Warren Mackenzie, U.S.A., Wide Footed Bowl, shino glaze with iron brushwork.

Paul Soldner, U.S.A., untitled, wheel thrown and altered, low temperature salt fired, unglazed, 29" x 35" x 31".

James F. McKinnell, U.S.A., Flat Bowl, porcelain, clear glaze over wax and engobe brush decoration, black luster lines, touches of mother of pearl luster, 12-3/4" diameter.

Nan McKinnell, U.S.A., Double Walled Porcelain Pot, thrown and altered, celadon glaze, 4-1/2" x 5-1/2".

Maurice Grossman, U.S.A., Ganesha Shrine, 1997, slab construction, molded surface application, raku fired, 8" x 14" x 4". Photo by the artist.

David Shaner, U.S.A., Pillow Form - Mirror Opening. Photo by Marshall Noice.

Marie Woo, U.S.A.,
Wall Piece, stoneware,
20″ diameter. Photo
by R.H. Hensleigh.

William Parry, U.S.A., OB #26 (Off Butterfly - back), 1987, stoneware clay, slip glaze, cone 6,
35″ x 18″ x 13″. Photo by Brian Oglesbee.

T.S. Haile, U.K., Orpheus, 1941,
stoneware, with pigments and glaze.
Courtesy of the Everson Museum of Art.
PC 63.30. Photograph © Courtney Frisse.

Richard Shaw, U.S.A.,
Open Book, porcelain.
Courtesy of the Everson
Museum of Art. PC
80.230.b. Photograph
© Courtney Frisse.

Val Cushing, U.S.A., Storage Jar,
stoneware, 20″ high.

Richard Zakin, U.S.A., untitled, 1995, colored clays,
11″ high.

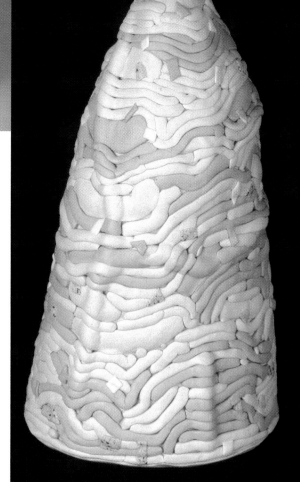

Don Reitz, U.S.A., Punch Out, 1999, wood fired, cone 11, 10" x 6".

Gertrud and Otto Natzler, U.S.A., Earthenware Vase, 1958. Courtesy of the Everson Museum of Art. PC 60.12. Photograph © Courtney Frisse.

7 CLAY BODIES

1. Definition of a Clay Body

A clay body may be defined as a mixture of clays or clays and other earthy mineral substances which are blended to achieve a specific ceramic purpose. Many clays found in nature serve very well just as they are. In brick making, for example, it would be uneconomical to have to do much mixing or blending of raw materials, and, in fact, clay that will do quite well for common brick manufacture is found in many localities. Similarly, many clays can be dug out of the ground, kneaded with the right amount of water, and made into pottery without making any additions. Such clays might be called natural clay bodies. The potter, in pre-scientific times, relied largely upon such clays for his raw material and made few or no additions to them. Sometimes, however, adjustments were made for better working properties. For example, some sand might have been added to reduce the shrinkage and lessen the tendency of the clay to warp when dried and fired.

However, the demands potters make of clay as a material today usually make it necessary to blend two or more materials to achieve the desired results. Such demands may, for example, be extreme plasticity to make the clay suitable for throwing, or complete density at a given firing temperature, or whiteness and translucency when fired, or the property of casting, as a fluid slip, or the development of certain desirable colors and textures. In order to arrive intelligently at suitable mixtures for a given use, it's vital to understand the physical properties of clays and their response to firing, and also the physical and thermal properties of other materials used in clay bodies.

2. The Ways in Which Clay Bodies Need to Be Altered to Make Them Useful

In practice it is usually necessary to make additions to a natural clay in order to have it serve the practical needs of forming and firing. The ways in which it might be desired to change a clay for practical purposes may be listed as follows:

1. Changes of color or texture. It may be desired to alter the fired color of the clay to make it either a lighter or a darker shade, or to increase or decrease its granular roughness or texture.
2. Changes in plasticity. It may be desired to make a clay more plastic or less plastic.
3. Changes to decrease shrinkage or to improve drying and firing with a minimum of warpage or cracking.
4. Changes to lower the maturing temperature or to raise the maturing temperature. Or, stated another way, changes that will increase or decrease density at a given temperature.
5. Changes to improve the fit of glazes.

Leaving aside changes in color and texture for the moment, it can be seen that all adjustments in clays involve either: (a) adjustment of its physical properties to give the desired plasticity, workability, and shrinkage, or (b) adjustment of its reaction to firing, either raising or lowering the degree of heat necessary to bring about the desired degree of density.

Changes of the first type are made by adding clays or other materials of more or less plasticity and of varying particle size. Changes of the second type are made by adding clays or other materials of more or less fusibility.

3. Porcelain as an Example of a Clay Body

An example of a clay body would be the type of mixture or blend of materials used in making white, translucent porcelain, fired at about 1300°C. The proportion of materials found satisfactory for such a body is approximately as follows:

China clay or kaolin	5 parts
Feldspar	3 parts
Silica	2 parts

China clay by itself would not be practical for making porcelain because its high melting point, 1500°C or more, would require an impractical degree of heat to bring about fusion and translucency or glassiness. Therefore, feldspar would be added, which, by itself, melts to glass at a temperature of about 1300°C. This material, acting upon the clay, brings the whole mass to the point of fusion. It is further necessary to add silica or powdered quartz for the double purpose of improving the resistance of the body to warping and of giving hardness and stability to the semi-glassified final body. As will be seen later, the silica also enables the glaze to fit to the body more easily.

While the above composition may fire to a pure white, translucent body, it will be difficult to use in making pottery because of the nonplastic character of the mixture. The clay is apt to be too mealy and crumbly to model or throw, and is likely to cast too rapidly in molds and be difficult to smooth and finish. To correct these troubles, a more plastic clay must be added, such as a ball clay. While such an addition may correct the working properties of the body, it would also decrease the whiteness of the fired clay because of the higher iron content of the ball clay. Some compromise must then be made, either with whiteness or with workability. A practical porcelain body, then, might have approximately the following composition:

China clay	4 parts
Ball clay	1 part
Feldspar	3 parts
Silica	2 parts

Final adjustment of such a body would depend on the exact temperature to be used, the kinds of clays available, and the fusibility of the feldspar. The combination of china clay and feldspar and its firing at elevated temperatures were essentially the closely guarded secrets of the Chinese potters in their manufacture of white, translucent porcelain. The plasticity of the kaolins in China usually made it unnecessary for them to use plastic materials of the ball clay type; and their clay bodies, of marvelous purity of color and translucency, were rightly the envy of European potters. The method of compounding and firing porcelain bodies was rediscovered in Europe in 1710 by Herman Boettger, in Meissen, Germany.

4. The Method of Arriving at a Suitable Blend of Materials

The logic involved in formulating a porcelain body is obvious, given the desired end product and the nature of the ingredients. But how are the relative amounts of the various ingredients arrived at? In practice this is done empirically, or by experimentation and testing. The primitive potter who added more sand to his clay until it would dry without cracking and fire without breaking was making a clay body. He proceeded by empirical methods, and although he may not have known the logic of his procedure, eventually he arrived at workable compositions.

Actually, most potters proceed today in much the same fashion. If a clay does not work properly by itself, we correct its bad habits by making additions of other clays, or other materials, to it. Theoretically, in the light of our relatively complete knowledge of the chemistry and physics involved in physical and thermal reactions, it might be possible to predict with some accuracy what any combination of clays might do in a body fired to a given temperature. But such a prediction would still need to be tested to be verified. The ceramist generally proceeds by making predictions or guesses, and then, through trial and error, arrives at a mixture that works well in practice. This is the way clay bodies were typically developed in the past, and is still the major approach today. However, since the development of the personal computer, we can now make use of ceramic industry computer software programs, such as *Insight*, to greatly simplify the trial and error approach and solve problems through chemical composition comparisons.

For the potter who may or may not have access to computers and ceramic software programs, what is of most interest is the physical character of the ingredients, such as plasticity and grain structure, and their thermal behavior, such as shrinkage and fusibility.

For convenience, all the materials which go into clay bodies may be thought of as being plastics, i.e., clay; or as fillers, which are nonplastic materials like silica, grog, or calcined clay; or as fluxes, such as feldspar or frit. Plastics lend the necessary workability and plasticity to a clay body, and even a clay body which is to be used in casting or pressing needs to have a certain degree of plasticity. The fillers enable the clay to dry out safely without undue warping or cracking, and they decrease the amount of shrinkage. The fluxes control the fusion or hardening point of the clay and make it fire to a satisfactory degree of density at whatever temperature is being used.

5. Formulating a Stoneware Body

As an example of the kind of thinking that goes into the formulation of a clay body, and of the way empirical testing of such a body might proceed, the following example is given.

Suppose the aim is to formulate a stoneware body for use in general pottery making, and particularly for working on the potter's wheel. It might be desirable for the clay to mature to a nearly vitreous body at 1280°C, to shrink no more than 13%, and to be relatively free from warping, deformation, and cracking. This is an easier problem than making a porcelain body, because it is much more likely that some naturally occurring clay will serve as a complete body with little or perhaps no adjustment. The first step in formulating such a stoneware body will be to find a clay that will be, as nearly as possible, serviceable without any alteration. Suppose that the best natural, unadulterated clay available has the following characteristics:

Plasticity - good, but not quite good enough for the intended use.
Shrinkage - a total drying and firing shrinkage of 10% at cone 9.
Water absorption of fired clay - 6%.
Warping or cracking - none.

From these data, which can be obtained by a few simple tests for plasticity, shrinkage, and absorption (see Appendix), it will be seen that in this instance a further increase of plasticity is needed and that the fusibility of the clay needs to be increased to make it mature into a denser, less absorbent fired structure at this particular working temperature. Since the shrinkage of the clay is only 10%, somewhat more plastic clay can be added without the danger of increasing the shrinkage unduly or causing excessive warping. The stoneware clay, in other words, is not quite plastic enough and does not mature at the temperature at which it's ideal to work, and it must be changed to make it satisfactory for use.

The next step might be to make a chart, indicating a series of predictions or guesses as to the best combinations of materials for the purpose. Either a few or a great many tests might be made. Usually it is better to start with a few trials, since the results of these preliminary trials may give a more precise indication of what further work needs to be done. The first tests might be made as indicated in the chart below, which should be read downwards.

	#1	#2	#3	#4
Stoneware clay	55	45	60	50
Ball clay	20	20	15	15
Silica	15	15	15	15
Feldspar	10	20	10	20

The chart shows four different bodies, all made by adding differing volumes of other materials to the original stoneware clay.

Test #1 represents an estimate of exactly what materials need to be added to solve the problem and make a workable body. The twenty parts of ball clay are added to increase the plasticity of the mixture. The ten parts of feldspar are added to lower the fusion point of the clay and to make it more dense at the intended temperature. The fifteen parts of silica are added to ensure good drying, give a harder fired body, and to improve the chances of glaze fit.

The question is: How are these figures arrived at? Actually, they depend upon knowledge of the materials being added and are based largely on previous experience with similar problems. In other words, until recently, there were really no fixed rules for formulating clay bodies. As has been done throughout history, the potter usually proceeds by trial and error rather than on the basis of exact theory. The ceramic chemist or consultant nowadays uses ceramic calculation software to minimize the likelihood of error and to get closer to a suitable clay body in a shorter period of time. Knowledge of raw materials then comes into play as chemical calculation procedures are no match for the sensitivity found in a potter's fingertips. It is there that the quality of a clay body is most accurately determined.

Since it is uncertain exactly how body #2 will actually perform or fire and since it represents merely the best guess out of many possibilities, other combinations may also be made. In body #2, silica and ball clay are held constant, and an additional ten parts of feldspar are added at the expense of the stoneware clay. This mixture covers the possibility that the ten parts of feldspar in body #1 might not be enough. Bodies #3 and #4 are the same as #1 and #2, except that the ball clay content is lowered by five parts and the stoneware clay is increased by five parts. This covers the possibility that the original twenty parts of ball clay in #1 and #2 might be too high and cause excessive shrinkage.

In such a group of tests the number of variables in the series is held to a minimum. If new variables are introduced in each test, interpretation of the results becomes difficult. If several ingredients are changed in one test, it may be impossible to know exactly what material or combinations of material caused the fired result.

As the next step, the four bodies indicated on our chart would be mixed up, made into plastic samples, and tested. Tests for plasticity are inexact, but in practice, if ware is made from the test bodies by throwing or jiggering, a fairly good idea can be obtained of their workability. Other properties may be determined from fired samples. Suppose that, after firing to cone 9, the four body tests were evaluated as below:

	#1	#2	#3	#4
Dry shrinkage	5%	4.5%	4%	4%
Plasticity	good	good	good	good
Total shrinkage	13%	12%	11%	11.5%
Absorption at cone 9	5%	2%	5%	2%
Warping	none	none	none	none

These results show that the addition of ball clay in #1 has corrected the plasticity toward a point near the objective. Body #2 and #4 are too dense, which indicates the presence of too much feldspar, and #1 and #3 are not quite dense enough, which indicates that the proper amount of feldspar would probably be somewhere between 10% and 20%.

The next set of tests would aim at further adjustments of the body toward the desired objective, and the final choice of a body composition might be as follows:

Stoneware clay	52
Ball clay	20
Silica	10
Feldspar	18

The empirical process of formulating body compositions is somewhat like cooking - the proof of the pudding is in the eating. For most potters and ceramic artists, this is the only practical way to work, and until the advent of personal computers, the only way. Computers and software programs are still beyond the financial reach of many, so the empirical method remains the method most used by potters. The recipe is improved over a series of variations until it performs, in practice, as desired. The number of ingredients is usually not great, and the individual behavior of each ingredient may be well known. For this reason, formulating clay bodies is not particularly difficult and may usually be accomplished with fewer tests than are required in the case of originating glazes. The tolerance of minor variation in a clay body is great. Any one of the ingredients may be changed by 5% or 10% without making an easily detectable difference. In studio work or small-scale production, the exact control of body composition is less necessary than in large-scale industry, where complete uniformity of results is essential. Sometimes, however, after a clay body has been used for a considerable time, difficulties in production and firing may appear which were unnoticed at first, and minor adjustments may be needed to correct the body. Some of these difficulties may be through changes in the mined materials, or the complete loss of a material as the mine gets played out or closed for economical reasons. In such a situation, a rational attack on the problem, based on the known properties of the original materials, may save a great deal of time.

6. Clay Bodies Designed for Particular Forming Methods

Not only must clay bodies be designed for a particular firing temperature so as to give, at that temperature, the desired color, texture, and degree of hardness and density required; they must also be designed for particular forming methods. Clay may be shaped into objects either by modeling, throwing, jiggering, pressing, dry pressing, or slip casting in molds. Each of these methods of shaping demands certain physical properties in the clay. For example, a clay for throwing on the wheel must be very plastic, while for modeling or pressing much less plasticity is required and may, in fact, be a disadvantage because of the excessive shrinkage of highly plastic clay. Some clays which are quite adequate for some processes will not work at all for others. It is unlikely, for example, that a clay that casts well will be good for wheel work.

7. Throwing Clays

In throwing, potters make extreme demands on the plasticity of clay. A really good throwing clay should not take on water readily while being worked, and should stand well and hold its shape even when soft and thin in section. While it is possible to throw simple forms from very granular and nonplastic clays, the complete range of possible thrown shapes demands a dense, highly plastic, and cohesive clay, with just enough rough material in it to furnish a slight "tooth" to aid the clay in standing while wet and soft at the end of the throwing operation. In throwing clays, potters must be prepared to accept a high shrinkage and some tendency toward warping, and the ware must, as a consequence, be carefully managed in drying and firing.

As a general rule, throwing bodies are made with as small a percentage as possible of nonplastic substances in them, such as silica and feldspar. A single, naturally occurring clay may be an excellent one for throwing, and such clays are not unusual, especially in earthenware types of clay. If such natural bodies are unavailable, a combination of several plastic clays of various kinds may do as well. Ball clay is almost always used to increase plasticity. When the proportion of ball clay rises to about 30%, however, trouble with shrinkage and drying may begin and the body may become unpleasantly sticky.

Adding flux to a throwing body is something of a problem, because nonplastic powders such as feldspar, talc, or frit may seriously decrease the plasticity. Some nonplastic materials such as nepheline syenite may also cause deflocculation to occur in clay bodies stored for more than three months. This causes thixotropy to occur, where the clay gets softer to the point of being nonworkable. If a dark-burning clay is desired, this difficulty may be overcome by adding a red clay of low fusibility and high plasticity, which acts as a flux.

Although throwing clay must be plastic and dense, every thrower discovers that a clay that is too smooth and fine-grained throughout will not stand up in large or tall forms. For making such forms, and especially for pieces more than about 12″ high, a clay with some tooth to it is necessary. Grog, fine sand, or coarse clay in a throwing body seems to give it the necessary bones or structure to make it stand up. It has been found that grog sized to pass through the 30-mesh screen and to stay on the 80-mesh screen is most suitable for throwing clay. If the grog is too fine, it decreases plasticity and makes the clay wet too rapidly; if, on the other hand, the grog is too large in grain size, it makes the clay excessively abrasive to the hands. A rough fire clay or ground silica clay may be added to throwing bodies in place of, or in addition to, grog. In general, about 8% to 10% of granular material will greatly improve the performance of a throwing clay. If more than 10% of grog is present, it may be found that the clay wets too rapidly during throwing and is insufficiently plastic.

A potter can make only so large or tall a pot with any given clay. Each clay body will reach a point where it will not stand in a higher cylinder, but will slump down. No matter how skillful the thrower is, he cannot achieve a taller piece than his material will allow in structural strength. It is for this reason that the skilled thrower is very much concerned with the composition of his clay. He wants a material that will allow him to achieve the full range of form and scale his skill permits. And, once accustomed to one certain clay, the potter may find it difficult to throw well with any other. It is true that many beginning pottery students struggle along with clay mixtures which the most skilled thrower would find impossible to manage, and in ignorance they tend to blame themselves rather than the material for their failures. The right clay body for wheel work is very important, and a large part of the creative pleasure in throwing pottery lies in the possession of a dense, fat, well-aged, and responsive clay.

Bentonite may be added to a clay to improve its workability on the wheel. Bentonite swells and forms a gel when wet, and the presence of a small amount of it in a clay body will greatly increase plasticity. If more than about 2% of bentonite is used, however, the clay may become excessively sticky and be difficult to wedge. Too much bentonite also may cause drying problems.

Macaloid, a montmorillonite clay and similar in use to bentonite, has approximately twice the plasticity of bentonite and so should be used at half the quantity of bentonite. It should be mixed with warm water before being added to a clay body.

Other more recently developed products such Veegum "T," Hectobrite, etc., are now being used and may be more available. In general, the families of bentonites, smectites, and hectorites all produce good plasticizing abilities. Many of these highly beneficiated bentonites are surface treated with organic polymers to increase their properties. A polymer is any long-chain organic chemical, from nasal mucus to seaweed to the excrement of stressed out cabbage worms, which is a form of a slime. The slimes may be dehydrated but regain their properties when water is added.

8. Modeling Clays

Making clay mixtures that will be good for modeling is a relatively simple problem. Since modeled objects such as sculptures, tiles, architectural pieces, or large hand-built pots are usually rather thick, a clay is required which will dry out rapidly and safely with little danger of cracking. The clay must also fire safely, especially during the initial stages of heating when water is being driven from the clay. A large amount of grog brings about these necessary properties in a modeling clay. The usual amount of grog is 20% to 30% and it may be coarse or smooth, depending on the textural effect desired. A coarse fire clay may be used instead of, or in addition to, grog. Some coarse fire clays by themselves make splendid modeling clays. Some processes, such as building intricate shapes in coils or ropes of clay, or the making of extreme shapes may call for considerable plasticity as well as for coarse texture. Mixtures of very plastic clay, such as ball clay, with coarse material, such as fire clay and grog, may give the right degree of plasticity without unduly increasing shrinkage or making drying and firing difficult. A small percentage of bentonite, or other plasticizer, from 1% to 3%, up to 2% or 3%, has been found useful in giving added cohesiveness and "stand" to a modeling clay. Modeling clay that is too smooth and greasy can be very unpleasant to work with, and even a small amount of experience will make the modeler appreciate a good, rough-textured, plastic clay which can be finished off either smoothly by pressing or burnishing-in the grog or roughly by scraping the surface.

Lightweight clay bodies may be made by mixing combustible aggregates with the plastic clay. These burn out in firing, leaving pits or voids in the fired structure. Sawdust, coffee grounds, groundup fruit pits or nutshells, or the like can be used. In the plastic state such organic additions to the clay act somewhat in the manner of grog, adding toughness and facilitating drying. During the firing, complete combustion of the aggregate occurs, usually without difficulty if a normal firing cycle is followed. Lightweight bodies have been found useful for large pieces and for architectural elements where weight is a factor.

Pearlite, or perlite, is sometimes used to make a lightweight body. This mineral, a volcanic ash, is very light. It is added to the body just as a grog would be added.

9. Casting Clays

A clay body that will cast well must be designed with the physical nature of casting slips taken into account. The process of casting requires a fluid suspension of clay in water, which will flow readily but will not settle in the molds. The clay slip must pour smoothly from the mold, leaving a surface free from lumps or roughness. Furthermore, pieces which are cast must not wet the mold unduly, must release themselves from the mold upon drying, and must not have an excessive shrinkage or warpage.

An ordinary mixture of clay and water will not cast well in a plaster mold. For one thing, a great deal of water is required to make clay flow as a liquid suspension. Usually it takes about as much water as clay, by weight, to make a slip. Such a slip, although it will flow, has the serious disadvantage of a tendency to settle, leaving water at the top and a heavy sludge at the bottom. Also, when such a slip is drained out of the mold, it will leave a roughness and lumpiness where the excess clay has drained away. Upon drying, the piece is very apt to stick to the mold in spots and to shrink and warp excessively because of the high water content of the clay.

Casting, then, would not be a practical way of making pots unless there were some way of cutting down on the amount of water required to make a fluid slip. The process that achieves this result is known as deflocculation. When clay and water are mixed together to form a slip, they are said to be in a flocculent condition. That is, the minute grains of clay are gathered together in clumps or "flocks," and each grain of clay, instead of floating separately by itself in the water and thus flowing easily over and around its neighboring particles, is drawn into a globule of many particles. These flocks or clumps of clay grains require a lot of water, relatively, to make them flow.

The tendency of clay particles to draw together into groups when suspended in water can be explained by electric attraction.

In order to decrease the amount of water needed in the clay slip, it is necessary to disperse the clay particles, to break up the flocks, so that each particle of clay is floating by itself. This is accomplished by adding to the clay some substance - usually an alkali such as sodium silicate or soda ash - which is known as an electrolyte. An electrolyte has the effect of changing the electrical charge on some of the particles of clay and thus causing them to repel one another and to float individually in the water rather than clinging together in groups.

In practice, only a very small amount of electrolyte, or deflocculant, is necessary to prepare a casting slip. Between .3% to 1.5% of the weight of the clay will usually be sufficient. The most commonly used deflocculants are sodium silicate and soda ash. Sodium silicate is the familiar "water-glass." It is a compound of soda and silica made by fusing the two into a glass, which is then dissolved in water by heat and pressure. The relative amounts of silica and soda and the amount of water present in sodium silicate vary, and various brands will have different formulas. It is well always to use the same type of sodium silicate to be sure of consistent results in deflocculation. The sodium silicate is weighed out in a beaker, rather than measured, even though it is a liquid. Soda ash, which is also commonly used as a deflocculant, is a crystalline powder, readily soluble in water. It may be weighed out and then dissolved in the water with which the slip is to be made. It is common to use a combination of both soda ash and sodium silicate, in about equal parts, for deflocculating slips. Soda ash and sodium silicate are still the most common deflocculants, but Darvan 7 from the R.T. Vanderbilt Co., and Spinks 211 from the Spinks Clay Co., are just two of the newer, more stable and less sensitive products on the market. They are sodium poly acralates.

When a deflocculant is used in making a slip, very much less water is necessary to make a smooth-flowing liquid suspension. Whereas in a mixture of clay and water about equal parts of each by weight are required to make a slip, in a deflocculated slip something less than half this amount of water will be needed. Most casting slips contain from 35% to 50% of water to the weight of the clay, by weight. This amount of water, if no deflocculant is used, is barely enough to make a clay plastic enough to model. It is surprising what a potent effect a small amount of deflocculant has upon the physical nature of a mixture of clay and water.

The usual casting slip, then, has about thirty-five to fifty parts of water to the dry ingredients by weight, and .3% to 1.5% of deflocculant, or mixed deflocculants, by weight of the dry ingredients. In other terms, one hundred parts of clay would require thirty-five to fifty parts of water and between one third and one and one half parts of deflocculant. In mixing a casting slip, the best procedure is to weigh out the water and the dry ingredients first. Then the deflocculant is carefully weighed out and added to the water and stirred until it is thoroughly dispersed. Then the dry ingredients are gradually added, while being mixed continuously. Unless the deflocculant is first added to the water, the mass of clay may remain so heavy as to make mixing impossible, even when all the water is added.

Although sodium silicate and soda ash are the most commonly used deflocculants, others are sometimes used, such as sodium based water softeners such as Darvan and Calgon. Sodium hydroxide is a strong deflocculant, but it has the disadvantage of being caustic and must be handled carefully. Sodium pyrophosphate, which is usually sold as a wetting agent or cleaning aid, may also be used. Tetrasodium pyrophosphate, another soda compound, has been found to be effective in deflocculating some clays that do not seem to respond to other deflocculents. Sodium tannate, an organic compound, is also sometimes used.

Some clays do not deflocculate at all and cannot be used in casting slips. Common surface clays containing considerable iron or free alkali are usually difficult, if not impossible, to make into practical casting slips. The more pure clays, such as kaolin and ball clay, usually can be readily deflocculated and make good casting slips. Many buff-burning stoneware clays and fire clays also deflocculate and cast well.

The problem is, of course, to determine the minimum amount of water and the proper amount of deflocculant that will be required. To determine the amount of deflocculant and water needed for a clay body to make it into a serviceable slip, the following procedure may be employed. First, the clay body is thoroughly mixed with an excess of water. This serves to thoroughly intermix all the ingredients of the body, such as clay, silica, and feldspar. After it has been mixed, the slip is partially dried out in a plaster vessel and then allowed to become bone-dry. Drying in a dryer or oven at slightly more than 100° will ensure complete drying. The dried clay is then pulverized in a mortar to a powder which will pass through a 20-mesh screen. It is next weighed out in fifty-gram packets. The test is usually made on a total amount of 500 grams of clay. Water is next measured into a clean bowl. Since the aim is to defloc-culate 500 grams of clay, it can be assumed that at least 300 grams of water will be needed, since slips seldom, if ever, contain a smaller percentage of water than this. The clay is added to the water fifty grams at a time, and each addition is stirred so that it is completely mixed into the water without lumps. After about 250 grams of clay have been stirred in, it will be noted that the mixture is becoming pasty and is no longer fluid. At this point some deflocculant is added. This is accomplished by slowly adding sodium silicate, drop by drop, from a burette. To facilitate the flow of drops of fluid from the burette, the sodium silicate may be reduced in viscosity by mixing it with an equal part of water, which will thus make a 50% solution. After a few drops of the defloc-culant have been added, the slip will again become very fluid and more clay can be added until the slip is again too stiff to flow. Then another drop or two of the deflocculant can be added. Clay, sodium silicate, and more water are thus added until all the clay has been put into the mixture. Then it can be noted how much sodium silicate is missing from the burette - the amount required to deflocculate the given amount of that particular clay. If the amount of water required goes higher than fifty parts of water for each hundred parts of clay, it is not likely that the casting slip will be satisfactory, since the large amount of water will cause excessive warping and shrinking, and may make the pieces stick to the molds. If the slip does not deflocculate at all on the first test, but remains thick and nonfluid, some other deflocculant or combination of deflocculants may be tried. If these do not work, it may be that no matter what deflocculants are used, the particular clay being tested will not make a satisfactory casting slip.

After making a test for deflocculation, it is well to let the slip stand for an hour or more to determine whether or not it has a tendency to gel. If it does, too much or too little deflocculant may have been used. It is important that casting slips remain in a fluid state even when not being stirred. If the trial slip is cast into a small mold, its performance in actual casting may be checked. If the slip drains from the mold, leaving the piece with a smooth, regular interior, it is working well. Sometimes the slip is not fluid enough and leaves bumps, lumps, or "curtains" on the inside of the piece. In this case its viscosity will have to be adjusted by changing the kind or amount of deflocculant, by increasing the water content, or by altering the formula of the body, perhaps substituting clays that are better casters for those causing the trouble.

It is sometimes quite difficult to get a slip to behave perfectly in practice, and in large-scale manufacture the condition of the slip is always of concern. Minor adjustments may be necessary after a slip has been thoroughly tested over a period of time by daily use in casting. Sometimes difficulties arise from the alkalinity of the water, from a change in the water, from subtle changes in the clays used, from the moisture content of the dry clays or other materials used, or from mechanical difficulties in mixing and getting the air stirred out of the slip. All these difficulties are, of course, curable, but it sometimes takes careful and perhaps extended testing to remove the cause of the trouble.

After pottery is cast in molds, there is usually a spare part at the top that must be trimmed away to form the finished edge. The scrap from such trimming is perfectly good clay, and the potter will want to reclaim it and use it again. The trouble is that the scrap has some deflocculant left in it. Not all the deflocculant is there, because some of it migrates into the mold along with the water that is sucked out of the slip during the casting process. It is hard to tell just how much more deflocculant should be added to scrap to make it similar to its original condition. The usual practice is to keep the scrap and add to each new batch of slip a certain amount of scrap, either dry or in the damp state. By rule-of-thumb it can be determined just how much additional deflocculant should be added to the mix to take care of the deficiency in the scrap.

Cast pieces frequently stick in the molds, which causes warping and cracking. This trouble may be caused by too much water in the slip, or by a combination of materials in the slip, which makes it too plastic and sticky. If neither of these conditions is present, the trouble must be sought in the condition of the molds, which may be wet or may have surfaces sealed over with soap, grease, or other foreign matter. Sometimes slips that contain free iron oxide tend to stick in the molds, and if a red slip is wanted, it is better to rely on red-burning natural clays, if possible, rather than on an addition of iron oxide.

Deflocculants have a corrosive effect on plaster molds, and for this reason the less deflocculant a slip contains, the better. The sodium silicate and soda ash penetrate the mold as a solution in the water of the casting slip, and they tend to stay in the mold, except for some of the material that forms as a delicate fuzz on the surface of the mold when it dries. The surfaces of the molds are, of course, subject to mechanical wear in addition to the chemical deterioration caused by the deflocculant, and for this reason molds cannot be expected to last beyond a certain number of casts. Hardened plasters such as Hydrocal, Hydrostone, and Ultracal are now being used for molds to cut down on this problem.

The length of time required to make a casting of normal thickness will vary according to the differences in casting slips. Slips that are quite nonplastic and contain a high percentage of silica, feldspar, or other nonclay substances will cast rapidly. The wall of solid clay which forms on the mold in the case of such nonplastic slips offers little barrier to the flow of water toward the mold, and a thick coating is rapidly formed. On the other hand, slips that are highly plastic will be slow casters. Slips that are very nonplastic are exceedingly hard to cast because of their drying speed, and also because they are difficult to trim and have so little strength in the leather-hard state that it is difficult to get the pieces out of the molds. More plastic compositions make for more leisurely casting, easy trimming and handling, and a higher percentage of good pieces. The usual casting time for a normal clay and for a vessel with normal thickness is from ten minutes to half an hour, depending on the condition of the mold, the type of piece, and the exact thickness desired.

In formulating bodies for slip casting, the factors of deflocculation and casting properties must be taken into account. Since casting does not require any manipulation of clay in a plastic state, the plasticity of the clay can be very much less than that required for bodies to be thrown. Actually, too much plasticity in a casting clay can be a source of difficulty. In practice, casting bodies usually have not much more than 50% of clay in them, the rest being made up of nonplastic materials such as silica, feldspar, and other fluxes. Some ball clay, however, is usually necessary in a slip to ensure adequate dry strength and to make trimming and handling easy. Clays are selected which are known to cast well, and some clays that might be otherwise desirable may have to be passed up because they cannot be made to deflocculate. Other than the factors of plasticity, castability, and the balance between plastic and nonplastic ingredients, the usual principles prevail in the formulation of casting bodies. A body that casts well is usually not plastic enough for throwing; but frequently a body can be made that will cast well and will also press and jigger well.

10. Bodies for Jiggering and Pressing

If objects are to be made on the jigger wheel, the clay body must be of medium plasticity and must dry with minimum shrinkage and warpage. Pieces are usually left on the mold after jiggering, and the drying shape must accommodate itself to a new position on the mold as it dries and shrinks to a smaller size. This requires a clay of some toughness, yet one that does not shrink excessively. A blend between the ball clays on the one hand and the more nonplastic kaolins, stoneware clays, or earthenware clays on the other will give the desired properties for any given process or system of drying. There is no way of predicting beforehand exactly what any given combination of clays will do when subjected to a particular process, such as jiggering. In arriving at a suitable jiggering clay, there is no substitute for trial-and-error testing.

Bodies that are to be pressed from plastic clay may be considerably less plastic than those bodies that are to be formed by jiggering. In pressing, the clay must be soft enough to flow into the cavity of the mold while under pressure, but the plasticity of the clay is not much of a factor except insofar as plasticity and strength are related. Pressed ware is commonly handled immediately after pressing and must be strong enough to retain its shape.

11. Color and Texture in Clay Bodies

The natural colors of fired clay may range from pure white or grey, through light tans, buff, red or orange-red, through brown and dark brown to black. This range of color, although it is predominantly warm and rather limited in hue, is actually sufficient to give a wide selection of color for various kinds of pottery. In texture, clay may range from the very smooth to the extremely rough. The color and texture of fired clay is very reminiscent of the rocks, sands, and outcroppings of the earth; in fact, the color of ceramic pieces is usually produced by iron oxide, just as the color of the earthy substances around us is produced by iron in one form or another. We respond sympathetically to the color of fired clay, perhaps because it shares this earthy or rocky color that we associate with the landscape. Almost everyone has a liking for the simple, honest texture and color of bricks, flowerpots, and other fired clay objects such as drain tile and red roof tiles. This earthy range of color comes about very easily and naturally in ceramics, and though it is easy, as we shall see, to alter the color of a clay body, the colors of natural clays when fired are more often than not found to be very pleasing.

Almost all clays contain enough iron to give them a slightly warm tone when fired. The pure white clay is certainly the exception; most of the surface or common clays have enough iron in them to give a pronounced brown, tan, red, or buff when fired. Other coloring oxides are apt to be in clay besides iron, notably manganese, but these are usually in such small quantity that their coloring effect is overwhelmed by the iron. Some clays, however, are so contaminated with iron, manganese, and other metallic oxides that they will fire a very dark brown or black. Most clays fire to a buff, pink, red, or brown. The presence of lime tends to bleach the red or brown color normal in an ironbearing clay.

Not only does the presence of iron have an effect upon the color of the fired clay, but, perhaps as important, the temperature of firing and the atmosphere in the kiln vitally affect the color of the finished piece. For example, one clay might be a light pink color when fired to cone 08. At cone 04 it might be a brick-red color, and at cone 1 it might be a chocolate brown. At cone 6 it might be almost black and cinder-like in texture. If fired at cone 04 in a reducing atmosphere or cooled in a reducing atmosphere, the same clay might be black. Any given clay, in other words, will yield a great variety of colors, depending on how it is fired. The effect of reducing or smoky atmospheres on fired clay is dealt with in detail in a later section, but, in general, reduction has the effect of bringing out cool rather than warm

tones. On clay with only a small amount of iron, reduction will produce grey or grey to buff colors. Those clays which normally in oxidation burn to a red color will in reduction tend to be black. Or, if the atmosphere of the kiln is uneven, the same piece may exhibit colors of black and red resulting from flashing or the partially reducing conditions prevailing near one side or part of a piece. Bricks are sometimes deliberately fired in this way to give a mottled color.

The rich brick-red color of fired clay is possible only when the clay is fired somewhat short of vitrification. When the firing for any given body proceeds to a certain point, the production of glass in the clay body will result in tones of brown, grey-brown, or black, rather than red. In fact, paving bricks often show a greenish darkness, because the glassy phase is so colored by iron.

The color of clay may be altered by adding coloring oxides. If darker tones of red or brown are desired, iron oxide may be added. If a light-burning clay is given an addition of 2% to 4% of iron oxide, it will burn red or brown. Red iron oxide is usually used for this purpose. One disadvantage is that the iron oxide is very potent in color in the raw body, and the potter's hands, tools, and clothing become stained a deep rust color. Yellow iron oxide reacts almost identically to red, without the staining problems associated with red iron oxide. Iron oxide acts as a strong flux in clay, and the addition of more than a small percentage of iron may make the body too fusible for the intended temperature. Tests may easily be made to determine just how much iron should be added to get the desired effect.

Black iron oxide may also be used to color clay bodies. It is coarser in particle size than the red iron oxide and may result in a somewhat speckled color in the fired clay. Black iron oxide may not oxidize completely in firing and may result in a somewhat greyed color as compared to the red oxide. It does not have the disadvantage of staining.

If a very dark color or a mottled or speckled appearance is desired, other coloring oxides or combinations of oxides may be used. Combinations of iron oxide and manganese dioxide will give tones of grey-brown to dark brown or black. About 2% of manganese dioxide is enough to darken a clay appreciably. Used alone, manganese dioxide will give grey-brown colors, with more or less prominent specks. This is due to the relatively coarse particle size of the manganese. If very prominent specks or splotches are desired, granular manganese may be used. Manganese ground to pass the 80-mesh screen will be found to be sufficiently coarse to give a very strong speckled color. If a black color is desired, combinations of iron, manganese, copper, and cobalt may be used. The tolerance level of firing such a body is usually very tight and the manganese content is likely to flux the body, fusing quite quickly and giving a firing range of only two cones before pyroplastic deformation starts to set in. Cobalt and copper oxides are very strong fluxes and also, being very soluble in glass, will color any glaze put over them. For these reasons, they should be used sparingly, if at all, in clay bodies; furthermore, they are expensive. However, if a specific colored clay is desired for the work in hand, any mineral colorant or prepared stain may be used. In general, for practical reasons of expense and firing, the amount of coloring oxide added to a clay body should be held to below 3%, but in some cases, and with some colorants, it may rise to as much as 20% in order to get special effects. Here, as in compounding most ceramic materials, the nearer one can stay to natural materials, the better the results are apt to be. It is better to use naturally occurring red clay than to doctor up a white clay by putting iron into it, but to get a good color response in the ochre, yellow, blue, or green range, a white clay has to be the base.

Pink clays may be made by adding copper carbonate or oxide to a white body - usually porcelain - to about 3% and fired in reduction. Blues are produced by adding stains prepared from cobalt oxide, greens from copper and chrome, and the like. Color manufacturers furnish body stains prepared for this purpose. They have been widely used in the tableware industry to produce ware colored all the way through, so that when a blue plate is chipped, the clay body underneath is blue, which makes the flaw less noticeable.

Texture in clay may be of two sorts: a texture which is actually a roughness, and a visual impression of texture, which results from broken color, spots, specks, or splotches. If an actual roughness is desired, grog in varying amounts and types may be added to the clay. Grog is clay that has already been fired and then ground into granules. It may be purchased in a variety of types, such as fire clay grog, which is usually buff color, or porcelain grog, Molochite which is white. Or grog may be prepared by

grinding any fired clay, such as red bricks or specially prepared mixtures. Grog is ground, then screened for size. A grog that will pass the 20-mesh screen is quite coarse and will give a very rough and earthy texture if it is added to a clay body in the amount of about 15%. Grog that will pass the 40-mesh screen could be considered of medium size and could be used to give tooth to throwing bodies. Sometimes very coarse grog is used - 10-mesh or even bigger - for large terracottas or for sculptures or other objects where good drying is needed and where a heavy texture is desirable. Rough fire clays, silica clays, or shales may have the same effect as grog in making a rough texture in clay bodies. The fire clays are apt to slake down over a period of time, however, and while the freshly made-up clay may be quite rough because of the presence of a rough fire clay, after the clay has tempered for a month or so it may be found that the fire clay has softened and that the body has become considerably more smooth. Some fire clays, by themselves, are very excellent workable clays, of a rough and ready sort, for modeling and for certain kinds of pottery. Shale is very hard and slakes only very slowly, if at all. It can be used as a grog if its color and fusibility are right for the intended heat treatment and finished appearance.

Although rough and groggy bodies are obviously not suitable for tableware or for certain other ceramic products, they do have an appeal, both visual and tactile, which makes them a very suitable medium for sculpture, for hand-made pottery of various sorts, and for many kinds of useful and ornamental ceramic objects. The effort of potters, historically, has, of course, been directed toward ever smoother and more refined clay bodies. This development culminated in the appearance of pure white, vitrified porcelain in China. While this achievement may always remain as an ideal, modern ceramists tend to maintain an open mind about all types of ceramic effects and to use roughness where roughness is called for, either practically or aesthetically.

Texture of a visual sort, which is the result of spots or specks, can be induced in a clay body by adding coloring oxides in granular form, which will burn to a darker color than the surrounding areas of clay. Manganese has already been mentioned in this connection. Also frequently used is ilmenite, which is an ore containing iron and titania. Ilmenite and rutile, another iron and titanium colorant, can be purchased in various grit sizes. Material passing the 80-mesh screen will give a prominent black speck to clay. Iron in granular form will also give very prominent specks and splotches. Sometimes rust scrapings, blacksmith's scale, or iron filings are used for this purpose. The size of the iron particles and the temperature of firing will determine the nature of the spots. Another source of black specks may be grog from red brick or shale which, when carried to sufficient temperature, will reach the point of fusion and will produce a strong dark speck. Materials that induce dark specks will, of course, influence the glaze also, especially high-temperature glazes, which are strongly influenced by the clay body beneath them. The amount of material added to a clay to bring about specks will depend on what is used and the density or strength of the specks desired. In general, about 2% of ilmenite will give a very noticeable effect, and in a high-fired body, about 5% of red brick grog will give strong speckled texture. Trials must be made to determine the most suitable composition for any given situation.

White specks may be introduced into a darker clay body by adding a white or light grog. Porcelain grog, or Molochite, is very suitable for this purpose. After the object has been made and before it has been fired, it may be necessary to sponge, sandpaper, or scrape the surface to reveal the white grog; otherwise the grog will remain covered, even at the surface, by a thin film of clay and will not be noticeable. The combination of black and white specks in a brown or grey clay may give extremely handsome textures that are akin to granite.

As in the case of colors in clay bodies, those textures that occur naturally are often the most pleasing in the finished product. Specks, for example, that are too prominent and too evenly spaced and too unrelated to the other colors of body and glaze have an artificial appearance. This kind of contrived texture is often noticeably out of place on low-fired ware being made to simulate high-fired stoneware. The virtues of each material and of each process and firing temperature speak best for themselves.

It is risky to combine clay bodies of differing compositions in one piece, because the differences in drying shrinkage, firing shrinkage, and maturing temperature may cause them to break apart or develop cracking. It is inadvisable, for example, to make a pot from one clay and then fasten on an appendage such as a handle made from another clay. Although this is the usual scenario, one artist I know combined several clays as disparate as from porcelain through various grogged stonewares to a stoneware with grog as coarse as 1/4″ in diameter. The inevitable tension cracks in the pieces were filled with dental amalgam, the idea coming while having a tooth filled. The result was like an abstract landscape with heavily grogged clay as the rocky foreground with silver seams and the porcelain, suitably covered with a bluish celadon glaze, as the sky. There is almost always a solution, often very creative in its own right, to solve a problem.

Pieces may be made which incorporate clays of differing colors. In this case a light-colored clay is used as the basic composition. Darker variations of it may be made by adding iron, iron chromate, manganese, or body stains. These darker variations, since they are essentially the same composition and vary only in the small additions made to influence color, can be freely combined with the lighter clay body. Marbled or agate ware is made in this way. Alternating layers of dark and light clay are pressed together, and the resulting mass is wedged and thrown on the wheel. The result is a random streaking of light and dark. Or slabs of the combined clays may be cut and recombined in such a way as to give complex geometrical patterns. They may also be combined in designs by cutting and assembling in blocks, as in the Japanese process called Neriage or Neri Kome. Cross-cut slices become prepatterned slabs. The slabs are then pressed in molds or are used in hand-building or slab constructions.

Another example of the use of two clays of differing color on one piece is the sprigged design on Wedgwood pots, where white cameo-like figures are applied on various colored, but most often blue backgrounds.

12. Earthenware

Earthenware is usually fired at temperatures below cone 1, and the fired clay remains somewhat porous and open in structure. The vast majority of the world's pottery has been earthenware because of the wide prevalence of earthenware clay and the relative ease of reaching the kiln temperatures necessary to fire it.

Earthenware has a soft tactile quality and a feeling of lightness quite different from denser forms of pottery. Although more fragile than stoneware or porcelain, it is not so brittle. The color range of earthenware encompasses a beautiful palette that includes various warm greys as well as red, orange, buff, ocher, and brown. These body colors, combined with the brilliant colors of low-fired glazes, make earthenware an ideal medium for color expression.

Earthenware bodies are usually made up of common red- or buff-burning clays, with only enough other materials added to achieve good working and firing properties. In almost every part of the world there are clays readily available that serve quite well for making earthenware, and the abundance of such clays partly accounts for the fact that man has depended everywhere upon pottery for the utensils of daily life. Common red clay is usually quite plastic and suitable for modeling, hand-building, throwing, pressing, or any process that makes use of the plastic clay in forming. The presence of iron oxide in nearly all of the secondary clays found near the surface of the ground accounts for the typical color of earthenware clays, and also accounts for the relatively low temperatures needed to make sound, serviceable ware from it.

In formulating bodies for earthenware, the best plan is to rely largely on one natural clay. Most of the common red clays fire to a fairly dense and hard state in the range from cone 06 to cone 1. The first step is to locate a good source of supply for such a clay. Many ceramic supply houses sell common red clay that is serviceable for earthenware. However, the cost of such clay, especially if it must be freighted for a long distance, may make it advisable to look into local sources. If potters are willing to do the work, red clay can be located and dug in most localities. Or a local brickyard or flowerpot factory may have available an excellent earthenware clay ready for use.

Once a clay has been located, the next step is to test it to find out what its characteristics are. Tests for plasticity, shrinkage, and absorption should be made at the various temperatures. It will then be known what additions must be made to the clay to make it work well with the intended processes and firing temperature. The additions are apt to take one of the following forms:

1. If the clay is too refractory - that is, if it does not become hard enough at the temperature at which it must be fired - some flux must be added to it. This flux might be iron oxide, talc, or a frit.

2. If the clay is too fusible and becomes too dense at the intended firing temperature, refractory materials must be added such as kaolin, ball clay, stoneware clay, silica, fine grog, or fire clay.

3. If the clay is too sticky and shrinks too much, it will need the addition of more nonplastic material such as silica, kaolin, grog, or fire clay.

4. If the clay is mealy and not sufficiently plastic, it will need the addition of some more plastic material such as ball clay or bentonite.

5. If the color of the clay is to be changed, iron or other coloring metallic oxides may be added.

Tests must be made to determine not only the necessity for changes in the clay but also the amount of the additions which will result in the most serviceable earthenware body.

The chart on page 107 indicates some typical earthenware body compositions for firing in the range of cone 06 to cone 1. These bodies are based on the following hypothetical red clays, which represent, however, common types.

Red clay #1. Very plastic and sticky. Fires to a dark brown, very dense mass at cone 04. Total shrinkage at cone 04 is 13%. Absorption at cone 04 is 1.5%.

Red clay #2. Good plasticity. Fires to a terracotta color at cone 04. Total shrinkage at cone 04 is 11%. Absorption, 6%.

Red clay #3. Fair to poor plasticity. Fires to a light buff at cone 04. Total shrinkage, 8%. Absorption, 13%.

Clay #1 is too plastic and too fusible; #2 is about right; #3 is not plastic enough and does not mature sufficiently in the intended range of temperature.

The compositions A, B, and C are adjustments designed to correct the red clay #1. This clay is, by itself, too plastic and too fusible. It may be adjusted by adding more refractory clays and silica. The compositions D, E, F, and G are based on clay #2, which by itself is close to being satisfactory. In E, a small amount of ball clay is added to increase the plasticity. In F, fire clay is added, which might make the clay better for modeling or for large pieces. In G, both ball clay and some frit are added to make a slightly denser body.

The compositions H, I, J, and K are designed to

	A	B	C	D	E	F	G	H	I	J	K
Red clay #1	75	50	75	-	-	-	-	-	-	-	-
Red clay #2	-	-	-	100	90	90	90	-	-	-	-
Red clay #3	-	-	-	-	-	-	-	75	60	50	85
Kaolin	15	-	-	-	-	-	-	-	-	-	-
Ball clay	-	-	-	-	8	-	5	20	25	25	
Stoneware clay	-	25	-	-	-	-	-	-	-	-	-
Fire clay	-	15	25	-	-	10	-	-	-	-	-
Talc	-	-	-	-	-	-	-	-	-	20	-
Body frit	-	-	-	-	-		5	5	5	-	10
Silica	10	10	-	-	-	-	-	-	-	-	-
Bentonite	-	-	-	-	-	-	-	-	-	-	3
Iron oxide	-	-	-	-	2	-	-	-	-	5	2

correct clay #3, which is too lean and does not mature sufficiently in the intended range of temperature. Plastic clay, bentonite, and fluxes are added to overcome the difficulty.

If no red clay is available for making a red earthenware type of body, kaolin, ball clay, and iron oxide may be used together with some flux to bring the clay into the lower range of temperature. A typical composition for such a clay body might be:

Kaolin	25
Ball clay	30
Body frit	17
Talc	5
Silica	10
Iron oxide	3

The difficulty with compositions of this sort is that when the necessary amount of flux is added, the percentage of plastic material is apt to be too low to make a good clay for throwing. For casting, however, such a mixture might work better than a body made largely from natural red clay. For all plastic processes it is better, simpler, and cheaper to make earthenware clay bodies as nearly as possible from common, natural, red-burning clay.

White or very light earthenware bodies may be made by combining light-burning clays such as kaolin, ball clay, or stoneware clay with fluxes suitable for the intended temperature. In bodies of this type, the problem centers around the type of flux to be employed and the development of sufficient plasticity in spite of the necessarily large amount of non-plastic material. Actually, the number of fluxes that can be used in white earthenware is severely limited. Feldspars, with the exception of nepheline syenite, are too refractory to have much influence on a clay body below about cone 1. In practice, talc, frit, nepheline syenite, or combinations of these must be relied on.

Frits sold for use in clay bodies are usually leadless and of a somewhat higher melting point than glaze frits. The use of frit in a clay is an effective way of making it mature at a low temperature; however, it has the serious disadvantage of shortening the firing range. A natural red clay body may have a comfortable firing range of four or five cones, whereas a body fluxed with a frit may have to be accurately fired to within two cones. If it goes slightly higher in firing, it may warp, slump, and begin to fuse; or, if it is slightly underfired, it may remain too soft and chalky. Another problem in using frit in clay bodies is its tendency to deflocculate slightly when the clay is stored moist over a period of time. Most frits are slightly soluble, and the frit in a clay may dissolve to the extent of releasing enough sodium to cause deflocculation. This causes the plastic clay to become limp, soft, and impossible to form. The tendency may be counteracted by the use of about .5% of aluminum sulfate or magnesium sulfate in the clay, which tends to neutralize the alkalies causing the trouble. But soluble salts added to the clay may bring about other difficulties, such as efflorescence or the forming of scum on the surface of the clay.

Talc has been widely used in commercial clay bodies sold for use by hobbyists and schools. With the use of talc a body can be formulated which is white and which matures at a low temperature and has a long firing range. Talc has the property of forming fairly low-melting compounds with the clay and silica of the body. The only difficulty is that a great deal of talc must be used to make a clay tighten and mature at cone 01 or below, if no other flux such as iron or a frit is present. The result is that talc bodies are relatively nonplastic and are really only suitable for casting. If casting is the only forming process to be employed, however, a talc body may be satisfactory in every way.

Combinations of talc, frit, and nepheline syenite may be used to make low-fired clay bodies of extreme density or even translucency. If the fluxing ingredients are increased sufficiently, the composition may approach that of glass, with, of course, an attendant sacrifice of plasticity in the clay. Low-fired simulations of porcelain may be made from combinations of white-burning clays and fluxes. While pottery made from material of this type may have the virtue of density or possibly translucency, it will not be mistaken for true porcelain because of its glassy and rather cheap appearance. It is interesting that before European potters discovered the method of making true porcelain, the Italian potters attempted to make porcelain by adding ground glass to white clay and firing it at the same low temperatures they employed for making earthenware. The Persian potters, who admired tremendously the porcelain wares from China, also attempted to make white translucent wares in their kilns, which were not capable of attaining the necessary high temperatures for true porcelain. They probably employed ground alkaline frit or soda ash to bring down the fusion point of white clays. None of these attempts to simulate porcelain was very successful.

The chart at the bottom of the page indicates typical compositions for white or light buff earthenware to be fired at cone 04.

Bodies A, B, and C use combinations of frit, talc, and nepheline syenite for flux. Sufficient ball clay is added to ensure reasonable plasticity. B and C contain some stoneware clay, which lends a buff tone to the body. Bodies D, E, and F are talc bodies, with talc used in amounts up to 40%. When this much talc is present, the entire remainder of the body is made up of ball clay. Bodies G, H, and I contain a great deal of flux and tend toward a dense glassy structure.

Another type of earthenware body is that employed in the manufacture of inexpensive white tableware. Such bodies are usually fired at cone 2 to cone 5. At this relatively higher temperature the problem of body composition is simple, and white-burning clays, together with some feldspar, talc, and silica, result in fired ware which, although it is slightly porous and presents no difficulty in firing such as warpage or slumping, is reasonably hard and serviceable in use.

High-temperature earthenware, low-temperature stoneware, or porcelain fired in the middle range of temperature, from cone 1 to cone 6, have the virtue of hardness, strength, density, and durability of glaze. In clays fired at these temperatures some of the virtues of stoneware can be achieved, while at the same time there remains the possibility of the brilliant and varied color typical of lower firing. Since less flux is required in middle-range bodies, plasticity is easier to achieve. In general, there is much to be said for the range of cone 1 to cone 6 as a working temperature for pottery making. On the one hand, the softness of glaze characteristic of the lower-fired wares is avoided, and, on the other hand, the difficulties of high firing, with its attendant wear

	A	B	C	D	E	F	G	H	I
Kaolin	25	-	25	-	-	-	15	25	-
Plastic Florida kaolin	15	25	-	-	20	-	25	-	40
Ball clay	30	20	25	60	50	60	10	25	10
Stoneware clay	-	15	10	-	-	-	-	-	-
Frit	15	10	15	-	-	5	10	-	15
Talc	5	10	-	40	20	30	20	20	20
Nepheline syenite	-	10	10	-	10	5	20	30	15
Silica	10	10	15	-	-	-	-	-	-

and tear on kiln and kiln furniture, to say nothing of expense, are avoided. In formulating a dark-burning, middle-range body, as in the case of lower-fired earthenware bodies, it is well to start with a clay which by itself matures at about the right temperature. Middle-range clays of this sort are much rarer than clays that mature at around cone 04, but they can be located or purchased.

The following chart indicates some typical formulas for earthenware bodies in the middle range of temperature, cone 1 to cone 6.

	A	B	C	D	E
Common red clay	30	-	25	-	-
Stoneware clay	25	-	35	-	-
Middle-range clay	-	75	-	-	-
Ball clay	25	15	20	20	20
Kaolin	-	-	-	30	35
Fire clay	10	10	-	-	-
Silica	10	-	10	10	20
Nepheline syenite	-	-	10	30	10
Talc	-	-	-	10	15

A, B, and C are dark-burning plastic clays. In A, thirty parts of fusible, low-fired red clay are balanced by stoneware clay and ball clay to make a cone 4 body, which burns to a medium red color. In B, a middle-range red clay is used, and is altered only by the addition of some ball clay and fire clay. In C, a lighter color clay is made by keeping the red clay content at twenty-five parts and making the stoneware and ball clay total fifty-five parts. Ten parts of nepheline syenite are added for flux. D is a vitreous white casting body in which nepheline syenite and talc are used together as a flux. E is a commercial-type white earthenware body.

13. Stoneware

Vitreous, grey, buff, or brown ware, fired in the range of cone 6 to cone 14, may be considered stoneware. The name comes, of course, from the dense, hard, impervious character of the body.

In some ways the formulation of stoneware bodies is simpler than earthenware because the higher heat makes less flux necessary. As in the case of earthenware, the best solution is to find a good stoneware clay which, by itself, comes near to answering the needs of plasticity, fired density, and color. Many fine stoneware clays are available, particularly in the central and eastern parts of the United States. They may be used straight, or altered slightly for more plasticity or for a desired change of color, texture, or glaze fit. A good natural stoneware clay should be plastic enough for throwing, fire to a tan, grey, or light brown color, and be fairly dense at cone 6.

The relatively higher heat of stoneware firing makes possible the use of feldspar as the principal body flux. Feldspar is an ideal body flux because it has a long firing range, is cheap, and presents no difficulties or hazards.

For texture, grog and fire clays may be used. Some fire clays are actually quite similar to stoneware clay, although they may have a higher firing range and be coarser and less plastic. For rougher types of bodies, combinations of stoneware clays and fire clays are ideal. Common sand is sometimes used instead of grog, but if more than about 10% is added, dunting may occur.

When no natural stoneware clay is available, adequate bodies for high firing may be made up from kaolin, ball clay, feldspar, and silica, with iron oxide or red clay added for color. Such bodies, however, may lack the plastic quality of a natural stoneware body.

Fired stoneware should have an absorption of 3% or less. At its best it is dense and impervious and has a rich earthy color and texture.

The following chart gives some typical cone 8 to cone 10 plastic stoneware compositions:

	A	B	C	D	E	F
Stoneware clay	80	75	40	30	-	20
Sagger clay	-	-	20	-	-	-
Ball clay	10	15	20	30	30	15
Kaolin	-	-	-	-	40	25
Red clay	-	-	-	10	5	-
Feldspar	10	10	10	-	15	20
Silica	-	-	10	-	10	20
Fire clay	-	-	-	30	-	-

Body A is largely of stoneware clay, with only enough ball clay and feldspar added to improve the plasticity a little and to make the clay fire to a denser mass. B is similar, but somewhat more plastic because of the increased ball clay. C is a somewhat less plastic clay in which sagger clay has been used and ten parts of silica are added to ensure glaze fit. D is a rough type of body with a large percentage of rough fire clay. E is a stoneware body that relies mainly on kaolin and ball clay instead of on stoneware clay for its plasticity, and that is colored by a small addition of red clay. F is a stoneware body designed for casting or jiggering.

14. Raku

Bodies for raku usage are generally similar to stoneware with an added amount of grog or other aggregate material to protect the ware from excessive thermal shock from quick heating and cooling cycles. Grog additions of up to 30% are often used. Some of the clay content may be replaced with Kyanite, an aluminum silicate that develops long fibrous crystals in the body matrix.

15. Porcelain

Porcelain is a vitreous whiteware of more or less translucency fired to cone 9 or more. It is made by combining white-burning clays with feldspars and silica. The relatively high heat acting upon the fluxes in the clay results in a dense, impervious body which approaches glass.

Compounding porcelain bodies is actually quite simple since the ingredients are few and the best proportioning of the ingredients is well established in practice. The main difficulty is that, if only pure and white-burning clays such as the kaolins are used, the clay body is so nonplastic that it is hard to make anything out of it, even by casting.

The proportion of five parts of clay, three parts of feldspar, and two parts of silica may be taken as the starting point in formulating porcelain bodies. The clay must be divided between kaolin and ball clay to make the body workable. If extreme whiteness is not desired, more ball clay may be used, and the body as a result will "pot" with less difficulty. Usually, in the interests of uniformity in case slight changes occur in the composition of the clays, several kaolins are used. If a soft feldspar such as nepheline syenite is

used, less of it will be needed to bring about translucency. The silica content may vary, but if it exceeds about 25%, dunting may result. The proportioning of the materials depends, of course, on the exact firing temperature, and a body designed for firing at cone 14 will have a good deal less feldspar in it than one designed for cone 9.

Some kaolins, particularly those from certain parts of Florida, are relatively plastic, and the use of these clays helps in the formulation of porcelain bodies which are white and yet reasonably workable. The exceptionally iron-free kaolins from England and from Georgia in the United States tend to be quite nonplastic. Since some ball clay is necessary, the selection of the kind is critical, since ball clays vary a great deal, both in plasticity and in iron content. English ball clay is perhaps the best for porcelain since it is both highly plastic and relatively iron-free. English ball clay contains considerable carbon, which must be screened out before the clay is used.

Some typical porcelain compositions are given below:

	A	B	C	D	E	F	G
Georgia kaolin	35	25	25	5	30	25	-
Florida kaolin	10	15	-	40	15	15	10
English ball clay		5	10	25	-	15	10	-
Kentucky ball clay		-	-	-	10	-	-	-
Feldspar	30	30	25	-	20	-	25
Nepheline syenite		-	-	-	25	-	30	-
Silica	20	20	25	20	20	20	20
Grolleg kaolin	-	-	-	-	-	-	50

A is a very white cone 10 to cone 11 body. Its small ball clay content makes for low plasticity. B is essentially the same body but modified by an increase in the ball clay, which makes for better workability but some sacrifice of whiteness. C is composed of equal parts kaolin, ball clay, feldspar, and silica. Although somewhat grey in fired color, it casts and trims well. In D, plasticity is partly achieved by a high percentage of Florida kaolin. E is a body for cone 12 to cone 14. It has a smaller than usual percentage of feldspar. F is designed to mature at cone 9 and relies on nepheline syenite instead of feldspar for flux. G is a body based on the English grolleg clay. This will produce a fine translucent body at cone 10 to cone 12. Porcelain clays containing nepheline syenite and stored for more than three months are likely to deflocculate and become thixotropic, making it almost impossible to use without drying and re-wedging. All porcelain clays may be difficult for wheel work without the addition of a small amount, 1% to 3%, of white-firing bentonite or macaloid, or polymer-based plasticizer.

Sometimes, in addition to the materials used for the above bodies, a small amount of lime is introduced into porcelain bodies to act as an auxiliary flux or catalyst. For this purpose, 1% or 2% of calcium carbonate or dolomite may be used.

In oxidation, porcelain bodies tend to be creamy white in color. When fired in reduction, the small amount of iron present in the body gives a blue-grey tinge, which, like blueing in the wash, gives the appearance of brilliant white.

Bodies used commercially for the production of vitreous china are essentially the same as porcelain bodies. In the manufacture of china, the body of the ware is matured in a first firing, without glaze. In this bisque firing, since the ware is not glazed, it can be supported by special refractory setters, or by nesting in silica sand, and this prevents much of the warping or deformation which would otherwise occur. The ware is glazed in a second firing at about cone 4, usually with a lead boro-silicate glaze. In true porcelain, as distinguished from china, the body and the glaze are both matured in a high firing. This means that the ware must survive the high fire without support from refractory setters, and one of the difficulties of making porcelain is that the body, as it nears maturity, becomes so soft and glass-like that warping and slumping are very apt to occur.

Careful design of the shapes and careful setting and firing will get around most of the difficulty, but losses in porcelain making are inevitably high. The advantage of true porcelain is that not only is the body vitreous and translucent, but the glaze is very hard, scratchproof, and lustrous, and the contact between glaze and body is so intimate and so indistinct that the glaze, instead of appearing as a glassy coating, appears as an integral part of the body.

Although porcelain can be made to cast and jigger well, it is very difficult to achieve a porcelain body that will be good for throwing. This is due to the inherently nonplastic character of white clays. If sufficient ball clay is put in the body to make a highly plastic clay such as is needed for wheel work, the fired result will be cream color or grey rather than white. Bentonite also, when it is used to increase plasticity, makes the body grey. The following bodies, designed for throwing, indicate the kind of compromise which often must be made to obtain plasticity:

Porcelain body	1	2
English china clay	10	30
Florida kaolin	20	15
Tennessee ball clay	26	15
Feldspar	24	20
Silica	20	20

If a white body is to be used for throwing, it should be made up well in advance to allow for aging, which may make a considerable difference. One cup of vinegar to one hundred pounds of clay greatly aids in aging of clay. Since white clays, even at their best, are far from being as plastic as the darker clays, it is well to confine the thrown shapes to simple ones of modest size. If extreme thinness and translucency are desired, the pots can be trimmed down when leather-hard to the proper cross section. To avoid warping in thrown porcelain, very careful handling and drying are necessary. And in making any kind of porcelain, great care must be taken to prevent contamination with iron or other impurities that would cause specks. All the utensils used must be clean. When dark clays are being used in the same workrooms where porcelain is being made, it may prove impossible to keep the white clay clean.

16. Ovenproof and Flameproof Bodies

An advantage of pottery over most other types of vessels is that it is serviceable for use in cooking in the oven and microwave. Casseroles, bean pots, warming pots, and other cooking wares have the advantages of being inexpensive, durable, and of retaining heat and keeping food warm for a long time. Pottery cooking vessels may be not only serviceable, but handsome enough in appearance for use on the table.

Pottery intended for use in the oven must be made so that it will not crack either from the shock of being placed in a hot oven or of being taken out of the oven and quickly cooled to room temperature. Actually, if reasonable care is exercised in use, most earthenware, stoneware, or porcelain pots will serve quite well for oven use. However, pieces that will last for years in normal cooking use may break if subjected to some unusual heat shock, such as would result from placing the piece directly over a flame, or cooling it suddenly by placing it in cold water while it is still hot from the oven.

One kind of cooking ware that has been widely used in the past is made of an open, porous, nonvitreous or underfired body. Soft ware of this sort is loose enough in structure to accommodate itself to the rapid expansion and contraction which result from heating and cooling. French provincial cooking ware and most Mexican pottery bowls and casseroles are of this type. Such ware is not apt to crack from heat shock, and may even be used directly over a low charcoal fire. The resistance to cracking in this case results not in the formulation of the body but merely in the fact of its being underfired. Such porous cooking pots have the disadvantage of being soft and easily broken, and they tend to be unsanitary. Since glazes on underfired bodies seldom fit, crazing is common and permits the penetration of liquids from the food into the body of the ware.

Most stoneware glazed with a fitting glaze is suitable for use in the oven. However, if a pot is specifically intended for oven use, certain factors should be taken into account to increase its durability and resistance to shock:

1. The body should be formulated with as little silica content as possible. This means selecting clays low in silica and high in alumina, eliminating clays that contain much free silica, and avoiding the addition of silica to the body. Free silica in the body has a high reversible expansion when heated, and is the principle cause of failure in heat shock. Free silica in the body may be the cause of residual strains in the body incurred during cooling when the piece was fired. Such internal strains may not show up until a piece is used in the oven, at which time it may crack when heated or cooled.

2. Some feldspar should be included in the composition of the body. Feldspar, acting as a flux, tends to take up free silica in the body and incorporate it into glassy compounds of relatively low expansion. Talc may also function in this way and is often included in bodies intended for oven use. Lithium bearing feldspars such as petalite, spodumene, or amblygonite are best for these bodies. Amblygonite

is sometimes sold as low-solubility spodumene.

3. High firing temperatures are desirable. At the higher temperatures any free silica in the body is more apt to be taken into combination with the other oxides present. If properly compounded, bodies fired at cones 10 or 11 will be more successful than those fired at cones 8 or 9. However, the body should not have a porosity below 3% or 4%.

4. Compact, spherical shapes will be more resistant to cracking than flat, extenuated forms. Forms with sharp angles or corners should be avoided. Pieces intended for oven use should have an even cross section throughout, and should not be excessively thin or excessively thick.

5. The body should not contain appreciable amounts of iron, especially if fired in reduction.

6. Ovenproof and flameproof bodies are best fired in oxidation, as reduction, particularly early body reduction, will inhibit the growth of mullite crystals in the matrix of the body. Mullite forms a network of needle-like crystals which give strength and resistance to thermal shock.

7. Glazes should fit, but should not be under excessive compression. Glazes should be applied evenly to both the inside and outside of the pot. The same base glaze should be used on both the outside and the inside. Glazes should not be thickly applied.

If the above precautions are followed, it may be found that fitting a glaze to the body is difficult and that all of the favored glazes craze. The only solution is to develop glazes of low-expansion characteristics. (The problem of glaze fit is discussed in a later section.)

While the making of ovenproof pottery is a fairly simple matter, making ware to be useful over direct flame is difficult. The shock of heating and cooling is much more sudden and intense, and bodies that will give excellent service in the oven often will fail when placed directly over a burner on the stove. However, that problem has been solved. One type of body that will withstand almost any heat shock is an extremely high-fired high-alumina porcelain in which all free silica has been converted to fused silica or mullite. Laboratory porcelain is of this type, similar to Corningware, and may be placed directly over a flame without danger of cracking. In fact, laboratory porcelains may be heated to red heat on one side only and still not break, and they may be plunged into cold water while very hot without failure. Such a body requires a firing at cone 18. At this elevated temperature the silica either becomes fused into vitreous silica or is incorporated into crystalline structures of mullite. Little or no free silica remains in the fired body. Therefore, the thermal expansion of the body is extremely low; hence also its high resistance to shock. The ceramic bodies used for spark plugs, which are also high in alumina, are able to withstand millions of cycles of sudden, drastic heating and cooling without failure. The high temperatures involved in making shock-proof porcelains, and the exacting manufacturing techniques involved, make them out of reach financially for the average studio potter.

Flameproof ware has been successfully made from high lithium bodies. Lithium, used as a body flux, has a low coefficient of expansion, which makes it useful for controlling the resistance of the fired body to heat shock. Petalite ($LiO_2 \cdot Al_2O_3 \cdot 8SiO_2$), a natural lithium spar, is the preferred material. Most formulas call for between 30% and 50% of petalite in the body. The clays used may be divided between ball clay, kaolin, or stoneware clay; in fact, if highly silicious clays are avoided, the kind of clay used seems to have little effect on resistance to heat shock. A small amount of auxiliary flux may be used somewhat as a catalyst. Following is a typical petalite body designed for resistance to heat shock:

Petalite	45
Feldspar	5
Ball clay	35
Stoneware clay	10

For best results such a body should be fired to at least cone 11. Higher firing ensures that all of the free silica in the body will be combined with the petalite to form lower-expansion lithium compounds. Very careful firing is necessary because, if the ware is either overfired or underfired, its resistance to heat shock may be impaired. It will be seen that such a body, containing only about 50% clay, will not be highly plastic. Some bentonite may be added to improve the plasticity sufficiently so that simple forms may be thrown on the wheel. Casting presents no difficulty. Small amounts of iron or red clay may be added for color, and the ware may be fired in either oxidation or reduction. Glaze fit can present a difficult problem because of the extremely low expansion of the body. Most glazes will craze

over such a clay. Thinly applied slip glazes have been successfully used. Glazes high in lithium may also fit well. Petalite, spodumene, or lepidolite have been used as sources of lithium for glazes.

To test a body for resistance to flame, a small flat dish is made about 7″ in diameter, with a rim 1″ high. Water is placed in this and it is put on an electric hot plate and heated until the water has boiled off. After five minutes of further heating, the dish is plunged into cold water. If a body survives this heating and cooling for several cycles, it may be considered flameproof. Such a test is actually much more severe than the normal use of a piece in cooking.

17. Reinforced Clay Bodies

Before they are fired, objects made from clay have a low tensile strength. The stresses which always accompany drying shrinkage often cause cracking, especially in large objects or in those that are complex in shape. While the relatively compact and spherical shapes common in pottery usually dry and shrink without cracking, forms that have appendages, varying cross sections, extended elements, or angular joints are much more prone to difficulty in drying. Very large forms, since they tend to dry unevenly, are particularly subject to drying cracks. The tendency of clay objects to crack upon drying and the fragility of the dried material have tended to limit both the range of form and the scale of works in ceramics.

To help overcome the difficulties caused by drying shrinkage, fibrous material may be added to the clay. One of the earliest references to such a technique is the story in the Bible of the Egyptian Pharaoh's spiteful order depriving the Israelites of straw for their brick making (Exodus, ch. V). The use of straw as a reinforcement in adobe bricks was known to prehistoric man. The straw, mixed in with the plastic clay when the brick is made, gives a greatly increased dry strength because of the tensile strength of the embedded fibers.

Primitive potters also sometimes used fibers to reinforce their clay. Microscopic examination of certain pre-Columbian American pots reveals that cattail fuzz had been mixed into the clay. Such hairy fibers interlaced in the clay body gave it increased tensile strength; upon firing, these fibers were burned away, leaving barely noticeable voids. Any sort of fiber may be used for this purpose, and clays containing fibrous material, particularly if the fibers are strong, will show greatly increased dry strength and resistance to cracking. If considerable fiber is used, however, the resulting voids in the fired body may result in a loss of fired strength and density.

Woven cloth may be used as well as fiber to increase the strength of unfired clay bodies. Cheesecloth, for example, may be embedded in the walls of clay objects. The embedded cloth will inhibit cracking, especially at joints and corners where stress is apt to be critical. Such reinforcing cloths must be of a very open weave so as not to produce cleavage planes in the clay, and the cloth must be beaten or smeared well into the clay. The use of such reinforcing cloths, if they are well buried within the wall of the object, will have no discernible effect on the fired piece. The cloth burns away in the fire without difficulty.

Reinforcing cloth may be used with a deflocculated clay slip as well as with plastic clay. A fired clay facsimile of lace can be made by dipping actual lace into deflocculated slip. The slip clings to each element of the lace, which burns away in the fire. This technique has been much used on figurines.

Clay slabs may be made by dipping any open-weave cloth such as burlap or cheesecloth into a heavy deflocculated slip and building up a thickness by the addition of several layers. Such slabs may then be shaped in any way desired and can be used for building. They may be joined by transitional elements also made from cloth and slip. Plastic clay, which will have approximately the same water content as the slip, can be used for finishing or additions. Structures built up in this way will have extremely high dry strength and will not crack even if dried rapidly or carelessly.

The use of organic and therefore combustible fibers as described above always results in voids in the finished piece, which to some degree weaken the fired structure of the clay. To obviate this disadvantage, other additives such as fiberglass or nylon fiber may be used. Fiberglass, used either as strand or as cloth, has all the advantages of developing strength in the unfired clay object obtained with other types of fiber. But in the fire, if temperatures of cone 6 or more are achieved, it melts and survives in the clay as a network of glassy threads. These glassy passages, instead of detracting from the strength of the clay, as in the case of voids left by the burning off of organic fibers, may actually increase the modulus of rupture of the fired body.

If fine fiberglass strand is mixed directly into a clay body, the resulting mixture will have increased cohesiveness in the plastic state and greatly increased dry strength. About .5% to 1% of fiberglass to the weight of the clay has been found to be effective. Clay reinforced with fiberglass strands holds up very well in the various hand-building techniques, and warping and cracking are practically eliminated. The mixture may be thrown on the wheel with a noticeable increase in the possible range of form. If the tools are kept sharp, trimming may be accomplished as usual. In the fired piece, thread-like lines of glass will be noted permeating the structure. Glazing may be done as usual, and the presence of the fiberglass will not exert any noticeable influence on the color or texture of the surface. If fiberglass strand is to be added to a clay body, the mixing is best done by combining the dry materials with the fiberglass in a dough mixer or muller-type mixer and adding just enough water to achieve plasticity.

Fiberglass cloths may be used much in the manner described above. A very open-weave cloth must be used, and one that has not been coated with plastic. Light fiberglass cloth of the type made for sheer draperies has been found to be suitable. Tough slabs of great tensile strength both in the plastic and in the dry state may be made from fiberglass cloth and deflocculated slip. Any desired thickness can be achieved by adding layers of slip-dipped cloth. The range of form and scale of objects made from such membranes exceeds that which is possible using plastic clay alone. A thick slip containing no more than about 35% water has been found to be suitable. Slips made with water and clay alone, without deflocculents, cannot be used because they will have too great a shrinkage and will lack density.

The firing of objects made with fiberglass and clay combined presents no difficulty. In the early stages of firing the fiberglass disintegrates and loses its character as a fiber. Later, as the fire advances, it melts. The reaction of the clay body to the fire is not noticeably affected because the actual percentage of fiberglass is small - in any case, no more than about 1% of the weight of the clay. Therefore, its fluxing action is not significant. Fiberglass may be used with any type of clay body, including porcelain.

The incorporation of fiberglass in clay bodies gives a tensile strength lacking in clay alone, and complex forms that would ordinarily crack in drying can easily be made. Very large pieces can be made successfully with little risk of cracking. Dry strength is enormously increased. If reinforced with fiberglass, joints or the corners of slab-built pieces will not come apart on drying. In sculpture especially, the process has great potential.

The use of fibers and cloth as reinforcement in clay was developed by the author in a series of experiments begun in 1963. The process of using fiberglass in clay was invented and perfected by Daniel Rhodes in 1965.

The use of fiberglass, unfortunately, has some negative aspects in that the material can cut hands and cause allergies. Its use in clay bodies has largely been superseded by the addition of chopped nylon fiber in place of fiberglass. The benefits are equal to using fiberglass without the attendant problems. The methodology is basically the same.

18. Paperclay

A recent development in fiber-reinforced clays has been the research since 1989 and through the early 1990s by Rosette Gault. Her use of paper pulp in clays has made huge changes possible in the making of many forms of pottery and sculpture. Paperclay is now a licensed product made commercially by a number of ceramic materials suppliers. Here she talks about the process, its methodology, and its potential.

"Paper makers have known for a long time that up to 30% to 40% of clay in a paper pulp recipe can be an improvement to paper. In ceramics, we never considered that adding pulp to clay in inverse proportions would be worthwhile. Manmade fibers were more uniform, had less drawbacks in comparison. Pulp fibers are irregular lengths and introduce organic matter into the clay. The risk of smelly buckets was to be avoided. The trace mineral contribution of paper to a clay recipe could be a bother. Most who worked with paperclay, following the conventional methods of figure making, wanted fiber strength to interrupt fractures during forming.

"It turns out that the so-called drawbacks mentioned are, in fact, an essential prerequisite ingredient for a clay body that is more versatile to handle than normal. When pulp fiber is mixed in clay, the irregular, hollow, water-absorbent tube-like fibers wick water like capillaries through the clay body. The flexible hollow fibers shrink and expand with the clay body as it shrinks in drying or re-wetting. When the pulp is blended with clay slip, it becomes like a liquid "Velcro" that stiffens and snags espe-cially well in the micro-pores of the bone-dry paper-clay or paperclay bisque. This means that, in practice, freedom to improvise over bone-dry armature clay structures or figures is now a reality for a maker.

"One by one, kiln openings at sites all over the world in recent years told the story. Experiments with the unorthodox possibilities of paperclay over the last ten years (suggested in my articles, books, and lectures) proved reliable. Paperclays respond to imagination and practical needs of a maker in ways that were previously inaccessible in ceramics.

"Ceramic paperclay (P'Clay®, New Century Arts, POB 9060, Seattle, WA 98109) has nearly double the green strength for ease in handling and transport to kilns. Those who dip glaze greenware for once-fire projects report better adhesion of glaze. The list of advantages continues from there. Fresh soft wet paperclay can be modeled directly over bone dry, and sometimes even over bisque. Repairs and improvisation to greenware (or even bisque!) such as broken fingers, handles, feet, trim, et al. are likely to succeed.

"Base clays from one side of the planet to the other - stoneware, porcelain, terracotta, earthenware, high fire, low fire, raku, pit - can be blended with paper pulp in volume proportion from 5% to 49%, most typically somewhere between one third to one quarter by volume of pulp to slip. Unlike paper mâché, which has too much paper in it to fire, the higher proportion of clay in ceramic paperclays remains after fire for durability and structure. Those who want to adapt one of the "old-style" so-called "sculpture" or "raku" base clays with maximum grog or sand content ought to reduce the ratio of grog or other additives at least by half or one third before adding pulp. Due to huge variety in clays and papers worldwide, the volume method is a more reliable all-purpose "get started" guide than a specific weight.

"Papers, too, may be recycled in the mix. Newsprint, out-of-date brochures, writing papers, egg cartons, are suitable. Since most ink burns out in the fire, there is little effect on the ceramic result. Turn shredded or torn papers, or even toilet rolls, into pulp by blending them in a soup of water to wet fluffy consistency before scooping out of the water with a household sieve. The object is to disperse the pulp fibers uniformly throughout the clay slip to an oatmeal consistency. Pour out over a plaster drying bat and wedge up soft clay from there.

"It is possible to force paperclay dry too. Pots in

the kiln fire (especially above cone 4) will expand, contract, and "move on their own" (like teapot spouts) in a hot kiln. Why not put the fresh work through a mini-version of similar stress to find out right away where or if cracks or spontaneous movement will occur. Repair, reinforce, or compensate as needed. A paperclay structure that is stable after force-drying episodes is likely dependable in kiln fire later.

"The repertoire of potential surface textures of the paperclay slip (P'Slip®) is expanded to include 'paper-like, fluid paste icing, thick smear or waves.' Those who still prefer smooth traditional burnish or terra sigillata surfaces will be pleased to find them still possible over paperclay.

"The glazed result is indistinguishable from a nonpaperclay without detailed inspection by electron micrograph. The voids from the paper fibers are very small and even in bisque they would be hard to see. The lighter weight might be the only clue. In fact, the paper burns off at approximately 120°C. When it's gone, all the rules of normal clay will apply. The paper can not rescue overfired or poorly formulated base clay blends.

"Today we see evidence of continued variation and innovation in paper-reinforced clays. These include sand cast structures, fired combinations with metals and chicken wire, public art commissions, free-standing outdoor figures, murals, tiles, innovations with latex and plaster mold forms, design and models of prototype master making in industrial labs, installations, 'big-burn' events, free-standing constructions of string or twigs dipped in P'Slip and fired out, glass slumping, and progress on 'double recycle' for building materials (i.e. blend scrap glaze/clay with recycled paper to fire to a water-tight tile).

"Because of its higher 'success rate,' use of P'Clay in elementary schools, either for fire or as affordable painted greenware is growing too. Teachers of special needs children and adults report proven advance in self esteem, which is heartwarming news.

"I see potential application of the medium that could affect every corner of contemporary ceramic art and science in the future. I am thankful to the hundreds of people behind and in front of the scenes whose efforts and experiments have collectively inspired this to be well underway.

"Today, there is my informational website - www.paperclayart.com - to serve the ever-growing community of interest. For those who do not wish to make their own batches, the ready-made pre-wedged P'Clay blend is a real convenience and can even be thrown on the wheel!

"Compensation for cracking and loss is so much an essential element of practice with potter's clay that it was never questioned. The day one figures out how to avoid the cracks with certainty is understood to be one of the essential prerequisites to success in the field. Once that point is attained, one can begin to produce work that is fresh and genuine. With paperclay, fears of cracking and loss are less during the critical attention to detail and finish stages of the process too. As a result more attention and time can now be directed to the bottom line - fresh imagination for surface and forms that will stand the test of the fire and time.

"The potential for an advance in artistic integrity and pleasure in the 'territory of paperclays' is underway. This new variation on an ancient approach opens up a huge range of possibilities, allowing the artist who works in clay a freedom to work with far less fear of loss in the final product. Expanded construction methods, from throwing and hand-building to exploration of unconventional forms of clay work, are now possible through this revolutionary process. The future for this new variable on an old methodology looks to be very secure. It will be interesting to speculate on what other new clay developments are just around the corner awaiting discovery."

19. Warning

All reinforcing materials may carry with them some health hazards. Fiberglass contains fine strands of glass that may severely irritate the skin. Fine nylon fiber is probably better all around than fiberglass but may have side effects from inhalation of fine fibers. Organic additions such as paper or cloth can develop molds that may cause nasal, respiratory problems and allergies. Molds can be inhibited by the use of fungicides and bactericides, but who knows what secondary problems that may cause. One other problem with reinforced clays is that since they can easily be used to patch and repair badly made work, the quality of craftsmanship is likely to suffer as poor or ill-conceived work can be saved too easily and fired into permanence.

8 ENGOBES, SLIPS, AND TERRA SIGILLATAS

1. Engobe Composition

An engobe, or a slip, is a layer of liquefied colored clay, or paste, applied to the surface of a piece of pottery to change its color or to add some decorative accent. The terms engobe and slip generally mean the same thing; the word engobe is more commonly used in North America and the word slip is more common in Europe, particularly the U.K. The main difference is a technical one, in that slips are generally applied to unfired greenware, and engobes are sometimes formulated to be usable over the top of bisque-fired ware. There are many ways of coloring and applying these liquids or semi-liquids. An important part of the art of pottery decoration is concerned with the compounding, application, and glazing over of slips, engobes, and terra sigillatas. The use of layers of surfacing variations helps to develop a richness of surface similar to all the variables of painting and printmaking combined. A direct relationship between graphic skills and pottery surface enrichment can emulate anything from thin watercolor to thick acrylic, oil paint, or impasto. The thickness of these coatings, as well as what glazes may cover them and the way they are fired, will define the final result.

Engobe compositions must be so designed that the engobes will (1) cover the ware with a suitably dense coating of the desired color, (2) cling to the ware during the shrinkage which accompanies drying and firing, (3) vitrify or harden at a temperature similar to, or somewhat lower than, the maturing temperature of the clay on which they are to be used, and (4) survive under the glaze coating without being dissolved into the glaze and without checking or peeling. Actually, all of the conditions are rather easy to satisfy, and engobes usually have very wide tolerances in composition, application, and firing range.

Very useful engobes may be made by adding coloring oxides to the particular clay which is being used for the ware. For instance, if one has a good throwing clay, a darker-colored engobe can be made of it simply by adding some iron oxide and manganese, perhaps 2% of each. Such an engobe may be painted with a brush or roller, dipped, trailed, or sprayed onto a pot, and it will stick well, provided the piece is still damp and has not begun to shrink.

The difficulty with such an engobe is that it is best applied to fairly wet clay; otherwise, if the engobe is applied when the clay is leather-hard, since the pot has already undergone part of its shrinkage, the engobe may loosen and peel off when it shrinks. Another difficulty with such engobes is that the only colors possible are those that are darker than the clay body, since it is impossible to alter a clay mixture toward lighter values without radically changing the kinds and proportion of clays in the mixture.

To get around these difficulties, engobe compositions are designed to have less shrinkage than the clay upon which they are to be applied and to be made up of light-burning materials so as to be essentially white, unless colored with added coloring oxides. To ensure whiteness and opacity, tin oxide or zirconium oxide are frequently added.

The materials that go into engobes may be conveniently divided into groups consisting of (1) clays, (2) fluxes, (3) fillers, (4) hardeners, (5) opacifiers, and (6) colorants.

The clays used in engobes are usually chosen for whiteness and for their relative shrinkage. Combinations of kaolin and ball clay usually fill the requirements of an engobe. If more shrinkage is needed, the ball clay can be increased relative to the kaolin, and if less shrinkage is needed, the kaolin can be increased. In most engobes the amount of these two clays together will total between 40% and 70%.

The fluxes used in engobes will vary with the maturing temperature and possibly the color requirements. For higher temperatures, cone 1 to cone 14, feldspar is the best choice. For the lower ranges of temperature some leadless frit, perhaps used in combination with talc, is used. Small amounts of calcium may be added as an auxiliary flux.

For a filler, silica is used. Engobes usually contain a generous amount of silica. It lessens the shrinkage and lends the desirable property of hardness to the engobe, and it also increases the likelihood of glaze fit. The usual percentage of silica in engobe compositions is 15% to 30%. Pyrophyllite, a nonplastic aluminum silicate, may be used as a filler. It functions in engobes and clay bodies like a preshrunk calcined clay.

For hardening, a little borax added to engobes has been found to be useful. Borax, being soluble, tends to recrystallize in the engobe when it dries on the ware, and this forms a tougher, harder coating which is less subject to damage in handling. Organic binders, such as sugar or gums, may be used for this purpose, but they have the disadvantage of spoiling with age.

For opacity, zirconium oxide may be added to the engobe. For the darker colors this is not really necessary. But if an opaque and very white engobe is needed, the opacifier helps to ensure whiteness and enables the engobe to be applied more thinly without loss of opacity. Tin oxide works equally as well as zirconium oxide and generally gives a better, less cream-colored white, although it is more expensive. What is used really depends on the results desired.

The chart shows some typical engobe compositions. In engobes, as compared to glazes, there is a rather broad tolerance for differences in composition. Sometimes a material in an engobe may be increased or decreased by 10% or so without making any noticeable difference in the fired result. What is required of an engobe is that it sticks to the ware during the drying process without cracking, peeling, or breaking loose at the edges, and that, in firing, it does not come loose from the surface of the ware, dissolve in the glaze, or upset the fit of the glazes. Although engobe tests may be rather hard to evaluate, adjustments in the raw shrinkage of the engobe and in its

Engobe Compositions

Temperature Range	Cone 08-1			Cone 1-6			Cone 6-11		
State of ware to which engobe is applied	Damp	Dry	Bisque	Damp	Dry	Bisque	Damp	Dry	Bisque
Kaolin	25	15	5	25	15	5	25	15	5
Ball clay	25	15	15	25	15	15	25	15	15
Calcined kaolin		20	20		20	20		20	20
Leadless frit	15	15	15			5			5
Nepheline syenite				15	15	20			5
Feldspar							20	20	20
Talc	5	5	15	5	5	5			
Silica	20	20	20	20	20	20	20	20	20
Zircopax	5	5	5	5	5	5	5	5	5
Borax	5	5	5	5	5	5	5	5	5

flux can easily bring about a working combination of materials.

2. Coloring Oxides in Engobes

Engobes provide a great opportunity for the creation of surface variation and texture beneath the glaze, like textured or spackled stucco on walls and ceilings. They may be colored with any of the coloring oxides which are used in glazes (see Chapter 19 for color and colorant information). The colors resulting from such additions, when seen under the fired, transparent glaze, are very similar to the colors produced by the direct addition of the coloring oxide to the glaze, but the textures may be radically different. A higher percentage of coloring oxide must be added to engobes than to glazes to obtain a similar hue because of its density or opacity. Coloring oxides may be used in a great variety of combinations to obtain many colors. As would be expected, cobalt added to an engobe gives a blue color, copper gives green, and so on. These colors reach full saturation only when the engobe is covered with the glaze, although they can have wonderfully variable and subtle colors without glaze.

Since engobes are essentially clay coatings on the ware, the colors which seem most suitable may be those in the earthy range, such as black, brown, tan, light grey, and grey-blue. However, if any comparison to painting a house with a brick or timber frame covered with grey or white plaster is made, the coatings beneath the paint are just as important as the paint itself. Particularly pungent reds, greens, yellows, or blues had perhaps best be achieved with glazes rather than with engobes. Highly textured or spotty colors can easily be obtained from engobes by adding granular materials such as granular manganese, ground red brick or shale, or granular ilmenite.

The following list gives the typical amount of coloring oxides added to engobes, and the probable resulting color:

2% iron oxide	–light tan
4% iron oxide	–brown
6% iron chromate	–dark brown
1% iron chromate	–light grey
2% iron chromate	–medium grey
1% cobalt oxide	–medium blue

1% cobalt oxide	} –grey-blue
2% iron oxide	
3% copper oxide	–medium green
10% vanadium stain	–yellow
6% manganese dioxide	–purple-brown
3% granular manganese	–speckled brown
6% rutile	–creamy tan
3% iron oxide	
2% cobalt oxide	} –black
2% manganese dioxide	

More about color additives and the use of stains is given in a later chapter.

The glaze used over engobes has an important influence on the color and the quality of the engobe. Alkaline glazes, for example, will have their peculiar brilliance of color when used over colored engobes. Clear glazes used thinly over engobes, give the effect of merely wetting the engobes and revealing every detail of texture or brushwork. Lead glazes have a tendency to dissolve the engobe, and if a high-lead glaze is to be used, the engobe composition should include an ample amount of silica and opacifier.

Semi-opaque glazes over engobes may give very beautiful, partially veiled effects. Subtle gradations of color and texture may result from the glaze, partially concealing and partially revealing the engobes. If an engobe is used that is heavily loaded with iron oxide, manganese oxide, or other dark coloring oxides, it will bleed through semi-opaque or opaque glazes and give mottled, rich textural results, especially if the thickness of the glaze is varied.

3. Vitreous Engobes

An engobe that has a very low shrinkage because of the small amount of plastic clay in it, and that matures to a dense opaque coating over the ware, may be called a vitreous engobe. It is essentially the halfway point between a clay and a glaze. Vitreous engobes may be applied on either dry or bisque ware with safety, since they have little shrinkage and can accommodate themselves to the already shrunken ware. If bisque ware is decorated with vitreous engobes, the glaze may be applied directly over the engobe without the necessity of firing on the engobe. This process has the advantage of not requiring the careful timing necessary in slip decoration over damp ware. Bisque ware may be stored and given an engobe decoration at any time. Another advantage of decoration with vitreous engobes over bisqued ware is that the decoration, if it is not satisfactory, may be washed off and another one may be applied in its place. Vitreous engobes have the disadvantage of not giving the freedom of technique that is possible on damp ware. It is not advisable to use slip trailing, as this is apt to peel off, and other techniques, such as sgraffito, which depend on a damp and soft base of clay for their effect, are not at their best with vitreous engobes.

Vitreous engobes are compounded with a minimum amount of clay, just enough to give good adhesion. About 10% to 20% is usual. The filler, usually silica, may be present in a higher quantity than in the case of normal engobes for application to damp ware. Usually the flux is also increased. Vitreous engobes are more like glazes in their composition and may be thought of as underfired, very opaque glazes which are put on under the regular glaze to influence color and to achieve pattern. Since vitreous engobes are usually glazed over when they are still raw, some gum or hardener in the composition is almost a necessity. When vitreous engobes are used on ware, the glazing techniques are somewhat limited because of the danger of disturbing the engobe coat. Spraying the glaze may be quite satisfactory, but dipping and pouring may loosen the engobe and cause checking, peeling, or cracking.

4. Techniques of Applying Engobes

A great variety of engobe application techniques are possible. Engobes may be applied by painting, dipping, brushing, trailing from a syringe or slip trailer, or by spraying. Resist patterns may be made with wax, liquid latex, or cut paper attached to the ware by dampening with water. Linear patterns may be scratched through the engobe into the damp clay beneath - the familiar sgraffito technique.

When a glazed surface is not necessitated by function, engobes without any cover of glaze may be used to add color or texture to the clay surface. If sufficient flux is used, the engobe can be hard and durable, and a wide variety of colors can be produced by adding coloring oxides or stains. There is a useful range of surfaces which lies somewhere between clay and glaze in character; in fact, some very underfired glazes have a potential use in producing dry, earthy surfaces suitable for sculpture, murals, or the outside surfaces of pots.

Engobe decoration has the virtue of plasticity, ease of application, and a close relationship to the clay, which makes it, perhaps, more homogeneous with the pot than most kinds of decoration carried out in the glaze. Slip or engobe decoration is, of course, associated with the earthy, natural, and frequently very beautiful wares of the Pennsylvania Dutch, the English earthenwares of the pre-industrial era, and the peasant wares of central Europe. The warm, earthy colors of these wares, their spontaneous, rapidly done, and unaffected patterns, and their sturdy functional shapes make them still a standard of excellence for slip-decorated pottery.

5. Terra Sigillatas

Terra sigillata is actually a type of engobe rather than a glaze. It is a Latin term that means "sealed earth." It is familiar as the burnished, usually black, surface seen on the classical wares of the Greeks, the red "Arretine or Samian" wares of Roman patricians, and on the pottery of many other cultures, most notably in pre-Columbian Central and South America. It may have a dense, rather waxy surface, usually red, brown, or ochre in color.

The black glaze on ancient Greek pottery is a form of terra sigillata. This glaze, which has the appearance of a black varnish, was actually a slip made from a fusible red clay. The black color is the result of reducing conditions in the kiln. That the Greeks were able to produce both black and red color on the same pot was formerly something of a ceramic mystery. The answer is simple, however. They reoxidized their pots toward the end of the fire, which turned the body color to red. Those areas that had been painted with sigillata remained black because in their sintered, partially fused state they were relatively immune to the effects of the oxidation. (For further information on traditional Greek terra sigillatas and their beautiful use, see *The Techniques of Painted Attic Pottery* by Joseph Veach Noble, Watson Guptil, New York, 1965.)

Historically, terra sigillatas have normally been made with red clays, but almost any clay can be made into a sigillata. Usually terra sigillata is made by separating the finer fractions of a common iron-bearing plastic clay. The slip so obtained is spread on the ware in a thin coat and fired to a low temperature. Using cream to white firing ball clays and kaolins, sigillatas can be made to take color and produce a surface effect not unlike watercolor. Books referring to terra sigillatas usually state that these surfaces can't be fired higher than cone 04, often even less, without losing the smooth sheened surface typical of this process. Although to some extent this is true, by firing terra sigillatas up to cone 10, some of the sheen will undoubtedly be lost but the opportunity is given to develop a surface that is like matte vellum or ivory, particularly over a porcelain clay. This gives the potter yet another possibility of surface that may be a basis for color or painting.

To prepare terra sigillata, clay and water are mixed until the resultant slip is quite thin, having a specific gravity of 1.2 or less. Some deflocculant may be added to the slip to aid in keeping the particles floating. About .3% of sodium hydroxide or 1% of soda ash or 1% sodium silicate to the weight of the dry clay has been found to be a satisfactory deflocculant for most clays. The usual weight ratio of clay to water is approximately four of clay to ten of water. A typical light sigillata might consist of the following:

> 10.5 lb. dry ball clay or kaolin (4.77kg)
> 3 U.S. gallons water (11.35 liters)
> 1 to 2 oz. deflocculant (50 grams)

Ball milling may help to separate and float the particles of clay but is not generally necessary. After thorough mixing, the slip is allowed to settle for a minimum of a day. The water from the surface, along with suspended grey to black scum of carbonaceous matter, is then decanted off. Then, about the top third of the clay slip in the vessel is skimmed off for use; the rest is either discarded or dried to a thick slip and used as a painting medium with anything from a paintbrush to a palette knife. When making a colored sigillata, it is sometimes difficult to correctly measure a dry colorant in relation to a liquid slip. One liter of liquid sigillata is approximately one kilogram (1,000 grams). An addition of ten grams of dry colorant would give approximately 1% saturation and one hundred grams of colorant would give approximately 10% saturation.

Terra sigillata can be colored with a wide range of colorants, from basic oxides and carbonates to underglaze or body stains. In a terra sigillata, the color will be rendered partly opacified by the opacity of the basic materials, whereas in a slip or engobe the color will be totally opaque.

Terra sigillata may be applied by dipping, painting, or spraying on damp or dry ware. It is usually best applied very thinly; otherwise, the layer of slip may crack during shrinkage. The Greeks, however, often used it in a thickened state and painted it on with wide brushes, as close examination of their pots sometimes shows. The surface may be burnished before firing by rubbing with a hard smooth instrument like the back of a spoon or alternatively, with a soft cloth or chamois leather to develop a softer sheen. I find that the soft side of an old sweatshirt works perfectly well. A terra sigillata fired in a low-temperature reduction will turn a beautiful black sheen. A standard white clay slip painted in designs over a terra sigillata will give a mix of sheen and matte black when fired in low-temperature reduction or reduced in combustible material as in the methods of reducing raku.

The color range of a typical terra sigillata is about the same as that of clays. Clays should be selected that are already very fine in grain structure. Different clays can be blended for color effects.

Although terra sigillata may make a piece of low-fired pottery somewhat impervious to moisture, it does not seal off the surface of the clay as positively as does a glaze.

PART II

GLAZES

INTRODUCTION

Since the original publication of this book in 1957 and its subsequent second edition in 1973, there have been vast changes in the ceramic world. New materials have arrived as new deposits are found and mined; old ones have gone as mines get played out or become uneconomical for production, and much ceramic technology has changed beyond recognition. Research into materials for space travel and exploration have given us wonderful new materials for kiln construction and other uses. We are the beneficiaries of many inventions in industrial research. Perhaps the most significant changes in all our lives have come from the development of the computer. In the ceramic field, it is the personal computer, or PC, that has revolutionized the way we learn about, calculate, and store vast amounts of data.

Previously, we would have needed a huge library to hold all of the information on the technology of ceramics. Now, with the aid of the Internet, various software programs, and interactive "chat rooms" of like-minded people, the technical side of this medium is being understood and expanded in ways never before imagined. Earlier methods of calculation required the use of slide rules and/or longhand methods of approach. Today, we can have our mathematics done in the flick of an eye by computers that take the drudgery out of this part of the process. Unless you have the brain of a rocket scientist or actuary, this part of the ceramic process has usually been an anathema to the great majority of people trying to understand this incredibly complex medium. With freedom from this form of labor the artist can now begin to understand in ways never before possible, and thus can approach glaze and color development in more creative ways.

Glaze calculation software has been developed by a number of people around the world to solve their particular problems, but the ones most in use in North America are *HyperGlaze*, a program for the Apple Macintosh computer designed by Richard Burkett, and *Insight*, a program for both IBM and Apple computers designed by Tony Hansen. I have asked both of these authors to comment on their programs and the flexibility they make possible. I also queried Ron Roy, a ceramic consultant. Roy is a potter and clay/glaze consultant to both potters and suppliers. He uses calculation software extensively to help solve clay and glaze problems as well as to develop new products. You'll find their comments in Chapter 13.

The basis of success in any glaze development, however, must remain the formation of a knowledge bank of the materials we use, and the behavior of those materials in conjunction with others at varying degrees of temperature. There is no better way of learning than to gather information by testing the materials and observing how they melt at different temperatures and how they interact. Gradual understanding of the reactions taking place and careful note-taking will allow the novice and master alike to understand the behavior of sintered materials. Observation is one thing and theory is another. Reinforced with software programs as both data bank and calculator, the potter can combine the observed with the theorized to develop a personal direction in his or her work.

There are many ways to go about the development of the ceramic surface, some no-tech, some low-tech, and some high-tech. The great thing about glaze development is that you can choose your personal approach at whatever level you feel comfortable. Many well-known potters absolutely hate to deal with calculation in any way and do all of their glaze and color development by purely empirical processes of "try it and see." They usually get to know a small number of favorite materials quite intimately and develop their palette and surface variation within fairly tight parameters. There is nothing wrong with this way of working. It has been in use for at least 5,000 years, and chemical calculation processes for only a little over a hundred years. People are often inhibited by the combination of chemistry, mathematics, and analytical methods - the high-tech approach. In between no-tech and high-tech are a wide range of places that different people view as "comfort zones," areas where they feel comfortable, until it doesn't quite make it for them any more. Then they can effect a change if they wish. No single method is right or wrong; they all add to the combined experience of this medium. It is a matter of personal choice. No matter how you do it, working with the ceramic surface is a process of discovery. It has no end and few limitations.

I feel that a general overview of the differing approaches is warranted here. When developing glazes you first have to ask yourself a few questions. In setting about the necessary research for changes to this book, I sent a short questionnaire to a number of North American artists and teachers particularly respected in the glaze development area. I am greatly indebted to them all for their extensive and thoughtful responses. Their names are in the Acknowledgments at the beginning of the book. I asked them their various approaches to developing the surfaces of their work.. Most of the responses here are from Val Cushing, although a great deal of similarity in response occurred from all the respondents.

Q. What are your thought processes when developing a new glaze?

A. Most answers to this question tabulated a similar number of steps:

a. What temperature will it be?

b. What atmosphere and firing method will it be? Oxidation, reduction, electric, gas, oil, wood, dung, soda, salt, raku, primitive, pit or saggar, earthenware, stoneware, porcelain, etc.?

c. What surface texture? Glossy, satin, matte, dry?

d. What light transmission? Transparent, translucent, semi-opaque, opaque?

e. What color range is wanted? Intense, pastel, subtle, jazzy, etc.?

f. What specific colors are wanted? Reds, blues, greens, yellows, earth colors, etc.?

g. Is it for food vessels, sculpture, or other decorative use?

These questions establish the direction that potters should go in starting the technical journey to achieve the end in mind. It should always be in relation to the concepts and ideas being developed concerning the nature of the work in hand. How will the glaze suit the forms and how will the surface suit the function, if there is one?

Q. When developing new glazes do you think out the desired surface and potential color, then (a) use a known recipe that is somewhere close to what you want, then adjust it, (b) calculate a glaze from limit formula basics, (c) use a computer software program, (d) develop it empirically from previous experience and knowledge of material, or (e) use a combination of the above. If you answer (e) what combination of methods do you use?

A. The general response here was that most used a combination of methods, particularly at different stages of their careers. Early approaches are colored by the teacher who inspires the student. Students who are lucky enough to receive a good technical background from a knowledgeable teacher will be taught empirical observation in conjunction with calculation processes. This immediately ties together the numbers game of theory with the evidence of what happens in reality. The shorter this distance, the more easily and thoroughly the potter will gain mastery over the glaze-making aspect of this medium. A healthy combination of curiosity, visualization, observation, and testing will give the potter the tools necessary for personal exploration.

Q. What is the most important factor for you when developing glazes, surface, or color potential?

A. Certain kinds of surfaces demand the use of specific materials, particularly fluxes. Fluxes are also the main controlling factor in the development of specific color. (More explanation of this will be stated in later chapters.) Sometimes the desired color response conflicts with the materials needed to develop a specific surface. With a great deal of experience, it is possible to achieve most colors on most surfaces, but many years of study and observation are necessary to do this. It is probably best to decide on the color range you want to work with and select the materials to get that color response. Calcium and magnesium, the least color-affecting fluxes, can be used to change the subtleties of surface.

As you can see, there are a number of approaches to glaze making. They basically fall into the following categories:

1. Play with basic raw materials and test them individually by firing at a variety of temperatures. Observe the results and make notes on their behavior. Then mix those that melt extensively with those that are sluggish in different ratios until suitable glaze melts are achieved. Even the most oddball and unlikely materials, like eggshells, bones, organic materials, soap powders, and photo chemicals may have great potential. This is the "try it and see" or "kitchen" method and gives the potter a good understanding of the physical potential or the behavior of materials under heat. This understanding is the basis necessary to make the most out of the following approaches.

2. Use recipes or formulas from other potters, books, and magazines, either as is, or, if you're knowledgeable enough, change them to suit your own needs. Interchanging fluxes and comparing results is always a great learning process. Applying stripes of liquefied colorant solutions will give far greater concepts of a glaze's potential.

3. Calculate glazes longhand by one of three methods - Unity Molecular Formula (UMF), percentage analysis, or ultimate analysis.

4. Use one or more computer software programs based on the above methods to take the drudgery and possible inaccuracy out of longhand methods.

5. Any combination of the above four is likely to lead to greater understanding of both materials and their chemistry. Very experienced ceramic artists juggle between them all from the knowledge that, for certain types of surface, some methods work better than others.

No matter which form of calculation you use, there are things that no description or calculation can do for you. It will not tell you three major things:

1. What the visual and tactile quality of surface will be: glassy, glossy, satin, vellum, matte, crystalline, or dry.

2. Which materials to select for a glaze to obtain specific colors or textures - what it looks like and how it responds to additions of colorants and opacifiers.

3. How the same glaze will vary in differing firing conditions and kilns.

These are things that only observation and experimentation will give you. A recipe or formula can only go so far. The rest is up to you.

No wonder it all seems so complicated! However, deep down, glaze making is simply an elevated form of cooking at high temperatures. As with cooking, the better you know the ingredients, the more creative the dish! The more you experiment and test, the greater your knowledge and observation skills will become.

So where do you start? Some start with formulas and glaze calculation, and some with direct working with materials and observation. From my experience, most people prefer to work in the latter way and learn to develop glazes by direct response and intuitive manipulation of materials. Looking at materials tests and seeing how the most mundane and oddball of materials has potential for use is both fun and instructive. There is no doubt that, to some extent, you have to do this anyway in glaze and color development, but the potential problem here is that the "kitchen" method of working doesn't give the serious potter some of the tools needed to solve complex technical problems that may occur. If technical problems are not an issue in the type of work being done, then the "try it and see" approach, particularly with respect to color development, is certainly adequate and has been practiced for millennia. It is worth remembering that you don't need to know it all, but you do need to know what impacts on your work really well!

From the potter's point of view, the study of glazes is more complex than that of clay and clay bodies. More materials are involved, and the number of variables which must be taken into account is considerably greater. Unlike the needs of factory production or industrial ceramics, the potter doesn't usually need this depth of technical understanding. In the main, we are artists and not ceramic chemists. In dealing with clay, simple rule-of-thumb methods of formulation and control will usually suffice. However, with glazing, more exacting procedures are required if any degree of predictability is expected. Even if the potter uses only prepared glazes purchased from a supply house, he will still have to gain control over application and firing in order to get good results.

Some knowledge of chemistry will be helpful to the student of glazes but it is not absolutely necessary. In trying to describe what actually happens in the formation of glazes, we speak of atoms, molecules, and chemical reactions. But these things are not apparent in the finished pot and remain for the potter somewhat in the realm of abstraction. It should be emphasized that formulating, applying, and firing pottery glazes is a craft more akin to alchemy rather than a science. The value of the work ultimately resides in the finished product rather than in the procedures by which it is produced, no matter how involved or difficult these procedures may be. The degree to which the ceramic artist delves into the mysteries of glaze making will depend on his interest and on the kind of ceramics he wishes to make. Such a limited involvement with glaze study does not automatically impose any limitation on the value of his work; in fact, very fine results often come from concentration on the use of a few glazes. Or the potter may be drawn to certain elusive colors or textures which will require many hours of laboratory work and testing for realization. In any case, the rules and methods of glaze formulation and calculation should be considered as practical aids rather than as ends in themselves.

With glazes, slips, and decorative processes, the potter enters the world of color and two-dimensional surfaces. As an art, pottery has occupied a unique position somewhere in between sculpture and painting; that is, pottery forms that are highly dimensional and voluminous in character have been clothed in colors, textures, and motifs which relate to painting and drawing. This marriage between form and graphics has not always been a happy one. But in the best examples of pottery, there is a successful fusion of two- and three-dimensional elements in a way that is quite unusual and does not suggest a hybrid art. In most of the traditional pottery workshops of the past, glazing and decoration was considered a separate craft and was assigned to specialists who took no part in the actual shaping of the pots out of clay. But the individual potter today, who usually carries out all processes himself, must be something of a master of both form and color, a synthesizer and welder of many elements into unified wholes. It is scarcely surprising that in this difficult task some artists put their emphasis primarily on form, restricting themselves to simple glaze effects, while others prefer to work with less concern for form and more for the more painterly qualities. The history of pottery could be studied from these two viewpoints - form and surface. The Chinese, during the earlier periods at least, seemed more concerned with form than with surface, while the Greek and Persian potters tended to regard pottery shapes as so many blank canvases upon which their marvelous fantasies of line and color could be spread.

As a medium of surface embellishment, and aside from practical qualities such as durability, glazes have some uniquely valuable properties. The total range of glazes, from low-fired to high-fired, permits an almost limitless palette of surface and color. Transparency and opacity can be controlled, as well as reflectance and matteness. Color blending, controlled areas of color, linear patterns, textures, and flow can all be manipulated. Depth of color is possible, and one layer may be applied over another to give an optical mingling of tones and hues. Because of the large number of variables in the reactions of glaze materials, glazes are almost unbelievably various in color and texture, and historically glazes have been used for widely differing aesthetic purposes. Poles apart are the old Chinese Ju glazes, for example, with their dense opaque surfaces, resembling smooth white marble when seen in moonlight, and the incredibly brilliant domes and facades of the Persian mosques at Isfahan, with their thousands of square yards of shimmering blue and turquoise glazed tiles. The blazing color of Hispano-Moresque lusters, the earthy roughness of German salt glaze, the pure cool whiteness of Ming Dynasty "Blanc de Chine" - all of these are varying examples of the glazer's art.

The chapters which follow show the history, materials, and methodology of the glaze-making process. The range of possibilities is endless. What other medium has this potential for discovery? Of mixing together diverse powdered rocks and creating a thin film of a new rock over the forms you make. Making new rocks is an endlessly fascinating scenario for the potter. Where else can you re-create the act of creation in such a direct way? Choice of direction and choice of process is yours for the taking. Use whatever methodology works best for you to get where you want to go. Be afraid of nothing! Glaze making is about options.

9 THE NATURE OF GLASS AND GLAZES

1. Silica as the Basis of Glass

Glazes on pottery are similar to other kinds of glass, and to understand pottery glazes one must first understand something of the nature of glass as such. Although glass is an extremely abundant and important substance in our daily lives, few people have much understanding of what it really is and what it is made of.

Glass is difficult to define in nontechnical terms. Actually, it is a noncrystalline substance of more or less transparency and translucency, which has been formed by the cooling of a melt of earthy materials. Plastics, which may be transparent or translucent, are organic in origin and thus would not come within this definition.

In describing the nature of glass, we must consider the phenomenon of melting and the tendency of matter to crystallize. All the materials of which the earth is formed were, at the beginning, in a vaporous or liquid state. This was because elevated temperatures prevailed during the early stages of the formation of the earth. As the earth cooled, it solidified or froze - at least the outer crust did. The interior may be assumed to be hot enough still to be in the liquid state; that is, it would be in the liquid state if the pressures prevailing deep in the earth were removed, as sometimes happens in the case of volcanic action.

The state of matter, then, is strictly dependent on its temperature, and the same substance may be a liquid, a vapor, or a solid, depending on how hot it is. Water is a very familiar example of this. We know it as steam, as a liquid, or as a solid (ice). And a substance which we think of as being permanently solid, such as a rock, may be reduced to a liquid or to a vapor if sufficient heat is applied to it. At the first atomic explosion at Los Alamos, the sands around the tower holding the bomb were liquefied by the heat.

When a substance cools from the liquid phase to the solid phase, it ordinarily assumes a crystalline state. Most of the earthy substances of the crust of the earth are crystalline. When a substance is in a crystalline state, its molecules are arranged in recurring sequences or patterns that repeat themselves three-dimensionally. A crystalline substance might be compared to a pile of building blocks in which each block is placed in a similar relationship to its neighboring blocks. Different substances form crystals of different shapes and arrangements. Salt, for example, crystallizes in forms whose planes meet at right angles. The recurring pattern of a crystalline substance is known as the crystal lattice. The form of the crystal may be repeated on a larger scale, so that pieces of quartz, for example, will have a shape bounded by planes meeting at the angle characteristic for the crystal of that substance. It will be seen that if crystals are to pack closely, with their faces meeting, only a certain number of shapes are possible. It was, in fact, predicted mathematically how many different crystal forms were possible before this number was verified by observation.

When a crystalline substance is heated, the bonds between the molecules become weakened, and the molecules are no longer able to maintain their fixed relationship to one another. This decrease in bond and the more helter-skelter arrangement of the molecules, which makes for fluidity, we call melting. A molten substance has no crystalline structure.

When a melted or liquefied substance is cooled, the molecules tend to re-form into a regular lattice. The material solidifies or freezes, and is again in the crystalline state.

When, as sometimes happens, a substance cools and solidifies without a crystalline structure reforming, it retains some of the characteristics of a liquid. Such a "solidified" or "supercooled" liquid is glass, which may be thought of as a melted liquid that has managed to cool and solidify without recrystallizing.

Some oxides have a greater tendency to form glass than others. Most important among the glass-forming oxides is silica, which in practice is the basis for all useful glasses. Silica melts at 1710°C. This is, of course, a relatively high temperature, and is beyond the reach of most kilns and furnaces used in ceramics. When silica melts, it is a clear liquid, without crystalline structure. When silica cools, it has a tendency to remain in the amorphous or glassy state; that is, the crystalline structure of the original material does not re-establish itself. This is particularly true if the silica is cooled rapidly. Silica, then, by itself, is a material which readily forms a glass when melted and cooled. Furthermore, pure silica glass is exceptionally hard, durable, resistant to the attack of acids, and resistant to breaking from heat shock. It would be the ideal glass for many practical purposes except for the difficulty of melting the material and the impracticality of forming it into useful objects when it is in the molten state.

In nature, glass is rather unusual. The normal geologic processes allowed molten material to cool very slowly; and, as the molten liquids froze, they had a chance to crystallize. Obsidian and some other minerals, however, are true glasses.

Glass, then, may be thought of as a chilled liquid from the melting of earthy substances. While it acts like a solid, it is nevertheless elastic, more or less transparent or translucent, and lacking in crystalline structure.

2. Making Glass

Glass objects made from silica alone would be superior for most practical purposes. Some vessels for laboratory and special uses are, in fact, made from pure silica. But the difficulty of melting and forming such objects makes them too expensive for ordinary use.

Silica is, however, the basis of all practical glasses and, to facilitate its melting and fabrication, fluxes are added to it. These fluxes lower the melting point and make possible the melting and forming of the glass at reasonably low temperatures. Soda and lime are usually used for this purpose. All these materials - silica, soda, and lime - are very abundant and cheap, and, as a result, glass can be made in great quantity and at low cost. Silica is usually used in the form of a white sand. The soda is added as soda ash, and the lime as crushed and ground limestone. The ingredients are heated in a clay crucible or tank until they melt and fuse together as a liquid. The temperature at which this fusion takes place will depend on the exact composition of the batch, but most commercial glasses are made at around 1500°C. The tank or bath of glass is kept at a high enough temperature to prevent its freezing, and some of the molten material is then drawn off and fashioned into glass objects by blowing, pressing, drawing, or rolling. After the object is made, it is placed in a low-temperature furnace and allowed to cool slowly. This annealing is necessary to prevent strains in the glass which might cause it to crack.

Compounds of lead and potassium are also used in glass to obtain different properties in the finished material. Color is obtained by adding metallic oxides, such as iron oxide, manganese dioxide, gold chloride, or cobalt.

Ordinary glass is predominantly silica, fluxed by the additions of other materials that lower its melting point, facilitate making it into objects while molten, or lend other desirable properties to the finished product, such as color. The glass industry has developed a great many kinds of glass which, in addition to filling the practical need for containers and cooking vessels, has supplied the optical trade and other scientific consumers with glasses of many valuable specific properties.

3. The Distinction Between Glass and Glazes

The subject of glass as such is only briefly touched on above, since the primary concern here is with glazes for the ceramic surface. A distinction must now be made between glass and glazes. Although pottery glazes are true glass, their composition is adjusted for the rather specialized function of sticking onto the surface of clay. Glass to be fashioned into bottles, window glass, and the like must be of quite a low viscosity; in other words, it must be fairly runny when molten. In pottery glazes the glass must, on the other hand, be quite stiff when melted, so that it will hold its position on the surface of the clay and not run off during the firing. This stiffness in pottery glazes is primarily achieved by the addition of alumina to the mixture. Alumina has the property of increasing the viscosity of the glass, and for this reason it is present in only small amounts in ordinary glass. However, it is possible to make pottery glazes from glass which is low in alumina, and, in fact, some special colors and surfaces are achieved only in the absence of alumina.

Glazes, like any other glass, are predominantly silica, with just enough other material added to make them melt at the desired temperature and to give the desired texture and color. The art and science of glaze making involves the proper selection, apportioning, mixing, application, and firing of glaze materials to get the desired result.

An obvious distinction between glazes and glass is that glazes are made by blending the unmelted raw materials - the silica and other constituents of the glaze - and spreading these blended materials on the surface of the pottery where the glaze or glass is formed or melted in place. Glass, on the other hand, is melted first into a bath of molten liquid material and then fashioned into objects. A glaze may be defined as a glassy coating melted in place on a ceramic body, which may render the body smooth, nonporous, and of a desired color or texture.

Enamels, which are outside the scope of the present work, are essentially the same as glazes, except that they are melted onto metals rather than onto ceramic bodies. Enamels are usually fired at lower temperatures than glazes.

10 EARLY TYPES OF GLAZES

The knowledge of ways to form glazes on pottery is of great antiquity, dating back to at least 5,000 B.C. Some authorities claim dates as early as 12,000 B.C. Since glazes were made in many parts of the world long before the beginnings of any scientific knowledge of chemistry, it is clear that the processes involved must have been essentially simple and the raw materials abundant. Before discussing in more detail the chemical makeup of glazes, we might well consider the methods used by the ancients in glazing their pottery. Their results were in no way inferior to the best of present-day glazed ware - results achieved by strictly empirical methods which had no basis in scientific knowledge or theory.

1. Egyptian Glazes

The Egyptians, who undoubtedly made the first glazed ware, utilized the soda compounds found in abundance in the desert areas of the Near East. The turquoise glazed beads, ornaments, and small sculptures, which are known as Egyptian paste, are probably the earliest glazed objects. The glaze on Egyptian paste is formed by mixing soluble sodium salts into the clay, which, during drying, deposits on the surface where it forms a glaze when fired. Such glazes may have been made accidentally at first. There are two likely scenarios. First, the rocks in the area are generally of highly fusible natron. When the rocks were placed to form a fire pit, the side facing the fire would get enough heat and alkaline ash to cause the surface to melt. Early examples are of fused stone. Second, it is quite likely that when objects were being modeled from the desert clays and talcs, some of the soda ash so prevalent in the desert could have become mixed in by chance. The observation of these primitive fusions, and the capitaliza-

tion on it in works of art and utility, is a good example of the way man has advanced his techniques. It was discovered that the addition of copper-bearing minerals to the mixture resulted in bright blue and turquoise glazes. The vibrant color of this type of glaze is irresistibly beautiful, yet technically there is no great difficulty in producing it from a few readily available materials. (This type of glaze is discussed in more detail in a later chapter.)

A great technical improvement over Egyptian paste, in which the glaze-forming materials were mixed right into the clay, was the practice of applying the glaze materials on the surface of the ware and thus enabling a more exact control over the thickness and color. This advance, which occurred in Egypt in very ancient times, resulted in the first glazes, which were made, applied, and fired much as we do today. Glazes were fused on objects carved from steatite as well as on pieces made from clay. They were very simple in composition, probably being made up of soda ash, sand, and a little clay for adhesion. Such a combination of raw materials would have been found easily in the Near East and would melt to a glaze at a very low heat.

2. Early Lead Glazes

The highly alkaline glazes invented and used by the Egyptians had some serious drawbacks, such as difficulty of application, a tendency to craze and even to peel or fall off the ware after firing, and a certain amount of solubility, especially if put to use in cooking. Many of these difficulties were overcome by the discovery of lead as a glaze material. This important advance probably occurred in ancient Syria or Babylonia. It was found that lead, presumably in the form of lead sulfide, or galena, when ground to a powder and dusted or painted onto the surface of the clay, would fuse in the kiln to a smooth and shiny glaze. Lead compounds are fairly common in nature, and the procuring of the raw materials must have presented no great problem. The lead glaze was superior to the alkaline glaze in practicality, if not in beauty. It was easy to apply, was not subject to so many flaws in firing, and it fitted the clay better and was more durable in use.

Simple lead glazes are easy to make and may involve only a few materials. The potters of medieval England and Europe merely dusted galena powder on the damp pots, thus getting a sufficient coating of lead to form a glaze on the fired piece. A fairly practical glaze can be made from two parts of lead oxide together with one part of pulverized sand and one part of common red clay. Such a glaze will be smooth, bright, and brown or amber in color, similar in appearance to lead-glazed country pottery commonly made in both Europe and America. Apparently there was no awareness of the danger of lead poisoning until the 19th century.

In the Near East the Syrians and Babylonians learned to make various colored lead glazes by mixing in metallic oxides, such as copper, iron, and manganese; and some of their ceramics, notably the large architectural tiles and reliefs, represent a very high development in glaze making. The knowledge of lead glazes spread to China, and some of the earliest glazes in that country, dating from about 500 B.C., were made with lead. Some of the early Chinese lead-glazed wares have weathered and become iridescent as a result of the decomposition of the glaze, and now look quite unlike their original state.

3. Ash Glazes

In China the pottery kiln was improved, and thus the attainment of higher temperatures was made possible. All the wares of the Near East were fired at about 1050°C or less. In China, kiln firings of 1200°C or more became common in early times - as early, perhaps, as 1500 B.C. This development, made possible by the downdraft chamber kiln, which conserved and utilized the heat from the wood fire rather than letting it escape from the chimney, permitted the creation of new types of glazes that melted at higher temperatures.

An early type of glaze was formed by the ashes of the fire, which were blown through the kiln by the draft of the fire, lighted on the ware (if it was unpro-

tected), and formed a glaze on its surface. Wood ashes contain considerable alkalies, such as potash and soda, in addition to silica and some alumina that give them a relatively low fusion point. Some old Chinese and Japanese pots have a glaze on one side only, or on the shoulder, which can be accounted for by the ashes in the firing chamber. Or ashes were sometimes dusted or painted on the surface of the ware before firing, which resulted in a thin glaze.

If a sufficiently high firing temperature is employed, a very durable and satisfactory glaze can be made from wood ashes, feldspar, and clay, in about equal parts. This is a good example of the simplicity of glaze compounding, at least where a high degree of control is not essential. All these materials were readily available to the ancient potter, and he needed only to discover them and to control them by rule-of-thumb methods. No knowledge of chemistry was involved. (Further information about ash glazes is given in a later chapter.)

4. Slip Glazes

Higher firing temperatures also made possible the slip glaze, or glaze made up mostly or entirely of clay. Some of the most beautiful of the old Chinese glazes are of this type. When higher firing temperatures were reached, potters found that some clays, such as common red earthenware clay, would melt in the kiln and form a brown to black glass. Such clays are relatively fusible, due to the presence of iron and other impurities. Most common surface or red-firing clays will melt at about 1250°C, and some will fuse at even lower temperatures.

To make a slip glaze, it's necessary merely to spread a fusible, iron-bearing clay over a pot made of a more refractory clay and then fire to a sufficiently high temperature to form a glaze from the coating clay. The fusion point of slip glazes may be lowered by adding some flux, such as ashes or feldspar.

5. Feldspathic Glazes

Another extremely simple kind of glaze is the feldspathic glaze, or glaze made up largely of feldspar. Here again, relatively high temperatures are required to melt such glazes, and for this reason they remained the exclusive property of Asiatic potters for over two thousand years, since only there were kilns constructed that could reach the necessary heat. Feldspar by itself will melt to a glass at about 1250°C. This one material, when pulverized and spread on the surface of a pot, may give a very beautiful milky white glaze; in fact, some of the masterpieces of early Chinese pottery were probably glazed in just this way. Feldspar is a very common mineral and very easy to identify and to crush into a fine powder. Its fusion point can be lowered by merely adding a little ground limestone. Some of the most beautiful glazes known to the art are simple combinations of only three materials: feldspar, limestone (calcium carbonate), and quartz (silica), all of which are common minerals available almost everywhere.

6. Salt Glazes

Salt glazing, which is described more fully later, is mentioned here as an example of a glaze which is simple to make and does not require either numerous materials or a knowledge of chemical reactions. Salt volatilizes in the kiln at about 1200°C, depositing a film of sodium on the clay object. Further temperature rise will melt this to bond with the silica and alumina in the clay to develop a sodium-alumina-silicate glass on the ware.

We have considered some of the ways in which glazes were made in the past, before any technology existed that made possible a scientific knowledge of what the materials consisted of or of how they behaved in various combinations when melted. In general, potters combined various earthy minerals in proportions which, by trial and error, were known to give the desired result, and they fired their glazes to a temperature sufficient to fuse the glaze. Recipes were handed down from one generation to the next, and secrets of glaze making were closely guarded. That such methods worked well enough is evidenced by the magnificent achievements of the past. It is also evident that glaze making is not very difficult or technical; otherwise it could not have been done so successfully in the past. It has been, and still is, a matter of combining a few common materials and subjecting them to the right degree of heat. The most beautiful effects in glazes come about naturally and are, by and large, the outcome of reactions the potter has stumbled upon rather than invented.

Although fine glazes were produced in the past without any exact knowledge, present-day technology has made glaze making immensely easier for the potter. For one thing, the raw materials can be obtained in prepared and ground form and can be assumed to be uniform in composition. In former times the potter had to dig, grind, and prepare his own materials. The composition would likely vary, depending on the source. Our knowledge now permits the rapid compounding, adjusting, changing, and control of glazes for any desired result. This, together with the relatively exact control with which we can fire our ware, makes for more certain results than were formerly possible. However, there is still enough uncertainty left in the process to keep it interesting, as any experienced potter will testify.

11 THE OXIDES AND THEIR FUNCTION IN GLAZE FORMING

Before getting into the materials and methods of glaze development, I feel that it is helpful to have general information on two specific points - chemical formulation known as *Unity Molecular Formula (UMF)* and *frits*. Being armed with this information makes understanding considerably less forbidding.

Glaze making is not so much chemistry as alchemy and many people get turned off before being turned on, as it all seems so complicated. Glaze making can be likened to cooking - it takes years to become a master chef, but simple cooking is within everyone's reach.

Unity Molecular Formula divides the role that chemicals play in the glaze into three groups or columns. Simply put, these columns represent on the <u>left,</u> the fluxes, which melt the silica and are the prime contributors to color development; in the <u>center,</u> the amphoterics or stabilizers, usually clays, which act to bond the glaze to the clay and inhibit excessive fluidity, like a glue; and on the <u>right,</u> the glass formers such as silica, which need to be melted by fluxes. The relationship between the three columns determines the ratio of materials in the glaze. This, in turn, determines the temperature at which the glaze will mature. The three columns are often thought of as representing the blood/fluxes, muscle/clays, and bones/glass former.

Frits are combinations of materials usually formulated for the use of the ceramic, glass, or enamel industries. They are made to eliminate the problems of solubility and toxicity in the basic material, and to give a reliable source of these materials into a glaze. A huge variety of reliable and stable frits is now available through many companies worldwide. These allow the potter to incorporate otherwise unstable, toxic, or soluble materials into the glaze structure.

1. Oxidation and the Oxides

Most earthy materials, including those we use for glazes, are in the form of oxides. The finished, fired glaze is a mixture or melt of various elements, all in oxide form. Since in ceramics we are continuously dealing with oxides, an understanding of the term is essential. An oxide may be defined as the chemical combination of any element with oxygen. Oxygen is a very prevalent element, and in the course of geologic time most of the elements on the surface of the earth have entered into combination with it. In some cases it has taken eons of time to effect this oxidation, but in the case of some other elements, such as silicon, oxidation is rapid and the element is unstable in the presence of oxygen. Oxygen is, of course, ever present in the atmosphere and in water, and is thus always available for chemical combination.

We are all familiar with oxidation, even if we do not know it by this term. Combustion is an example. The carbon of wood, coal, or oil combines with the oxygen of the air, and the result, burning, is a chemical reaction which gives off heat and light. The product, carbon dioxide, is a gas which becomes part of the atmosphere. The residues, such as ash, consist mostly of material which was already in oxide form and so did not enter into the reaction.

Rusting is another familiar example of oxidation. The iron (Fe) combines with the oxygen of the atmosphere of the air or of water and becomes rust or iron oxide (Fe$_2$O$_3$). The metal chromium does not oxidize under ordinary atmospheric conditions; so it is added to steel to keep it from rusting - stainless steel is an alloy of steel and chromium.

Like most chemical reactions, oxidation is facilitated by heat. When the crust of the earth was still hot, oxidation of the elements that composed it was more rapid and complete than it would have been at lower temperatures. For this reason almost all earthy materials are oxides. In ceramics we subject the materials to relatively high temperatures, and finished ceramic products are composed altogether of oxides, even when materials which are not in oxide form, such as the carbonates, are used in compounding them.

The study and control of glazes is made much simpler and more understandable if the glaze is considered in its final, fired, melted state rather than in its unfired condition. After the glaze has been heated and fused, it is made up of elements in the oxide form. The relationships between these various oxides - that is, their relative amounts and the effect they have on one another during fusion - are what we are really concerned with in compounding glazes. The distinction must be kept in mind between these oxides in the fired glaze and the raw materials we combine to make the glaze. For one thing, many glaze materials have more than one oxide in them. Clay, for example, has both alumina and silica, and feldspars commonly have three or more elements in them. Furthermore, some glaze materials, such as whiting (CaCO$_3$), are carbonates rather than oxides, although the end result from such a material in the finished glaze will be an oxide - in this case, CaO. In other words, there is a real distinction between the raw materials, which we combine to make glaze, and the finished, fired, melted glaze.

The oxides that enter into the finished glaze will be considered first, and then the raw materials from which these oxides are derived.

2. The Glaze Oxides

A listing of all the commonly used glaze oxides includes the following:

PbO	lead oxide
Na$_2$O	sodium oxide
K$_2$O	potassium oxide
CaO	calcium oxide
MgO	magnesium oxide
BaO	barium oxide
Li$_2$O	lithium oxide
SrO	strontium oxide
Sb$_2$O$_3$	antimony oxide
B$_2$O$_3$	boric oxide
ZnO	zinc oxide
Al$_2$O$_3$	aluminum oxide
TiO$_2$	titanium oxide
SiO$_2$	silicon dioxide

Comparatively few oxides are found in glazes and glass. There are enough, however, so that an almost infinite number of combinations is possible. This is what accounts for the great variety of glazes. It should be emphasized that the oxides listed above are the oxides that form the glaze itself and that, with some exceptions, these oxides do not lend any color to the glaze. The exceptions are lead oxide, which gives a faint yellowish color to glazes, and combinations of lead and antimony, which give the color known as Naples yellow. First we shall discuss the glaze itself, and later study the way in which it may be colored. In practice, glaze colorants are usually added in small percentages to the batch of materials which forms the glaze.

3. The Function of the Oxides in Glazes

Something should be said here in a general way about the oxides which have been listed as entering into glaze composition. For one thing, no two of them behave exactly alike. Each oxide has a particular contribution to make to the glaze. Calcium, barium, and strontium behave more nearly alike than any others, and sodium and potassium are similar. The only oxide indispensable to glaze making is silica, and all the rest are oxides which may or may not appear in any particular glaze. Sources for the various glaze oxides are abundant and relatively cheap.

Silica is the most important of the oxides listed. By itself it will form glass, given enough temperature. It should be thought of as the material which forms the main body of the glaze, and the other materials should be thought of as modifiers. Most glazes contain a preponderance of silica. The oxides listed above in the first group may all be thought of as fluxes, or oxides that cause the silica to melt. It will be noted that the oxides listed are all metallic oxides or alkaline earths. Although they vary widely in melting point and in chemical activity or inertness, they all have the effect of making silica melt at a lower temperature than it would by itself. The alumina, which is used only in very small amounts in glazes, has the effect of stiffening the melt. It prevents the melted glaze from running down the vertical walls of pots, and it also serves to prevent the formation of crystals in the glaze when it is cooling. For this reason it is left out of glazes that are meant to show crystals, but it is present in almost all other glazes.

4. How Glazes Melt in the Kiln

Before we discuss the glaze-forming oxides in more detail, the actual history of a glaze should be described, from its compounding to its melting and solidifying. Such a description should help in visualizing the part the various oxides actually take in making up the finished glaze.

The raw materials of glazes, described in detail later, are either rocks or minerals such as silica and feldspar, which have been ground to a fine powder, or they are materials that have been prepared by precipitation or other chemical methods, and are supplied in the form of fine dry powder. Glaze materials are usually fine enough to pass through a screen having 200 meshes to the inch. When the various ingredients of the glaze have been combined and mixed with water, a mass of material is obtained, which is composed of particles of various materials lying next to one another. In this state the glaze is applied to the ware in a coating uniformly composed of small particles of the various original raw materials. The more thorough the mixing of the glaze, the more intimate the contact will be between the various materials.

As the glazed ware is heated to red heat and beyond, changes begin to occur in the glaze. Whatever volatile materials are contained in the glaze, such as carbon and sulfur, will be driven off, and the glaze will then be composed entirely of oxides. As the heat advances, these oxides will begin to chemically react on one another and fusion will begin.

Fusion may occur at first in the reaction of two or more of the materials, and the glass so formed may then promote the fusion of additional oxides until all are drawn into the melt. In most glazes this fusion occurs rather gradually with the advancing heat. Finally all the separate solids of the mixture will have lost their identity in the melt, which will be of uniform consistency. Fine particle size in the raw materials promotes fusion by bringing the various materials into more intimate contact. When the heat of the kiln subsides, the glaze chills into a solid mass of glass coating the ware. This glass or glaze is actually a complex solution or mixture of the various oxides rather than a chemical compound of definite composition.

When glazes are melted onto clay bodies, there is always a certain amount of reaction between the two, especially in higher-fired ware. As we have seen, when clay approaches vitrification in the kiln, there is a certain amount of glass formed in it, and the oxides which make up the clay are activated by the high temperature. The fluid glaze likewise is active and tends to eat down into the clay a bit, taking some of it into solution and perhaps dissolving iron and other impurities from the clay surface. Microscopic examination of a section of a glazed piece will show an intermediate zone between clay and glaze which is partly glaze, partly clay, called interface. This reaction between clay and glaze serves to make the glaze adhere firmly to the clay body. In porcelain it may be difficult to establish the line where clay stops and glaze begins, since in this case the two are much alike. Lowfired ware shows little reaction between glaze and clay, and for this reason it is sometimes very hard to fit a glaze onto an underfired, soft clay body.

5. Silica - SiO$_2$

Silica is the fundamental oxide of glass. Pottery glazes are largely made up of silica, and the other ingredients put into glazes are actually put in to modify it toward a lower melting point, or to lend to it some other property such as alkalinity, opacity or matteness. Low-fired glazes, those which mature at 1050°C or less, contain about two parts of silica to one part of the other ingredients of the glaze combined. High-fired glazes, those melting at 1250°C or higher, will have three or four times as much silica as all the other ingredients combined. About 60% of the crust of the earth is made up of silica - a fact which indicates the hardness, durability, and resistance to chemical change or solution of this oxide. These are the desirable properties it adds to glazes, and it is a general rule of glaze making that as much silica as possible be added to the glaze. High-fired glazes are of superior hardness compared to low-fired glazes, because more silica can be incorporated in them.

Vitreous silica has a low coefficient of expansion, and for this reason its presence in the glaze controls the fit of the glaze to the body. (This will be treated more fully in the section on glaze faults.)

Silica has no undesirable properties when used in glazes, except that, when present in excessive amounts, it may cause the glaze to be underfired at the intended temperature or it may cause devitrification or the formation of crystals in the cooling glaze. No glaze colors are adversely affected by silica.

6. Alumina - Al_2O_3

Although alumina is used in relatively small amounts in glazes, it contributes importantly to the working properties of the glaze, and the only glazes commonly made up without alumina are those intended to develop crystals during cooling.

Alumina is refractory and does not melt by itself until about 2040°C. For this reason not much alumina can be added to a glaze without causing it to be underfired and dry in appearance.

The presence of alumina in a glaze makes the melted glaze more viscous and less apt to run off vertical surfaces. This is a valuable property in glazes for use on pottery. Another valuable function of alumina is the prevention of recrystallization during the cooling of the glaze. Without alumina many glazes would devitrify in cooling and would have rough surfaces, opacity, or mottled textures. Alumina in the molten glass acts as a retardant in keeping the other materials from getting together in the crystalline state.

Alumina also adds to the hardness, durability, and tensile strength of glazes. Because of its high melting point, it lends opacity and matteness to any glaze if used in amounts beyond a certain critical limit, dependent on glaze composition and the firing temperature.

7. Sodium Oxide - Na_2O

The oxide of sodium is very active chemically and functions in glazes as a strong flux or melter. It is a very useful oxide in glazes from the lowest temperature range to the higher-fired glazes. Those containing a lot of sodium may be brilliantly colored by the addition of metallic coloring oxides. The presence of the soda lends a strength and brilliance to the color. One of the most outstanding examples of this is the turquoise blue that results from the addition of copper oxide to a glaze high in soda. The so-called Egyptian blue is a color produced by this combination.

Sodium has the disadvantage of having a very high coefficient of expansion, which causes glazes high in sodium to craze on most pottery bodies. Other disadvantages of high-soda glazes are their tendency to be soft and easily worn or scratched, their slight solubility in acid, and their tendency to weather and deteriorate. Many of the masterpieces of ancient Persian pottery are now in bad condition because of the weathering of the soda glazes. Still another difficulty with soda is that there are few natural sources that are insoluble. Many feldspars contain soda, however, and modest amounts can be added to a glaze in this form.

Used in moderate amounts and in combination with other fluxes, soda is a very useful oxide in glazes over a wide range of temperature. It is an important constituent of ordinary glass, which is largely composed of silica, soda, and lime.

8. Potassium Oxide - K_2O

Potassium oxide is very similar to sodium in its action in glazes. Actually, these two oxides behave so much alike that they are frequently described by the symbol "KNaO," which means a blend of sodium and potassium in any proportion. Potassium has the same advantages and the same disadvantages as sodium. Its color response is brilliant and similar to that of sodium, with some differences in color, depending on whether soda or potassium predominates in the mixture. Manganese in a soda glaze gives a reddish purple color, for example, while in the presence of potassium it gives a blue-purple. Potassium has a slightly lower coefficient of expansion than sodium, but it is still very high and causes crazing.

Potassium is a very active flux and is useful in glazes at all temperatures. Its only natural source in insoluble form is feldspar, and when considerable amounts of potassium are required in a glaze, a frit must be used.

9. Lead Oxide - PbO

Lead oxide is probably the most dangerous material used for the development of glazes. Without proper usage and studio cleanliness, it is dangerous to the person making the glazes, as well as to the user of wares with glazes which may be unsafe for foods and storage. It has been largely banned from the educational and commercial ceramic worlds and its use in glazes for functional ware is strictly controlled by governmental agencies like the Food and Drug Administration. There is a further discussion of lead problems later in this section.

Unfortunately for the potter who is not making functional objects, the elimination of lead from his assortment of glaze materials also eliminates a wide range of possible color development. Lead is absolutely needed to develop many ceramic colors. If the work being made is purely for decorative use and cannot be used for cooking in, eating from, drinking from, or storing things in, there is no reason why lead glazes should not be used to make possible the full range of the potter's palette. Used carefully it is a marvelous material for the glaze maker.

Lead oxide is used in glazes as a flux. Lead and silica alone will give a fairly good glaze, similar to that used on low-fired Mexican pottery. Most glazes the world over have contained lead as the principal fluxing ingredient. Generally speaking, it is the most useful and dependable melting flux in the lower and middle ranges of temperature.

Lead oxide has the advantages of a very low melting point, a favorable effect on most coloring oxides, and the tendency to produce a smooth, bright glaze free from blemishes. It has a fairly low coefficient of expansion, which makes lead glazes very easy to fit to most pottery bodies without crazing. Lead glazes may easily be made clear, transparent, bright, opaque, matte, or textured by varying the composition and adding suitable opacifiers and matting agents.

Lead as a material for glazes is valued for its dependability. It melts gradually, surely, and smoothly; and glazes fluxed with it are relatively free from defects unless accidentally reduced in the firing. In addition to these practical advantages, lead glazes can be used to produce rich, brilliant, deep colors in a very wide variety of hues.

There are some disadvantages in the use of lead oxide in glazes. None of these disadvantages in any way disqualifies it for use in pottery, however. For one thing, lead-glazed ware must be fired in an oxidizing atmosphere. In modern practice this is scarcely a disadvantage, since kilns are ordinarily fired with a clear, smoke-free atmosphere. Lead oxide does reduce easily, however, and if ware is in direct contact with flame or smoke during firing, it may be blistered and blackened. Another limitation of lead oxide is that above about 1200°C it becomes volatile. For this reason lead glazes are seldom used above about cone 6. Of course, at the higher temperatures other dependable fluxes such as feldspar are available; so the use of lead is unnecessary. The volatilization of lead oxide accounts for the tendency of the interior of kilns and kiln furniture to become glazed over after numerous firings of lead-glazed ware. Lead glazes have the reputation of being harsh and shiny in surface, and the devotee of stoneware glazes tends to underestimate the creative possibilities of the lead glaze. Actually, lead glazes can easily be controlled to any degree of matteness or dryness and do not need to be bright and garish in color and texture.

One serious drawback to the use of lead oxide in glazes is that as a raw material it is poisonous, and appropriate precautions must be taken in using it to avoid the possibility of lead poisoning. Lead poisoning is caused by the ingestion of lead compounds into the system, either by mouth, by breathing vapors or dusts, or by getting lead into open cuts in the skin. The symptoms of lead poisoning are various, and it is difficult to cure, since lead taken into the system tends to remain there. Painters using lead paint have frequently suffered from lead poisoning, and in England during the last century, pottery workers using lead glazes became so subject to lead poisoning that regulations were established prohibiting the use of raw lead compounds.

Lead poisoning is a serious matter, and the possibility of contracting it while working with glazes should not be discounted. Every possible precaution should be taken when raw lead glazes are being used. Glazes should be applied by dipping or painting and never by spraying. Dust must be kept under control, and care must be taken that even minute quantities of lead do not contaminate food or get onto the ends of cigarettes. Lead poisoning is the result of accumulations of lead in the system, and even the smallest amount taken in daily will, over a period of years perhaps, reach the critical level.

Lead which has been fritted with silica or other oxides is not poisonous, and, wherever possible, lead should be introduced into glazes in fritted form. This is particularly true in classroom work where it may be difficult to enforce the safety rules necessary in the use of raw lead glazes. Lead silicates or lead frits are considered nonpoisonous if they contain at least two molecules of silica to one of lead oxide. Before introducing a lead frit as a regularly used material, the potter should seek assurance from the manufacturer that it is non-toxic.

Another aspect of the problem of the poisonous nature of lead is that some lead glazes, after being fired on the ware, are soluble in weak acids. Therefore, appreciable quantities of lead may be dissolved into such foods as fruit juices, vinegar, tomatoes, and especially certain soft drinks. While the amount of lead ingested from the single use of a plate, bowl, or beaker may be extremely small, continued use of a lead-glazed pot may cause severe lead poisoning and even death. However, the danger arises only from improperly compounded and fired glazes, and can easily be avoided. The only lead glazes that are hazardous to health because of solubility are those that contain an excessive amount of lead relative to silica and the other glaze oxides, and those fired at very low temperatures. To be safe, lead glazes should have at least three molecules of silica to one of lead, and preferably this ratio should be higher, to be on the safe side. The glaze should also include several oxides from the RO and R_2O group and as much alumina as possible without inhibiting proper fusion. Lead glazes on ware intended for table use should be fired to at least cone 04 and preferably higher.

There is some evidence that glazes fired in the static atmosphere of the electric kiln are more soluble than those fired in gas or oil-burning kilns. Thickly applied glazes give more lead release than thin ones. Copper oxide in a lead glaze greatly increases its solubility in acid, and for this reason copper should not be used as a glaze colorant in lead glazes. Solubility and lead release may be increased by underfiring, and for this reason lead glazes should always be fired to their proper maturing temperature.

Unfortunately, if the composition of the glaze is not known, there is no way to tell if a glazed pot is potentially hazardous just by examining it; only a leach test in dilute acid can determine the possible solubility of lead in the glaze. A standard test for lead release from ceramic glazes has been developed by the United States Food and Drug Administration, Division of Compliance Programs, Bureau of Foods.

Understandably, buyers of pottery have become suspicious of all glazes, even of high-fired, lead-free ones. This is unfortunate, because the vast majority of pottery glazes, including lead glazes, are perfectly safe to use. One exception is the type of lead glaze often used in raku ware, commonly very high in lead and often containing boric acid which, when present with lead in a glaze, increases the solubility of the lead. Such raku glazes, fired to cone 08 or lower, are appreciably soluble in certain foods, and should never be used on such tableware as cups, pitchers, plates, or other containers. Since the raku maker can never know how his pieces will eventually be used, he should probably avoid using lead glazes for pieces that could be used as food containers. Please see the following four-point list.

1. Lead compounds such as white lead and red lead are poisonous and must be handled with great caution.

2. If lead is introduced into a glaze in the form of a lead silicate or frit, the risk of poisoning incurred while handling the glaze or applying it to the ware is minimized.

3. Eating and drinking from certain high-lead, low-fired glazed pottery may be hazardous.

4. Lead glazes compounded by using sufficient silica and alumina and by including several oxides besides lead among the RO and R_2O group may be perfectly safe to use.

Unfortunately, in many ceramic textbooks found in libraries around the world, or even on potters' bookshelves, there are often potentially problematic glaze recipes. Even with all the information that has been around for years, these books are often the unwitting source of recipes for amateur potters who sometimes mix the glazes in ignorance of the problems. Without knowledge of lead glaze recipes or use, my credo has always been - if in doubt, leave it out!

10. Calcium Oxide - CaO

Most glazes contain calcium oxide. Since it is a common and inexpensive material and contributes only desirable properties to glazes, it is one of the most valuable glaze ingredients.

Although calcium oxide has a very high melting point, 2570°C, its principal function in glazes is that of a flux. In high-fired glazes, calcium oxide may be the principal flux, but in lower-temperature glazes, other fluxes such as lead, zinc, or sodium must be used along with calcium to cause the glaze to melt. Calcium contributes to the hardness and durability of glazes. It causes no difficulty in firing, and few glaze faults can be traced to it.

Calcium oxide has little effect upon the colors obtained from coloring oxides. In high-fired reduction glazes the grey-green color known as celadon is favored by the presence of considerable calcium oxide in the glaze.

The presence of calcium in low-fired glazes high in lead oxide or sodium oxide renders them harder and more insoluble.

When too high a percentage of calcium oxide is used in a glaze, it will produce a matte, dull, or rough surface. This is due to the refractory character of the material when present in more than the amount needed, and to devitrification caused by the limited solubility of calcium silicate in the melt. Calcium oxide is useful in producing glaze surfaces that are slightly dull. By increasing the amount of calcium in some glazes, a dulled surface can be achieved without affecting the transparency of the glaze very much.

11. Barium Oxide - BaO

Barium is a potentially toxic glaze ingredient. The function of barium oxide and calcium oxide in glazes is somewhat similar. Barium is refractory, and it must be used in smaller amounts than calcium, especially in low-fired glazes. In high-fired glazes barium oxide is a moderately active flux.

Barium is commonly used to produce matte glazes. In most types of glazes barium produces a soft satiny matte surface which is very attractive. When the amount of barium used is too great, very

dry surfaces will result. When considerable boron is present in a glaze, additions of barium oxide will not produce matteness.

The presence of barium oxide in high-fired glazes favors the development of celadon and iron-blue colors in reduction firing. Brilliant copper-blue glazes may be obtained when the barium content is high. With nickel, pinks, plums, reds, and purples are possible in oxidation above cone 4. With small amounts of chromium, acid yellows, yellow-greens, and chartreuse are possible.

12. Magnesium Oxide - MgO

Magnesium oxide is used principally as a high-temperature flux. It is too refractory to be of much use in low-fired glazes, except to lend opacity and matteness. In high-fired glazes magnesium oxide may give a smooth, buttery surface to the glaze. This is especially the case in reduction firing. High-fired reduction glazes containing magnesium oxide are usually opaque, smooth and dense, and pleasant to the touch. An excess of magnesium oxide will cause dryness in a glaze and may also contribute to such difficulties as crawling and pinholing.

When cobalt is added to glazes containing magnesium oxide, the resultant color is purple rather than the usual blue. At very high temperatures, and where considerable magnesium oxide is present, this purple may be mottled with streaks of pink or red. With small amounts of nickel, lime to olive greens are possible.

13. Zinc Oxide - ZnO

Zinc oxide is a very useful flux in the middle and higher range of temperature. Used in small amounts, it may be a very active flux, and when added in larger quantities, it may produce matteness and dryness. It is little used in glazes fired at temperatures below cone 01, because at the lower temperatures it does not have much fluxing power.

Although zinc oxide is not nearly so strong a flux as lead oxide, it has been employed as a substitute for lead. The so-called Bristol glaze was developed in England to avoid the use of lead. This type employs zinc as the principal flux, with calcium, magnesium, and barium used as auxiliary fluxes.

As an additional flux in glazes which contain lead, feldspar, or boric acid, zinc is a very valuable material. It is an aid to smooth, even, trouble-free glazing. However, glazes that rely mostly on zinc for flux are apt to crawl and may be subject to pitting and pinholing; also, the colors may be mottled and broken. A little zinc is a good thing but a lot of it is likely to cause trouble.

The presence of zinc oxide has a pronounced effect on the colors obtained from several coloring oxides. When iron and zinc are both used, the resulting colors are apt to be dull and rather dingy. On the other hand, copper and zinc together produce brilliant turquoise greens. When zinc and chrome are used together, brown results rather than green. When zinc and tin are both used, the glaze may become slightly pink or brownish. Zinc and titania together are useful in promoting crystalline development in glazes. Because of these rather special color reactions, the high-zinc glaze is not commonly used.

14. Strontium Oxide - SrO

The function of strontium in a glaze is very similar to that of calcium and barium. It produces similar colors to those produced using barium and is often used as a barium replacement. It is a little more fusible, however, and should be used at 75% of the volume required for barium to effect a similar melt. It may be substituted for calcium oxide where a more active melt is desired in a glaze at a given temperature. Since strontium is more expensive than calcium and has no pronounced advantages over calcium, it is little used.

15. Antimony Oxide - Sb₂O₃

Antimony is sometimes used as an opacifier, although it is in no way superior to tin or zircon for this purpose. It is used principally to produce the stain Naples yellow, which results from the combination of lead oxide and antimony oxide.

16. Lithium Oxide - Li₂O

Lithium oxide is useful as a highly active flux, and its action in glazes is somewhat similar to that of sodium. As an alkaline material its color response is similar to, but more pungent than that of sodium and potassium, but it has a low expansion and therefore is less likely to cause crazing. Lithium oxide is rather expensive, which has kept it from being used very much. Even in small amounts it has the ability to give a great deal more punch and interest to glaze surfaces and colors.

17. Boric Oxide - B₂O₃

Boric oxide is a low-melting-point substance with strong fluxing power comparable to lead oxide or sodium oxide. It is a very useful glaze ingredient which has come into common use in modern times. The only natural source of boric oxide that is not soluble is calcium borate. Therefore, except where this material is used, boric oxide is introduced into the glaze in fritted form. Since colemanite and its substitute, Gerstley borate, are no longer being commercially mined, various frits or similar materials are being produced to fill the void. Cadycal 100, Laguna borate, Pemco Frit 54, and Ferro Frit 3134 have similar effects in the glaze melt. Boric oxide can be used as the main flux in a glaze or as an auxiliary flux, and it can be used from the lowest to the highest temperatures. It forms borates that reduce the expansion of the glaze, and so is useful in the correction of crazing.

Boric oxide intensifies the effect of coloring oxides, and in this respect it is similar to sodium and potassium. When even a slight amount of iron is present, it may produce milky or opalescent blues. It may also cause broken or mottled color effects with the various coloring oxides.

Glazes for commercial tableware are commonly made with both lead oxide and boric oxide used for flux, and such glazes - the so-called "lead boro-silicate" glazes - are notable for their smoothness, freedom from pits or other blemishes, long firing range, and good wearing properties.

12 GLAZE MATERIALS

1. Preparation of Raw Materials for Use in Glazes

The important oxides that enter into the composition of glazes have been briefly described. Next, the raw materials used to obtain these various oxides will be discussed. The distinction between the oxides that make up the fired glazes and the raw materials that are combined to make up the glaze batch must be kept in mind. Some raw materials yield only one oxide in the finished glaze. Calcium, which yields only CaO in the finished glaze, is an example. Other raw materials may yield several oxides in the finished glaze. Cornwall stone, for example, yields six different oxides - sodium, potassium, calcium, magnesium, aluminum, and silica, plus trace amounts of titanium, iron, and fluorine - a very valuable material for the glaze maker working at higher temperatures. If the ceramist is to use his raw materials intelligently, he must know what oxides are in them and what they contribute to the final result.

While the beginner may feel that there are a bewildering number of materials from which glazes can be made, the number of possible materials is actually severely limited. About twenty-one materials include all those commonly used. Of these twenty-one, about nine are used relatively little. A good working knowledge of about a dozen materials is needed to approach the subject of glaze making intelligently. Here we are not considering the materials that color glazes and influence their texture, but only the materials used to make up the body or structure of the glaze itself.

Most of the commonly used glaze materials are derived from common rocks and minerals. It is a mistake to think that glazes are made up from obscure, expensive, or rare materials. Actually, in most localities, glazes can be made up from minerals common and easily obtained in nature. For example, some of the most beautiful of all high-fired glazes are composed of feldspar, silica, limestone, and clay. All these minerals are common and can be located and identified easily. In practice, however, it is seldom worthwhile for the potter to prepare his own glaze materials, because the materials he would be digging and laboriously grinding would be in no way different or superior to the prepared materials he could get from a supplier.

Glaze materials are supplied and used in the form of finely ground powders. Some materials, such as flint (silica), feldspar, dolomite, whiting (calcium), talc, and clay, are natural materials which are mined and then ground to the desired degree of fineness. Other materials are the product of chemical processes, such as precipitation. Whether the material is derived from natural minerals or is the result of chemical preparation, the common standard for particle size is a grind that will pass through a 200-mesh screen. Fine grinding tends to make all the materials used for glaze making look very much alike, and the potter must take care not to get materials mixed up or to lose the labels from sacks or bins.

With the exception of lead compounds and barium, all basic glaze materials are nontoxic. Some of the soluble materials are caustic, however, and care must be taken to avoid prolonged contact with the skin. Care must also be taken to avoid breathing silica dust. Prolonged breathing of dusts containing silica may cause silicosis, a disease of the lungs; to avoid this hazard, all glaze spraying should be done in well-ventilated spray booths, and the dust around the working areas should be kept to a minimum. Modern methods of dust control have practically eliminated the problem of silicosis from the pottery industry.

Glaze materials do not deteriorate either in the

raw state or when mixed with water into glaze slips, and they may be kept indefinitely. Most glaze materials are relatively inexpensive, and the higher cost of prepared glazes, which may be purchased from some suppliers, represents more the cost of preparing, packaging, and selling the glaze than the cost of the raw materials. Some coloring oxides and stains for glazes are expensive, but these are used in relatively small quantities.

The materials used in glazes should be insoluble in water. This practical consideration rules out many common materials that otherwise might be useful in glazes. For example, sodium silicate could be used for glazes as a source of sodium were it not for its solubility in water. (The problem of solubility in glazes is discussed in the section on frits.)

2. Silica, Flint, Quartz - SiO_2

Flint is used in glazes as the main source of silica. In mineralogy flint is a variety of quartz - usually grey, black, or brown - which has an extremely small crystalline structure (crypto-crystalline). Potter's flint may be made by grinding any form of crystalline quartz into a fine powder. Silica is insoluble and chemically inert. It is abundant and cheap.

3. Clay - $Al_2O_3 \cdot 2SiO_2 \cdot 2H_2O$

Clay is used in glazes as a source of aluminum oxide, and since all glazes require silica, its silica content also contributes to the glaze. Clay also contributes some desirable physical properties to the raw glaze. Kaolin or china clay is ordinarily used, since it is relatively free from iron and thus does not give any color to the glaze. Ball clay, stoneware clay, or earthenware clay may be used in glazes, but the higher iron content of these clays will give a tan or brown tint to the glaze and may also lower its fusion point somewhat.

Besides furnishing alumina and silica to the glaze, clay acts as a floatative in the raw glaze batch, helping to keep the other ingredients from settling to the bottom of the slip. Clay also helps to give the raw glaze coat on the ware a toughness which makes it less apt to be smeared or damaged during placing in the kiln.

Ordinarily all the alumina called for in a glaze is supplied by clay and by feldspar. However, it is possible to introduce alumina in the form of aluminum hydrate or aluminum oxide. But since these materials are much more expensive than clay and do not lend the same desirable physical properties, there is no advantage in using them except for specific textural effects.

In calculating glazes the theoretical composition of kaolin is used ($Al_2O_3 \cdot 2SiO_2$), although many clays are known from chemical analysis to be considerably different from this in formula. Ball clay, for example, always has more silica in it than the amount in the theoretical formula for kaolin. But such variations have a negligible effect on the glaze, since the amount of clay in a glaze is small in any case. When glaze recipes include more than about 12% of clay, calcined clay may be used to lessen shrinkage.

Slip glazes, which are composed entirely or largely of clay, are discussed in a later section.

4. Feldspar

Feldspar is one of the most important glaze materials. It is used in almost all glazes, and in high-fired glazes it is often the principal material and provides the principal flux. Feldspar, as has been noted, is one of the constituents of granite, and it is one of the most common and widespread of minerals.

Feldspar is made up of (a) an alkaline portion consisting of sodium, potassium, or calcium, singly or in combination; (b) alumina; and (c) silica. Formulas for pure feldspars are as follows:

Orthoclase	$K_2O \cdot Al_2O_3 \cdot 6SiO_2$
Albite	$Na_2O \cdot Al_2O_3 \cdot 6SiO_2$
Anorthite	$CaO \cdot Al_2O_3 \cdot 2SiO_2$
Spodumene	$Li_2O \cdot Al_2O_3 \cdot 4SiO_2$

The formulas represent the theoretical composition of these minerals. Only hand-picked specimens in nature would have a composition corresponding to the formula.

A commercial feldspar would be more apt to have a formula something like this:

K_2O	.74	Al_2O_3	1.026	SiO_2	6.34
Na_2O	.26				

Here the first column indicates that sodium as well as potassium is present. The alumina and the silica are both present in higher amounts than in the theoretical composition. Commercially available feldspars have trade names such as "Custer Feldspar" or "Kona F4 Spar." These trade names have no mineralogical significance, but the suppliers of feldspars maintain a reasonably uniform composition for any feldspar marketed under a given name. Producers may blend the rock from different parts of the same quarry, or from different quarries, to keep the material uniform in composition. The producers of feldspar furnish a chemical analysis of the material being sold, from which the formula can be calculated.

Different feldspars vary rather widely in composition. Those feldspars having a high amount of potassium are favored for additions to clay bodies. Feldspars high in soda are favored for glaze making because of their relatively lower fusion point. When a glaze recipe calls for just "feldspar" without specifying any particular brand or kind, various kinds may have to be tried to find out which gives the desired result. More exact methods of glaze calculation call for specific kinds of feldspar.

Feldspar is useful in glazes because of its relatively low melting point and its incorporation of the alkalies potassium and sodium in an insoluble mineral. It is, in effect, a kind of natural frit. Most feldspars will melt by themselves, with no other material added, at about 1250°C, and will sinter into a hard mass at considerably less than that temperature. Calcium, dolomite, or talc added to a feldspar in amounts of 5% or 10% will bring down its fusion point 50° or more. The fusible nature of feldspar is due to its content of sodium, potassium, or lithium.

When temperatures of cone 10 or more are available, extremely simple glazes can be made largely of feldspar, with perhaps small additions of whiting, dolomite, or talc. Glazes very high in feldspar have a tendency to craze because of the quantity of sodium or potassium present. They often have a milky, semi-opaque quality which is very beautiful. Some of the classic old Chinese wares, notably Lung Ch'uan ware of the Song Dynasty, was probably glazed with highly feldspathic compositions. One of the advantages of high firing is that a few simple materials can be made to yield such beautiful glazes.

Some feldspathic materials are so different from the ordinary feldspar that they are called by other names. Nepheline syenite, for example, is a feldspathic rock that has an unusually high amount of sodium and potassium in relation to the amount of silica present. It has the formula:

$$
\begin{array}{llll}
K_2O & .254 & Al_2O_3 & SiO_2 \\
Na_2O & .746 & 1.108 & 4.652
\end{array}
$$

The lower melting point of this material makes it very useful in compounding glazes, especially those in the middle range of temperature. Nepheline syenite is also very useful as a body flux in clays where a lower maturing temperature is desired.

Cornwall stone is another feldspathic material in common use for both glazes and bodies. It is produced in Cornwall, England. A typical analysis is:

$$
\left.\begin{array}{ll}
CaO & .304 \\
Na_2O & .340 \\
K_2O & .356
\end{array}\right\} Al_2O_3 \quad \left\{\begin{array}{l} SiO_2 \\ 8.10 \end{array}\right.
$$
$$
1.075
$$

In Cornwall stone, the lime, soda, and potassium are about equal, and the silica is higher in proportion to the alkalies than in most feldspars. Cornwall stone is also likely to have a number of valuable trace elements.

5. Calcium Carbonate, Whiting - $CaCO_3$

Calcium carbonate or whiting, is the most common source of calcium oxide in glazes. It is made by grinding limestone, chalk, marble, or other calcite minerals. Whiting of exceptional purity is made by precipitation.

6. Magnesium Carbonate - $MgCO_3$

Magnesium carbonate is used as a source of magnesium oxide in glazes. It is either made from magnesite, or it may be a precipitated material made from mixtures of magnesium sulfate and soda ash. The precipitated magnesium carbonate is very light and fluffy in texture. It tends to mix more easily into the raw glaze than the ground magnesite.

7. Dolomite - $CaCO_3 \cdot MgCO_3$

Dolomite is a natural mineral containing calcium and magnesium carbonates in equivalent parts. It may be used in glazes whenever both magnesia and calcia are called for.

8. Barium Carbonate - $BaCO_3$

Barium carbonate is the usual source of barium oxide in glazes. The material is prepared from the mineral barytes (barium sulfate) by precipitation with soda ash, following reduction to sulfide. It is poisonous and should be handled with great care.

9. Talc - $3MgO \cdot 4SiO_2 \cdot H_2O$

Talc may be used in glazes wherever both magnesia and silica are desired. It is prepared by grinding the natural mineral steatite. Talc frequently contains some calcium as an impurity, which contributes to its action as a flux in glazes. Talc is used as a flux for clay bodies, especially low-fired bodies.

10. Strontium Carbonate - $SrCO_3$

Strontium carbonate is prepared from the mineral celesite ($SrSO_4$). Its action in a glaze is similar to other alkaline earth materials, calcium and barium. It affects color in much the same way as does barium, but doesn't carry the same health hazards. In a glaze 75% of strontium will give the same melting power as 100% of barium. Since it is considerably more expensive than calcium or barium and its action in glazes is very similar, it is seldom used.

11. Calcium Borate, Colemanite, Gerstley Borate - $2CaO \cdot 3B_2O_3 \cdot 5H_2O$

Note: At the time of writing this edition of this book, colemanite, or Gerstley borate, has ceased to be mined. Since the material has been in constant use for years and many glazes, particularly lower-temperature and raku glazes, have been dependent on it, I have decided to leave its description in this list. There will be other similar materials come on the market, such as Cadycal 100, Laguna borate, or numerous formulated frits which produce similar results in glazes. I have no doubt that one particular favorite variant will come to dominate those that are available, but, as yet, that hasn't emerged.

Calcium borate is a natural mineral containing both calcium and boron in a relatively insoluble form. It is valuable as a glaze material since it is the only source of boric oxide in an insoluble form except for frit. Its composition tends to be somewhat variable, which has limited its use in large-scale pottery manufacture. It is, however, a favorite material of the studio potter. Calcium borate, when it is used as the principal flux in glazes, often gives a broken, mottled texture which can be very attractive. This is particularly true if rutile also is used. Also, glazes with considerable boric oxide in them tend to be bright and colorful. Calcium borate may also lend a milky, blue opalescent quality to a glaze. When combinations of lead and calcium borate are used, the resulting glaze may be very reliable, smooth, and of long-firing range. Calcium borate may be used alone as the flux for very low-fired glazes. The slight solubility of calcium borate may give it a tendency to flocculate the glaze slip. It may be noticed that a glaze that has been made up to a normal consistency with water will, after standing for a day or two, become thick and pudding-like, and will require more water to make it right for application. This excess of water may result in trouble by causing cracks in the dried raw glaze, and perhaps subsequent crawling.

12. Litharge - PbO

Litharge, or lead monoxide, is made by spraying molten lead into a furnace with a current of air. Because of its relatively low oxygen content, litharge is probably more subject to reduction in firing. Besides this disadvantage, it is relatively coarse in particle size compared to the other materials yielding lead oxide.

13. White Lead - $2PbCO_3 \cdot Pb(OH)_2$

White lead, or basic lead carbonate, is prepared by treating the metal lead with acid and carbon dioxide gas. The result is a finely divided white powder, free from impurities and insoluble in water.

White lead is the preferred form of raw lead for use in glazes. Its advantages are its purity of composition and its fine particle size. The fine particles keep the material from settling rapidly in the glaze slip. White lead fuses very readily, perhaps partly because of the mixing that results from the escape of carbon dioxide gas from the material during heating.

14. Red Lead - Pb_3O_4

Red lead is prepared by roasting litharge (PbO). It is cheaper than white lead, but it is not commonly used in glazes because of its coarse particle size, its tendency to settle out in glaze slips, and its objectionable red color, which stains the hands, clothing, and tools. It does not fuse quite so readily in the kiln as white lead. Red lead is commonly used in preparing frits, where none of these disadvantages apply and where its higher lead content is an advantage.

Both white lead and red lead are poisonous and must be handled with due precautions.

Lead silicates, made by a fusion process, are now commercially available. These are nonpoisonous. They are reliable in composition and are easily incorporated in glazes. However, they must still be used with great care, as adding some colorants, notably copper, to these frits may reactivate the toxic problems of the original material.

15. Zinc Oxide - ZnO

Zinc oxide, the only available source of zinc for glazes, is made from the ore sphalerite (ZnS). The raw zinc oxide may cause cracking and crawling of the glaze coating. In these cases zinc oxide should be used in the calcined form.

16. Antimony Oxide - Sb_2O_3

Antimony oxide is the only common source of antimony in glazes. It is little used, except to produce Naples yellow stains from combinations of lead and antimony.

17. Soda Ash or Sodium Carbonate - Na_2CO_3

Soda ash is soluble and is therefore little used in glazes with the possible exception of high-temperature Shino-type glazes. It is a major source of sodium in glass and in frits. It is used as a defloculant for clay slips.

18. Bone Ash, Calcium Phosphate - $4Ca_3(PO_4) \cdot 2CaCO_3$

Bone ash is sometimes used in glazes, although its most important use is in providing the flux in china bodies. The material is made by calcining bones or by precipitation. Bone china has been made in England since the early part of the last century, and it is known for its extreme thinness and translucency. In glazes bone ash functions as an opacifier and as a source of calcium. The phosphorus in the glaze causes an opalescence which arises from the presence of countless small entrapped globules in the glaze. In a high-fired glaze, a small amount of bone ash may induce opacity and opalescence. Some famous old Chinese glazes, notably the glazes on Chün or Jün wares of the Song Dynasty, are known to contain phosphorus, and their blue opalescence may be due to the presence of this material, which was possibly introduced into the glaze in the form of an ash. Bone ash also has a particularly interesting effect on some colorants, notably iron, copper, and cobalt.

19. Cryolite - Na_3AlF_6

Cryolite, or sodium aluminum fluoride, is an interesting material because it makes sodium available in a natural and unfritted form. It may be used wherever sodium and alumina are called for in a glaze. It adds the characteristic color response of sodium or of highly alkaline fluxes. The fluorine content, however, may cause difficulties in the form of excessive boiling of the glaze during melting, with the possibilities of pitting or pinholes.

20. Lepidolite - $(HO_2F)_2 \, KLiAl_2 \, Si_3O_{10}$

Lepidolite is a lithium mica and is sometimes used as a source of lithium in glazes. It has a lower fusion point than most feldspars, and the lithia will serve to make most glazes more shiny than when a potash or soda spar is used. Lepidolite, however, seems to cause boiling and pitting in some glazes.

21. Spodumene - $Li_2O \cdot Al_2O_3 \cdot 4SiO_2$

Spodumene, a lithium feldspar, is used in glazes as a source of lithium. Substitutions of spodumene for feldspar in glazes may tend to correct crazing. Amblygonite, a low-solubility spodumene material, is a very useful material in mid to high-temperature glazes.

22. Lithium Carbonate - Li_2CO_3

Lithium carbonate is used as a source of lithium in glazes. It offers the possibility of making glazes which have a brilliant color response, without the necessity of resorting to soluble materials or to frits.

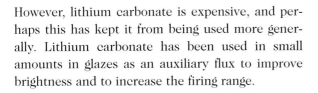

However, lithium carbonate is expensive, and perhaps this has kept it from being used more generally. Lithium carbonate has been used in small amounts in glazes as an auxiliary flux to improve brightness and to increase the firing range.

23. Fluorspar - CaF_2

Fluorspar has been used in glazes as a source of calcium. While it is commonly used in the enamel and glass industry as a flux and decolorizer, its usefulness in glazes has not been definitely established. It does, however, have some interesting attributes when used in conjunction with colorants, affecting cobalt, copper, and iron in subtle, yet different, ways to the norm.

24. Pearl Ash, Potassium Carbonate - K_2CO_3

Pearl ash is soluble, and for this reason it is seldom used in glazes. It is used, however, as a source of potassium in frits.

25. Niter, Potassium Nitrate - KNO_3

Niter is highly soluble and is seldom used raw in glazes. It is used in frits as a source of potassium.

26. Borax - $Na_2O \cdot 2B_2O_3 \cdot 10H_2O$

Borax may be used in glazes as a source of both sodium and boric oxide. But it is soluble, and for this reason is of limited use except when it is incorporated into a frit. Small amounts of borax, however, are sometimes very useful in lowering the fusion point of a glaze slightly and making it heal over and melt more smoothly. Small amounts of borax in a glaze or slip help to form a tougher coating on the ware. A thin crust of borax crystals develops on the surface of the raw glaze or slip.

The materials described above include all the commonly used glaze materials. Of those listed, there are several that are very seldom used, and others that are used largely in the compounding of frits. All these materials are best thought of as glass makers and should not be confused either with the various oxides of which they are made up or with the materials, to be discussed later, which are used to color and to influence the texture of glazes.

The great variety of glazes possible and the variety in the temperatures at which they melt is achieved by blending these materials in various proportions. In the next chapters, methods of arriving at workable combinations of materials are described.

LOW-FIRE PIECES

Cone 018 to Cone 1 Approximately

Dick Lehman, U.S.A., "Nub Handled Bottle," thrown and burnished grolleg porcelain clay, sagger-fired with sumac and leatherleaf, 11" high.

Jimmy Clark, U.S.A., "Pastoral," 1999, pinched, decorated with terra sigallata, pit-fired with resist slips, stripped and sanded, 15-1/2" x 9-1/2".

Piero Fenci, U.S.A., Japanese Pillow with Goose Head, 1998, raku-fired terracotta, 8″ x 15″ x 14″.

Richard Zane Smith, Untitled Corrugated Vessel, clay, 1988, 19-1/2″ x 18-3/4″ x 18-3/4″. Collection American Craft Museum, New York. Gift of the artist and Gallery 10, Inc. Photo by Eva Heyd.

Steven Forbes de Soule, U.S.A., Triangulated Vessel #4, thrown and altered bowl with layered copper and silver glazes and underglazes, raku-fired, 11″ x 16″.

Harvey Sadow, U.S.A., Gulfstream Series, 1984, ceramics, multiple raku-fired, 12″ x 11″.

Eiko H. Amano, U.S.A., Kimono Tile, raku-fired copper raku glaze with low-fire overglazes, wax resist line work, 14" x 11-1/2".

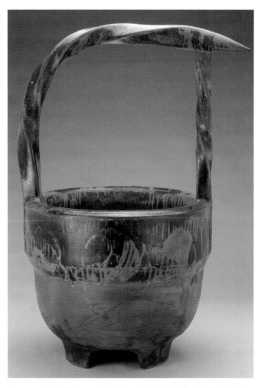

James Watkins, U.S.A., Bird Basket (Double Walled Caldron), 1995, raku-fired with copper wash glaze over clear glaze, 37" x 20".

Steven Forbes de Soule, U.S.A., Triangulated Vessel #3, thrown and altered bowl with layered copper and silver glazes and underglazes, raku-fired, 14" x 13".

Piero Fenci, U.S.A., Origami Handbag, 1998, raku, 18" x 16" x 10". Photo by Harrison Evans.

Harvey Sadow, U.S.A., Smokey Cape, 1991, ceramic vessel, multiple raku-fired with eutectic slips, 10″ x 12″.

Richard Hirsch, U.S.A., Alter Bowl with Weapon Artifact #2, 1995, low-fired glazes on bowl, terra sigillata, raku-fired base, acrylic lacquers, 23″ x 16″ x 12″.

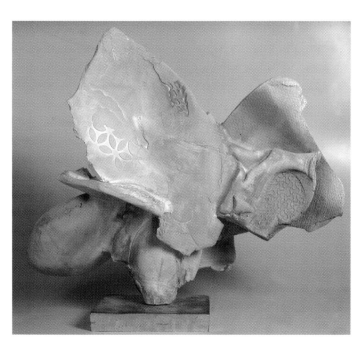

Paul Soldner, U.S.A., Sculpture, 1998, unglazed with slips and low-fired salt fuming.

Minako Yamane-Lee, U.S.A., Mini Raku Teapot, 3-1/2″ wide.

Steve Heinemann, Canada, Apparition, 1999, cast earthenware, multiple firings, 25″ x 19″ x 11″. Photo by Andrew Layerle.

Walter Dexter, Canada, Raku Vase.

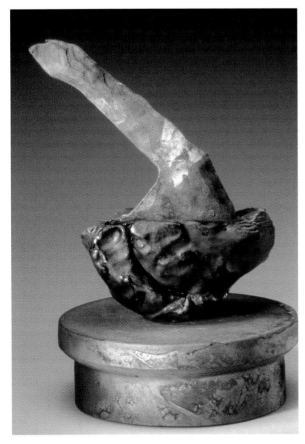

Richard Hirsch, U.S.A., Pedestal Bowl with Weapon Artifact #14, 1997, low-fired glazes, lacquers, 44″ x 32″ x 13″.

James D. Watral, U.S.A., Neo Apulian Vessel No. 7, 1991, earthenware, glaze copper leaf, 23″ x 24″ diameter. Photo by Harrison Evans.

William Brouillard, U.S.A., Mesabi, 1996, hand-built, thrown and assembled earthenware, fired to cone 03 in oxidation, 20" x 26" x 34".

Susanne Stephenson, U.S.A., Spiral Dance II, terracotta, 18-1/2" x 16" x 14". Photo by John H. Stephenson.

Rosette Gault, U.S.A., Wall Work, 1980, fired earthenware, sandy glaze, 26cm x 28cm x 1cm. Photo by Roger Shreiber.

Juan Granados, U.S.A., First Harvest, 12 green oval-shaped forms on floor, earthenware, glaze, stains and oxides, 18" x 108" x 186". Photo by Jon Q. Thompson.

Greg Payce, Canada, Wake (detail), 1997, work comprised of 15 vases lined up on a shelf with lips touching, wheel thrown, terra sigillata over textured slip, whole work 240cm long x 18cm deep x 27cm high. Photo by Marc Hutchinson.

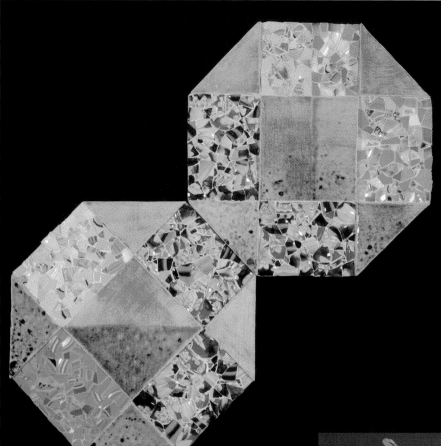

Susan Tunick, U.S.A., English China Duo, wall relief, clay medallions inset with ceramic shards, each 14-1/2" x 1-1/2". Photo by Peter Mauss, Esto Photographics.

Linda Arbuckle, U.S.A., Biscuit Jar: Seasonal Event, 1999, majolica on terracotta, 8-1/2" x 9". Photo by the University of Florida Office of Instructional Resources.

Elaine Parks, U.S.A., Garden House Series, 1997, two colors low-fire clay, slab built, cut and assembled, 10" x 5" x 5". Photo by Thomas Dix.

Pauline Pelletier, Canada, Vase, earthenware, fractured, glazed, copper and iron oxides with gold lusters, cone 04, reconstructed, 24cm x 33cm. Photo by Pierre Fortin.

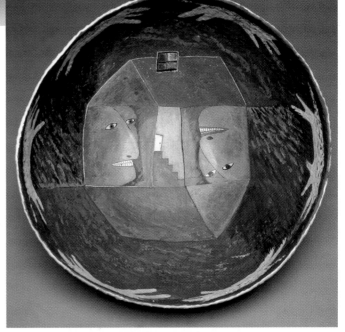

Heather Driver Kerslake, Canada, untitled, 1994, bowl (interior), hand-built earthenware, 16cm x 43cm. Photo by Ellen Tobin.

James D. Watral, U.S.A., Neo-Apulian Vessel, 1997, earthenware, glaze, copper leaf, 6" x 17" diameter. Photo by Harrison Evans.

Jean Cappadonna-Nichols, U.S.A., In Front of Every Woman…, hand-built white earthenware, glazes and stains, 39-1/2″ x 25-1/2″ x 13-1/2″. Photo by Bill Martin.

Dan and Nisha, Canada, Triple Elephant, white earthenware with underglazes. Photo by Vivian Gast.

Ann Tubbs, U.S.A., Two Watering Cans, stoneware, majolica, 11″ and 12″. Photo by Stephen Johnston.

Richard and Carol Selfridge, Canada, Imari Geisha Teapot for Van Gogh Tea Ceremony, terracotta, majolica, 48cm high.

Gail Kendall, U.S.A., Tureen, earthenware.

Posey Bacapoulos, U.S.A., Oval, majolica on terracotta, 4-1/2" x 9" x 4". Photo by D. James Dee.

Fausto Salvi, Italy, untitled, 1999, majolica form, 20cm x 10cm x 7cm.

Walter Ostrom, U.S.A., Dutch Treat, majolica plate, 11" diameter.

Keith Wallace Smith, U.S.A., Incarceration, 1999, terracotta, matte glaze, iron, 27" x 27" x 34". Photo by Allen Cheuvront.

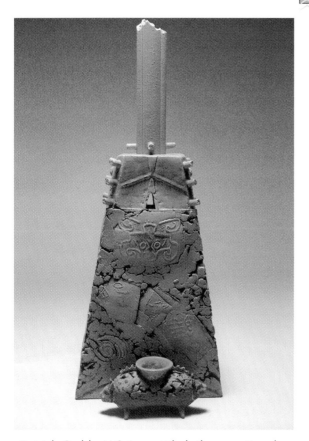

Patrick Crabb, U.S.A., untitled, three sectional pieces, press molded and wheel thrown, electric kiln glazes, 33″ x 13″ x 4″. Photo by the artist.

Don Hee Suh, Korea, Left Alone, earthenware sculpture, fired at cone 04, 10″ x 23″.

Jan Edwards, U.S.A., Two Fish Plate, red earthenware, underglazes, clear glaze, and paper resist, 12″ x 12″. Photo by Bill Bachhuber.

Don C. McCance, U.S.A., Sterility Head, soup tureen, 13″ x 17″.

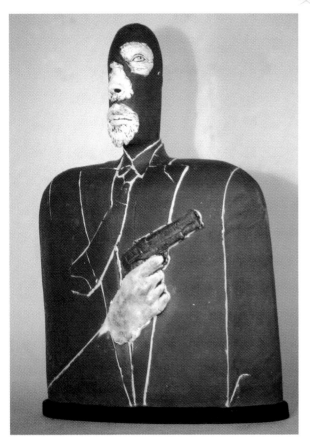

Verne Funk, U.S.A., Assassin, slab built, press mold additions, dark clay, white clay, slip, glaze, bisque 04, glaze 06, 28" x 21" x 8". Photo by the artist.

Nan Smith, U.S.A., Guardian (detail of ceramic figure), 1997, airbrushed underglaze and glazed earthenware, 26" x 18" x 28". Photo by Allen Cheuvront and Associates.

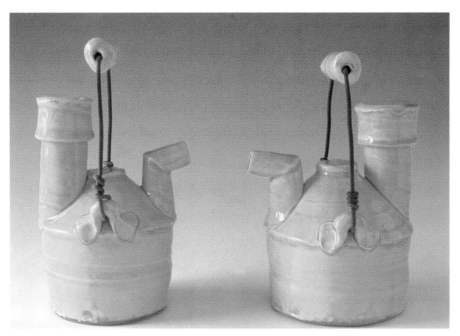

Linda Christianson, U.S.A., Two Cooking Oil Cans, 2000, electric fired earthenware, red clay, white slip, clear glaze and umber wire.

Dot Kimura, U.S.A., untitled, shaped hardware cloth into form, dip and spray paper clay on the form, bisqued then gray sandy crater glaze, rutile and iron oxide wash, fired at cone 06, 18" high. Photo by Dave Harrison.

Don Reitz, U.S.A., untitled, 1985, black clay, vitreous engobes , clear glaze, oxidation fired, 16" x 8".

Marti Mocahbee, U.S.A., untitled, wheel thrown red clay, low-fire with hand-painted underglazes, clear glossy food-safe glaze.

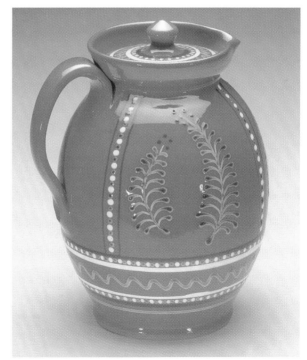

Hal and Eleanor Pugh, U.S.A., Lidded Pitcher, redware clay, trailed slip decoration, 10" x 6-1/2". Photo by Juan Villa, Inc.

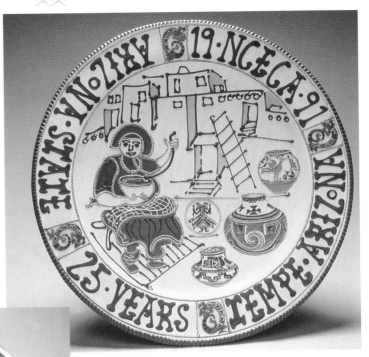

Irma Starr, U.S.A., NCECA Dish, at museum
at the University of Arizona.

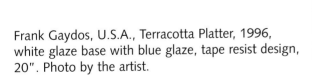

Diego Romero, (Cochiti Pueblo) Weight Lifter,
bowl, native clay, black and silver paint, kiln fired,
10" diameter.

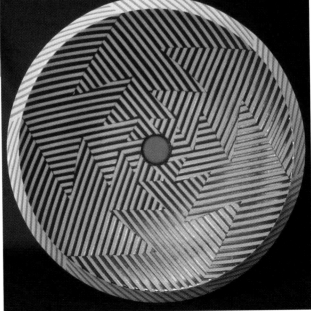

Frank Gaydos, U.S.A., Terracotta Platter, 1996,
white glaze base with blue glaze, tape resist design,
20". Photo by the artist.

Angela Gallia, U.S.A., The Blue Chair, coil built earthenware, colored with Cerdec stains and commercial underglazes. 15″ x 22″″ x 14″.

Bruce Breckenridge, U.S.A., Boyle Heights #2, 1993/94, ceramic tile, majolica, 88″ x 198″. Collection of the Apache Corp., Houston, Texas.

Kathleen Nez, U.S.A., (Navajo) Gallup Black on White, lidded casserole, stoneware, kiln fired, 6-1/2" x 10-1/2".

Neil Forrest, Canada, Trivet: Stage & Floor, 1995, earthenware, Egyptian paste, mortar and grout, 26" x 24" x 3". Photo by Jennifer Corsen, Halifax, NS.

Walter Ostrom, U.S.A., Fish Vase, majolica, thrown and altered, 11" high.

John H. Stephenson, U.S.A., Zone Two, terracotta wall piece, 22" x 28-1/4" x 3-1/2".
Photo by the artist.

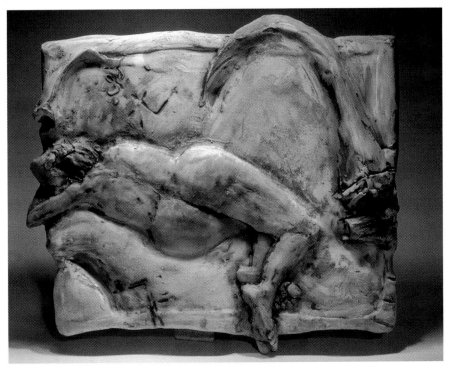

Denys A. James, Canada, Arch Series, figurative wall relief, terracotta, oxidation,
cone 05, with slips and stains, 17" x 23" x 4". Photo by Denys James.

Les Lawrence, U.S.A., Wedgwood Plate, 1999, faux Lenox laser decals, china paint, 12" diameter. Photo by John Dixon.

Verne Funk, U.S.A., Split, white clay, wheel thrown, underglaze pencil glaze, bisque 04, glaze 06. 15" x 15" x 2". Photo by the artist.

Akio Takamori, Teapot. Courtesy of Schein-Joseph International Museum of Ceramic Art. 1991.33. Photo by Brian Oglesbee.

Kurt Weiser, U.S.A., Flight, teapot, cast mold from original thrown and altered piece, cone 10, porcelain with clear glaze, overglaze enamel fired at cone 018, 9-1/2" x 11" x 4-1/2".

Kinichi Shigeno, Canada, Heeled Boots, overglaze enamels on oxidized porcelain.

Kurt Weiser, U.S.A., Covered Jar, cast piece, mold made from original thrown and altered piece, cone 10 porcelain with clear glaze, overglaze enamel fired at cone 018, 19" x 12" x 9-1/2".

13 GLAZE CALCULATIONS, THEORY, AND OBJECTIVES

The process of glaze calculation requires accurate processing of information in order to be of any use to the potter. Unfortunately, most people get frustrated by the combination of mathematics and chemistry, turning instead to using glaze recipes from books and magazines to have glazes for their work. Until fairly recently, to compare, calculate, alter, problem-solve, or develop glazes, the longhand approach was the only way. With the development of calculators some of the burden was resolved but it was not until the development of personal computers that it became possible to quickly do all the procedures mentioned above. Some people realized the potential of the calculation process through computers and developed software programs to bypass the slower methods of calculation. Following are the descriptions of such programs by Richard Burkett, developer of *HyperGlaze* and Tony Hansen, developer of *Insight*. *HyperGlaze* and *Insight* are currently the most used programs in North America.

Visuals of the computer screen interface are included to show what it looks like, although it is a little like looking at still photographs of a movie. The speed and flexibility of the programs can only be appreciated through use.

1. *HyperGlaze*

by Richard Burkett

"Manipulating the characteristics of glazes on a chemical molecular basis has come a long way from hand glaze calculation. Computer software now makes calculating the molecular formula of a glaze very fast and effortless. This in turn allows a look at glazes from a different and useful viewpoint: the interactions of the various ceramic oxides. Ceramic engineers have been doing this for decades, using calculators and slide rules. The information they have compiled on glazes and glaze materials is often in Unity Molecular Formula (UMF) or percent-by-weight format. With the software currently available, potters can quickly compare glaze recipes to understand better how they work. Modifications of the glaze based on computer feedback of the characteristics of a formula are equally fast.

"*HyperGlaze* is one such computer program for Macintosh® computers that helps maintain a database of glazes, clays, and ceramic materials. In only a few seconds, the software calculates the chemical makeup of glazes and clays from the information in the materials database. The recipes and the calculated unity molecular analysis are stored in a famil-

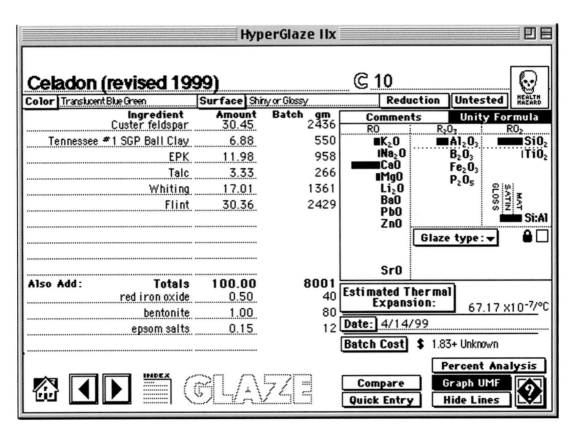

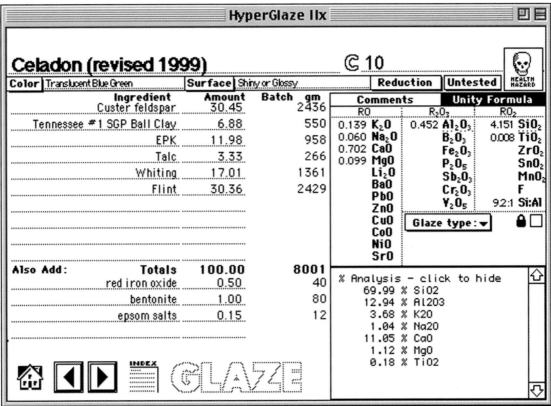

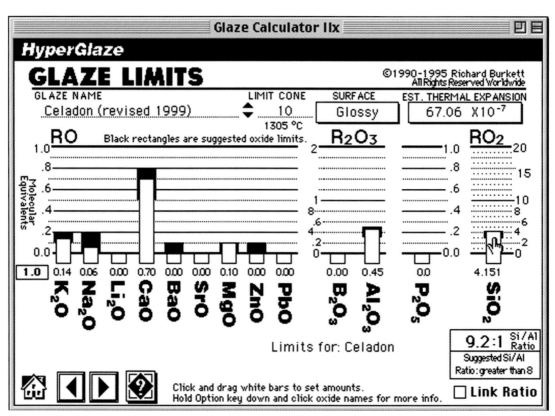

HyperGlaze IIx

Celadon (revised 1999)   © 10

| Color | Translucent Blue Green | Surface | Shiny or Glossy | | Reduction | Tested |

Ingredient	Amount	Batch gm
Custer feldspar	30.45	2436
Tennessee #1 SGP Ball Clay	6.88	550
EPK	11.98	958
Talc	3.33	266
Whiting	17.01	1361
Flint	30.36	2429

Comments / **Unity Formula**

revised from the original to use whiting instead of wollastonite (gets lumpy - needs screening) Original recipe found by Linda Litteral 1998 undergrad. Original revision of glaze was just a

Health Hazards

Talc: wear a NIOSH approved dust mask when handling dry material
Flint: free silica-wear a NIOSH approved dust mask when handling dry material

Also Add:	Totals	100.00	8001
	red iron oxide	0.50	40
	bentonite	1.00	80
	epsom salts	0.15	12

Date: 4/14/99

Batch Cost $ 1.83+ Unknown

Percent Analysis
Compare / Graph UMF
Quick Entry / Show Lines

Glaze Calculator IIx

HyperGlaze

GLAZE LIMITS

©1990-1995 Richard Burkett
All Rights Reserved Worldwide

GLAZE NAME	LIMIT CONE	SURFACE	EST. THERMAL EXPANSION
Celadon (revised 1999)	10 / 1305 °C	Glossy	67.06×10^{-7}

RO Black rectangles are suggested oxide limits. R_2O_3 RO_2

Molecular Equivalents

1.0	0.14	0.06	0.00	0.70	0.00	0.00	0.10	0.00	0.00	0.00	0.45	0.0	4.151
	K_2O	Na_2O	Li_2O	CaO	BaO	SrO	MgO	ZnO	PbO	B_2O_3	Al_2O_3	P_2O_5	SiO_2

Limits for: Celadon

$9.2:1$ Si/Al Ratio
Suggested Si/Al Ratio: greater than 8

Click and drag white bars to set amounts.
Hold Option key down and click oxide names for more info.

☐ **Link Ratio**

iar format, making use of the software extremely intuitive. Notes on the glaze (application, testing, surface, textures, color, etc.) are all stored with each recipe. *HyperGlaze* also calculates a batch recipe alongside the percentage recipe for any size batch in grams, decimal pounds, or pounds and ounces. The cost of the recipe, a percentage oxide analysis, and its estimated thermal expansion are also calculated at the same time.

"Since artists are generally visual people who are not always comfortable with numbers, *HyperGlaze* will also display the chemical makeup of the glaze as a bar graph of the relative amounts of all the oxides. This makes it quick to find a glaze that, say, is high in calcium oxide if that's needed to get the color desired. *HyperGlaze's* visual format is used also to view a bar graph of the recipe against limit formulas for glazes of various types. The limit formulas in *HyperGlaze* help the potter to better understand how a glaze compares to similar recipes, how it may likely melt, and how colorants may react with the various fluxes in the glaze. New glazes that fit specific needs of a colorant or surface can be quickly formulated.

"*HyperGlaze* even automatically calculates limit formulas from any set of glazes in the recipe database. These custom limit formulas can then be installed into *HyperGlaze*. Glazes can then be adjusted on the molecular level simply by dragging the oxide amount bars on the graph up and down to change the individual oxide amounts. *HyperGlaze* adjusts the fluxes to maintain unity at all times. It also allows the silica and alumina amounts to be adjusted either individually or together in a set ratio to maintain matte or gloss glaze characteristics when changing the working temperature of the glaze. If it's necessary to change the cone at which the glaze is used, the software will automatically adjust the temperature of the recipe, one cone number at a time either up or down.

"As glaze ingredients disappear from the world market (notably Albany slip and Gerstley borate are no longer available), computer software like *HyperGlaze* lets the potter easily calculate new recipes which use other ingredients to obtain a chemically identical glaze. This is one of the areas in which computer software really excels: calculating ingredient substitutions. Another area of glaze calculation that benefits from computer software is in adjusting the fit of a glaze to a clay body, altering the tendency of a glaze to craze or shiver. The estimated thermal expansion of a glaze can be calculated from its percentage analysis by weight. The recipe can then be changed a little at a time to increase or decrease thermal expansion, so that the glaze will fit the clay.

"The database features of glaze software allow the potter to find similar recipes, even if the ingredients are not the same, or find ingredients that are good substitutes for other ingredients not readily available. These searches are automated so the computer does the work of looking through hundreds of recipes or analyses."

Richard Burkett, Associate Professor of Art
The School of Art Design & Art History, SDSU,
San Diego, CA 92182-4805
http://www.sdsu.edu/art
e-mail: richard.burkett@sdsu.edu
voice mail: (619) 594-6201
The CeramicsWeb:
http://art.sdsu.edu/ceramicsweb/

The other program in common use, particularly in industry and in clay manufacturing, is *Insight* by Tony Hansen.

2. *Insight 5* Ceramic Glaze Calculator

by Tony Hansen

"*Insight 5* is a ceramic glaze calculator that can be used to formulate and adjust glazes. It is focused on calculations rather than record-keeping.

Compact, fast, and highly interactive
Side-by-side recipes with independent calculations
Paper and eBook instruction manuals
Customizable oxides and materials lists
Recipes can be saved in individual files

Analysis and unity/non-unity formula calculation types with LOI support
Interactive formula-to-batch calculations
Calculates ratio, expansion, recipe cost

"*Insight 5* was first released in 1988 and has been used worldwide since. It is compact, fast, and highly interactive. It employs an in-memory database to maintain data in the oxides and materials lists, control the way calculations are done, and generate material records from calculations. Notes can be entered for each recipe. Controls are within easy reach to set conditional unity, ratio, oxide and recipe level calculated properties, loss on ignition, and recipe totals. *Insight 5* is an excellent teaching tool for demonstrating the principles of formula/analysis/unity, limit formulas, LOI, and material-oxide relationships."

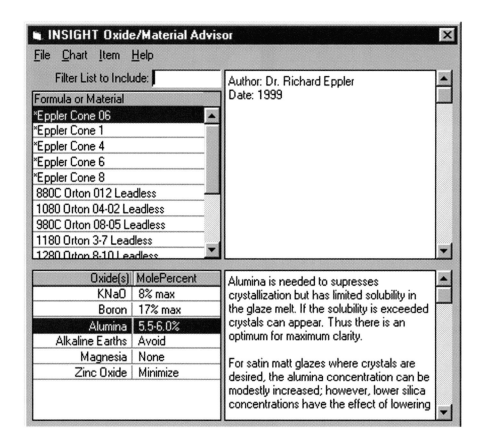

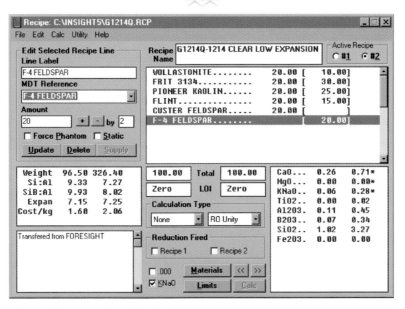

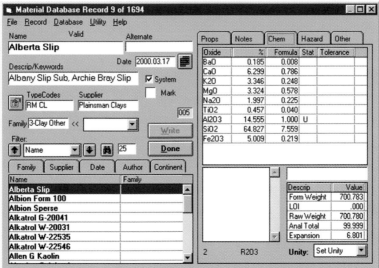

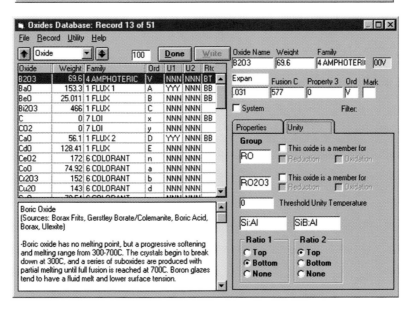

One consultant who uses computer software in addition to his forty-year hands-on experience in the ceramic world is Canadian potter Ron Roy.

3. Computer Glaze Calculation Programs

by Ron Roy

"If you had asked me ten years ago if there was anything new in the future to help potters deal with clay and glazes, I would have said no. We will just have to keep guessing - the better our experience, education, and knowledge of materials and the role of oxides, the better we would be able to guess, but it would still be a guessing game.

"That was before I started using a computer and glaze calculation software. While it is true that calculating the Seger molecular formula has been with us for well over one hundred years, the process was slow and laborious. I had tried it and could never get the same answer twice. And it was time-consuming to the point that discouraged even small changes.

"Now I can get the molecular formula in an instant - change the number of materials and their amounts and every time get the new molecular formula in the blink of an eye. This is the kind of job computers were invented to do.

"So how do I use this incredible tool? I am a technical consultant to two clay manufacturers and hundreds of studio potters. I use calculation software many times each day to solve clay and glaze problems - everything from simple glaze faults, substitution of materials, and originating new glazes and bodies for specific needs.

"Much of my work is in the area of clay/glaze fit problems. It is possible - now common - to attach an expansion number to each oxide. This means for each glaze we get a calculated expansion/contraction number which, for most glazes, is useful when reformulating to improve glaze fit. It is a matter of substituting lower expansion oxides for higher to fix crazing. There are some glazes that are so unbalanced they are not fixable in a way that retains the original look, but for most glazes on most bodies, it is not only possible, but most potters can use this aspect as soon as they learn how to use the calculators.

"The key to successful use of a glaze calculation program is the analysis of the materials we use. Most of those materials come from mines that will provide typical analysis. If the materials are local and there is no analysis, then it is simply a matter of sending a sample to a lab, entering that analysis into whatever program you are using, and using it like any other.

"It is true that there are variations in the materials we use - everything dug up will have some variation - but on the whole this does not seem to be a limitation. I can still fix glazes in spite of some variations in raw materials. In fact, without calculation software I would have a very difficult time dealing with the problem.

"Let's take the example of Gerstley borate - a variable material and no longer available. Because I have several analyses for GB I can reformulate using what I know (the variations) and simply substitute in a frit or other source of boron, make the necessary adjustments to the other oxides, and the glaze will be the same. If I keep the alumina/silica ratio the same, the surface will be the same. If I keep the calculated expansion the same, the fit will be the same. If I keep the oxide balance close, the color response will be the same.

"The same applies to clay bodies. For instance, if you have a recipe from twenty years ago and two of the clays are no longer available, and you have analysis for those clays (I have always been able to find them), you can substitute available clays and get the same results. Some will say that particle size is an important factor in this process but that can be compensated for as well.

"I talk from direct experience here. There have been many times when a clay or glaze material has been unavailable for one reason or another. I have had to reformulate whole families of clay bodies and most times have done it the first time I tried.

"I would recommend using calculation in conjunction with the empirical method - at least in the beginning until confidence is built up. Short line blends of a crazing glaze - lowering the calculated expansion more each time - is most useful. It is then possible to find an approximate calculated expansion for that glaze on that clay body. This will eventually result in having a calculated expansion number which will be useful when dealing with other glazes on that body. The knowledge built up using this method will gradually allow faster and more accurate results.

"I could write a book about what I have learned over the last few years - and probably will. Certainly I only have enough space here to whet the appetite.

I give workshops in the use of calculation software. If you are interested in being on my mailing list, contact Ron Roy through *Ceramics Monthly Magazine* at: editorial@ceramicsmonthly.org."

Following are descriptions of the pre-computer methodology of glaze calculation. It is long, confusing and often unwieldy to work with, but for many, the only way of understanding and working with the process.

4. The Necessity for Different Recipes for Glazes

A good question might be why two or three recipes for glazes, once they had been found to be effective, would not do for all pottery making. To the uninitiated it would certainly seem that potters are too preoccupied with the matter of glaze composition. Actually, however, there is a real need for a great variety of glaze compositions. For one thing, pottery is fired over a wide range of temperature. The lowest-fired wares are heated to about 800°C, and the highest are fired at about 1400°C. Obviously, the same glaze would not be satisfactory at all temperatures, since a glaze which will melt at a low temperature will volatilize or run off a pot at a higher temperature. In practice, any one glaze composition is useful for a temperature range of, at most, about 30°C. For this reason various recipes are required for each range of temperature.

Another reason for numerous glaze compositions is the demand for a variety of surface qualities. Glazes may be bright or dull, opaque, transparent, translucent, shiny, matte or dry, thick or thin, and all the gradations in between. All these surface qualities result from varying the content of the glaze.

Color in glazes results from the addition of small amounts of coloring oxides to the glaze. Various glaze compositions, however, strongly influence the resultant colors, and the makeup of the glaze itself must be controlled if certain desired colors are to be obtained.

5. Grouping Oxides According to Their Function in Glazes

It has been noted that in formulating, changing, or studying glazes, it is convenient to think of the glaze as a completed melt, containing only oxides as they have resulted from the combining and melting of the raw materials. Some method of representing the relative amounts of these oxides in a glaze is a necessity, and also necessary is a method of determining what materials, and in what quantities, will yield the desired kind and amount of oxides in a glaze. The empirical formula and the calculation of glazes from the empirical formula have been devised to fill this practical need.

The empirical formula is a method of representing a finished or melted glaze in terms of the relative amounts of the various oxides present. Empirical here means that the formula is a device for convenience and calculation rather than a true chemical formula. In this sense the empirical formula, as it is used in work with glazes, is a somewhat arbitrary device. Nevertheless, it does represent a real relationship between the oxides in the glaze, and for this reason it is of great assistance to the ceramist in any work which deals with glaze composition. The convention of the empirical formula as a method of representing glaze composition has been universally accepted among ceramists, and it has been helpful not only in the solving of practical problems of glaze composition but also as an aid to the understanding of glazes.

According to the empirical formula, the oxides common to glazes are arranged in three groups or columns as follows:

RO, R_2O (Blood)	R_2O_3 (Muscle)	RO_2 (Bones)
PbO	Al_2O_3	SiO_2
Na_2O	B_2O_3	
K_2O		
ZnO		
CaO		
MgO		
BaO		
SrO		
Li_2O		

This classification groups together those oxides which, in general, perform a similar function in the melting of the glaze. The oxides in the first column tend to act as melters, or fluxes, and they promote the fusion of the silica, in the last column, which may be thought of as the more passive oxide in the reaction. The alumina, in the middle column, occupies a somewhat neutral position in the reaction. It does not act as a flux, and yet it influences the nature of the melt. The oxides in the first column are essentially basic or alkaline in their reaction, the silica in the last column is essentially acid, and the middle column oxides are neutral. The different groups are named according to the proportion with which the oxides of that group combine with oxygen. The first column is called the "RO" column, which means radical combined with one atom of oxygen or some element combined with one of oxygen. The second column is called the "R_2O_3" column, which means some element combined with oxygen in the ratio of two to three. The last column is called the "RO_2" column. The analogy of "blood, muscle, and bone" has been used by glaze makers for centuries to describe the function of materials that make up glazes.

This grouping of the oxides gives a clearer picture of the function of the various oxides in a melting glaze. Of course, all the oxides in the first column are not equally active as fluxes, but that, in general, is their function. They serve to attack the silica and cause it to melt. Some of the oxides in the first column, although they may function in glazes as fluxes, are in themselves very refractory substances.

6. The Theory of Atomic Weight and the Method of Stating the Quantities of the Oxides in the Formula

Having briefly described the manner in which the oxides are grouped in a formula, we now consider the method of reporting the quantity of each oxide present in the glaze. These quantities are expressed as the relative number of molecules of each oxide present rather than as the gross or actual weight of the oxide present. The reason for this will be evident when it is considered how widely differing are the weights of the various molecules. To make this more clear, a word should be said about atomic weights.

Scientists have identified 118 separate elements, 92 occurring naturally and the remainder man-made. The smallest indivisible units of these elements are known as atoms. Chemists have discovered that the atoms of different elements vary widely in weight. The atoms of the element lead, for example, are very much heavier than the atoms of the element oxygen. Hydrogen is known to be the lightest element. In making a relative scale of weight, hydrogen was assigned the value of one, and the weight of the atoms of all the other elements was expressed in terms of their relationship to the weight of the hydrogen atom. Oxygen, which is sixteen times as heavy as hydrogen, is given the atomic weight of sixteen. Silicon is twenty-eight times as heavy as hydrogen. Thus all the elements have been assigned a weight. This weight does not refer to pounds or grams, but to the relative weights of the atoms of the elements in terms of the weight of the hydrogen atom.

Atoms combine in specific relationships to form the various substances of nature. These groups of atoms are called molecules. A molecule may be defined as the smallest part of a substance which can exist separately. Water, for example, is made up of hydrogen and oxygen. The water molecule consists of two atoms of hydrogen tied to one atom of oxygen, and it is written with the symbol H_2O, which simply means two hydrogen atoms to one oxygen atom.

The weight of any molecule is expressed in chemistry as the sum of the weights of the atoms it contains. Thus the water molecule H_2O is twice the weight of hydrogen, or two, plus the weight of oxygen, which is sixteen, making a total weight of eighteen. The weights of the various atoms and the weights of the various oxides used in ceramics are easily determined by consulting a chart of atomic and molecular weights, and they therefore do not need to be calculated each time. But an understanding of the basic principle of atomic and molecular weight is necessary to an understanding of glaze calculation.

Another example of the calculation of the molecular weight of a substance will make the method clear. Suppose, for example, the aim is to determine the weight of silica, SiO_2, which contains one atom of silicon to two atoms of oxygen. Multiplying the atomic weights by the number of atoms indicated in the formula and adding the total, the molecular weight is as follows:

$$
\begin{aligned}
O_2 \quad & 16 \times 2 = && 32 \\
Si \quad & 28 \times 1 = && \underline{28} \\
& && 60 \text{ - molecular weight of } SiO_2
\end{aligned}
$$

This same method is used in determining all molecular weights. More complicated substances, such as feldspars or frits, merely involve more arithmetic.

The reader who has studied chemistry must forgive this brief digression on some very elementary facts. If, on the other hand, the reader does not know any chemistry, a certain amount of confusion about the method of dealing with substances in terms of atoms and molecules is to be expected. But unless some understanding of elementary chemistry is gained, calculating glazes may remain a meaningless juggling of numbers and symbols.

If the idea of molecular weight is understood, the method of stating the quantities of the various oxides in the formula can be described. These quantities are always expressed in the relative numbers of molecules present in the glaze rather than in terms of the weights of the various oxides present. To make a simple analogy, suppose a basket is filled with apples and oranges. This is analogous to a glaze in which are melted two different oxides. If it's necessary to know the relative quantity of apples and oranges, the best way is to make a count of each. Or better, it might be said that there is one orange for every two apples, for example, which gives an exact idea of the relative quantities. It wouldn't be logical to say that there are five pounds of oranges and three pounds of apples. So it is in describing a glaze. It's necessary to know how many molecules of silica there are in relation to the molecules of lead oxide, calcia, alumina, etc. In other words, the question is: What is the balance or relationship between the various components of the glaze? As has been seen, the molecules of the glaze are of widely varying weight - lead, for example, being several times heavier than silica. But in describing a glaze in a formula, the *relative number of molecules* of each substance is what is of interest, regardless of their weight.

For example, the formula for a simple lead glaze might be:

PbO   1   Al₂O₃   .2   SiO₂   1

This formula means that, in relative quantity, there is present in the finished glaze one molecule of lead oxide, .2, or one fifth, of a molecule of alumina, and one molecule of silica. The fact that the alumina is reported as being less than one molecule will give an idea of the rather arbitrary nature of the empirical formula, since in actuality, parts of molecules do not exist in this way. However, the formula may give an exact idea of the numbers of molecules in the glaze relative to one another.

A graphic representation of the glaze given above may help to make the meaning of the formula more clear:

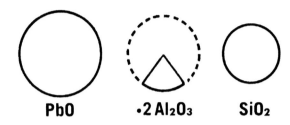

Here the molecules of the various oxides are represented by circles of various sizes which correspond to the discrepancy in weight of the different substances. Lead is heavier than silica. One circle each of lead and silica are shown, since the formula calls for a relationship of one to one. The alumina is represented as one-fifth (.2) of the whole alumina molecule. Of course, in actuality, even the smallest visible fragment of a glaze would contain billions of molecules; so the formula does not tell anything about the total number of molecules in any given quantity of glaze. But it does give an idea of how many molecules of one thing there are in relation to the molecules of the other substances present.

7. The Unity Formula

Note: In the calculation information and exercises that follow, I have left the use of lead intact as it is the only flux that can entirely fill the RO column. All others must be mixtures of a number of single fluxes or compounds.

As a basis for comparison, it has been accepted as a convention that all the oxides in the first column of the empirical formula be made to add up to one. This greatly facilitates the comparison of one formula with another. Since all the oxides in the first column act in general as fluxes, the numerical relation between the flux in a glaze formula and the silica can be seen at a glance. According to the unity formula, a glaze that contained lead oxide and calcium oxide in the proportion of one molecule of lead oxide to one molecule of calcium would be written:

PbO   .5
CaO   .5

And if these two oxides were present in a glaze in this proportion, the formula might be:

PbO .5

  Al$_2$O$_3$ .5   SiO$_2$ 1

CaO .5

In this formula there is one molecule of silica for each half molecule of lead oxide, calcia, and alumina. When the sum of the fractional amounts in the first column adds up to one, we say that the formula is a unity formula.

Since the oxides in the first column perform a roughly similar function in the glaze, it is convenient for these always to add up to one, as a basis of comparison with silica. It can be seen at a glance, then, how many silica molecules are associated with the fluxing portion of the glaze. Of course, it would be possible always to write the silica portion of the glaze as the figure one and to state the other oxides as quantities relative to one. One trouble with such a system would be that the amounts of oxides in the first column would turn out to be such small fractional amounts that calculation would be more difficult and inexact.

Most of the confusion about the calculation of glazes centers about two points. One point is that the figures refer to molecules or parts of molecules rather than to weights or fractions of weights. The other point is that the amounts in the first column are arbitrarily made to add up to one and that all the other quantities are expressed in amounts relative to this.

8. Calculating Recipes of Glazes from Their Formula

Glaze calculation is a method of finding out what raw materials to mix up to yield, in a melted glaze, the balance of oxides indicated in a formula. It also is a method of determining the formula of any glaze recipe. It is important to distinguish between the formula of a glaze, which reports only the oxides present and their quantities, and the batch or recipe of a glaze, which tells only what raw materials go into making up the glaze and their quantities.

Suppose, for example, that the following formula is given, and the aim is to find out what materials to weigh out in the laboratory to make a glaze which, when fused, will have this composition:

PbO – 1   SiO$_2$ – 1

Although there is no alumina present, and only one oxide present in the first column, this is a correct unity formula, since the sum of the first column is one. At first it may seem logical that the way to make up a batch of this glaze would be to take one pound (or gram) of lead oxide and one pound or gram of silica and mix them together. But it can't be done this way because, since the lead oxide molecule is much heavier than the silica molecule, the result would be too many silica molecules and not enough lead oxide molecules. Therefore, to find out what to weigh out to arrive at a glaze formula, first raw materials must be chosen that will yield the desired oxides. These materials must then be weighed out in quantities that will yield the right molecular ratio between the oxides as called for in the formula. In this case, the goal is a ratio of one lead oxide molecule to one silica molecule. For the glaze litharge, PbO, and silica, SiO$_2$, might be used. To get the right quantity, the molecular weight of the material is multiplied by the quantity called for in the formula:

PbO 1x 223 (molecular weight of litharge) = 223 parts of litharge

SiO$_2$ 1 x 60 (molecular weight of silica) = 60 parts of silica

The answer, 223 parts of litharge and 60 parts of silica, may be weighed out in ounces, pounds, or carloads, and if this proportion were kept, the resultant glaze would have the proportion of one molecule of lead oxide to one of silica. The calculation is made necessary by the difference in the molecular weights of the substances involved.

To give a slightly more involved example, suppose the aim is to determine the batch or recipe of the following formula:

PbO .8   SiO$_2$ 1

CaO .2

Here, for each .8 molecules of lead oxide and .2 molecules of calcium oxide, there is one molecule of silica present in the finished glaze. The problem of calculating the batch or recipe for this glaze is to find the proper quantity and kind of raw materials to furnish the oxides in the amounts shown in the formula. Looking over the list of available raw materials, note that lead oxide can be supplied by litharge, whose formula is PbO and whose molecular weight is 223. Calcium oxide can be supplied by whiting, whose formula is $CaCO_3$ and whose molecular weight is 100. Silica can be supplied by flint SiO_2, whose molecular weight is 60. Actually there is some latitude of choice in filling most formulas - choices governed mostly by commonsense. Having decided what materials to use, it must now be determined how much of each material is needed to fill the formula. As in the previous example, this can be calculated by multiplying the amount of the oxide called for in the glaze by the molecular weight of the raw material that supplies this oxide.

PbO	.8	x	223	=	178.4 parts of litharge
CaO	.2	x	10	=	20 parts of calcium
SiO_2 1	.0	x	60	=	60 parts of silica

The answers constitute the batch weight of the glaze, i.e., the relative amount of raw materials that must be weighed out to fill the formula.

It will be noted that the batch does not add up to 100 and is not a percentage composition. But it is a recipe that shows the relative amounts of each material. To be able to add percentages of colorants, opacifiers, and texturizers, it is convenient to make the batch to a percentage composition. To make the total come to 100, so that each quantity in the recipe will be a percentage of the whole, the sum of the recipe is divided into each figure in the recipe and then multiplied by 100, as follows:

Litharge	178.4	÷ 258.4 =	.690	x 100 =	69.0	
Calcium	20	÷ 258.4 =	.077	x 100 =	7.7	
Silica	60	÷ 258.4 =	.233	x 100 =	23.3	
	258.4				100.0%	

The two simple examples given above illustrate how the formula can be converted into a recipe. This procedure would be followed when, for example, a new glaze had been formulated on paper and it was desired to find out what ingredients to weigh out for an actual sample glaze.

9. An Example of Calculating from the Batch to the Formula

Glaze calculation makes possible the determination of the formula of any given batch or recipe of raw materials. Suppose, for example, that the goal is to determine the empirical formula for the following mixture:

Calcium	10	parts by weight
Litharge	50	parts by weight
Silica	40	parts by weight
	100	total

This recipe tells the amount of each raw material to weigh out for the glaze, but it does not tell how many molecules of silica there are in the mixture relative to the number of molecules of lead oxide and calcium oxide. It is this relationship that must be known to deal intelligently with the composition.

To find the empirical formula of the above recipe, divide each quantity of material by the molecular weight of that material:

Calcium	10 ÷ 100 = .100
Litharge	50 ÷ 223 = .224
Silica	40 ÷ 60 = .666

The answers here are known as molecular equivalents. The problem has already been solved in effect, because the relationship between .100, .224, and .666 tells the relative quantity of molecules of each substance in the glaze. It remains only to arrange these answers according to the empirical formula and to make the first column add up to one, or reduce it to unity. So the formula is written:

PbO	.224	SiO_2	.666
CaO	.100		
	.324 total		

As the formula now appears, the first column falls short of one (unity). The next step is to divide each quantity in the whole formula by the sum of the quantities in the first column, which in this case is .324:

PbO	.224 ÷ .324 = .691
CaO	.100 ÷ .324 = .309
SiO_2	.666 ÷ .324 = 2.05

We may now write the formula in final form:

PbO	.691		
		SiO_2	2.05
CaO	.309		
	1.000		

Unless the division and multiplication are carried out to the fourth place, the sum of the first column is apt to be short of one by one or two thousandths. This is too small a quantity to be of any significance in glazes.

The essential methods of glaze calculation are illustrated in the examples given thus far, and if the principles involved in them are understood, more complicated problems can be dealt with without difficulty. The objectives of glaze calculation are: (a) to state the molecular formula in a clear way which will give a basis for comparison, (b) to translate the molecular formula into a recipe of materials which will yield in the finished glaze what the formula calls for, and (c) to arrive at a molecular formula from any given recipe of raw materials.

Table of Ceramic Raw Materials

Material	Raw Formula	Molecular Weight	Equivalent Weight	Fired Formula	Fired Weight
Alumina Hydrate	Al_2O_3 1.0	137.97			
Aluminum Oxide	Al_2O_3 1.0	101.94			
Antimony Oxide	Sb_2O_3	292	292	Sb_2O_3	292
Barium Carbonate	$BaCO_3$	197	197	BaO	153
Bentonite	K_2O 0.3848, Na_2O 0.2087, CaO 0.0601, MgO 0.3428 } Al_2O3 1.071, Fe_2O_3 0.105 } SiO_2 5.434	522.1	-	-	-
Bone Ash (Calcium Phosphate)	$Ca3(PO_4)_2$	310	103	CaO	56
Borax	$Na_2O \cdot 2B_2O_3 \cdot 10H_2O$	382	382	$Na_2O \cdot 2B_2O_3$	202
Boric Acid	$B_2O_3 \cdot 3H_2O$	124	124	B_2O_3	70
Calcium Borate (Cadycal 100)	$2CaO \cdot 3B_2O_3 \cdot 5H_2O$ $Ca_2B_6O_{11} \cdot 5H_2O$	412	206 / 197	$CaO \cdot 1.5B_2O_3$ / $CaO \cdot 1.5B_2O_3$	161
Calcium Carbonate (Whiting)	$CaCO_3$	100	100	CaO	56
China Clay (Kaolin)	$Al_2O_3 \cdot 2SiO_2 \cdot 2H_2O$	258	258	$Al_2O_3 \cdot 2SiO_2$	222
Chromic Oxide	Cr_2O_3	152	152	Cr_2O_3	152
Cobalt Carbonate	$CoCO_3$	119	119	CoO	75
Cobalt Oxide Black	Co_3O_4	241	80	CoO	75
Copper Carbonate	$CuCO_3$	124	124	CuO	80
Copper Oxide	CuO	80	80	CuO	80
Copper Oxide Red (Cuprous)	Cu_2O	143	80	CuO	80
Cornwall Stone	CaO .304, Na_2O .340, K_2O .356 } Al_2O_3 1.075 } SiO_2 8.10	667	667	Unchanged	667
Cryolite	$Na_3 \cdot AlF_6$	210	420	$3Na_2O \cdot Al_2O_3$	288

Table of Ceramic Raw Materials (Continued)

Material	Raw Formula	Molecular Weight	Equivalent Weight	Fired Formula	Fired Weight
Feldspars: Potash Feldspar (theoretical)	$K_2O \cdot Al_2O_3 \cdot 6SiO_2$	556	556	Unchanged	556
Soda Feldspar (theoretical)	$Na_2O \cdot Al_2O_3 \cdot 6SiO_2$	524	524	Unchanged	524
G200 Feldspar	K_2O 0.6 Na_2O 0.30 } Al_2O_3 1.05 } SiO_2 6.16 CaO 0.1	559	559	Unchanged	559
Custer Feldspar	K_2O .69 Na_2O .31 } Al_2O_3 1.05 } SiO_2 7.05	615	615	Unchanged	615
Kona F-4 Feldspar	Na_2O .48 K_2O .32 } Al_2O_3 1.02 } SiO_2 5.60 CaO .20	508	508	Unchanged	508
Nepheline Syenite	K_2O .25 Na_2O .75 } Al_2O_3 1.11 } SiO_2 4.65	462	462	Unchanged	462
Kaolin, Calcined	$Al_2O_3 \cdot 2SiO_2$	222	222	$Al_2O_3 \cdot 2SiO_2$	222
Iron Chromate	$FeCrO_4$	172	172	$FeCrO_4$	172
Iron Oxide Red (Ferric)	Fe_2O_3	160	160	Fe_2O_3	160
Iron Oxide Black (Ferrous)	FeO	72	72	FeO	72
Fluorspar (Calcium Fluoride)	CaF_2	78	78	CaO	56
Lead Carbonate (White Lead)	$2PbCO_3 \cdot Pb(OH)_2$	775	258	PbO	223
Lead Monosilicate	$3PbO \cdot 2SiO_2$	789	263	Unchanged	789
Lead Oxide (Litharge)	PbO	223	223	PbO	223
Lead Oxide (Red)	Pb_3O_4	684	228	PbO	223
Lepidolite	K_2O 0.0235 Na_2O 0.0160 Li_2O 0.9517 } Al_2O_3 1.0270 MgO 0.0089 } Fe_2O_3 0.0021 } SiO_2 3.019 343.2 MnO_2 0.0053	-	-	-	-
Lithium Carbonate	Li_2CO_3	74	74	Li_2O	30
Magnesium Carbonate	$MgCO_3$	84	84	MgO	84
Manganese Carbonate	$MnCO_3$	115	115	MnO	71
Manganese Dioxide	MnO_2	87	87	MnO	71

Table of Ceramic Raw Materials (Continued)

Material	Raw Formula	Molecular Weight	Equivalent Weight	Fired Formula	Fired Weight
Nickel Oxide Green	NiO	75	75	NiO	75
Nickel Oxide Black	Ni_2O_3	166	83	NiO	75
Niter	KNO_3	101	202	K_2O	94
Petalite	$Li_2O \cdot Al_2O_3 \cdot 8SiO_2$	608	608	Unchanged	608
Plastic Vitrox Clay	K_2O 0.4513 Na_2 0.045 CaO 0.075 MgO 0.275 Al_2O_3 1.000 Fe_2O_3 0.127 SiO_2 10.975	844.79	-	-	-
Potassium Carbonate (Pearl Ash)	K_2CO_3	138	138	K_2O	94
Pyrophyllite	$Al_2O_3 \cdot 4SiO_2 \cdot H_2O$	360	360	$Al_2O_3 \cdot 4SiO_2$	342
Potassium Bichromate	$K_2Cr_2O_7$	294	294	$K_2O \cdot Cr_2O_3$	294
Silica (Flint, Quartz)	SiO_2	60	60	SiO_2	60
Sodium Carbonate (Soda Ash)	Na_2O_3	106	106	Na_2O	62
Sodium Nitrate	$NaNO_3$	85	107	Na_2O	62
Spodumene	$Li_2O \cdot Al_2O_3 \cdot 4SiO_2$	372	372	Unchanged	372
Strontium Carbonate	$SrCO_3$	148	148	SrO	120
Talc (Steatite)	$3MgO \cdot 4SiO_2 \cdot H_2O$	378	126	$3MgO \cdot 4SiO_2$	360
Tin Oxide	SnO_2	151	151	SnO_2	152
Titanium Dioxide (Rutile=impure TiO_2)	TiO_2	80	80	TiO_2	80
Wollastonite	CaO 1.0 } SiO_2 1	116			
Zinc Oxide	ZnO	81	81	ZnO	81
Zirconium Silicate (Zircopax)	$ZrO_2 \cdot SiO_2$	183	183	Unchanged	183
Zirconium Oxide	ZrO_2	123	123	ZrO	123

This list includes most of the generally used materials. For more obscure materials, search computer programs or internet sources such as the American Ceramic Society (www.ceramics.org).

The availability of ceramic materials is subject to change. Since the first edition of this book, the following materials have ceased being produced:

Gerstley borate (colemanite)
Albany slip
Michigan slip
Kingman feldspar
Buckingham feldspar
Oxford feldspar
US spodumene
US lithium carbonate
US copper carbonate
litharge
red lead

Many new and replacement products have now come on the market, including:

Alberta slip
Cadycal 100
Laguna borate
Inclusion colors
Many new frits
A new generation of lead bisilicates
New rheological additives and polymers
New deflocculants

In the future we will likely see less of an array of ball clays from Tennessee and Kentucky, kaolins from Georgia, and the complete loss of lead in any form.

Glaze Calculation Using Materials Containing More Than One Oxide

1. The Table of Ceramic Raw Materials

The table of ceramic raw materials on pages 182-184 gives some of the necessary facts about the raw materials of glazes for use in glaze calculation. In practice we refer to some such chart for atomic weights and other information which it is difficult and, in fact, unnecessary to commit to memory. Two formulas are given for each material: its formula as a raw material and its formula after having been fired. This is necessary since many glaze materials are altered in composition by firing. Volatile constituents such as the carbonates are lost in firing. This is referred to as L.O.I. or loss on ignition. Raw calcium carbonate is $CaCO_3$; but when fired, it becomes calcium oxide, CaO. The carbonate, carbon dioxide or CO_2, was burned off. All the materials in their fired state are in oxide form. The molecular weight of a material may be different after it has been calcined, fired, or melted into a glass.

2. Equivalent Weight

The column labeled "Equivalent Weight" refers to the molecular weight of material that must be taken to yield one complete unit of the oxide which is desired in the glaze. In most cases the equivalent weight is the same as the molecular weight of the material. There are, however, exceptions where the equivalent weight is either more or less than the molecular weight. Six of these are given below:

Bone ash	$Ca_3(PO_4)_2$
Calcium borate	$2CaO \cdot 3B_2O_2 \cdot 5H_2O$
White lead	$2PbCO_2 \cdot Pb(OH)_2$
Red lead	Pb_3O_4
Niter (potassium or sodium nitrate)	KNO_3
Cryolite	Na_3AlF_6

In all these six materials the given formula of the material yields, when fired, either more or less than one molecule of the oxide which enters into the composition of the glaze. The molecular weight of the material has therefore been adjusted either to a higher or to a lower figure so as to give one molecule of the oxide in question. This adjusted, or equivalent, weight may be defined as that weight of a raw material that must be taken to obtain, in the glaze, one molecule of the desired oxide in fired form.

For example, red lead has the formula Pb_3O_4 and a molecular weight of 685. When red lead is fired, it becomes PbO. Note that PbO has more atoms of lead relative to those of oxygen than has Pb_3O_4. Also note that the formula of raw red lead is written Pb_3, which means three atoms of lead. Therefore, for a yield of one atom of Pb, divide the molecular weight of the red lead by three, giving an equivalent weight of 228.

In the case of white lead, divide by three also.

White lead has the formula $2PbCO_3.Pb(OH)_2$. When fired, the carbonate (CO_3) and the hydroxide (OH)$_2$ radicals are burned away, leaving three PbO. Therefore, to obtain the equivalent weight of white lead, divide its molecular weight, 775, by three, which gives 258.

In the case of niter the raw formula contains but one atom of potassium. Since the fired unit, K_2O, has two atoms of potassium, multiply the molecular weight of the raw niter, 101, by two to get the equivalent weight, 202.

A similar situation occurs in the case of cryolite, Na_3AlF_6. Here the goal is to obtain one molecule of Al_2O_3. Since cryolite contains only one atom of Al, its weight must be doubled. Doubling Na_3 gives, in the fired formula, $3Na_2O$.

Calcium borate as a raw material is conveniently written $2CaO.3B_2O_3.5H_2O$. It is awkward to handle this formula in calculating because there are two units of calcium; so the formula is split in two, giving instead one unit of CaO and one and one-half units of B_2O_3. This cuts the weight from 412 to 206.

The equivalent weight used in the case of these six materials is admittedly a rather arbitrary device, chemically. But it does simplify calculating, and if the equivalent weight is used consistently for all materials, no discrepancies in calculating will arise from this source. If the figure equivalent weight is not used, the six materials discussed above must be calculated each time with reference to their formula and to the fact that they do not yield one oxide unit.

3. Feldspar Formulas

The feldspars in the raw material table are represented by formulas which are identical with the empirical formula already described. The alkalies and alkaline earths are grouped in the first column, which adds up to one, and the alumina and the silica are given values relative to those of the first column. The formula of a feldspar, or of any other material for that matter, is computed in the same way as the example described above in which a glaze batch was converted to a formula.

An example is now given of the manner in which the formula of a feldspar is derived from its chemical analysis. Suppose that a feldspar has been given quantitative analysis and is found to have the following composition:

SiO_2	66.2
Al_2O_3	18.4
CaO	1.6
K_2O	10.8
Na_2O	2.0

These figures, as reported by the chemist, refer to the actual percentages by weight of the various oxides found in the particular feldspar. They do not mean that there are 66.2 molecules of silica to each 18.4 molecules of alumina, but rather that there are 66.2 grams or pounds of silica to each 18.4 grams or pounds of alumina. The purpose of converting the analysis as given above into a formula is to get at the relative quantity of molecules of each oxide present.

As in the example involving lead oxide and silica in a glaze, divide each item in the percentage composition by the molecular weight of the oxide, which gives the molecular equivalent or relative number of molecules of each oxide.

% Composition		÷	Molecular Weight		Molecular Equivalents
SiO_2	66.2	÷	60	=	1.103
Al_2O_3	18.4	÷	102	=	.180
CaO	1.6	÷	56	=	.028
Na_2O	2.0	÷	62	=	.032
K_2O	10.8	÷	94	=	.114

The molecular equivalents can now be set down in their appropriate columns:

CaO	.028		
		Al_2O_3 .180	SiO_2 1.103
Na_2O	.032		
K_2O	.114		
	.174		

Since the first column adds up to .174, this is not a unity formula; and, to make it come to unity, all quantities of the formula are divided by .174, which results in the formula in its final form:

CaO	.160		
		Al_2O_3 1.04	SiO_2 6.39
Na_2O	.184		
K_2O	.655		
	.999		

We now have the formula of the feldspar in terms of the relative numbers of molecules of the various oxides present. To obtain the formula weight of the feldspar, the quantity of each oxide present in the formula is multiplied by the molecular weight of that oxide, and the resultant sums are totaled, as follows:

$$
\begin{array}{lrclr}
CaO & .16 & \times & 56 & = 89.6 \\
Na_2O & .184 & \times & 62 & = 11.40 \\
K_2O & .665 & \times & 94 & = 61.6 \\
Al_2O_3 & 1.04 & \times & 102 & = 106.1 \\
SiO_2 & 6.39 & \times & 60 & = \underline{383.4}
\end{array}
$$

$$571.5 = \text{formula weight of the feldspar}$$

Two of the feldspars listed on the raw materials chart are theoretical, or typical, compositions rather than commercially available materials. Most of the minerals found in nature do not conform exactly to the composition that has been determined by mineralogists to be typical. In the case of feldspars, only hand-picked specimens would be apt to conform exactly to the theoretical composition. Commercially mined feldspars usually have two or three alkaline constituents, and the proportion of alumina and silica is rarely like the ideal composition. To make an accurate calculation of a glaze, the formula derived from the most recent analysis must be used.

4. Calculation of the Batch from the Formula of a Simple Lead Glaze

When glazes contain materials which have more than one oxide in them - and this is true of almost all workable glazes - the arithmetic or calculation becomes somewhat more complex. For example, the following glaze, although it is a very simple one, involves the addition of clay as a material; since clay contains both alumina and silica, it will serve to illustrate the method of calculation where one material yields two different oxides.

$$PbO \quad 1 \qquad Al_2O_3 \quad .2 \qquad SiO_2 \quad 2.5$$

The experienced glaze maker can see at a glance that this glaze could best be made up by combining some material that yields lead oxide, such as litharge or white lead; clay, which would take care of the alumina; and silica. The problem is to determine how much of these materials to use to get the ratio of

oxides indicated in the molecular formula. Let us say that litharge is chosen for the lead content of the glaze. As in the previous examples, the quantity of lead oxide called for, 1, is multiplied by the equivalent of litharge, 223, giving 223 parts as the amount of litharge to use in the recipe. The clay used to supply the alumina has the formula $Al_2O_3 \bullet 2SiO_2 \bullet 2H_2O$ and the equivalent weight of 258. Taking .2, the amount of alumina called for in the formula, and multiplying it by 258, the batch weight for the clay is obtained - 51.6. But with each molecule of alumina in clay there are associated two molecules of silica. Therefore, when the formula is supplied with .2 of alumina, it's also getting along with it .4 of silica. This amount partially fills the amount of silica called for in the formula, but there still remain 2.1 molecules of silica to be filled with the material flint. Taking then, 2.1, the amount of silica needed, and multiplying it by 60, the equivalent weight of silica, the result is the batch weight for silica, 126.

The arithmetic involved in this simple calculation will be made more clear if the calculation is arranged in tabular form, placing across the top all the oxides in the formula and their quantity and, in the vertical column to the left, arranging the raw materials to be used in satisfying the formula.

A table such as this is usually kept in calculating glazes to help keep track of the amount of the various oxides supplied by the raw materials.

	PbO 1	Al$_2$O$_3$ .2	SiO$_2$ 2.5
Litharge 1	1		
	0		
Clay .2		.2	.4
		0	2.1
Silica			2.1
			000

$$
\begin{array}{lrcl}
\text{Litharge} & 1 & \times 223 = & 223 \\
\text{Clay} & .2 & \times 258 = & 51.6 \\
\text{Silica} & 2.1 & \times 60 = & 126 \text{ Batch weights of} \\
& & & \text{recipe}
\end{array}
$$

The important method involved in the above calculation is the manner in which the amount of clay is figured, since it is supplying two different oxides to the glaze. It should be noted that when .2 of the material is taken, it's a fractional amount, less than one part. With this .2, comes, of course, .2 of everything in the material, not only .2 of alumina but .2 of the silica as well. When a quantity of a material is introduced, the quantity applies to all the components of the material. Actually, what was done in this example is to introduce .2 or one-fifth, of the clay molecule, and naturally this one-fifth part contains one-fifth of the alumina, or .2, and one-fifth of the silica, or .4. Of course, a molecule cannot actually be divided in this fashion, and the arbitrary nature of the calculation should be kept in mind. But, as we have said, the method does permit an accurate translation of the formula into terms of actual raw materials.

5. Calculation of a Glaze Containing Both Clay and Feldspar

The method of handling materials which supply more than one oxide to the glaze will be clarified by another example involving both clay and a feldspar. Suppose the goal is to calculate the recipe of a lead glaze with the following formula:

PbO   .8 Al_2O_3 .25 SiO_2 2.00
K_2O .2

The first step is to construct a chart in which the oxides can be tabulated and kept track of as they are filled or satisfied by the raw materials. As before, the oxides of the formula are posted horizontally at the top, and the raw materials are placed in a vertical column at the left.

	PbO .8	K_2O .2	Al_2O_3 .25	SiO_2 2.00
White lead .8	.8			
Potash feldspar .2			.2	1.2
		.2	.05	.8
Clay .05			.05	.1
			00	.7
Silica .7				.7
				0

Here lead oxide in the formula is the start and is filled with .8 of white lead. Then the potassium oxide, K_2O, is filled by taking .2 of potash feldspar (orthoclase). In this case, for the sake of simplicity of calculating, I have used the theoretical composition of orthoclase as shown on the raw materials chart, even though such a material is not available commercially. With the .2 of feldspar also comes .2 of everything in the feldspar, which has the formula K_2O 1, Al_2O_3 1

and SiO_2 6. This adds to the formula .2 K_2O (1x.2), .2 of Al_2O_3 (1x.2), and 1.2 of SiO_2 (6x.2), which quantities are posted in the chart as shown.

The next problem is to find out how much alumina and silica still remain to be added to the glaze. This is determined by subtracting the amount that came with the feldspar from the amount called for by the formula, namely, .05 of alumina and .8 of silica. The alumina is then filled with the material clay ($Al_2O_3 \cdot 2SiO_2 \cdot 2H_2O$). As in the previous example, .05 of clay, which satisfies the alumina of the formula, brings along with it twice that amount of SiO_2, or .1. Subtracting this amount from the remaining silica gives the quantity .7, the amount of silica which must be added with flint.

The molecular equivalents obtained by this procedure are now multiplied by the equivalent weights of the various raw materials involved, which gives the batch weights or recipe of the glaze, as shown below:

White lead	.8	x 258 = 206.4
Feldspar	.2	x 556 = 111.2
Clay	.05	x 258 = 12.9
Silica	.7	x 60 = 42.0

No matter how complicated the glaze is, or how many materials there are in it that contain two or more oxides, the procedure given in the above example is followed. Before giving a more complicated example of calculating, here are the steps in calculating a glaze recipe from a formula:

1. A chart is constructed, as in the previous examples, which makes it possible to keep track of the quantities as they are added. Then all those oxides in the first column of the glaze that occur singly in the raw materials are satisfied. Such oxides as lead, barium, and zinc occur in raw materials which yield no other oxide. If they are taken care of first, only those oxides found in materials containing two or more oxides will remain to be calculated.

2. The oxides in the first column are filled, which come from materials having more than one oxide in them.

3. The feldspar is calculated.

4. The remaining alumina is satisfied with clay.

5. And, finally, what silica remains to be satisfied after the addition of feldspar and clay is filled with flint.

6. Selection of Raw Materials for Glazes

Someone who has not become very familiar with glaze materials may feel puzzled as to what raw materials to use to satisfy a glaze formula. Questions are apt to arise, such as: Should the sodium in the glaze be filled with borax or with feldspar? The following general rules may make the reasons behind most choices more clear:

1. Soluble materials are avoided, and the glaze is satisfied wherever possible with insoluble natural raw materials or with frits.

2. As few materials as possible are used.

3. Use of natural raw materials which contain two oxides is preferred to adding the two oxides in separate form. For example, it is better to satisfy a glaze containing both calcia and magnesia with dolomite, which contains both of these oxides, than it would be to add whiting and magnesium carbonate.

4. Alumina is added in the form of clay or feldspar.

5. The silica still needed after the clay and feldspar have been added is added in the form of silica.

It will be seen that the glaze formula may be filled with raw materials in different ways. For example, the same lead glaze formula could be made up with either red lead or white lead. While it is true that the quantity and kind of oxides should be the same, the two glazes might not have exactly the same maturing temperature or the same characteristics. Different raw materials, in other words, influence the glaze, even though they may yield the same oxides in the finished glaze. This is due to the melting characteristics of the various materials and their interaction on one another during melting. Oxides added to the glaze in the form of naturally combined materials, such as feldspars, will cause a somewhat lower fusion point than if the same oxides had been added to the glaze in single materials. The selection of raw materials is critically important in glaze making, and if any glaze is to be duplicated exactly, the batch as well as the formula must be known.

7. Calculation of a More Complex Glaze

Now an example will be given of the calculation of a more complex glaze. Suppose the aim is to obtain the batch or recipe for a glaze whose formula is:

PbO .5
CaO .2
Al_2O_3 .25 SiO_2 2.8
B_2O_3 .15
K_2O .2
MgO .1

In studying this formula, it can be seen that several oxides in it can be supplied by materials which contain more than one oxide. The B_2O_3 may be supplied by calcium borate, since there is also CaO in the formula. The MgO may be supplied by talc, since this material yields both MgO and SiO_2. The K_2O would be best supplied by feldspar. A logical choice of materials would be white lead, feldspar, calcium borate, calcium carbonate, talc, clay, and silica.

As before, set up a chart that indicates the oxides called for in the glaze and the raw materials which have been chosen to fill the formula. The calculation is given below:

	PbO .5	CaO .2	B_2O_3 .15	K_2O .2	MgO .1	Al_2O_3 .25	SiO_2 2.80
White lead .5	.5 / 0						
Calcium borate .1		.1 / .1	.15 / 0				
Calcium carbonate .1		.1 / 0					
Talc .03					.1 / 0		.132 / 2.668
Feldspar .2				.2 / 0		.2 / .05	1.2 / 1.47
Clay .05						.05 / x	.1 / 1.37
Silica 1.37							1.37 / 0

In this calculation some new problems are encountered. It will be clear how the .5 of white lead was arrived at. With the calcium borate, the question is: How much calcium borate must be used to satisfy the .15 molecules of B_2O_3 called for in the formula? The formula of calcium borate, CaO 1, B_2O_3 1.5, will be seen to contain one and one-half times more B_2O_3 than CaO. It's necessary to divide the B_2O_3 as shown in the formula of the material in order to get the .15 called for in the glaze. In this case it will be seen that it's necessary to divide the formula of calcium borate by ten to get .15 of B_2O_3, which is one-tenth of 1.5, the amount of B_2O_3 in the formula of the material. Using the decimal system, multiply calcium borate by .1, which is, of course, the same as dividing it by ten.

This situation arises frequently in calculating. It's necessary to divide the formula of some material to get the desired fraction of some one oxide present. In this case the amount of B_2O_3 controls the amount of calcium borate to be put in the glaze, since all the B_2O_3 is to come from calcium borate. To find the factor, or amount, of calcium borate that will yield the right amount of B_2O_3, divide the amount called for in the formula by the amount that occurs in the material. Thus, in the case of the following calculation:

$$\frac{.15 \; B_2O_3 \; (\text{called for in the formula})}{1.5 \; B_2O_3 \; (\text{in the material calcium borate})} =$$

.1 (the amount of calcium borate that will yield .15 B_2O_3)

Having determined how much calcium borate may be used, namely .1, multiply all the oxides in calcium borate by .1 and post the answers on the chart. This gives a value of .1 for CaO (.1x1=.1) and, as expected, a value of .15 for B_2O_3 (.1x1.5). Calcium carbonate is next added, to take care of the remaining CaO. Next comes the MgO in the formula, which is to be supplied by talc. The formula of talc is 3MgO, 4SiO$_2$; so again a factor, or amount, for talc must be found, which when multiplied by the formula of talc gives .1 MgO, the oxide needed. Following the procedure given above the result is:

$$\frac{.1 \; (\text{amount of MgO needed in formula})}{3 \; (\text{amount of MgO in talc formula})} = .033$$

(amount of talc that can be used)

Now, multiplying all the oxides in talc by .033, the result is .033x3=.099, which is as near to .1 as arithmetic will go, and .033x4=.132 SiO_2.

The method used here for determining the amount of colemanite and talc which can be used to fill a formula is used whenever the raw material contains an oxide in its formula that is either more or less than one, provided that this oxide is the one being used to fill entirely some oxide requirement in the formula. The rule-of-thumb for finding the amount of a material to use may be stated:

$$\frac{\text{what is wanted in the formula}}{\text{what is present in the material}} =$$

the amount of the material that may be used

After subtracting the amount of silica obtained with the talc, carry out the calculation of the above problem in the same fashion as the preceding example. It remains, then, to multiply each of the figures obtained for the raw materials by its equivalent weight to obtain the batch of the glaze as follows:

Feldspar	.2	x	556	=	111.2
White lead	.5	x	258	=	129.0
Calcium borate	.1	x	20	=	20.6
Calcium carbonate	.1	x	100	=	10.0
Talc	.033	x	378	=	12.4
Clay	.05	x	258	=	12.9
Silica	.37	x	60	=	81.6

8. Calculation Involving a Complex Feldspar

An example is now given of a calculation involving a glaze which includes a particular feldspar, whose exact formula has been determined by chemical analysis and converted into a molecular formula. The problem is to calculate the batch of the following glaze:

K$_2$O .74

Al$_2$O$_3$ .35   SiO$_2$ 3.5

CaO .6

MgO .157

Since this hypothetical glaze is purely an example of the calculation process, any feldspar could be used. In this case, the no-longer-available "Buckingham feldspar" is used, which has the formula:

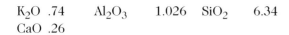

K_2O .74 Al_2O_3 1.026 SiO_2 6.34
CaO .26

In this example it will be seen that all of the K_2O and some of the CaO, Al_2O_3, and SiO_2 will be supplied by the feldspar. The rest of the formula can be made up with magnesium carbonate, dolomite, or talc to satisfy the MgO, and with clay and silica for satisfying the remaining alumina and silica.

A chart at the bottom of the page is constructed for ease of calculating:

In order to find out how much Buckingham feldspar can be used in this formula, the figure of K_2O .243 must be divided by .74, the amount of K_2O in the feldspar. This follows the method given in the previous problem, namely that of dividing the amount of the oxide needed in the formula by the amount which is supplied by the raw material. In this case, the answer is:

wanted in the formula - .243
have in the materials - .74 - .33 molecular equivalent of feldspar used to fill the formula obtained, .33, and the amounts are tabulated in the appropriate column. The MgO is then filled with dolomite, which brings with it an equal amount of CaO. The remaining CaO is filled with calcium carbonate, and clay and silica are used to complete the formula. The batch is determined in the usual way by multiplying the molecular equivalents of the various materials by the equivalent weights of the materials to obtain the batch weights:

Buckingham feldspar	.33 x 571 =	177.43
Dolomite	.157 x 184 =	28.88
Calcium carbonate	.357 x 100 =	35.7
Clay	.012 x 258 =	3.09
Silica	1.486 x 60 =	89.2
	Total	334.3

	K_2O .243	CaO .600	MgO .157	Al_2O_3 .350	SiO_2 3.50
Buckingham feldspar .33	.243	.086		.338	1.99
	0	.514		.012	1.51
Dolomite .157		.157	.157		
		.357	0		
Calcium carbonate .357		.357			
		0			
Clay .12				.012	.024
				0	1.486
Silica 1.486					1.486
					0

To bring this to a percentage batch for easy percentage additions of colorants or opacifiers, simply divide each ingredient by the total, as follows:

Buckingham Feldspar	177.43	÷-	334.3	=	53.07
Dolomite	28.88	÷	334.3	=	8.63
Calcium Carbonate	35.7	÷	334.3	=	10.68
Clay	3.09	÷	334.3	=	0.92
Silica	89.2	÷	334.3	=	26.68
				Total	99.98

These final figures can be weighed out as grams, pounds, kilograms or tons and will always be the same ratios.

Calculating Glaze Formulas from Batches or Recipes

1. An Example of Determining the Formula of a Glaze from a Recipe

An example is now given which will illustrate the derivation of a glaze formula from the batch or recipe. This has already been illustrated by a simple problem in Chapter 6. The following will indicate the method when numerous oxides are involved. Suppose that the need arises to know the formula of a glaze with the following composition:

Buckingham feldspar	45
Colemanite	10
Talc	10
Dolomite	10
Whiting	5
Zinc oxide	5
Clay	5
Flint	30

To find the formula of this combination of raw materials, start by dividing the quantity of each material by its equivalent weight. It will be seen that the procedure in solving this problem is essentially the reverse of the method used for calculating the batch from the formula.

Buckingham spar	45	÷	571	=	.078
Colemanite	10	÷	206	=	.048
Talc	10	÷	378	=	.026
Dolomite	10	÷	184	=	.054
Calcium carbonate	5	÷	100	=	.05
Zinc oxide	5	÷	81	=	.061
Clay	5	÷	258	=	.019
Silica	30	÷	60	=	.5

Next a chart is constructed which allows for the tabulation of the molecular equivalents of the various materials in a vertical column at the left. Across the top are arranged horizontally the oxides which are known to occur in the raw materials. Then the molecular equivalent of each raw material is multiplied by the quantity of each oxide in its formula, and the answer posted in the appropriate column. The totals of the columns are the number of molecular weights of the various oxides in the glaze.

The totals of the various oxides are now arranged as a formula:

K_2O	.057	Al_2O_3	.098	SiO_2	1.136
Na_2O	.020				
CaO	.152	B_2O_3	.072		
MgO	.132				
ZnO	.061				
	.422				

	K_2O	Na_2O	CaO	MgO	ZnO	Al_2O_3	B_2O_3	SiO_2
Buckingham spar .078	.057	.02				.079		.494
Colemanite .048			.048				.072	
Talc .026				.078				.104
Dolomite .054			.054	.054				
Calcium carbonate .05			.05					
Zinc oxide .061					.061			
Clay .019						.019		.038
Silica .5								.5
Totals =	.057	.02	.152	.132	.061	.098	.072	1.136

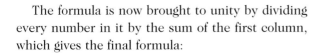

The formula is now brought to unity by dividing every number in it by the sum of the first column, which gives the final formula:

K_2O .132
Na_2O .047 Al_2O_3 .23 SiO_2 2.69
CaO .360
MgO .312 B_2O_3 .17
ZnO .144

2. Steps in Calculating from the Batch to the Formula

The steps in calculating from the batch or recipe of a glaze to the formula may be summarized as follows:

1. Divide the quantity of each material by the equivalent weight of that material.
2. Construct a chart with all the oxides in the materials arranged horizontally across the top and the raw materials listed vertically at the left.
3. Multiply the molecular equivalent of each raw material as determined in step 1 by the quantity of each oxide in its formula, and post the answers in the appropriate columns.
4. Add the columns for each oxide.
5. Arrange the quantities of the oxides in the manner of a formula.
6. Bring the formula to unity by dividing all quantities in it by the sum of the first column.

Practical Problems in Glaze Calculation

Discussion of some practical problems will make the reasons for calculating glazes clearer. Glaze calculation is a method of arriving at suitable compositions of materials for glazes, and for changing, adjusting, and comparing glazes without resorting to more trial and error in the laboratory than is necessary. Methods of arriving at original glaze compositions are discussed in a later chapter.

1. Comparison of Glazes

It is very difficult to compare two glaze recipes because the list of raw materials does not tell the relative amount of the oxides present, and it is the proportion of oxides in a glaze that is the controlling factor in melting and in surface quality. Glaze formulas, on the other hand, are easy to compare.

For example, suppose there were a comparison of the two recipes for cone 9 glazes given:

Glaze A		*Glaze B*	
Custer feldspar	52.2	Custer feldspar	149
Kona F4 feldspar	42.8	Dolomite	46
G-200 feldspar	93.9	Calcium carbonate	25
Dolomite	18.8	Clay	25.8
Talc	30.2	Silica	120
Calcium carbonate	45.0		
Zinc oxide	2.0		
Clay	30.9		
Silica	74.1		

Actually, Glaze A is a semi-opaque, satiny glaze and Glaze B is opaque and quite matte. But in the recipes as shown, it is rather hard to account for this difference, especially since in this case the recipes are not given in percentage amounts. It can only be guessed as to how much calcium oxide, or magnesium oxide, percentage-wise, there is in the two glazes.

Reduced to formula, the two glazes have the following composition:

Glaze A
K_2O .144 Al_2O_3 .367 SiO_2 3.120
Na_2O .096 Fe_2O_3 .002 TiO_2 .001
CaO .467
MgO .274
ZnO .020

Glaze B
K_2O .162 Al_2O_3 .348 SiO_2 3.936
Na_2O .073 Fe_2O_3 .002 TiO_2 .001
CaO .512
MgO .253

In the formulas it can be seen at once the relative amounts of the various oxides in the glazes and can compare them intelligently.

2. Substitution of Materials

Glaze calculation is useful in making substitutions of materials in glazes. If, for example, a particular frit or feldspar becomes unavailable, another material can easily be substituted with the knowledge of exactly how to change the recipe without altering the balance of oxides present in the glaze. To make such a substitution by trial and error would involve considerable laboratory work. It would be necessary to make numerous tests and fire them until the correct amount of new materials was arrived at.

Suppose, for example, that the goal is to continue using the following glaze even though "Ontario spar" was no longer available.

Ontario spar
K_2O	.75
NA_2O	.25
Al_2O_3	1.1
SiO_2	7.5

Formula weight = 647

Glaze
K_2O	.3
Na_2O	.1
CaO	.5
MgO	.1
Al_2O_3	.44
SiO_2	3.50

Glaze batch
Ontario spar	258.8
Calcium carbonate	40.0
Dolomite	18.4
Silica	30.0

Substituting nepheline syenite for Ontario spar:

Nepheline syenite =
KNaO   1 Al_2O_3 1.108 SiO_2 4.652

The revised batch is therefore:

Nepheline syenite	184.8
Calcium carbonate	40.0
Dolomite	18.4
Silica	98.4
Total	341.6

Although these two glazes are made up of different raw materials, their formula is the same. It is always more convenient to have the glaze batch add up to one hundred as the percentage additions of colorants and opacifiers is made easier. This is done by adding up the total ingredients (341.6), dividing each ingredient by this total, nepheline syenite = .55, calcium carbonate = .117, dolomite = .054, silica = .289, then multiplying by one hundred to get the final percentage batch:

Nepheline syenite	55
Calcium carbonate	11.7
Dolomite	5.4
Silica	28.9
Total	100.0

Frits, which are described later, are calculated in the same manner as feldspars.

3. Altering Glaze Formulas

There are many times when a potter feels it is desirable or necessary to change a glaze in order to alter its appearance, to make it mature at a different temperature, or to improve its fit to the clay body. Glaze calculation provides a method for making such changes rationally, with a minimum of trial and error. It is very difficult to make changes by altering the batch of a glaze, because the changed balance of oxides in the finished glaze cannot be accurately known. It is very simple, on the other hand, to make changes in the formula and to calculate the new glaze batch.

In practice, it is possible, and sometimes desirable, to change a glaze by simply adding some material. If the aim is to make a glaze more matte, for instance, clay could be added to the glaze in progressively larger amounts until the right surface quality had been achieved. But if the proposed alteration requires exact readjustment, it is much more logical to make the change in the formula. When making a change in the formula, it can be seen at a glance just how the ratio of the various oxides has been altered.

A simple example will illustrate the usefulness of glaze calculation in this connection. Suppose the following glaze at cone 04 is not bright and shiny enough:

White lead	154.8
Calcium carbonate	20.0
Potash spar	55.6
Zinc oxide	8.1
Clay	50.6
Silica	108.0

Calculate the formula of this recipe to be:

PbO	.6	Al_2O_3	.3	SiO_2	2.8
CaO	.2				
KNaO	.1				
ZnO	.1				

The formula reveals too much alumina and too much silica for a bright glaze at cone 04. The formula might be rewritten:

PbO	.6	Al_2O_3	.2	SiO_2	2.00
CaO	.2				
KNaO	.1				
ZnO	.1				

When calculating the batch from this formula, the revised glaze is:

White lead	154.8	÷ 336.3	=	46
Calcium carb	20.0	÷ 336.3	=	5.9
Potash spar	55.6	÷ 336.3	=	16.5
Zinc oxide	8.1	÷ 336.3	=	2.4
Clay	25.8	÷ 336.3	=	7.7
Silica	72.0	÷ 336.3	=	21.4
Total		336.3	=	99.9

4. Trying Out New Materials

Glaze calculation is very useful when some new material is being tried out in a glaze. If the chemical composition of the new material is known, it can be introduced into the glaze in the proper amount with a minimum of trial and error. Suppose, for example, that the wish is to try out some wood ash in a glaze. If the chemical analysis of the ash were available, its formula could be calculated the usual way of dealing with compound materials such as feldspars.

Chemical composition of an ash:

SiO_2	42.3%
Al_2O_3	12.8
Fe_2O_3	1.4
CaO	26.3
K2O	10.2
MgO	7.0

Formula derived from the chemical composition:

$$\left.\begin{array}{ll} K_2O & .15 \\ CaO & .63 \\ MgO & .21 \end{array}\right\} \begin{array}{l} Al_2O_3 \\ .15 \end{array} \left\{\begin{array}{l} SiO_2 \\ .94 \end{array}\right.$$

When the formula of the ash has been obtained, it can be used in a glaze with due regard for the amounts of various oxides present. In the ash given above it will be seen that the material by itself is too low in alumina and silica to be, by itself, a successful high-fired glaze. It would need the addition of clay, silica, and perhaps feldspar to make it practical as a glaze.

In a later section, the method of originating new glazes is described; according to this procedure, the ash described above could easily be incorporated into a new glaze which would be likely to perform in a predictable way. The method of originating new glazes will be more understandable in light of more information about the composition of glazes and the makeup of various types of glazes as discussed in the next two chapters.

The examples of glaze calculating given above cover all the problems encountered in calculating glazes from their formulas.

As stated at the beginning of this section concerning calculation, computer software programs generally take all of the mathematical drudgery out of calculation processes. They become a tool for quick and easy comparisons, simple calculation of replacement materials, and a fascinating opportunity to understand the basic structures of the glazes we use and develop. However, if a computer and the relevant software is not available, this is the method that needs to be followed. No wonder so many people are bemused and confused and go little further into this amazing medium!

14 THE COMPOSITION OF GLAZES

1. Fusion Points of Glazes

It is now necessary to consider in more detail the composition of glazes and the design of glaze formulas to control the temperature of melting, the texture, and the response to the addition of coloring oxides.

Combinations of oxides ordinarily have lower melting points than some of the oxides in the mixtures. When two oxides are intimately mixed and then subjected to heat, their melting point is often considerably below that of either of the oxides heated separately. The proportion of two oxides which has the lowest melting point is called the eutectic. This tendency of combinations of materials to have a lower melting point than either of the materials making up the combination is of great importance in glaze making, since it enables fluid mixtures to be made from combinations of largely refractory oxides. To verify this fact, make the following experiment: mix feldspar and calcium carbonate dry in three different proportions: 50% of each, 25% feldspar and 75% calcium, and 25% calcium and 75% feldspar. If these mixtures, together with pure calcium and pure feldspar, are made into mounds and fired on tiles in a kiln to about cone 8, the proportion of 25% calcium and 75% feldspar will have melted into a glass, while the feldspar will have only sintered into a stiff mass; and the calcium, changed by the fire into quick lime, will not have melted at all. Such "fusion button" tests are actually very useful in determining the effect on melting of various combinations of materials.

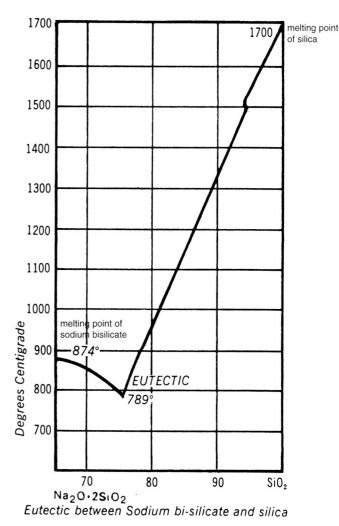

Eutectic between Sodium bi-silicate and silica

The diagram above illustrates the eutectic between sodium bisilicate and silica. Sodium bisilicate has a melting point of 874°C. Silica has a melting point in the neighborhood of 1700°C, yet when more silica is added to sodium bisilicate, its melting point is lowered to 789°C.

Glaze composition must be controlled so that, at the desired temperature, the glaze will melt and smooth itself out over the ware in a glassy coating. This fusion point is controlled by (a) the kinds of oxides present in the glaze and (b) the relative amount of these oxides. Melting is brought about by the interaction of the various oxides on one another when subjected to heat. Since most glazes contain numerous oxides, the reactions involved in the fusion of the materials into a glass are complex, and it is difficult to predict the exact temperature at which any given combination of glaze materials will melt. The formula of a glaze, however, gives a reasonably certain basis for predicting the melting point of the glaze within a cone or two.

The fusion point of a glaze may be lowered by:

1. Increasing the amount of active fluxes such as lead oxide, soda, or potash.

2. Adding more fluxing oxides to the composition of the glaze. For example, a glaze may be made to melt at a lower temperature by adding lead oxide, soda, potash, zinc oxide, or boric oxide.

3. Decreasing the amount of silica and alumina in the glaze.

4. Decreasing the more inactive fluxes, such as magnesia and barium oxide, in favor of more active fluxes.

5. Adding coloring oxides, such as iron, cobalt, or copper, which in themselves are active fluxes.

6. Grinding the materials more finely or introducing the oxides in the form of a frit rather than in the raw state, which may lower the melting point of the glaze.

The fusion point of a glaze may be raised by a reverse of these procedures.

It will be obvious that the melting point of any glaze must be known and under control before it can be successfully used, and that a glaze suitable for the lower ranges of temperatures will not be suitable for higher temperatures.

2. Fluxing Action of the Various Oxides

Chart 1 (page 198) shows the approximate tem-perature range of the fluxes commonly used in glazes, along with the approximate color in the kiln at the time. Each of these oxides, of course, has a specific melting point, and it will be seen that these melting points vary widely. Magnesium oxide, for instance, has a melting point of 2800°C, while lead oxide melts at 886°C. It must be remembered, however, that in combination with other oxides even a material which, by itself, has a very high melting point may function as a flux.

The chart shows each oxide represented by a solid line in that range of temperature, indicated by pyrometric cones, where it may be useful as a flux. The dotted portion of the line shows the temperature range at which the oxide may be less useful. The temperature range of these fluxes may be summarized as follows:

1. Lead oxide is an active flux from the lowest temperatures up to about cone 5. Beyond this temperature, lead becomes increasingly volatile and is seldom used.

2. Potassium and sodium are useful as fluxes throughout the temperature range. Both of these oxides are very potent fluxes.

3. The alkaline earths calcium, magnesium, strontium, and barium are active fluxes only at high temperatures, and below cone 4 they may inhibit rather than promote fusion.

4. Zinc oxide is useful as a flux from about cone 1 to the highest temperatures. Used in small amounts, it may function as a catalyst in promoting the fusion of other oxides.

Chart 2 (page 199) shows the approximate quantity of the various fluxing oxides found in glazes of various maturing temperatures. Such a chart is necessarily only approximate, since it does not take into account the interaction between the oxides, which is actually the controlling factor in the melting of the glaze. In this chart the quantity of the oxides is given for the different cones. By following the line for PbO, for example, it can be seen that at cone 04 about .7 of lead is apt to be found in a formula. Of course, if B_2O_3 were present in the glaze also, the amount of lead would be much less. The chart illustrates the fact that as the temperature advances, the more active fluxes - lead, soda, and potash - must be present in diminishing quantities, and the less active fluxes - CaO and MgO - may be

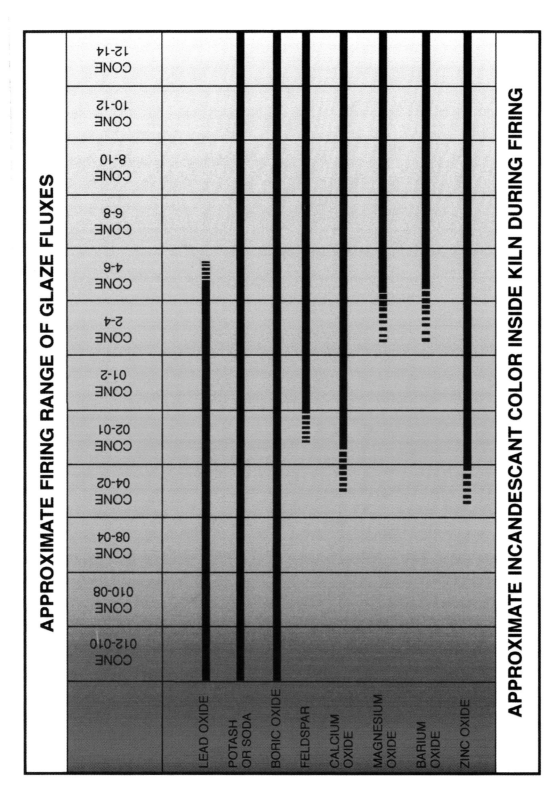

CHART 1

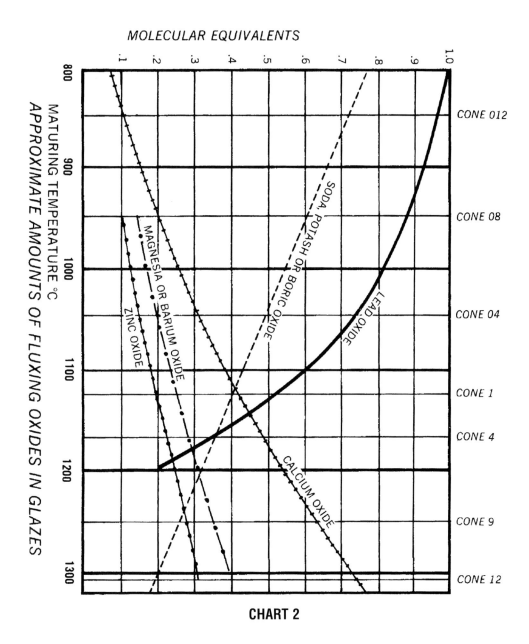

CHART 2

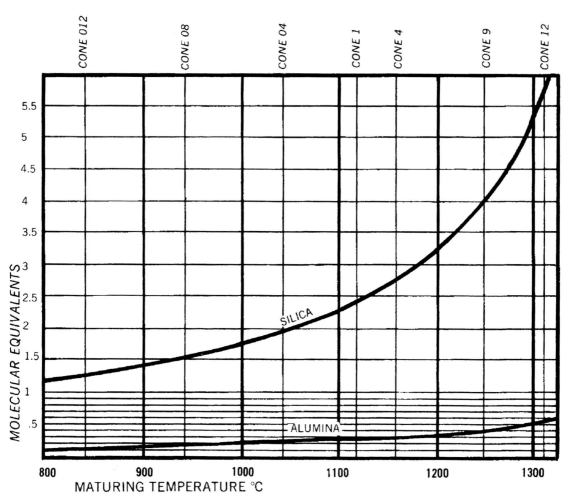

APPROXIMATE AMOUNTS OF SILICA AND ALUMINA IN GLAZES

CHART 3

increased in amount as the temperature becomes higher. It must be emphasized that such a chart may be used only as an approximate guide.

3. The Amounts of Silica and Alumina in Glazes

The amount of silica and alumina is always critical in glazes, since the amount of silica relative to the amount of the combined fluxes is the factor that largely controls the melting point. The amount of alumina always has a significant influence on the surface and texture of the glaze. Chart 3, which is constructed similarly to Chart 2, shows the probable amounts of silica and alumina found in glazes of various maturing temperatures. The amount of these two oxides increases with the temperature. However, it will be noted that there is more similarity between high and low-temperature glazes with respect to the amount of silica and alumina present than there is with respect to the makeup of the RO column and the amount of oxides in it. The amount of silica relative to the amount of alumina is shown graphically in this chart, and it illustrates the relative preponderance of the former. In general, the relative quantity of these two oxides is quite constant at the various temperatures. The general rule is that the silica will be three times the alumina, plus one, but there are so many exceptions to this rule that it can seldom be applied. It will be noted from the chart that even in the lowest temperature glazes the amount of silica does not usually fall below one molecular equivalent, and that even in the highest temperature glazes the amount of alumina does not exceed one molecular equivalent. An excess of silica in a glaze makes it too refractory and may cause devitrification. Not enough silica will make a glaze soft and liable to crazing. Too much alumina will cause glazes to be harsh, matte, opaque, and scratchy in surface, while not enough alumina will cause the glaze to run from vertical surfaces. Again, the amount of silica and alumina in

a glaze is dependent on what other oxides are present and in what amount. For example, if a large amount of some powerful flux such as lead is present in a glaze, the amount of silica and alumina can be correspondingly higher. Since silica and alumina lend the valuable properties of hardness, durability, and fit to glazes, they are introduced in as large amounts as possible.

4. Limit Formulas

Another way of stating the amounts of the various oxides which are apt to be found in glazes of various temperatures is the limit formula. The limit formula indicates the maximum and minimum amount of each oxide likely to occur in a glaze of a given maturing temperature. Limit formulas could be constructed for each pyrometric cone, but in practice a limit formula for each range of four or five cones is sufficient to aid in the formulation of glazes.

Since the amounts of the various oxides in any glaze are very much determined by the kind of oxides present and their relative quantity, limit formulas can serve to indicate the composition of glazes only in the most general fashion. For example, if the limit formula for cone 9 glazes indicates that magnesia may be found in amounts ranging from zero to .35 molecular equivalents, it serves to remind us only of the outside limits for the use of magnesia; and when it comes to assigning an exact amount for this oxide, the amount of B_2O_3 present must be known, as well as how matte the glaze must be, how much alumina is present, and other such facts which, taken together, determine the amount of MgO correct for a particular glaze. There are many variables to consider.

In spite of the fact that limit formulas assign values to the various oxides only within broad limits, they are useful in indicating the composition of glazes in a general way. The following limit formulas are given for the different temperature ranges and types of glazes.

Limit Formula Examples

Cone 012 - 08 Lead Glazes

PbO	.7 - 1	Al_2O_3	.05	SiO_2	1. - 1.5
KNaO	0 - .3				
ZnO	0 - .1				
CaO	0 - .2				

Cone 08 - 01 Lead Glazes

PbO	.7 - 1	AL_2O_3	.1 - .25	SiO_2	1.5 - 2.00
KNaO	0 - .3				
ZnO	0 - .2				
CaO	0 - .3				

Cone 08 - 04 Alkaline Glazes

PbO	0 - .5	Al_2O_3	.05 - .25	SiO2	1.5 - 2.5
KNaO	.4 - .8				
CaO	0 - .3				
ZnO	0 - .2				

Cone 08 - 04 Lead - Calcium Borate

PbO	.2 - .60	Al_2O_3	.15 - .2	SiO_2	1.5 - 2.5
KNaO	.1 - .25	B_2O_3	.15 - .6		
CaO	.3 - .60				
ZnO	.1 - .15				
BaO	0 - .15				

Cone 2 - 5 Lead Glazes

PbO	.4 - .60	Al_2O_3	.2 - .28	SiO_2	2. - 3.
CaO	.1 - .40				
ZnO	.0 - .25				
KNaO	0 - .25				

Cone 2 - 5 Calcium Borate Glazes

CaO	.2 - .50	Al_2O_3	.2 - .28	SiO_2	2. - 3.
ZnO	.1 - .40	B_2O_3	.3 - .6		
ZnO	.1 - .25				
KNaO	.1 - .25				

Cone 2 - 5 Lead Boro-Silicate Glazes

PbO	.2 - .3	Al_2O_3	.25 - .35	SiO_2	2.5 - 3.5
KNaO	.1 - .40	B_2O_3	.3 - .6		
CaO	.35 - .5				
ZnO	0 - .1				

Cone 8 - 12 Stoneware or Porcelain Glazes

KNaO	.2 - .40	Al_2O_3	.2 - .28	SiO_2	2. - 3.
CaO	.4 - .70	B_2O_3	.1 - .3		
MgO	0 - .35				
ZnO	0 - .30				
BaO	0 - .30				

15 TYPES OF GLAZES

What has been said so far about glaze composition applies in a general way to all glazes. A more detailed examination of various types of glazes will help to clarify the reasons for the use of various materials. These various types of glazes will be considered as base, or colorless, glazes. The coloring oxides will be described later.

Glazes are extremely varied in appearance, with an almost infinite range of possible color and texture. However, all glazes do fall into a few distinct types. The fact that these types shade into one another makes any exact system of classification rather arbitrary; however, an understanding of glazes is greatly advanced by learning the characteristics of the most important types.

Glazes can, of course, be classified according to the temperature at which they mature. Glazes are also classified as to whether they are raw or fritted, an important distinction in the consideration of glaze batches. Fritted glazes are discussed more fully in a later section.

1. Low-temperature Alkaline Glazes

An alkaline glaze is one which depends on the alkalies, i.e., sodium, potassium, or lithium, for its flux rather than on lead, the alkaline earths - calcium, barium, strontium, and magnesium, or boric oxide. Any glaze that matures below about cone 02 might be called a low-fired glaze. Low-temperature alkaline glazes have been used for centuries to obtain colorful decorative surfaces for pottery. This is the general type of glaze used for the most beautiful of the early Islamic wares of Persia, Mesopotamia, and Egypt, as well as some of the more colorful types of Chinese pottery.

The characteristics of glazes of this general classification are (1) fluid melting and a tendency toward a glassy appearance, (2) softness, (3) a tendency to craze on most clay bodies, and (4) the property of brilliant color when coloring oxides are added to the glaze. Soda and potash are very active fluxes, and their presence in considerable quantity in a glaze makes for rather sudden melting at low temperatures. The danger of overfiring is naturally increased by the presence of violent fluxes in the glaze; and highly alkaline glazes, especially if the alumina content is low, may be difficult to fire and may run excessively if the intended temperature is even slightly overreached. As will be seen from the limit formula for this type of glaze, the sodium or potassium content may be as high as .7 molecular equivalents.

The presence of sodium or potassium in a glaze favors the production of brilliant strong colors from the addition of various coloring oxides. In alkaline glazes copper oxide gives intense hues of blue-green, turquoise, or blue. The famous "Egyptian blue" color which appears on ancient Egyptian faience is an alkaline glaze colored by copper. Cobalt in an alkaline glaze gives an intense blue. Iron gives strong shades of straw color or brown, and manganese gives rich hues of violet and grape-purple. The colors from these coloring oxides are more intense and scintillating in low-fired alkaline glazes than in any other type.

Although the alkaline glaze is tempting from the standpoint of color, some practical disadvantages must be allowed for. For one thing, the highly alkaline glaze is almost impossible to fit to a clay body without crazing. The causes and cures of crazing are discussed in detail later, but in this connection it may be said that the only way alkaline glazes can be made to fit is by bringing the composition of the clay so near to that of the glaze that the working properties and plasticity of the clay are seriously impaired. However, on decorative wares that do not need to be impervious to liquids and on vitreous wares with an impermeable body, the tendency of alkaline glazes to craze may not be a serious disadvantage. Their color and brilliance, in any case, are at their best on decorative rather than on utilitarian ware. The network of lines formed by the crazed glaze may in itself be considered a decorative embellishment. Acceptable crazing is euphemistically referred to as "crackle."

Another difficulty with highly alkaline glazes is the fact that, outside of the feldspars, insoluble sources of potassium and sodium are few. In low-temperature alkaline glazes the feldspars cannot be used as a source of significant amounts of alkali because they bring in too much alumina and silica. The use of feldspar as the principal flux is therefore limited to the high-temperature glazes. The choice, then, in compounding low-fired alkaline glazes is one either of using soluble materials such as soda ash or borax or of using frits containing the desired soda and potash. Considering the practical difficulties encountered in the use of soluble glaze materials, it is usually best to use fritted material.

Highly alkaline glazes are soft and easily scratched, and for this reason they are not suitable for use on ware intended for hard usage. Such glazes may also be slightly soluble, even after they are fired. Glass which is composed of sodium and silica alone, without any other oxide being present, is soluble. In glazes solubility is highly undesirable because it leads to the deterioration and destruction of the glaze by weathering in contact with water or the weak acids in foods. For this reason alkaline glazes must contain enough of the alkaline earths, calcium, barium, and magnesium, or alumina to prevent solubility. Alkaline glazes sometimes come from the kiln with a slight scum on them which can be scraped off. This is a sign of solubility, as is the tendency to become dull after a little use or exposure to water. Such glazes need more calcium, zinc, magnesium, or alumina in them to stabilize the glass and render it insoluble.

Alkaline glazes may be either transparent or opaque, depending on the presence of opacifiers or on the balance of oxides in the glaze. If an alkaline glaze contains an excess of silica, it may have an opaque sugary texture. If a clear alkaline glaze is desired to give the bluest color obtainable from copper, the alumina content of the glaze must be kept very low. This will, of course, make the glaze subject to running and therefore short in firing range.

Highly alkaline glazes have a high surface tension when melted, and this makes them subject to crawling. The glaze may draw up into beads of glass on the surface, leaving bare spots on the ware. This is most apt to happen when the glaze is being melted on already vitrified ware.

2. Lead Glazes

Lead glazes are extremely useful at temperatures ranging from the lowest ordinarily used for pottery glazes, about cone 012, up to about cone 6. Lead glazes have many advantages. They are reliable, easy to control, colorful, and durable enough for most purposes. The invention of lead glazes in the Near East, which occurred about 2500 B.C., was a milestone in the history of ceramics because for the first time really practical glazed ware became possible. Since then, most of the glazed earthenware in all parts of the world has been glazed with lead. Familiar historic lead-glazed wares include the glazed architectural terracottas of ancient Syria, the glazed tomb sculptures of the Tang Dynasty in China, the tankards and jugs of medieval Europe, the peasant wares of central Europe and England, Bennington pottery in the United States, and the colorful majolica and slip-decorated wares of Spain, Italy, and Mexico.

Lead oxide melts by itself at 886°C and cools to form a glass. The glass formed from fused lead oxide alone is too soft, however, to form a durable and insoluble glaze for pottery. But when lead is melted with silica and other oxides, it forms a practical and beautiful glass. The "crystal" used for the finest glasswares is a lead glass, and it is valued for its exceptional clarity and luster. The low melting point of lead oxide makes it possible to fuse lead glazes at relatively low temperatures, not much above red heat.

The charts and the limit formulas on pages 198, 199, and 202 indicate the approximate amounts of lead oxide required in glazes at various temperatures. In the low-fired glazes the amount of lead may be nearly all of the RO portion of the glaze. In the cone 4 to 6 range the amount of lead will be about

.3 molecular equivalents. Beyond cone 6 lead begins to reach its volatilization point and can no longer be used with consistent results. Above cone 6 feldspar, rather than lead, is the most commonly used flux. When lead glazes are used at temperatures above cone 6, some of the lead content of the glaze is burned out or lost by volatilization, and the glaze remaining on the piece may be dry and underfired in appearance.

Lead glazes flow to a smooth, even, glassy surface, and one of the distinguishing characteristics of lead-glazed ware is a bright shiny surface. Lead glazes are not necessarily shiny, however, since they can easily be matted or dulled by the addition of barium oxide or alumina. But the lead glaze is normally bright and smooth, and in ware which is to be used for food, this is a definite advantage.

The color range of lead glazes is wide. Most of the coloring oxides, when added to lead glazes, yield soft, bright, pleasing colors. Copper produces a rich grassy green color. While this green can be very beautiful, it may lack the appeal of the turquoise color which copper produces in an alkaline glaze. Manganese in a lead glaze is a soft brownish purple. Iron yields exceptionally warm and beautiful hues of tan, brown, and reddish brown. Small amounts of iron, up to 2%, give pleasing tan, honey color, or amber. Higher percentages of iron will give deep amber, brown, or red-brown, depending on the amount used. Transparent lead glaze used over red clay gives the familiar red-brown color of Mexican pottery, or the more subdued tan or brown of old European or Pennsylvania Dutch slipware.

Lead glazes that are opacified with tin oxide have a pleasant creamy quality. Iron and tin together in a high-lead glaze give a warm, mottled cream to rust color which is often very beautiful, especially over textures or patterns in relief in the clay, which are emphasized by the glaze. Base glazes fluxed with lead are used to produce the so-called aventurine glaze, which is a crystalline glaze colored with iron, and also chrome-red glazes, which are made at very low temperatures of between cone 012 and 06. Both of these kinds of glazes are described in more detail in the section on special glazes.

Lead glazes fired at cone 2 to cone 6 have a more subdued color than the very active high-lead glazes at the lower temperatures. But the whole range of lead glazes can be handsome and adaptable to many purposes. When transparent, lead glazes may beautifully reveal slips or underglaze color; and when opacified, particularly with tin oxide, they make ideal majolica backgrounds or solid-color glazes.

The disadvantages of lead glazes include the danger of poisoning, which has already been described. Another disadvantage is the softness of lead glazes. Low-fired lead-glazed ware is easily scratched and in hard use will become covered with fine scratches that give the glaze a dull appearance. The lead glaze on old pieces is frequently badly worn or decomposed. In the case of ancient wares such as the pottery of the Han Dynasty in China or that of medieval Europe and Persia, the glaze may be mostly worn off or disintegrated by centuries of exposure to atmosphere and dampness. Lead glazes, after long exposure to moisture, may take on an iridescent color, which, in the case of some old wares, has undoubtedly enhanced a glaze that may originally have been quite garish and harsh in color when it first came from the kiln.

Lead glazes fired above cone 01 are relatively durable and give good service in all ordinary usage. Admittedly, lead glazes are not as durable as the more highly fired stoneware and porcelain glazes, but the potential of their color range and reliability may more than outweigh any deficiency in hardness.

Glazes containing some raw lead oxide are easy to apply because the lead, particularly if lead carbonate is used, makes the raw glaze dry on the ware in a hard coating, not easily dusted off or damaged in setting the ware in the kiln. However, if a glaze contains a very high percentage of white lead, cracking may be noted in the raw glaze coat. This is caused by the shrinkage of the white lead and can be corrected by replacing some of the raw lead with a frit or by adding a gum to the glaze.

Lead glazes will not withstand reducing atmospheres in the kiln and must be fired with an excess of air. Lead oxide is easily reduced to the metal lead. In a reducing atmosphere it turns grey or black, and the escape of gases from the glaze will most likely cause it to boil and blister. Prominent blisters on a lead-glazed piece may almost always be traced to reduction in the kiln. In electric kilns, or in kilns which can be controlled to give a clear atmosphere, lead glazes should not blister. Where gas, oil, or wood is used as a fuel, lead-glazed ware is ordinarily protected from direct contact with the flame by muffles or saggers. Fritted lead glazes are less liable to blister from contact with flame than are raw lead glazes.

3. Glazes Containing Boron

Boric oxide is a strong flux, and many glazes depend principally on it for fusion. There are few natural sources of boric oxide which are insoluble, and for this reason the oxide is commonly introduced into the glaze batch in the form of a frit. When available, colemanite or Gerstley borate provided a source of B_2O_3, which is practically insoluble; for this reason it became a very popular glaze material, especially with studio potters. Other materials such as Cadycal 100, Laguna borate, or frits like Pemco 54 and Ferro 3134, and others with similar properties will likely emerge to fill the void.

Very low-temperature glazes may be made with boric oxide, since its melting point is low - about 600°C. Combinations of boric oxide, soda, and lead may produce very fluid glazes at dull red heat.

The color response of glazes which contain considerable B_2O_3 is strong, with a tendency toward high-keyed color, more akin to the alkaline type of glaze than to lead glazes. Copper, in a high-boron glaze, gives a brilliant greenish turquoise, and cobalt a rich deep blue. Iron colors, however, tend to be rather dull and undistinguished compared to their brilliance in high-lead glazes.

Boric oxide may give a milky opacity to glazes. This opacity or opalescence results from the optical properties of the glaze. When traces of iron are present the glaze may be bluish in color. This tendency of high B_2O_3 glazes to turn a milky blue may be exploited to advantage by the addition of small amounts of coloring oxides such as copper, rutile, and ilmenite. The result may be spectacularly varied glaze surfaces of considerable interest.

Glazes high in boric oxide have a tendency to boil during melting, and when they reach complete fusion and smooth out, the remains of the boiling phase may appear as mottled spots or alligator-skin patterns. This surface texture is favored by the presence of rutile and zinc. Although the breakup of color may be very noticeable on a flat tile, the flow which occurs when the glaze is put on a vertical surface usually destroys it and results merely in some streaks.

The lead-boro-silicate glaze is commonly used on tableware. It is smooth, reasonably hard, and has a bright blemish-free surface. Such glazes, in the range of cone 2 to cone 6, are made by combining lead frits and boric oxide frits with feldspar, whiting, zinc, and other raw ingredients. In the tableware industry, glazes are carefully milled, precisely applied, and accurately fired in a clear atmosphere. This results in the flawless surface demanded by commercial standards.

4. Bristol Glazes

Bristol glazes are middle-temperature glazes, cone 2 to cone 6, which depend on zinc oxide as their principal flux. This type of glaze was developed in England to replace the lead glaze when the poisonous nature of raw lead compounds had become a health hazard in the growing pottery industry. In the middle range of temperature it is possible to make fairly fluid glazes without lead by carefully proportioning zinc oxide, calcium, and feldspar. The Bristol type of glaze is opaque, rather stiff, and not as smooth and bright as the typical lead glaze. It has the color response typical of high-zinc glazes, namely, rather poor and muddy colors from iron oxide, good greens and blues from copper and cobalt, and brown colors from chromium.

Calcined zinc oxide should be used in Bristol glazes to avoid the high shrinkage and possible cracking and crawling which may result from too much raw zinc in the batch. The Bristol glaze, because of its rather viscous and pasty consistency when melted, is very subject to pitting and pinholing. Since lead oxide is now available in fritted form, and since the Bristol type of glaze is difficult to use, it is actually an outmoded kind of glaze. The Bristol glaze can be handsome, however. It is at its best on ware which is light in color, rather thickly glazed, and colorful.

5. Porcelain and Stoneware Glazes

Leadless glazes fired above cone 6 or cone 7 may be called porcelain or stoneware glazes, depending on the kind of ware upon which they are used. Porcelain glazes are generally considered to be clear, smooth, colorless glazes made up with feldspar and calcium as the principal flux and fired to cone 9 or higher.

Porcelain glazes can be relatively simple in composition. Feldspar alone melts at around cone 9 or 10, and little other material need be added to it to make an acceptable glaze. For this reason high-fired glazes are generally simpler in composition than low-fired glazes. It is a simpler problem to make a glaze at cone 9 than it is to make one at cone 06. Heat works for the potter, causing simple combinations of materials to fuse, and the chemically more active and temperamental fluxes such as soda, lead, and boric oxide may be replaced by the more slow-melting alkaline earths and the minor amount of alkalies which are combined in feldspar.

Good high-fired glazes can be made from such simple combinations as: 85 parts feldspar and 15 parts calcium; or 60 parts feldspar, 20 parts silica, and 20 parts calcium. Some porcelain bodies are not too far from a glaze in composition and can be made into a glaze by the addition of about 20% more feldspar and 10% of calcium. Some form of feldspar is the most important ingredient of most high-fired glazes. Feldspar is really a natural glaze by itself, a frit formed by nature which combines the alkalies needed for flux with alumina and silica. Although all the different feldspars are quite similar in melting point, there is enough difference to make them not interchangeable in high-fired glazes, although in low-fired glazes a different feldspar may often be substituted without any difference in the fired result being noted.

High-fired glazes that contain considerable calcium oxide - .5 to .7 molecular equivalents - are usually transparent and tend to be bright. They have the dense, smooth, hard, jade-like surface which is admired in porcelain. In reduction, glazes of this type containing small amounts of iron will produce beautiful celadon colors, especially if small amounts of barium are also present. Copper reds may also be produced in glazes which are high in calcium oxide, especially if considerable sodium and potash are present.

High-fired glazes high in magnesia tend to be somewhat opaque, smooth, and "fat" in surface. The Chinese likened such glazes to "congealed mutton fat," and glazes of this character have been much admired on old Chinese stoneware. Certainly the high-magnesia glaze is one of the most beautiful in the whole range of pottery glazes. There is some danger of pitting and pinholing, however, because of the high viscosity of the glaze and also because there is some chance that overfiring will radically alter the appearance of the glaze by making it shiny and transparent.

High-fired glazes that contain considerable zinc oxide - from .15 to .3 molecular equivalents - may have a rather sugary look, with areas of matteness and shine on the same piece. Color is apt to be broken; and if the glaze contains rutile, the result may be highly textured. High-zinc glazes are temperamental, and pitting and pinholing may be hard to control.

In general, high-fired glazes have the advantages of being very hard, durable, and resistant to acids and to decay, and, if they are properly compounded and fired, they may be free from defects such as crazing and irregularities of surface. Besides these practical advantages, high-fired glazes have a sensuous appeal because of their dense hard surface and their characteristic soft muted colors. High-fired glazes appear to be more a part of the piece, more related to the clay of the pot, than do glazes matured at lower temperatures. In the case of porcelain, where the body itself is approaching a glassy condition, body and glaze may be very similar, and the line between the two is hard to detect even on a broken piece. At the higher temperatures there is more reaction between body and glaze. Stoneware glazes may be rock-like in color and texture and may reflect and reveal the earthy origins of pottery. The true character of stoneware glazes is very difficult to simulate at lower temperatures.

Brilliant color is not usually a characteristic of high-fired glazes, which are best suited for greyed, subtle colors. Strong colors are possible from copper and cobalt, but they do not have the vibrancy of the same colorants in low-fired alkaline glazes. At higher temperatures, manganese, iron, and vanadium yield noticeably more subdued colors than at the lower temperatures.

High-fired glazes have an appeal for the potter quite aside from the inherent practical advantages of the finished ware. Part of this appeal lies in the drama of extreme heat, which can melt and fuse hard earthy materials. At about cone 9 the color in the kiln becomes a bright yellow, and this color seems to symbolize the transmutations of the fire. Then too, the traditions of pottery reserve a special place for high-fired stoneware and porcelain, since these represented in their origin a magnificent technical achievement. The classic stonewares and porcelains of the Song Dynasty in China will probably always stand as pinnacles of excellence in the potter's art.

16 ORIGINATING GLAZE FORMULAS

1. Originating Glazes as Percentage Recipes

The question may arise as to how glaze formulas are arrived at and how the exact amounts in the formula are decided upon. Some information on this may be gained from the charts and limit formulas already given in Chapter 14. But here specific procedures will be outlined for originating new formulas.

Historically, glazes were originated by trial-and-error methods. Potters simply tried various materials in various percentages, rejecting those that did not work and making the most of those that did. We have the story of Bernard Palissy's long search for glazes which would simulate those then in use in Italy. He simply tried everything, even burning the furniture in his workshop to keep the kiln firing, hoping to hit upon the secret. Until late in the last century the whole art of glaze making was dependent on blind experimentation of this sort, and there was little scientific understanding of the results.

Modern-day potters can originate glazes very much in the manner of the old potters, by mixing, percentage-wise, various materials, trying them out in the fire, then changing the mix and trying it again as many times as necessary until it works. Even a rudimentary knowledge of the materials will enable potters to proceed in this way. Suppose, for example, that the goal was to make an original glaze recipe for a low-fired leadless glaze. An elementary knowledge of glazes provides some information as to the probable composition of glazes of this type. For one thing, it could be assumed that calcium borate would be present in about 25% to 60% of the batch. Silica would have to be present and would probably make up about 15% to 30% of the batch. Calcium would be desirable and could be present in about 5% to 15% of the batch. Feldspar would also be desirable and could be added up to about 25% of the batch. Clay, which aids in the working properties of the raw glaze, should be added and could make up to 15% of the batch. With general limits such as these in mind, the glaze composition could be theorized as follows:

Calcium borate	50	(for flux)
Silica	20	(for hardness, stability, and insolubility)
Calcium carb	10	(for insolubility, hardness)
Feldspar	10	(for insolubility, auxiliary flux)
Clay	10	(for suspension, to slow the melt)

This mixture would represent a guess, founded on some knowledge and experience, as to what materials would give a satisfactory glaze at the intended temperature. The next step would be to try the glaze in the fire to see how it melted. It might be found to be too fluid, runny, and glassy, in which case the amount of calcium borate could be cut to, say, forty parts, and the feldspar increased to twenty. Or the clay might be raised at the expense of the calcium borate. If a more fusible glaze was desired, the amount of calcium borate could be raised, and the clay, feldspar, and silica lowered. If a number of corrected recipes were fired and the results studied, a workable composition could result.

Similar procedures could be followed for any type of glaze. Of course, the typical composition of glazes must be known to avoid missing the mark by a wide margin, but even if the first tries are not successful, adjustments can be made in the light of a few simple principles of glaze formulation. If the glaze is too dry and appears rough and underfired, more flux is needed. If, on the other hand, the glaze is too soft and fluid and tends to run, the more refractory and hard-to-melt materials in the glaze, such as silica, clay, barium, magnesia, and calcium must be increased. The composition may, of course, be altered to make it more opaque, more transparent, more matte, or more shiny.

In originating low-fired formulas it is logical to start with some active flux such as lead, calcium borate, sodium, or boron and make additions to it. For high-fired glazes feldspar is the best starting point, and other materials can be added to this to bring about the desired fusion and surface texture.

Experimental low-fired glazes can be tried out in a kiln, using the raku method of rapid firing. The new glaze mixture is spread on a small bisqued tile and thoroughly dried out. It is then placed directly into a hot kiln through an opening in the door, using metal tongs. After ten or fifteen minutes the tile is withdrawn and the completed glaze can be studied. Working in this way, a dozen shot-in-the-dark formulas can be tried out in a few hours. The inexperienced glaze maker will be surprised at how many of his hunches do, in fact, come out as successful glazes. For the potter interested in specific color development, the decision of which fluxes to use is most important. A wrong choice of flux can cause much frustration. (See the book *The Ceramic Spectrum* by Robin Hopper for further information on specific color development.)

2. Using the Molecular Formula in Originating Glazes

The method of arriving at the composition of glazes by adjusting the percentage of materials as outlined above is necessarily somewhat hit-or-miss. The reason for this is that when, say, 10% of feldspar is added, it is very difficult to keep track of the oxides that have been added with this material. In the recipe the balance of oxides is not indicated,

and there is no logical way of comparing formulas or of making changes intelligently with reference to the oxide content of the glaze. When the formula is used, on the other hand, it is easy to originate glazes of known molecular composition, and the control over the amounts of the various oxides in the glaze makes the result much more likely to be practical. By using the formula, so much of one oxide can be put into the glaze and so much of another, until the formula is filled according to the balance of oxides which is known to melt at a given temperature, and then the recipe or batch can be calculated in terms of the various raw materials. This is where computer software programs like *HyperGlaze* and *Insight* come in very handy, quickly adjusting the formula to any change. The limits of the amounts of the various oxides that can be used at the various temperatures and for the various kinds of glazes is indicated in the limit formulas already given and in the graphs showing the probable amounts of the various oxides in glazes of different melting points. The amounts given in the limit formulas are determined experimentally and have no significance other than the fact that these amounts generally give glazes which melt at the indicated temperature. As has been pointed out, the limit formula can only state in a general way the composition of glazes, since there are so many materials involved that their interaction creates a great many variables. For this reason it is not possible to formulate glazes on paper with very much assurance that such compositions will work in practice. All new compositions must be tried and, more likely than not, adjusted before they perform as desired. In this sense making up new glazes is always experimental, and although the use of the molecular formula makes the result more certain to be successful, it by no means eliminates the necessity for testing and for trial-and-error experimentation.

3. An Example of Writing a New Formula for a Glaze

To formulate a new glaze intelligently, a specific temperature and kind of glaze should be aimed at. The temperature at which a glaze is to be fired is, of course, a critical factor in determining its composition. And the different qualities of texture, opacity, and response to coloring oxides are critically influenced by the composition of the glaze. For example, a typical problem might be the development of a transparent cone 04 lead glaze. To make up a formula for this type of glaze, the following procedure might be appropriate:

The limit formula for cone 04 glazes indicates that the amount of lead oxide is apt to be between .3 and .8 molecular equivalents. Within this rather wide latitude of choice, .6 might be taken as a likely amount. If a matte or rough-surfaced glaze was desired, a smaller amount might be tried. If the lead is assigned a quantity of .6 molecular equivalents, .4 equivalents remain to be satisfied in the RO column. Since it is desirable to include feldspar in practically all glazes, a figure of .15 might be assigned to "KNaO," which means either Na_2O or K_2O or both in indefinite ratio. These alkalies are associated with feldspar and in raw glazes are usually added in the form of feldspar or in some fritted material. There are now .25 equivalents yet to be added to bring the RO column up to 1. Again consulting the limit formulas, note that CaO may be present in glazes of this type in amounts from 0 to .3. Since this oxide is a valuable one to have in any lead glaze, .2 might be the amount decided upon. After this addition of CaO, .05 remains to be added. This might be filled with zinc oxide, barium, or magnesia. In this case let us say that zinc is added for promoting a smooth clear glaze. The RO column of the proposed glaze is now:

PbO	.6
KNaO	.15
CaO	.2
ZnO	.05

The limit formula indicates that the alumina in a glaze of this type may be between .1 and .25 equivalents. Since this design is for a clear glaze, a figure of .15 might be estimated. Less alumina than this might make the glaze too fluid; more might cause opacity in the glaze.

Silica, according to the limit formula, may vary between 1.5 and 3. Since a high figure for the lead has been indicated, the silica can be quite high also, and a figure of 2.5 might be decided upon. The glaze now reads:

PbO	.6				
KNaO	.15	Al_2O_3	.15	SiO_2	2.5
CaO	.2				
ZnO	.05				

With the arrival at a formula for the projected glaze, the next step is to calculate the glaze into terms of raw materials. From such a batch recipe a small amount of glaze can be weighed out and fired on a test tile. Sometimes a new glaze formula will come from the fire with just the intended properties, but more often some adjustments have to be made in the composition.

4. Originating a Formula Based on the Properties of a Particular Material

It will be noted that in the above example, when a value was assigned to the oxide "KNaO," the material feldspar was intended. Actually, when a new glaze formula is written, the raw materials must be carefully considered as well as the oxides, and new glazes commonly have as their starting point some raw material or combination of raw materials. Suppose, for example, that the relatively low melting point of the material nepheline syenite has been observed and the wish is to make a cone 9 glaze incorporating a high percentage of this material into its composition. The formula of nepheline syenite is:

.75	Na_2O	Al_2O_3	1.1	SiO_2	4.5
.25	K_2O				

This formula is fairly close to a cone 9 formula as it stands, and, in fact, nepheline syenite melts to a stiff glass at cone 9. However, it is too high in alumina and silica to be a practical cone 9 glaze, and the alkaline ingredients of the RO column make it craze on most bodies. It may be decided, then, since most cone 9 glazes have, at the most about .5 alumina, that the new glaze could be made up of about half nepheline syenite. Taking half of the nepheline syenite formula (.5) all the way through gives the following quantities:

.375	Na_2O	Al_2O_3	.55	SiO_2	2.25
.125	K_2O				

Here, in effect, the formula of the material has been split in two. The formula must now be filled in to bring it to unity. An addition of .4 CaO might be tried, since in cone 9 formulas it is common for this oxide to be as high as .7 equivalents. To fill in the remaining .1, MgO might be added, which could be

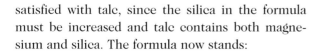

satisfied with talc, since the silica in the formula must be increased and talc contains both magnesium and silica. The formula now stands:

$$
\begin{array}{lll}
.375 & Na_2O & \\
.125 & K_2O & \quad Al_2O_3 \;\; .55 \quad SiO_2 \; 2.38 \\
.4 & CaO & \\
.1 & MgO &
\end{array}
$$

The glaze now appears to be workable except for the silica which, even after the addition of the talc, is too low. By bringing the silica up to a figure of 3.00, the glaze might be considered complete, and the glaze batch could be calculated using nepheline syenite, calcium carbonate, talc, and silica.

In this example the procedure was to (1) start with some material of known formula and melting characteristic, (2) decide how much of it can be used and divide its formula accordingly, and (3) fill in the rest of the formula with other materials.

After some acquaintance with the glaze-forming oxides and their quantitative balance in typical glazes, it is not difficult to write glazes which are very apt to work. There are, after all, a limited number of variables, and long experience has established, within general limits, the proportions most apt to be successful. The ceramist, in making up new glazes, will notice that there is actually a wide latitude in the proportions of materials in glazes. Glaze formulas may actually be altered considerably without radically changing the fired appearance or fit of the finished glaze. For instance, the amount of lead in a glaze may be cut down or increased by .2 or more molecular equivalents without making a noticeable difference. In making up new glaze formulas the aim is at rather broad targets and it's soon learned that combinations of glass-making oxides tend to melt rather easily in the fire, and that a little more of this and a little less of that may not make much difference in the end result.

If suitable melt for a given temperature is all that is required, this formula would probably have it. However, if a specific color is desired in the glaze, the selection of the particular fluxes that help to develop that color from coloring oxides or stains is paramount.

When aiming at some specific quality in a glaze, such as a particular degree of matteness or a certain response to color, a small change in the formula may have an important effect. It is in making such small adjustments that glaze calculation is an especially useful tool. For example, in a celadon glaze (this type is discussed later) a small amount of barium is known to produce a pronounced cool blue or green color by pulling out and dissolving iron from the body. In the formula of such a glaze an increase of barium by as little as .05 equivalents may make a significant change in the color of the glaze. Similarly, the exact degree of surface brightness in a glaze may be controlled by a fairly minor adjustment in the amounts of one or two oxides.

For most practical purposes existing and published glaze formulas can be relied on. The origination of new ones, however, is an exciting personal challenge. Properly interpreted, the results, will be very revealing as to the behavior of ceramic materials in the fire. It will be seen that mathematically there are a great number of possible variations in materials and the proportioning of materials for glazes of any given firing temperature.

Although the various methods of calculating glazes are very convenient in analysis, they are not particularly good at originating them. Experience has shown that the best glaze surfaces are visualized first. Many highly textured glazes that are beloved by potters are well outside the limit of formula norms. Original concepts of textured glazes which often contain extremely high amounts of different fluxes can be developed by trial-and-error. Once satisfactory results are obtained they can then be made into formulas for comparison purposes. Glazes that fall into these nonconforming limits are such favorites as lichen glazes, lizard-skin glazes, pitted shino, and dried mud-like nuka - basically anything where the limit formula for a given temperature is manipulated to be excessive in certain oxides.

In addition to the possible variation in base glazes are the large number of variations brought about by the additions of coloring oxides, stains, and opacifying agents. The sum of these variables is almost infinite. It is the resulting unexplored territory of new glazes that is tempting for the potter. The healthy urge toward experimentation and the great variety of colors and textures which may result from it have lent great vitality and interest to the art for centuries. Like the alchemists of old, potters are always chasing our own elusive version of the ultimate "gold" to clothe our forms, be it surface or color or both.

17 FRITTED GLAZES

1. Reasons for the Use of Frits

A frit is a glass that has been melted, quenched, and ground to a fine powder, ready to add as an ingredient to glazes or enamels. Various kinds of frits are extremely useful to the glaze maker.

One reason for using frits in glazes is to obtain certain valuable alkaline oxides in insoluble form. There are few insoluble sources of K_2O, Na_2O, and B_2O_3. Although sodium and potassium do occur in feldspar, they are associated with such quantities of alumina and silica that, especially in low-temperature glazes, their fluxing power is small. B_2O_3 is available to the potter in only one naturally occurring mineral which is insoluble: colemanite. As mentioned earlier, colemanite and its alternative, Gerstley borate, have ceased production in California. Substitute materials have been developed, and frits can also fulfill the same function within a glaze.

In order to make these desirable oxides available in insoluble form, they are fritted or melted up together with other oxides to form a stable, insoluble material which can be used like any other glaze ingredient.

Another reason for using fritted material is the poisonous nature of lead oxide. When lead oxide is fritted with sufficient quantities of other oxides, in most cases it can be rendered nonpoisonous. Whenever possible, it is advisable to use lead as a frit rather than in the raw state.

2. Hazards of Soluble Glazes

Since making frit requires special equipment and, at best, is apt to be a time-consuming process, and since commercially available frits are compara-tively expensive, the potter may be tempted to make use of soluble materials in his glazes, especially in those intended for low-temperature work. Soluble materials can be used successfully provided the necessary precautions are taken, and it is likely that much of the pottery made in the ancient Near East, including some of the most beautiful pottery ever made, was glazed with mixtures containing highly soluble materials.

The difficulties inherent in the use of soluble materials in glazes are:

1. Some of the soluble materials, such as pearl ash and soda ash, are caustic and may injure the skin unless rubber gloves are worn for protection.

2. If a glaze contains soluble material, the material dissolves in the water with which the glaze is mixed. This water must therefore be kept and not decanted off the glaze when the glaze has settled in storage.

3. In glazing, some water usually soaks into the body of the ware. If soluble material is present, it penetrates with the water into the body of the piece, leaving the glaze on the surface deprived of some of its material and altering, in effect, the composition of the clay and its behavior in the fire.

4. When the piece dries after glazing, concentrations of the soluble material may build up on edges, handles, or knobs. These concentrations of soluble materials may cause uneven melting.

5. When soluble glazes are stored for a period of time, they may become lumpy or filled with hard crystals or crusts that are hard to grind or mix again into the glaze.

6. Soluble materials are hard to keep in dry form. Some are hygroscopic, that is, they take on moisture

from the atmosphere and become hard and caked, making the material difficult to mix and grind.

Preparation and application techniques will occur to potters to overcome all these difficulties in the use of soluble materials. For example, materials can be stored in airtight containers, and glazes in covered jars. Ware can be bisqued to the point of vitrification and can therefore be impervious to saturation by soluble glaze. Drying can be controlled. Masks and gloves can be worn to give protection from poisonous and caustic materials. But frits have been developed to get around all these difficulties, and, except in special cases, it is better to use them.

One advantage in using fritted material, in addition to the simplification of glaze making and application techniques, is the smoother melting characteristics of already fired and melted material. Some of the volatiles of such materials have already been driven off, and, as a result, fritted glazes do not go through such a marked boiling or gas expulsion stage as raw glazes, and they are consequently less subject to pitting and pinholing. Fritted lead glazes, furthermore, are not so subject to reduction as raw lead glazes and can be fired more safely in gas kilns.

3. Methods of Preparing Frit

The method of preparing frit is simple and is essentially the same as that used for making glass. The weighed-out materials are placed in a furnace or crucible and heated until they are fused together into a mass of liquid. This red-hot liquid is then tapped out of the furnace and is allowed to flow into a tank of water, where the sudden cooling chills it and shatters it into small fragments. The glass is then ground in a ball mill until it is fine enough for use, usually 200-mesh or finer. Small batches of frit may be made in a pottery kiln by putting the raw material into a clay vessel or crucible and firing it in a glaze fire. When the frit is thoroughly melted, the crucible is lifted out of the hot kiln with tongs and the contents poured into a bucket of water. This requires great care, as pouring molten glass into cold water is likely to cause violent spitting of the glass.

4. Calculating a Frit Batch

Frit compositions are designed to give a high

yield of the desired oxides, usually the active fluxes PbO, K_2O, Na_2O, and B_2O_3, and to contain in addition enough other oxides to make the glass stable and insoluble. These other oxides may include SiO_2, Al_2O_3, CaO, ZnO, or MgO. Some typical frit formulas are given below:

$$\begin{cases} PbO & .94 \\ Na_2O & .02 \\ K_2O & .04 \end{cases} \quad Al_2O_3 \quad .08 \quad SiO_2 \quad 1.05$$

$$\begin{cases} Na_2O & .38 \\ CaO & .62 \end{cases} \quad \begin{matrix} Al_2O_3 & .38 \\ B_2O_3 & 1.2 \end{matrix} \quad SiO_2 \quad 2.8$$

$$\begin{cases} PbO & .85 \\ Na_2O & .15 \end{cases} \quad Al_2O_3 \quad .18 \quad SiO_2 \quad 2.5$$

$$\begin{cases} Na_2O & .65 \\ K_2O & .21 \\ ZnO & .08 \\ CaO & .06 \end{cases} \quad Al_2O_3 \quad 0 \quad SiO_2 \quad 2.3$$

It will be seen that the alkali content of some of these formulas is higher than could be obtained without recourse to some soluble materials. The silica and alumina are in low quantity relative to the RO groups. This relationship naturally makes for a low melting point.

The calculation of a frit batch is done in exactly the same manner as the calculation for a glaze. Suppose, for example, that a frit furnace is available and that the aim is to make a frit of the following formula:

$$\begin{matrix} Na_2O & .6 \\ K_2O & .2 \\ CaO & .1 \\ BaO & .05 \\ ZnO & .05 \end{matrix} \quad Al_2O_3 \quad .15 \quad SiO_2 \quad 2.5$$

This formula cannot be made up from insoluble materials because of the high content of Na_2O relative to the alumina and silica. Since it is a frit being made, however, soluble materials can be used in the batch, and in this case the raw materials of choice might be soda ash, feldspar, whiting, barium carbonate, zinc oxide, clay, and flint. The calculation is given below, in which the same method is used as that already given for glaze calculation.

18 GLAZE TEXTURES

1. Transparency and Opacity

So far, glazes have been considered as clear, colorless glass. Glazes, however, have a great variety of textures and colors, and the materials and firing treatments which determine these myriads of possible textures and colors must be understood by the ceramist. First, the varieties of textures will be considered, and later the problem of color.

Some glazes are clear - that is, the clay body or slip is visible underneath the layer of glaze. Other glazes are opaque and have the effect of an obscure or frosted glass, concealing what is under the glaze. Opacity in glazes may be due either to the nature of the glaze itself or to the presence in the glaze of opacifying agents.

Transparency may be thought of as the normal state of glazes; that is, if a glaze is fired to maturity and all the oxides in its composition reach a state of complete fusion, it will normally be clear and transparent. Many glazes, however, even though they do not contain any opacifying agent as such, are cloudy and opaque. Underfired glazes, for example, are opaque because of the lack of complete fusion. If firing is halted before the glaze is completely melted, some unmelted material may be floating in the glaze. These particles of unmelted materials may cloud the glaze in much the same fashion as dirt added to water makes an opaque muddy mixture. Glazes that are opaque because they are underfired will usually clear up and become transparent if the firing proceeds to the point of completely fusing the glaze.

Another cause of opacity is entrapped bubbles in the glaze. This may produce a cloudy or opalescent effect. Here the effect is analogous to suds in water, which may cause opacity without adding any actual solid particles. Bubbles in glazes are usually caused by the evolution of gas from the volatile materials of the glaze. Advancing temperature usually completes this reaction and clears up the glaze.

Opalescent, and hence cloudy, glazes may also be due to a mixture of glasses of differing indexes of refraction. This phenomenon frequently occurs in glazes high in B_2O_3 content. Such glazes may have a milky blue-white texture. In this case the glaze has the property of breaking up the light that passes through it, thus making it opaque.

Still another cause of opacity is the development of crystals in the glaze as it cools from a liquid to a solid. This phenomenon is known as devitrification. The crystalline solids, dispersed in the glaze or on the surface of the glaze, make it opaque. Such crystals may grow in the cooling glaze because of an excess of silica in the glaze, or the presence of rutile and zinc in glazes that are low in alumina, or from an excess or saturating amount of some coloring oxide such as iron or copper. Normally the presence of alumina in glazes prevents the formation of crystals in the glaze.

If some oxides in the glaze are increased beyond their normal limits at any given temperature, opacity may result. Zinc oxide, calcium oxide, barium oxide, magnesium oxide, or aluminum oxide, if present in more than a normal amount, will cloud the glaze.

Glazes which are opaque as a result of underfiring, opalescence, refraction, devitrification, or the imbalance of oxides are apt to clear up if the firing is carried to a sufficient degree of heat. This makes for rather uncertain results if opacity is desired in a glaze, and a surer way to achieve opacity is to add an opacifying agent. There are two opacifiers in common use: tin oxide and zirconium oxide. Both of these materials have a low solubility in glass; that is, they are not easily taken into the melt and remain in the cooled glaze as minute suspended particles. These suspended, unmelted particles make the glaze white or opaque. Tin oxide and zirconium oxide are usually added to a base glaze which by itself is essentially clear and transparent.

In many ways tin oxide is the preferred material to use as an opacifier. The discovery of its use in glazes, which occurred in the Near East over a thousand years ago, represented a great advance in pottery; it made white glazes possible. Tin oxide imparts a soft, pleasant texture to glazes and it enhances the colors derived from most of the coloring oxides. "Tin-glazed" ware - more correctly called "tin-opacified" glazed ware since the tin isn't a glaze - has been part of much of the wares of Persia, Spain, southern Europe, and the peasant wares of central Europe. The white, opaque glaze which can be made by the addition of tin to lead glazes has offered the ideal background for majolica decoration. About 5% of tin added to most glazes renders them opaque. A small addition of tin, 1% to 3%, may make a glaze semi-opaque and cloudy.

Zirconium oxide also gives opacity to glazes and may be used instead of tin oxide. It is usually prepared as a silicate of zirconium, some silica being combined with the zirconium oxide. Zircopax, Superpax, and Opax are trade names for such combinations. A higher percentage of zirconium oxide than of tin oxide must be used in glazes to achieve the same degree of opacity. About 7% of zirconium oxide will make most glazes opaque, and about 12% will produce white glazes. Zirconium oxide may be chosen as an opacifying agent because it is cheaper than tin oxide. However, it may give a somewhat harsher texture to the glaze and may not favor certain colors as tin oxide does. Zirconium oxide may also be useful as an opacifier in certain glazes containing chrome, where the presence of tin oxide will produce unwanted pink or brown colors.

Titanium oxide has useful properties as an opacifier although it will often pull small amounts of iron from the body or other glaze oxides and create a synthetic rutile. It will also contribute some texturizing qualities as it easily goes into a micro-crystalline state with many glazes. On a vertical surface these crystalline forms often turn into streaks like animal fur. Titanium also greatly affects some other colorants, turning iron to golden brown, copper to sage, and cobalt to milky green, for instance.

Semi-opaque glazes partially reveal what is underneath them, like a clouded glass. They are among the most attractive of all glazes. Semi-opaque glazes reveal, yet partially conceal, the slips or clays beneath them in a tantalizing way, like the dance of the seven veils. Unfortunately, they are very hard to control, and for this reason, although they are popular with studio potters, they are little used in industry. A semi-opaque glaze can be made by adding only enough opacifier to cloud the glaze without making it completely opaque. In semi-opaque glazes, the thickness of the glaze coating and the firing temperature become critical factors. If the glaze is applied a little too thickly, it may be opaque; if applied too thinly, it may be transparent. Also, if a semi-opaque glaze is slightly overfired, it may clear up and become too transparent; and if it is slightly underfired, it may be too opaque.

Semi-opaque glazes may result from any of the conditions described above as causes for opacity. In many cases, however, the effect is too dependent on exact firing temperature to be practical. The most practical semi-opaque glazes are those made by adding small amounts of tin oxide or zirconium oxide to an essentially clear transparent base glaze.

2. Bright and Matte Glazes

The surfaces of glazes may have more or less shine, reflectance, or brightness. A glaze with a dull surface, lacking in shine or reflections, is called a matte glaze. A completely melted glass or glaze is apt to have a bright shiny surface. This is because the glaze, as it melts, levels and flattens out to an exceedingly smooth surface. This smoothness of glazes is one of their practical features. A smooth surface is sanitary, is easily cleaned, and does not harbor dirt and germs in crevices or pits.

If a glaze is not completely melted in the fire, or if the viscosity of the glaze at the height of firing is still high, the surface of the glaze is apt to be slightly rough and therefore more or less matte. Underfired glazes are commonly matte as well as opaque. The development of crystals on the surface of the glaze may also cause matteness. Some of the most beautiful matte glazes are made in this way. Slow cooling naturally favors the matte glaze, especially if the matteness is the result of crystals in the glaze. Such matte glazes are called crypto- or micro-crystalline glazes to distinguish them from glazes with large visible crystals.

The addition of clay to glazes will cause matteness by making them more refractory and therefore somewhat underfired at the intended temperature. Similarly, additions of calcium to a bright glaze will give it a matte surface.

Barium oxide in excess of about .2 molecular equivalents will produce matteness in most glazes. The barium matte is particularly soft and frosty in appearance and is pleasant to the touch. Lead glazes which are made matte by the presence of barium oxide are among the favorite glazes of studio potters. Barium may not cause matteness in glazes high in B_2O_3, since this oxide forms a eutectic with barium, producing a fluid glass.

Matte glazes, although they are very attractive, have some practical disadvantages. They are hard to clean; and when used on tableware, they may make an unpleasant scratchy noise when scraped by silver. For these reasons smooth, bright glazes are usually preferred for tableware. Matte glazes are often very beautiful and their soft-looking surface, without sharp highlights or reflections, enhances the form of pottery.

The properties of matteness and opacity are related; that is, a matte glaze must also be at least semi-opaque, if not opaque, because the roughness of surface that causes matteness does not permit much transparency. An intriguing possibility is a slightly matte glaze, which, at the same time, is transparent enough to reveal the clay body or engobe beneath. Such effects are difficult to achieve. They are approximated by semi-opaque glazes applied thinly. The addition of calcium oxide may cause some dulling of the surface of a glaze without much affecting its transparency.

To summarize, matteness may be induced in glazes by:

1. Underfiring.
2. Increasing the alumina.
3. Increasing the calcium oxide or magnesia.
4. Increasing the silica to the point where devitrification will occur in cooling.
5. Including barium oxide in the glaze in amounts above about .2 molecular equivalents.

(A more extensive coverage on opacification and texturizing than is possible here is given in the book *The Ceramic Spectrum* by Robin Hopper.)

19 SOURCES OF COLOR IN GLAZES

1. Theory of Color in Glazes

Glazes on pottery, in addition to giving a tough, impervious, sanitary, and generally easily cleaned surface, have the virtue of an exceptionally wide range of color - color which has variety, depth, luminosity, and permanence.

Color in glazes may be due to the color of the clay, slip, or underglaze color beneath the glaze, as seen through the transparent glaze coating. Or glazes may be colored by metallic oxides dissolved in them. The latter is the most common and characteristic kind of glaze color. Glazes may also be colored by glassy coatings on their surface, such as overglaze enamels or luster films. "China painting" or the familiar decal decoration on tableware is composed of color in a low-temperature glaze matrix fired onto the surface of the prefired glaze.

Some metallic oxides - those of iron, copper, manganese, and cobalt - are readily soluble in glass. When dissolved in glass, they lend to it a characteristic color. The solution may be quite complete, and the effect in the finished glaze may be compared to the effect of adding a dye to water.

The color of any transparent body is the result of selective absorptions of certain wavelengths or color bands from white light. Some bands are absorbed more than others. The color seen (in glaze or glass) is that of the color band, or a combination of color bands, which is least absorbed.

The color given to a glaze by a certain metallic oxide is little related to the color of the oxide itself. Chrome is an exception, with its green. The color is sometimes that of the ion of the metal in a water solution of its salts. Here cobalt is an exception. Cobalt salts are pink in water solution. The fact seems to be that the vehicle, or solvent, strongly influences ion colors. Hence the variety of tints and even variety in color, when the same element is in a silicate melt with different modifiers of the glaze or glass.

In any glaze, the color that all colorants are likely to give is subject to change due to three basic variables:

1. The material makeup of the glaze.

2. The temperature at which the glaze is fired.

3. The atmospheric conditions in which it is fired or cooled - oxidation, reduction, or moderating between the two.

While only a few oxides are used as glaze colorants, the variables in the composition of the glaze, quantity of coloring oxide, application, and firing conditions are great, and in practice an almost unlimited number of colors can be made. It is this large variability that makes the study of glazes so fascinating.

The coloring oxides are described first; later the methods of combining and blending these oxides to obtain desired colors are discussed.

2. Iron Oxide

Iron oxide is perhaps the most important of the coloring oxides. It occurs in most earthy substances. The earth as a whole contains a very substantial percentage of iron, and, as we have seen, all clays either are fairly dark in color when fired because of the presence of iron oxide, or have smaller amounts of iron oxide present as an impurity even when the fired color is light. The characteristic browns, rusts, yellows, or greys of most rocks, sands, and soils are the result of the iron oxide present in these earthy materials.

Clear glazes which appear over clay containing iron oxide reveal colors of tan, brown, reddish brown, or yellow. There is a good deal of variety in these glazed-clay colors, a variety dependent on the amount of iron oxide in the clay, the type of glaze, and the temperature and atmosphere of firing. Immature clay bodies glazed with a clear glaze are brown, reddish brown, salmon, ochre, or yellowish pink. When a high-lead content glaze is used, the color of the clay is apt to be warm in tone; while alkaline glazes give cooler but bright hues of red-brown and yellow. Clay bodies with a small amount of iron oxide in them will appear buff, creamy, or yellow under clear glazes; while those containing considerable iron oxide will appear to be a dark reddish brown or chocolate color.

In the middle range of temperature, from cone 1 to 6, clays containing an appreciable amount of iron are apt to be hard-fired and mature, and under clear glazes they will be more grey and subdued in color than the lower-fired bodies.

Clay bodies fired at cone 5 or more are apt to be still more subdued in color. In such bodies iron oxide causes a very subdued brown or grey. Reduction firing, as described later, gives still another range of color to clay.

In most of the tableware industry, iron oxide is regarded as an impurity and a great deal of trouble is taken to avoid contamination of clays and glazes with iron. Many commercial ceramics, including tableware and sanitary ware, are traditionally white, and specks caused by traces of iron are regarded as serious defects. Ceramists have occupied themselves for generations in perfecting pure white porcelain - a feat mastered in China over 1,300 years ago. Whiteness no doubt has a prestige value because of the difficulty of achieving it and because of its association with the fine wares of the Orient and with the expensive early porcelains of Europe.

Factories producing whitewares must be equipped to prevent contamination by iron particles. Grinding mills are lined with porcelain blocks, and magnetic filters remove the larger particles of iron which may have gotten in clays and slips. The studio potter, however, tends to accept and even encourage iron in his materials and to make the most of the varied and sometimes earthy effects it naturally lends to pottery.

Iron oxide dissolved in glazes produces a wide range of color. If potters had only this one oxide to use as a glaze colorant, wares of great variety and color could be made. It is the most versatile of ceramic colorants. Subject to the three variables mentioned earlier, iron can give brown, green, gold, blue, red, yellow, pink, orange, burgundy, purple, grey, or black, In fact, the Chinese potters of the classic Song Dynasty period relied almost entirely on iron oxide as a colorant. The relatively wide range of glaze color that can be produced from iron is due to its ready solubility in glass, its sensitivity to changes in the composition of the glaze, and its sensitive response to atmosphere in the kiln.

Iron is usually added to glazes in the form of ferric oxide, Fe_2O_3. The mineral name for ferric oxide is hematite. It is commonly called red iron oxide because of its color, which is dense and strong, the color of barn paint (which is, in fact, made from iron oxide). Red iron oxide is the stable form of iron; and no matter what form iron is put into the kiln, in bodies or glazes, the oxidizing effect of firing converts it largely into Fe_2O_3.

Ferrous iron, or black iron oxide, which has the formula Fe_3O_4, may also be used as a glaze colorant, and in most cases it gives the same color as red iron oxide. As will be seen from the formula, it has a higher ratio of iron to oxygen than the red iron oxide, and for this reason may be expected to give somewhat darker colors when used in the same amount. Red iron oxide is finer in particle size than black iron oxide, and for this reason it is preferred whenever complete dispersion in the glaze is desired.

Yellow iron oxide, also Fe_2O_3, is a true iron oxide, not an ochre as is often mislabeled. It will give all of the colors ascribed to red iron without staining the hands and clothing.

Since common red clays contain as much as 8% iron, such clays can be added to glazes as a source of iron oxide. Most glaze recipes call for some clay; and, if red clay is used, the glaze will be colored as would be expected from a small addition of iron.

When rough, spotty, or speckled effects are desired, iron oxide may be added to the glaze in the form of crocus martis, an impure iron oxide, or in the form of red iron-bearing clay, slip clay, or as rust scrapings or ground black mill scale. Some clay-like minerals are loaded with iron, manganese, and other metallic oxides, and may be used to color engobes, bodies, or glazes. Barnard or "blackbird" clay is an example of this type of material. When it is used as a slip under high-fired glazes, the iron and other metallic oxides in Barnard clay bleed through, producing brown, tan, or grey coloration.

Iron oxide will produce warm hues in glazes ranging from light tan or straw color to dark brown or black. One percent of iron oxide added to a glaze will give a noticeable tint. Three percent will give a medium tint, 5% a strong tint, and over 7% will usually produce a dark brown or black. In high-temperature glazes containing bone ash, wonderful persimmon reds and oranges can be had with additions of iron to 15% to 20%.

In lead glazes iron oxide gives warm soft colors of tan, yellowish brown, amber, reddish brown, or dark mahogany brown. In low-fired glazes that are high in lead, rather brilliant tones of amber can be produced by additions of 2% to 5% of iron oxide as well as the possibility of creating "aventurine" glazes. At the higher temperatures, in the range of cone 01 to cone 5, when the lead content of the glaze is less, the colors produced by iron oxide are more subdued.

When iron oxide is used in a high-lead glaze which also contains tin oxide, a mottled cream color results, with red-brown areas where the glaze is thin, as on the edges of pots. Such glazes can be very handsome, especially over textured clay surfaces.

In alkaline glazes iron oxide gives cooler tones of yellow, tan, and brown.

If iron oxide is added to glazes which contain zinc oxide, the resultant color is apt to be rather dull and muddy. In general, base glazes that are high in lead oxide and are free of zinc oxide give the most handsome colors from iron additions.When iron oxide is added to most glazes in excess of 7%, a very dark brown or black results. Such blacks may be very bright and almost mirror-like in surface. Iron oxide is an active flux in reduction glazes, and even small amounts will make a glaze noticeably more fluid. In oxidation, iron behaves more as a refractory and usually becomes less fluid. Sometimes a glaze that is quite matte will become bright by the

addition of 2% or 3% of iron oxide.

If considerable iron oxide is used in a glaze, it has a tendency to crystallize out upon cooling. In the case of high-lead glazes these iron crystals may be brilliantly tinted with colors of yellow and red. The so-called aventurine glazes are produced this way.

Iron is very useful in modifying colors derived from other oxides. For example, glazes colored yellow, blue, or green by additions of vanadium oxide, cobalt oxide, or copper oxide may be greyed down and given depth and subtlety by the addition of small amounts of iron oxide.

In addition to producing a palette of warm colors, iron oxide also is used to produce the special and sometimes spectacular type of glazes known as celadon, saturated iron, and temmoku. These are described in a later section.

3. Copper Oxide

Copper oxide has been used since antiquity to produce colors of blue and green in glazes. Some of the earliest known examples of glazed pottery, made in Egypt about 3000 B.C., are glazed with alkaline glazes colored blue with copper oxide.

Copper carbonate, the most common source for copper oxide, is a light green powder, very fine in particle size, and having the formula $CuCO_3$. Black copper oxide is sometimes used. It is somewhat coarser in grain size, and, as will be seen from its formula, CuO, it yields more copper per unit of weight than does copper carbonate.

Copper oxide is highly soluble in glazes. It mixes thoroughly with the molten glaze during firing, even when not well ground into the raw glaze batch. Copper oxide, like iron oxide, is a strong flux, and its addition may make the glaze noticeably more fluid and bright in surface.

A 1% addition of copper oxide will give a light tint of color to most glazes - 2% to 3% will give strong color. More than 5% of copper oxide will give a dark or metallic surface, green or black in color, which often forms small crystals on the surface of glazes

Copper oxide added to a strongly alkaline glaze will produce a turquoise or blue color. This is the beautiful and familiar color we associate with Egyptian and Persian ceramics. The blue color is favored by the presence of little or no alumina, and, for intense hues, the soda or potash content must be high. About 2% of copper oxide added to an alkaline glaze will give a strong color. Copper-blue glazes may be opaque or, if transparent, may appear over a light body or slip which gives a maximum of reflected light passing through the glaze. Highly alkaline glazes usually craze on any ordinary clay body, but this defect may be tolerated for the sake of a very desirable color such as copper blue.

In lead glazes copper oxide gives various shades of green. Such greens are soft, warm, and similar in range of color to the green of plants. These greens may be beautifully modified by the addition of small amounts of other coloring oxides such as vanadium, rutile, iron, or nickel. **Note carefully**: Copper oxide should not be used in lead or lead-frit glazes applied to tableware because of its tendency to increase solubility and lead release in the finished glaze.

In glazes that rely largely on boron for their flux, copper oxide additions produce greenish turquoise colors. While these glazes may lack the singing brilliance of alkaline copper-blue, they can be very deep and beautiful, especially when opaque.

Copper in high-fired base glazes very high in barium will produce intense colors of blue or blue-green, either in oxidation or reduction. The blue color is rather unexpected in reduction firing, which normally brings about red or brown from copper. To achieve the brightest hues of blue the base glaze must contain 30% or more of barium. This is an abnormally high quantity of barium and may cause the glaze to be rather dry. Glazes made up of one part barium carbonate and one part feldspar have been successfully used with 2% of copper added. Glazes of this type are unsuitable for functional ware.

Above cone 8, copper oxide is quite volatile. It escapes from the glaze as a vapor which may influence the color of other glazed pieces in the kiln. In reduction firing, copper oxide gives the famous copper-red or oxblood color, which is described in a later section.

4. Cobalt Oxide

Cobalt oxide is the most stable and reliable glaze colorant. It gives a similar shade of blue in almost all types of glazes and under various firing conditions. The usual forms employed are cobalt carbonate, a light purple powder with the formula $CoCO_3$, or black cobalt oxide, CoO. The carbonate is usually preferred because of its fine particle size.

Cobalt oxide is the most powerful of the coloring oxides in tinting strength. A quarter percent (.25%) in a glaze is sufficient to give a medium blue. Half a percent (.5%) gives a strong blue, and 1% ordinarily gives a very dark blue. Amounts of more than 1% produce dense blue-black or black in a transparent glaze.

In alkaline glazes, cobalt oxide produces an extremely brilliant blue. Other types of glazes colored with cobalt oxide are somewhat less intense in color. When magnesia, in the form of dolomite, talc, or magnesium carbonate is present in the glaze in fairly large amounts, .2 equivalents or more, cobalt oxide tints the glaze a variety of colors from pink to mauve to lilac to purple-blue. In glazes fired at cone 9 or more, combinations of magnesia and cobalt oxide may give mottled effects, marked with spots or splotches of red, pink, and purple. Glaze colors of this kind are very hard to control or duplicate because they occur within narrow ranges of temperature and atmospheric variation.

The color resulting from cobalt oxide in glazes is so strong, insistent, and uniform in hue that most potters tire of it and lose interest in it. It is certainly true that cobalt oxide alone gives a rather harsh color. But the blue of cobalt oxide can be beautifully and subtly varied by the addition of other coloring oxides, such as iron, rutile, manganese, and nickel.

Glazes containing cobalt oxide may need to be thoroughly ball milled to eliminate a speckled or mottled appearance in the finished glaze.

5. Chromium Oxide

Chromium oxide is the most versatile coloring oxide, a veritable turncoat. It will produce red, yellow, pink, brown, or green glazes, depending on the three variables mentioned earlier.

In glazes that are free of zinc oxide and not excessively high in lead, chrome oxide gives a green color. This green is apt to be rather dense and heavy. It is usually not so attractive as the green resulting from copper oxide, especially if more than 1% of chromium oxide is used. Amounts of .5% to 3% of chromium oxide may be used for greens of various intensity. In low-fired lead glazes with above .7 equivalents of lead oxide and a low alumina content, chrome oxide may give brilliant orange or red color. The firing temperature of chrome-red glazes must be low, preferably below cone 08. One percent to 2%

of chromium oxide is enough to produce the color, which tends to be somewhat sugary looking because of crystals on the surface of the glaze. Or a soluble chromium compound may be used, such as potassium dichromate.

Low-fired lead glazes containing some soda as well as lead oxide may give a brilliant yellow when about 1% of chromium oxide is present. Here again, as in the case of the chrome-red glaze, the firing temperature is critical. Chrome-red glazes start to turn green at temperatures above cone 08, and by cone 04 very little, if any, red will be left.

Lead glazes colored with chromium are almost always toxic. They should not be used on food or drink containers under any circumstances.

Glazes containing both chromium oxide and zinc oxide are brown. Brown underglaze stains are often made from this combination of materials. Ordinarily only a small amount of chromium oxide is required to produce fairly strong tints in a zinc glaze, and when more than about 2% is used, the color is apt to be heavy and dingy.

When chrome oxide is added to a base glaze which also contains tin oxide, the resultant color is pink or brownish red. A small amount of chrome oxide, less than half of 1%, is sufficient to give a pink color in a glaze which contains 5% of tin oxide. Rich and varied tones of pink, greyed pink, and warm browns are possible with this combination, but true red cannot be achieved with chromium and tin. Red glazes are described in a later section.

When chromium and cobalt oxides are both added to a glaze, especially a glaze of the magnesia type fired in reduction at cone 9 or above, beautiful hues of teal, turquoise, and blue-green may be obtained. Small amounts of both chromium oxide and cobalt oxide give the most pleasing colors. Both oxides should be held to less than 1%.

Chromium oxide is quite volatile at cone 6 or above, and sometimes glazes containing tin oxide will be streaked with pink or brown by the volatilization of chrome from some piece nearby in the kiln, or even from a previous firing. Chromium oxide alone is quite refractory and does not dissolve in the glaze as readily as the oxides of iron, copper, or cobalt. Chrome oxide may be used as the green oxide of chrome, Cr_2O_3, or as potassium dichromate, $K_2Cr_2O_7$. This latter material, however, has the disadvantage of being both soluble and poisonous. In high barium glazes small amounts of chromium can give acidic yellow and yellow-green colors.

6. Manganese Oxide

Manganese gives a purple or brown color in most glazes. The usual source is manganese carbonate, $MnCO_3$, which is a very fine fawn-colored powder, or black manganese dioxide, MnO_2. Black manganese is used in bodies and slips where its coarser grain size, which tends to cause specks, may be considered an advantage rather than a disadvantage. Manganese, compared to cobalt or copper, is a weak coloring oxide, and 2% or 3% is usually required to give a pronounced color.

In highly alkaline glazes manganese gives a rich blue-purple or plum color. In lead glazes it gives a softer purple, less intense and tinged with brown. In glazes fired above cone 6 manganese tends to give rather neutral brown, and in a reducing fire it gives a very subdued brown.

In some lead glazes manganese carbonate may cause blistering, especially if the atmosphere in the kiln is not strictly oxidizing.

Combined with small amounts of iron, manganese oxide may give rich shades of cool brown. Combined with small amounts of cobalt oxide, it can produce deep violet or plum colors.

Manganese may be purchased in granular form. Depending on the glaze that it is included in, it can produce plum to black speckles which will run into fluid streaks at higher temperatures.

Manganese is a potentially dangerous material for the potter and dust masks should be used when handling powdered raw material.

7. Nickel Oxide

The common forms of nickel oxide used in glazes are green nickel oxide, NiO, or black nickel oxide, Ni_2O_3. Nickel oxide gives a wide variety of colors in glazes, but its most typical color is brown. The colors derived from nickel are rather uncertain, and for this reason it is little used by itself in commercial production as a glaze colorant. Small amounts of nickel oxide - below 1% - will give a grey color in most base glazes. When the amount is increased to 2% or more, brown may be expected. The color obtained with nickel oxide alone tends to be rather quiet, and sometimes dull and dingy. It is really most useful in modifying or greying the colors derived from other coloring oxides, and when about .5% of nickel oxide is added to glazes in addition to such coloring oxides as cobalt, iron, or copper, beautifully greyed or modulated hues may result.

In some cases nickel oxide may give strange and rather unpredictable color. In high-zinc base glazes, which are fired in reduction at cone 8 or higher, nickel may cause fairly bright yellowish or purplish tones, or even blue. In high barium base glazes plum to deep purple red may be achieved. These colors, however, are very uncertain and hard to repeat.

Nickel oxide is very refractory and, if added to already matte glazes in amounts exceeding about 2%, may make them excessively dry and rough.

8. Vanadium Oxide

Vanadium oxide is ordinarily used in glazes as a stain which is prepared by combining vanadium pentoxide, V_2O_5, with tin oxide. In such a stain the tin forms the bulk of the material. Vanadium stain gives a yellow color in glazes. Because of the rather small amount of vanadium oxide in vanadium stain, fairly large percentages are required to color glazes. Five percent will usually give a weak yellow, and 8% to 10%, a strong yellow. Since tin is present in the stain, it lends opacity to the glaze. If a base glaze already contains tin oxide and vanadium stain is added for color, the batch may have, as a result, too much tin, resulting in a pasty, underfired appearance. Vanadium is incorporated in a wide range of stains from yellow to blue.

9. Rutile

Rutile is an ore containing titanium oxide and iron oxide. It is used in glazes as a source of titanium, provided the color contributed by the iron is not objectionable. Rutile gives a tan or brown color to glazes. Its tinting power, however, is weak because of the relatively small amount of iron present, and it is more frequently used for its influence on the texture of the glaze than for its color. Rutile has the property of producing broken or mottled color in glazes that would otherwise have a smooth color and texture. The usual amount added to the glaze is 3% to 5%. In glazes containing B_2O_3, rutile may cause pronounced streaks or spots, particularly in those glazes which are opaque and lightly tinted

with some other coloring oxide, such as copper or iron. In more fluid glazes it will encourage opalescent blues to occur. In lead glazes the texture caused by rutile may be less prominent. Besides contributing to the breakup of surface color and lending a tan or brown influence to the glaze, rutile also serves to increase opacity, especially if used in amounts of 5% or more.

Rutile added to glazes containing copper, iron, cobalt, or chrome may give beautifully greyed and textured colors, and rutile glazes of various kinds are rightly favored by the studio potter for their rich variety and surface interest.

Rutile, which often comes from Australian beach sands, may be purchased in a granular form. This can impart a great deal of subtlety to all glazes, whether colored or not. It gives soft golden brown speckles.

The part rutile plays in the formation of crystalline glazes is described in a later section.

10. Ilmenite

Like rutile, ilmenite is an ore containing both titanium and iron. Ilmenite is a cruder ore and contains a higher percentage of iron. As a colorant it gives effects similar to those obtained from black iron oxide, especially if it is well ground into the glaze. Ilmenite is used mostly for its influence on texture and as a means of inducing spots or specks into bodies and glazes. When used in granular form, that is, as a coarse grind that will not pass through an 80-mesh screen, ilmenite will produce prominent specks or spots in a glaze. If other coloring oxides are also present in the glaze, these spots may be surrounded with minute halos of yellow which can give the glaze a highly complex and interesting surface. One percent to 3% of ilmenite is sufficient to give a marked color and texture. When added to clay bodies or engobes, ilmenite produces a darkening of color and a speckled, peppery appearance.

11. Iron Chromate

Iron chromate is used in glazes to produce shades of grey, brown, or black. In most glazes 2% will give a pronounced darkening of color. If the base glaze contains zinc, iron chromate will produce a brown color. If tin is present in the glaze, a pink or reddish brown may be expected from the addition of iron chromate. Brushwork in iron chromate on a tin-opacified glaze can produce black hazed with pink. In general, iron chromate, which has the formula $FeCrO_4$, colors the glaze about as would be expected from the combined addition of the two materials, iron and chrome. It is most useful as a modifier of other colors, although when a neutral grey is desired, iron chromate will sometimes give hues that can be obtained by no other combination of oxides. Iron chromate is commonly used in engobes to give a grey color.

12. Uranium Oxide

Uranium oxide gives yellow and red colors. After the restrictions placed on the use of uranium in 1942 this material disappeared from the pottery shop; when it again became available, its use was almost forgotten. It can be introduced into the glaze either as uranium oxide or as sodium uranate. Up to 10% of sodium uranate is used to produce yellow. In contrast to vanadium, which gives a rather warm yellow, uranium can be used to produce cool lemon-yellows. Bright red and coral glazes can be made by adding uranium to high-lead glazes at temperatures below cone 04. Up to 20% of uranium is used in a base low in alumina and calcium. Uranium reds are somewhat similar to chrome red. In reduction firing, uranium gives black. Even in a fused glaze it will remain radioactive.

13. Cadmium and Selenium

Cadmium and selenium are used to produce red glazes. They are ordinarily used combined in a glaze stain which is added as a colorant to a low-fired fritted lead-based glaze. The stain may contain about 20% selenium and 80% cadmium sulfide. In fact, the prepared "color" is a solid solution of CdSe and CdS. Stains of cadmium and selenium give a bright, almost spectrum red. The color is quite fugitive, however, and must be fired at a low temperature with a well ventilated kiln, even to the point of leaving the lid or door slightly open during firing. Rapid cooling of the glaze is necessary to prevent the red color from disappearing. In producing red colors from cadmium and selenium, it is best to purchase a prepared stain and to rely on the supplier's recommendation of a suitable frit to use for the glaze.

Cadmium and selenium should not be used for glazes on tableware, because any solubility of the glaze in the weak acids of food might release toxic compounds.

14. Other Coloring Oxides

Antimony is used to produce the color known as Naples yellow. Naples yellow stains are made by fusing antimony and lead together. The stain is unstable above cone 2.

Gold may be used in glazes to give a range of pink, red, and purple colors. Gold chloride is fused together with tin in a low melting flux to make a glaze stain. Its cost makes it impractical for use. Platinum may be used to make grey glazes, but is prohibitively expensive.

Silver and bismuth are used in lusters, as described in a later section.

In addition to the basic coloring oxides, a huge range of colored stains prepared for the ceramic industry are available to potters. Stains are mixtures of colorants and other materials prepared to give colors which otherwise may be difficult to achieve, such as yellows, reds, and oranges. Encapsulated or inclusion stains have recently been developed for this range of color.

(A more extensive coverage on colorants and color development than is possible here is given in the book *The Ceramic Spectrum*, by Robin Hopper.)

MID-FIRE PIECES

Cone 3 to Cone 6 Approximately

Rick Malmgren, U.S.A., Red & Blue Covered Jar with Cut Outs, stoneware, thrown and assembled, with copper red, temmoku and crawl glazes, cone 6 reduction, 19" x 11" x 11". Photo by Rick Malmgren.

Nancy Selvin, U.S.A., Teapot, terracotta, brushed and rubbed underglaze, hand-built over foam armature, 9″ x 9″ x 3″, with steel trivet. Photo by Steve Selvin.

Rudy Autio, U.S.A., Avalon, 1994, 34″ x 30″ x 18″. Photo by Chris Autio.

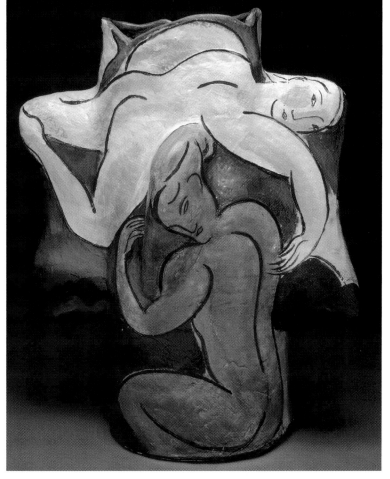

Fred Olsen, U.S.A., Afra Series, sculpture, colored slips, painted and airbrushed, slab construction using balloons for interior support, 24" x 24" x 10".

Sadashi Inuzuka, U.S.A., Exotic Species, 1998, ceramic, slip, 1000 sq. feet installation, various dimensions. Photo by Stuart Allen.

Trudy Ellen Golley, Canada, untitled installation floor piece, 1999, 2.9m x 2.1m x 10cm high, cone 4 oxidation. Photo by P.W. Leathers.

Charley Farrero, Canada, Bons Moments, 1998, wall sculpture, stoneware, slip-cast porcelain, hand-built and assembled elements, 42cm x 26cm x 13cm. Photo by A.K. Photos.

Scott Dooley, U.S.A., Teapot, Cream and Sugar, 1998, hand-built porcelain, textured with oxide underglaze, 12″ x 18″ x 5″.

Barbara Tipton, Canada, Red Hover, 1995, wheel thrown, altered and assembled stoneware, multi-fired to cone 6 and cone 5, 20cm x 34cm x 11cm.

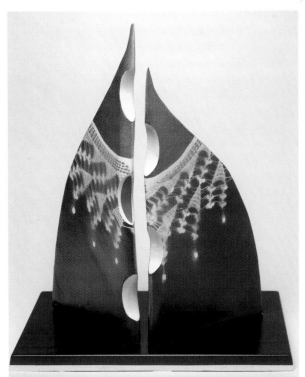

Sylvia Hyman, U.S.A., Fading Memories
(Relationship Series), 1992, porcelain, 18" x 16"
x 10-1/2". In the collection of Vta and Edgar Otte
in Hannover, Germany. Photo by John Cummings,
Nashville, Tennessee.

Leopold L. Foulem, Canada, Cup and Saucer with
Red Bull, 1999, ceramic and found objects.
Courtesy of the Prime Gallery, Toronto, Ontario.
Photo by Pierre Galnin.

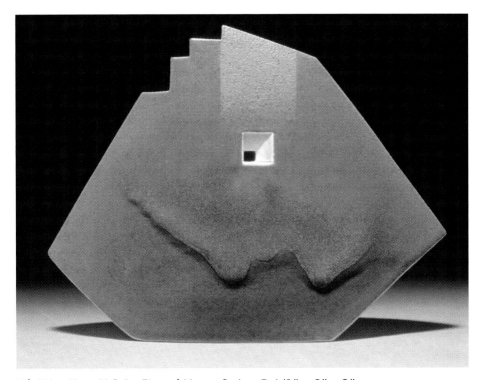

Yih Wen Kuo, U.S.A., Eternal Home Series, 5-1/2" x 8" x 3".

Yoshiro Ikeda, U.S.A., Pregnancy, off center wheel thrown and stretched, fired at cone 06, 15" x 18" x 18".

Rodger Lang, U.S.A., Cryptic Vestige #9 Serpent Guardian, 20" x 21" x 12".
Photo by John Bonath, Maddog Studio, Denver, Colorado.

Jerry Caplan, U.S.A., Prehistoric Pig, clay and nails. Photo by the artist.

Yih Wen Kuo, U.S.A., Dance with
Me, 33" x 22" x 10".

John Chalke, Canada, Pipes, 1998, 31cm l. x 17cm d.

William Parry, U.S.A., Sculpture KFS #3, 1981, stoneware, cone 6.

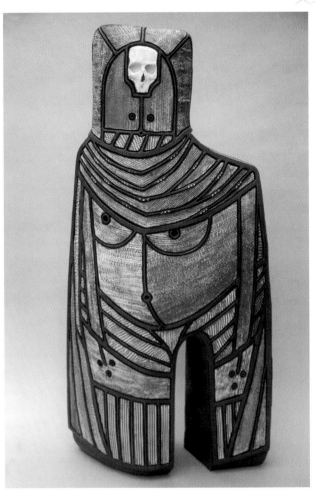

Bob Kinzie, U.S.A., untitled, 1999, piece sprayed with terra sigillata, bisqued, sprayed with patina (white slip) and rubbed away, fired to cone 6, 44" x 27".

Lana Wilson, U.S.A., Jumping Towards Hands, wall mosaic, glass, cement, iron sulfate formula (high barium glaze), fired to cone 6, refired to cone 04.

Cara Moczygemba, U.S.A., Hat Trick, 2000, ceramic, 17" x 8" x 5".

Lana Wilson, U.S.A., Ritual Bowl, movable parts on stand, cone 6 black engobe painted, then sponged off, red art formula brushed on and sponged off, fired to cone 06.

Walter Dexter, Canada, untitled.

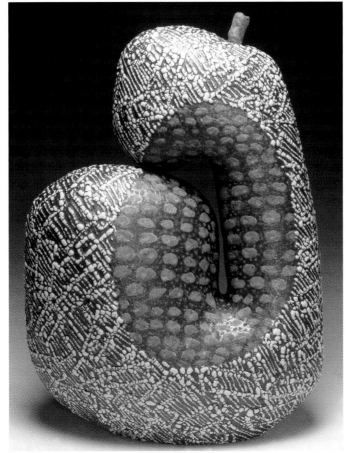

Yoshiro Ikeda, U.S.A., Zen Garden, 20" x 12" x 6".

20 METHODS OF COMPOUNDING AND BLENDING COLORED GLAZES

1. Additions of Single Oxides to Glazes

It is convenient to think of glaze colorants as materials which are added to an essentially colorless base glaze and to think of these added oxides as coloring or tinting the glaze to the desired hue. The glaze itself, minus any color influence, is referred to as the "base glaze." Sometimes the coloring oxides of a glaze are reported in its empirical formula in terms of molecular equivalents. In such cases they are calculated like any other material. Usually, however, the colorants are considered as additions to the base glaze and are expressed as an outside percentage. For example, a glaze said to contain 2% of iron will comprise one hundred parts of glaze and two parts of iron. If this method is used, the total of the glaze and the colorants added to it is actually more than one hundred. Since some glazes may have several oxides added to them for color, opacification, and texturing, it will be seen that it is more convenient and more logical to consider the base glaze as being a unit of one hundred parts.

It is very simple to develop a series of colored glazes using any base glaze which has been tested and found to melt properly at the intended temperature. When a new glaze is being worked out, it is common to concentrate first on the composition of the base glaze until it is working well and then, as the next step, introduce various colorants.

The first step in trying out some coloring oxides in a glaze is the simple addition to the glaze of a percentage of each of the coloring oxides. Amounts should be used which are known from previous experience to give an average concentration of color. If a separate test is made for each of the coloring oxides, the response of a new glaze to the various coloring oxides is determined at once, and further blending may be done more intelligently. The following list gives the approximate quantities of coloring oxides used to give tints of average strength:

Cobalt oxide or cobalt carbonate	.25%	to	7.5%
Iron oxide	1%	to	10%
Copper oxide or copper carbonate	.25%	to	10%
Chromium	2%	to	5%
Nickel	.5%	to	7.5%
Manganese	2%	to	10%
Iron chromate	1%	to	10%
Vanadium stain	4%	to	10%
Rutile	2%	to	10%
Ilmenite	1%	to	5%

It is good to make many tests using the basic colorants of iron, copper, cobalt, manganese, chromium, and rutile to determine the range of colors possibly resulting from various amounts of these oxides. Different concentrations of colorant from .25% to 10% and sometimes beyond, depending on the strength of the colorant and the will of the glaze maker, will give a wide palette. Some colorants, in some glazes, may make dramatic color changes as they become more saturated, and lighter, different tones may be achieved when the colorant reaches 7.5%. Combinations of colorants, opacifiers, and granular texturizers such as rutile, ilmenite, or manganese, will extend this palette to infinity.

When a transparent glaze is being tested, it may be advisable to also try a parallel series in which the same glaze is made opaque by the addition of 5% tin oxide or 10% zirconium. Color testing is always best done with white or light colored clays. When a transparent series is tried over dark clay the results may be somewhat disappointing because some of the colors, particularly the blues and greens, will appear dark and dingy, due to the dark color of the body underlying and influencing the color of the glaze. There are many different ways of simple cross-blending of colorants. Here we will look at three - two different line blends and a triaxial.

2. Line Blends

Although some beautiful glazes may result from the addition of single coloring oxides to a glaze, the most exciting glaze colors are usually the result of the addition of two or more colorants to the base glaze. Such additions may be arrived at by methodical blending or by adding combinations and quantities of oxides which are known to be congenial and promise to give good results. Testing may proceed on a hunch, or in the spirit of experimentation, by adding various materials to the base glaze just to see what will happen.

In methodical blending, the ceramist may anticipate that a certain percentage of his tests will prove to be unsatisfactory and will produce only muddy and unpromising colors. But there is also the probability that methodical blending will produce beautiful combinations which might not have been hit upon by other approaches.

The simplest type of methodical blend is the line blend, as shown in the chart 20-1. This kind of blend establishes a series of variations or mixes between two colors where diminishing amounts of one color or colored glaze are mixed with increasing amounts of another colorant or colored glaze.

The best method of blending glazes is to blend them in the wet state, mixed with water. One hundred gram batches are usually a convenient amount to work with, although for simple glazes of under four materials, fifty grams works quite well without the subsequent amount of discarded material. A line blend may reveal interesting combinations between two different colorants and/or opacifiers. This eleven point mix will give a wide color range. For very concentrated colorants such as cobalt and copper, a maximum amount of each color might be cut down to 5% or less, but from experience I have learned that heavy saturation of color often brings about some unusual, interesting and unexpected colors and textures.

	MIX 1	MIX 2	MIX 3	MIX 4	MIX 5	MIX 6	MIX 7	MIX 8	MIX 9	MIX 10	MIX 11
COLORANT X	10	9	8	7	6	5	4	3	2	1	0
COLORANT Y	0	1	2	3	4	5	6	7	8	9	10

20-1

Another type of line blend may be illustrated as follows:

1	2	3	4	5	6
	1-2	1-3	1-4	1-5	1-6
		2-3	2-4	2-5	2-6
			3-4	3-5	3-6
				4-5	4-6
					5-6

20-2

The top numbers, #1 to #6, may be any set of variables, such as additions of single coloring oxides to some glaze. For example, #1 might be a base glaze plus 2% of iron oxide, #2 might be the same glaze plus 3% of copper oxide, and so on. In the next row down, 1-2 is a half-and-half mixture of #1 and #2, 1-3 is a half-and-half mixture of #1 and #3, and so on. What this kind of blend actually accomplishes is to exhaust all the mathematically possible fifty/fifty combinations between the original variations in the top row. Such a blend can be rapidly prepared by wet blending after the glazes in the top row have been prepared with identical water content. This is a very valuable kind of blend, and it seldom fails to yield some subtle variations.

3. Triaxial Blending

When three materials or glazes are to be blended, a triaxial blending diagram is used. It appears as follows:

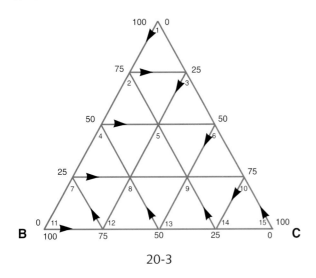

20-3

In this diagram, which is a fifteen point triaxial, the points on the line between A and B, between B and C, and between C and A are, in effect, simple diminishing amounts of the material at each apex: A equals ten parts of material A, B equals ten parts of material B, and C equals ten parts of material C. In this triaxial, as you come down the line A-B you get diminishing amounts of the A material. Similarly the line B-C and C-A give diminishing amounts of the materials chosen for points B and C. On the opposite side of the horizontal line A-B (shown with black arrowheads on the red lines) the colorant found in point C increases as that of point A decreases. This is, in fact, a line blend of these two materials. Adding the third material B, the lines read upwards and to the left (again shown with black arrowheads on the red lines). The C-A line reads downwards to the left (again shown with black arrowheads on the red lines). At all fifteen intersections or junctions of lines a one to fifteen number represents the mixture of what materials are at that point. Point five, for example, contains 5% of material A, 2.5% of material B, and 2.5% of material C. Point nine would contain 2.5% of material A, 2.5% of material B, and 5% of material C. A fifteen point triaxial is the simplest mix of three materials, although in effect there are only three points where there are three materials mixing together, points five, eight, and nine. For more complex mixtures, a twenty-one point or sixty-six point triaxial will develop far greater subtlety. However, in order to understand the process, it is usually best to start with the simple fifteen part one.

4. Methods of Making Glaze Variations Without Blending

All manner of variations may be made on any one base glaze without using any methodical method of blending, by simply planning some intended additions and trying them out. However, unless the experimenter is experienced enough to avoid unlikely combinations, much time may be wasted. For instance, the inexperienced potter may waste a day making tests that combine manganese and chrome as colorants in a glaze, whereas anyone who has worked much with glazes would know that this combination could result only in muddy colors. With a little knowledge, however, the ceramist may go directly to potentially promising mixtures and arrive at good glaze colors with less time spent testing than would be required by following some system of blending. Such a method also allows for the following of hunches and the trying out of unusual and strange combinations, some of which may prove worthwhile.

The following list is given as a general guide to combinations of glaze colorants. It does not extend to three colorants, and it should be emphasized that some of the best glaze colors do result from three or more coloring oxides in combinations with opacifiers or granular texturizers such as granular rutile, ilmenite, or manganese. The amount of colorant used, has, of course, a large influence on the resultant color.

When two or more coloring oxides are used in a glaze, the amount of each has to be reduced to avoid excessively dark colors. In general, a sparing use of coloring oxides gives the most pleasant glazes, unless deep, saturated colors are desired. Many glazes which seem attractive on a test tile, and which are in the middle range of value, can look very dull in a larger amount, as seen when used on a pot. It seems that the most attractive pieces of pottery usually have either light glazes or very dark ones. There are, of course, many exceptions to this rule.

Iron +
- cobalt–grey-blue
- copper–warm green, metallic green, black
- manganese–brown
- vanadium–ochre
- rutile–ochre, brown
- nickel–brown to grey
- chrome–blackish green

Copper +
- cobalt–blue-green
- manganese–brown, black
- vanadium–yellow-green
- rutile–warm or textured green
- nickel–grey-green
- chrome–green

Manganese +
- vanadium–yellowish brown
- nickel–grey or brown
- rutile–brown
- cobalt–blue-purple
- chrome–brown

Nickel +
- vanadium–grey, brown
- rutile–brown
- cobalt–grey-blue
- chrome–brown

Cobalt +
- vanadium–greyed yellow or mustard
- rutile–textured warm blue or grey-blue
- chrome–blue-green

Rutile +
- vanadium–ochreish yellow
- chrome–warm green

Chrome +
- vanadium–yellow-green

5. Use of Stains

In addition to the metallic oxides used to color glazes there are available also a great variety of stains and colorants which are commercially prepared for use as underglaze colors or glaze stains. The composition and use of these stains are discussed in a later section. All of these stains can be added to the glaze batch in the same way the metallic oxides are added. These commercial stains are prepared from the metallic oxides but are calcined with other materials to bring out certain colors. Some pink stains, for example, are made from combinations of chrome and tin oxide. Although the potter does not know exactly what oxides are contained in any particular commercial stain, since the manufacturers of such stains do not generally publish their formulas, he can use such stains effectively after finding out experimentally what colors they give in his particular base glazes. Actually, the use of commercial stains as glaze colorants has some advantages. Subtle tones of grey, pink, mauve, grey-green, or grey-blue can sometimes be arrived at more easily by using commercial stains than by adding very small amounts of chrome oxide, iron chromate, cobalt oxide, and the like to the glaze. The stains are also very useful as modifiers of other colors.

Commercial stains, whether labeled as underglaze, glaze, or body stains, are mixtures of metallic oxides, stabilizers, and fillers developed for use in the ceramic industry. Most have been calcined (prefired and ground) and show a fair indication of the color they will produce even when mixed together. Most are very stable in all temperatures and most atmospheres and are referred to as "zircon stabilized." They are usually opaque, and will stiffen a glaze when used in large quantities. Some allow the potter to employ oxides that would otherwise be highly toxic, notably antimony, cadmium, and selenium. They are extremely finely ground to produce maximum color without specking. They are produced by a variety of manufacturers worldwide with each producing its own variations which will probably be different from another company's stain bearing the same descriptive name. Some of the major stain makers are Pemco, U.S. and Europe; Ferro Corp., worldwide; Mason, U.S. and U.K.; Blythe, U.K., Johnson/Mathey, U.K.; Colorobbia, Italy and Spain; and dmc[2] (formerly known as Drakenfeld, Degussa, and Cerdec), the Americas. The colors derived from all ceramic colorants and stains are dependent on the basic makeup of the glaze itself. The wrong choice of glaze fluxes can eliminate certain colors but may favor others. This is why testing is so important to gaining a good understanding of the variables concerned.

6. Test Tiles for Glazes

Glazes are usually tried out on small test tiles. These may be pieces of clay about 1-1/2″ square and about 1/4″ thick. If the glazed surface is too small, it is difficult to get a good idea of the appearance of the glaze. If a hole is drilled through the top of the test tile, groups of related tests may later be strung together on a wire. Some sort of impressed texture on the face of the tile will give valuable information as to how the glaze will behave on rough or undulating surfaces.

Some potters make glaze trials on little tags of clay shaped somewhat like tombstones. They can be made very rapidly from a ball of clay about the size of a ping-pong ball. These little pieces stand upright in the kiln and have the advantage of showing the flow of the glaze on a vertical surface, which, after all, is the typical surface so far as pottery making goes. To test for the flow of glaze, flat tiles are sometimes propped up in the kiln at an angle.

Test tiles may be made on the potter's wheel. A shape is thrown resembling a dog dish. When it is leather-hard, the bottom is cut out to within 1″ of the sides, and the sides are then sliced up into segments about 1″ wide. These little segments, having a fragment of the bottom attached to them, will stand up in the kiln and make excellent testing pieces. They may have throwing marks on their surface, which is an advantage when testing glazes which are to be used on thrown pots.

7. Glazing and Marking Tests

It is advisable to bisque-fire test tiles before applying test glazes. There are several ways of applying glaze to test tiles. One way is to dip them, another is to brush them with the usual thickness of glaze. It is very informative to have both thick and thin variations of the glaze, as there can be very differing results from thickness of application. It is good to have several thicknesses of glaze represented. The whole appearance of a glaze may depend upon thickness of application, and each test should show these possible variations. This can easily be done by double or triple dipping or painting in making the test.

It is best to mark the back of the test tiles with an underglaze pencil, underglaze pen, or with a fine brush using red iron oxide mixed with water and a little gum to prevent smudging. Marking should be bold and legible, or the results of hours or even days of work may be lost.

To make a series of color tests of a base glaze, the glaze must first be carefully weighed out in sufficient quantity for the intended number of tests and then mixed thoroughly either by dry grinding in the ball mill, repeated sifting, or by mixing with water and thoroughly stirring to make sure all materials are thoroughly blended in the solution. Accurate weighing is important, since a small error in weighing say, half a gram of some oxide, may result in a significant error in the test. A small mistake in a test becomes a big mistake in a batch of glaze. In the case of very small amounts such as less than half a gram, it is best to weigh out one gram of material and then carefully divide the small pile of material into four or eight parts with the palette knife. Such mechanical divisions are more accurate than weighing, unless a very sensitive balance is available.

8. Recording Tests

The student of glazes will soon find himself swamped with paperwork. Orderly and complete records of experiments are necessary if the results of the tests are not to be forgotten or lost. It is a good plan to keep a record in one ledger of all the base glazes developed or used. These base glazes can be numbered or named for identification. In the ledger, along with the formulas and recipes of the base glazes, can be written the characteristics of each glaze, such as maturing temperature, surface, and application thickness. In another ledger can be recorded all tests fired. It is a good idea to assign a number to each test and to mark that number on the test tile. It does not work out well to try to mark all the facts about the test on the tile. If each tile is marked with a number, a corresponding number can be entered in the ledger, and there all the necessary information about the test can be written, such as the clay body, the base glaze, what the additions to the glaze were, etc. It is time-consuming to

write all this in the ledger, but it is a sure way of keeping track of what went into the tests, and memories tend to be short.

Equally important with recording what went into the tests is the record of the results. After a firing, a notation of what happened to the tests should be made in the ledger.

9. The Necessity for Testing

It may be wondered why it is necessary to do the seemingly never-ending testing which characterizes work with glazes. Like any other activity, glaze testing can certainly be overdone, and in ceramics it is common to find persons who seem to work exclusively at testing and never accomplish any finished results. However, a certain amount of testing is useful and necessary as a method of learning about the materials and processes of the craft. As in any other work, there is no substitute for experience, and making some actual glaze tests will be more instructive than reading about it. Facts which come to light in the course of practice tend to take their place and remain fixed in the memory as part of a potter's working knowledge. The greater the knowledge, the better the results.

Aside from the educational value of testing, the practicing ceramist will need to develop new colors and textures from time to time, and testing for new effects tends to sharpen interest and to keep the work alive and creative. The real problem of pottery making, however, is the application and use of colors and textures rather than the development of new ones. Any orderly worker with a healthy curiosity about ceramics can, in a relatively short time, develop literally hundreds of handsome glazes. The use of such glazes is another matter. More often than not, the best work in ceramics seems to make use of rather simple effects. The pursuit of hard-to-get colors and textures usually turns out to be a waste of time, and in tracking down some will-o'-the-wisp glaze the experimenter is usually overlooking dozens of perfectly good glazes which, with a little imagination, could serve his purposes just as well. Even the most spectacular glazes become tiresome when repeated too often or when they appear on banal forms.

Glaze testing can be greatly enlivened by the preparation of a few shot-in-the-dark tests for each firing. Glaze materials can be combined not with any logic or according to expected results but rather just to see what will happen. Tests of this sort often result in unusual and potentially useful surfaces and colors, and those tests which fail from a practical viewpoint are invariably instructive as to the reactions of the fired materials. While the main job of the potter in the lab is to bring the processes of glazing and firing under workable control, he should also be alert to the potential which lies in accident, and in those formations of color and texture which

happen as a result of his initiative but not his conscious plan. Always searching for the elusive surface and color for his individual expression, many potters make sure that there are some new glaze tests in every firing.

(A more extensive coverage on colorants, color development, and color blending than is possible here is given in the book, *The Ceramic Spectrum*, by Robin Hopper.)

21 GLAZE MIXING AND APPLICATION

1. Ball Milling

Glazes are prepared by mixing them with water to form a fluid slip. Intimate intermingling of the various materials of the glaze helps to promote melting, and for this reason it is necessary that all the materials in the glaze be thoroughly mixed. Most of the time ceramic suppliers sell well ground materials that do not require further milling, and when mixed with water into a glaze all that is required is to sieve the mix and the various materials will be thoroughly combined. However, some materials are found to be quite granular and may require further processing. Mixing and grinding can be accomplished in the ball mill, which is a rotating closed jar filled about one third full of rounded flint pebbles. The dry glaze and sufficient water are put in the jar and the cover is secured in place. The jar is then placed on the device which rotates it, and it is allowed to grind for about thirty minutes.

In the ball mill the action of the pebbles falling over one another thoroughly mixes and grinds the glaze slip. A mill must go at the right speed for efficient grinding. If it revolves too fast, the pebbles are carried around by centrifugal force and do not tumble on one another. If, on the other hand, the mill goes too slowly, there is not enough tumbling action. If the glaze slip is too thick, grinding may not take place because the pebbles will stick together. If it is done properly, milling a batch of glaze in a ball mill will produce a smooth, uniform slip in which any coarse materials or additions of coloring oxides will be thoroughly dispersed. Continued milling in a ball mill will serve not only to mix a glaze but also to grind the individual particles to smaller size. The ball mill can also be used to grind and mix dry batches of glaze. However, if such dry batches have considerable clay in them, it may be found that the material cakes against the walls of the jar instead of mixing.

2. Mixing and Screening Glazes

Most glaze materials are now supplied already ground to pass a 200-mesh screen and do not require further grinding. The glaze maker's problem is more one of mixing the various ingredients and dispersing the coloring oxides which have been added to the batch. Small batches of glaze can be satisfactorily prepared by mixing by hand in a mortar with pestle. Or, if no coarse material is used in the glaze, small batches may be mixed with a kitchen mixer or blender. For most work, screening is a very satisfactory method of mixing glaze. If coarse materials are a problem, dry glaze may be mixed by sifting it through a 30-mesh screen several times. Glaze slip can be mixed by screening it through a 60- or 80-mesh screen. If finer dispersion is required, or if there are some coarse particles to be screened out, a 100-mesh screen may be used. Glaze slip can be rapidly passed through the screen by bumping the side of the screen or by rubbing the surface of the screen with a paintbrush as the glaze is going through.

3. The Proportion of Water in Glazes

The amount of water to add to a dry glaze batch will depend on several factors. For one thing, some kinds of glaze take much more water than others. High-fired glazes which contain considerable clay or calcium borate, for example, will take much more water than fritted glazes. The consistency of the glaze is also controlled by the way in which the glaze is to be used. Glaze that will be applied to porous bisque needs to be quite thin, while glaze that will be dipped onto nonporous bisque must be thick. For normal application on medium-porous bisque the glaze should be about the consistency of light cream. If, during mixing, too much water is added to the glaze, the glaze may be allowed to settle and the excess water may be poured or siphoned off the top.

For any one glaze it is a good idea always to add the same amount of water for mixing. The consistency of glaze batches may be checked by the comparative weight of a given volume of glaze slip, by a hydrometer, or simply by the use of a wooden stick with a lead weight on the end of it, which, when allowed to sink into the glaze slip, will float at a similar level for batches of similar consistency. Marking the stick when the glaze is of appropriate thickness will make glaze thickness consistency constant.

Glazes are best stored in plastic, enamel, or wooden containers. If the containers are covered, no water evaporates from the glaze and it stays the same consistency. Galvanized iron containers such as buckets are not satisfactory because of the corrosive effect of many glazes on the zinc-coated surface. Glazes may, of course, be kept for an indefinite period provided no organic material such as gums have been added.

4. Suspenders, Gums, and Flocculents for Glazes

Many glazes have heavy ingredients in them which sink rapidly to the bottom of the glaze slip. To prevent this, a suspender is added. Raw clay in the glaze helps to keep all the ingredients from settling rapidly. If there is no raw clay in the glaze, an addition of 1% of bentonite usually corrects the difficulty without altering the fired glaze in any way. Some gums, such as sodium alginate, also help in keeping the glaze in suspension. All glazes settle to some extent, and it is very important to stir a glaze frequently while using it. Otherwise, some of the heavier materials will sink to the bottom and some of the glaze used may not be of the correct composition.

Gums are often added to glazes to make them dry on the ware in a tough coating that will not powder or mar when being set in the kiln. A small amount of gum will usually be sufficient. Gum arabic, gum tragacanth, or CMC - sodium carboxy methyl cellulose - is usually used for this purpose. These gums come in a solid form and must first be dissolved in alcohol or boiling water. About one cupful of gum can be dissolved in about half a pint of denatured alcohol. This solution is then added to about three quarts of water and is ready for use. For a gallon of glaze slip, about half a cup of gum solution can be used. One disadvantage of using gums is that their presence in the glaze causes spoiling. This can be prevented or delayed by adding a few drops of formaldehyde to the glaze. Sometimes sugar or molasses is added to the glaze to toughen the coating on the ware. When the glaze dries, the sugar crystallizes on the surface and forms a slight crust. It is sometimes necessary to harden the glaze coat before painting on it. This can be done by spraying it with a thin solution of either sugar water, syrup, or starch. This is often done to make majolica-style painting easier.

Acrylic binders may be added to glazes to increase the strength of the dried glaze coating. Acrylic mediums prepared for use with pigments in painting have been found to be very satisfactory. Such plastic mediums have the advantage of not fermenting or spoiling in the glaze slip. The quantity used depends on the degree of toughness desired in the glaze coating and may vary from one or two tablespoons of media to a quart of glaze slip to perhaps half a cup per quart for maximum strength. Acrylic binders may have a flocculating effect on the glaze slip.

All organic gums and binders burn out in the fire and have no effect on the finished glaze. In general, it is wise to use as little gum in glazes as possible; and it will usually be found that in studio work, where reasonable care is taken in handling the glazed ware, no gum is necessary.

In glazing vitreous, nonporous ware it is necessary to use a heavy glaze slip that will adhere to the surface of the ware in sufficient thickness. Such heavy glazes may be prepared by flocculating the slip with an addition of about .5% of aluminum sulfate or magnesium sulfate (epsom salts). The salts must first be dissolved in a small amount of hot water, then added to the glaze, which has already been milled with a normal amount of water. The addition of salts to the glaze has the effect of thickening it without making it lumpy. By adjusting the thickness of the glaze in this way, it can be made to adhere in any desired thickness on nonporous surfaces.

5. Glazing by Painting, Dipping, and Pouring

Glazes may be applied to pottery by painting, dipping, pouring, or spraying. For small-scale work, painting may be the best method. It is relatively easy to do and requires only a small amount of glaze. The glaze is applied with a soft brush in short, loaded strokes. It is usually necessary to go over a piece with two or three coats to be sure that all parts are evenly covered. Even though three coats are applied, the painted glaze often appears splotchy after firing because of an uneven coat of glaze. Another difficulty is that when the second and third coats are applied, the brush tends to pick up patches of glaze, causing thin spots. The only way to ensure a completely uniform coat of glaze by painting is to add some gum to the glaze and perhaps to tint each successive coat with a different color vegetable dye. Applying glaze with a lambswool or cellulose sponge roller may also help. These can be purchased from hardware stores in a variety of sizes.

Applying glaze by dipping and pouring has the advantage of rapidity and of producing a very even coat of glaze on the ware. It is quite easy to do but takes a relatively larger reserve of glaze, especially for bigger pieces. No glaze is wasted, however, since the only glaze used is what actually goes on the ware.

The methods used in dipping and pouring glaze on pottery vary according to the shape of the piece and the amount of glaze available. Smaller pieces can be completely immersed in the glaze, and the finger marks where the piece was held can be touched up later. In commercial production, dipping tongs are used to hold the ware securely at three points. Some skill and practice is required for successful dipping. The piece is held over the bucket with two or three fingers. It is then rapidly immersed, shaken vigorously while under the surface, then drawn out, emptied, and shaken to remove excess glaze. The whole operation should take only a few seconds. If the piece is held under the glaze for too long, an excessively thick glaze coat will be built up on it. The motions used in draining the piece of glaze should be studied to avoid drips and unevenness. In the case of very porous ware it may be advisable to dampen the ware before glazing to reduce its absorbency.

The insides of pieces may be glazed by filling them with glaze and then quickly emptying them. This is, in fact, the only feasible way of glazing narrow-mouthed pieces. The outside of the piece may be glazed later by dipping, pouring, or spraying.

Pieces can be glazed on the outside by holding them or supporting them upside down over a pan and pouring a cascade of glaze over them. If the piece is turned rapidly while the glaze is being poured on, very even glazing is possible. Sometimes, however, the variations in thickness which result from the different techniques of pouring glaze can be used decoratively to enhance the form of the piece.

One useful method of glazing the outside of a piece is to place a pan on a banding wheel. Then, on some kind of prop, the piece to be glazed is supported upside down in the pan. While the wheel rotates, the glaze is poured over the pot, the excess glaze being caught by the pan.

When pieces are to be glazed by dipping or pouring, their bottoms or feet can first be coated with wax to prevent the glaze from adhering. In this process beeswax or paraffin is melted and applied to the pot by dipping or painting. Some kerosene may be added to the wax to improve its consistency for brushing. Care must be taken to avoid splashing wax on any part of the pot to be glazed. Latex emulsions are also used; they have the advantage of not requiring heating, but unfortunately quickly wreck brushes. Resists done with latex emulsion must be allowed to dry before glazing is done.

Unless the bottom of a piece is cleared of glaze or it is held up during the firing on spurs or pins, it will stick to the kiln shelf.

6. Spraying Glazes

Small amounts of glaze can be sprayed on with

an airbrush, atomizer, or freon-propelled spray. For larger work glazes may be sprayed on the ware with a spray gun. Spray guns and airbrushes operate on compressed air and are similar to those used for spraying paint and other liquids. Glazes to be sprayed should be carefully ground or screened so they will not clog the spray gun. The ware to be glazed is usually rotated on a banding or decorating wheel while the stream of atomized glaze slip is directed toward it. The glaze lights on the piece in small droplets.

Spray glazing has the advantage of requiring very little reserve glaze. An average-size piece can easily be glazed with as little as one cup of glaze. At the same time, spraying is wasteful of glaze unless the glaze that does not light on the pot is collected afterward from the spray booth. However, in small-scale work, where many different glazes are ordinarily used, it is seldom feasible to save the glaze scraped off the booth.

As a method of glaze application spraying has some disadvantages relative to dipping and pouring. It is slow, and some find the noise of the necessary compressor and fan unpleasant. Also, it is difficult to build up an even coat of glaze with the spray gun. After the piece is covered, it is very hard to tell where the glaze is too thin, and some parts of a pot, such as places under the handle and around the bottom, may be almost entirely missed. Unless the glaze is checked by probing with a pin or knife, such thin places may not be detected until after firing. If the spray gun is held too far from the piece, the glaze coat may be excessively powdery because the glaze lights on the piece in small dusty granules.

If glazes are to be sprayed, an exhaust fan must be provided to carry off the dust. The operator should wear a dust mask to avoid the possibility of breathing toxic, carcinogenic, or respiratory-problem-causing glaze dust.

7. Thickness of the Glaze

It is difficult to specify how thickly glazes should be applied, since different glazes call for widely varying thickness. The average glaze is somewhat less than 1/32″ thick in the raw state. A heavy application is 1/16″. In some cases, such as transparent glazes applied on vitreous whitewares, the glaze coating may be 1/64″ thick or even less. In some oriental-style glazes such as nuka, chün, or shino, a thickness of 1/8″ is not unusual. The raw glaze coating is always considerably thicker than the finished, fired glaze because of the consolidation of materials which accompanies melting.

The thickness of the glaze has an important effect on its fired appearance. Some glazes, for instance, which are semi-opaque when thinly applied, may be completely opaque when they are put on more thickly. Transparent glazes, however, may have about the same appearance whether they are thick or thin, and for this reason they are easy to apply. The thickness of a glaze on the object can be gauged by scratching the raw glaze with a pin or knife point. The viscosity of a glaze in the container may be checked with a hydrometer when an optimum density has been decided on and recorded.

8. Approaches to Glaze Application

Applying glazes requires considerable skill and experience, especially if the exact reproduction of previously achieved effects is an objective. In such cases the thickness and evenness of the glaze is very important, and the thickness of the glaze slip, the porosity of the bisque, and the timing of the glazing operation must be brought under control.

While the exact duplication of glaze effects is mandatory for factory production, the average studio potter accepts the variations which come from the glazing process as natural, and he may prefer that his pieces not look exactly alike. In this spirit the irregular flow of the glaze as it cascades over the wall of a pot, the subtle differences in thickness that develop from pouring or dipping glaze, the skips that occur, leaving bare clay exposed, or even the revealed finger marks that show how the pot was held during glazing may all contribute to the expression of the piece. Glazing, with its complex variables, is a part of the creative process and, like finger touches in the clay, can reveal much about the spirit in which the pot was made. No one will mistake the irregularities that come from clumsy or inept glazing for those expressive nuances in the glaze which result from a technique that is skillful, intelligent, and relaxed.

Some glazing techniques are not possible to control closely, and they should be valued for just this reason; they ensure an element of surprise in the finished work. By courting the unexpected, the potter can sometimes reach beyond his usual range.

Dissimilar glazes can be applied one over the other. The fusion of the two in the fire may bring about mottled or streaked textures. Splashing or pouring gives rise to configurations of glaze which may enhance the form or give it tension or vividness. Japanese potters as early as the 16th century created splashed and drip patterns on ceramics which foreshadow "action painting" in contemporary art. They achieved poured-glaze effects that were at once spontaneous and free, yet perfectly integrated with the form of the pot.

Glazing that relies to some degree on accident or on chance variables seems to be more suitable in stoneware than in earthenware. The action of heat, especially at cone 8 to 11 in reduction, tends to pull the elements of the pot together; glaze and body become all of a piece and irregularities in application of glaze or slip can be accepted along with the variations imparted by the fire itself, such as flashing or color modulations. Irregularities in low-fired glazes are more apt to give the effect of ineptitude. If a complex technique is employed, using, for example, both underglaze elements such as slip or underglaze painting, combined with overglazes or lusters, the glazing process must be carried out with exacting control. Generally speaking, the lower firing ranges, especially if high color and figuration is involved, are much more demanding on the skill of the potter than are the higher-temperature effects, since the latter usually rely on a few simple combinations of materials along with the more complete fusion that higher firing achieves.

Normally, glazing is preceded by testing and trials or by previous experience which gives the glazer a more or less exact expectation as to how the finished pot will appear as it comes from the kiln. It is possible, however, to use the materials intuitively and to work almost completely in the realm of the unexpected. Feldspar or frit can be applied directly to the pot, or put on in layers, together with other materials such as Albany slip substitutes, calcium borate, or scrap glaze. Coloring oxides may be painted or rubbed on under or over the glaze or between layers. Glazes may be dusted on rather than applied as a fluid slip. Several layers can be dusted on successfully if some acrylic medium is sprayed on to fix the coatings of dust. Wax resist can be used to resist or block out areas when multiple layers of glaze are being dipped or poured on. If such improvisations are to be successful, the potter must have a good knowledge of what the various materials will do in the fire and of how they may react on one another. The best cooks work without recipes, but they know their raw materials intimately. If the glaze formula book is put aside and the attempt is made to work directly with the materials, a high degree of unpredictability must be accepted. The pot may be sacrificed by a bad hunch in glazing, or refiring may be necessary. Surface effects achieved in this manner, whether good or bad, can never be repeated. But, as an alternative to closely controlled work, glazing "without the book" can bring added excitement to the kiln-opening, and may also yield valuable insights into the action of glaze materials and their potential in the completion of pottery forms. The decision-making process of how to develop the surface is the artist's choice and there is an almost unlimited variety of possibilities. That is what makes this medium so exciting and so much fun.

22 FIRING GLAZES

1. Setting Glazed Ware in the Kiln

Glazed ware must be handled very carefully to avoid marring the delicate, unfired glaze coating. It is best to handle the ware as little as possible, but it usually must be picked up to remove any adhering bits of glaze from the bottom and to check for thickness. Also, care must be taken not to allow glaze from one piece to get on another, as this may result in unsightly smudges on the finished pieces. With experience, potters become accustomed to handling glazed ware skillfully so that no damage is done to the glazes.

Before setting glazed ware in the kiln, it is often wise to brush the inside of the kiln carefully, especially the crown and walls, to prevent loose crumbs of fire brick from falling on the glazed ware during firing. The kiln shelves and props should also be carefully dusted off. New kiln shelves are painted with a kiln wash consisting of two parts kaolin and one part silica, or equal parts alumina hydrate and kaolin, mixed with water to the consistency of heavy paint. More kiln wash may need to be added to the shelves after a few firings to cover up bits of glaze that may have dripped onto them. Dry applications of alumina hydrate sprinkled on the shelf will work just as well and give the ware some opportunity to move as it shrinks with the advancing temperature. Care must be taken not to accidentally brush the dry coating onto the ware placed below, or it will fuse to the glaze surface, causing unsightly blemishes.

The ware to be set in the kiln is arranged on a worktable according to size and intended position in the kiln. If the kiln fires unevenly, certain glazes may be used in the cool or hot spots to anticipate this. If pieces of similar height are grouped, it simplifies the job of deciding what height props to use for each shelf, and makes the setting easier. It is convenient to place the props first, three to the shelf, and then to nest the pots on the shelf, allowing about 1/8″ between pieces. When the shelf is filled, the next shelf can be lowered onto the three props. If the shelves have a tendency to wobble, a pad of plastic fire clay wadding or kaolin fiber blanket placed between the props and shelf may be used. The cone plaque is placed in a position easily visible through the spy-hole, the door is closed or bricked up, and the firing is begun.

2. Formation of the Glaze in the Fire

The first actual change in the glaze during firing is the volatilization of carbon and sulfur. Thus, at red heat, whiting, $CaCO_3$, becomes CaO. These changes cause no difficulties, and the heat of the kiln may be advanced quite rapidly during the early stages of firing, since there is no drying or dehydration to accomplish, unless work is being once fired, when a slower firing is best for the ware.

After red heat is reached, glazes begin to sinter, that is, they become caked onto the ware in a tough coating. This sintering is due to the beginnings of fusion in some of the ingredients of the glaze.

Actual melting in most glazes begins several cones below the maturing temperature. Most cone 9 glazes begin to melt at about cone 4. In the early stages of melting, the glaze becomes very rough and may crack like drying mud. As the melting proceeds and the glaze becomes more and more liquid, it settles down to a smooth layer on the ware.

Most glazes go through a boiling or bubbling stage during melting. Lead glazes, at a certain stage in melting, have large bubbles which can sometimes be observed through the spy-hole of the kiln, rising and breaking like bubble gum. Normally, when melting is complete, these bubbles disappear. The evolution of small bubbles in the melting glaze is thought to help in mixing the molten material and in bringing about complete fusion. If bubbling is still going on when the glaze begins to cool and harden, small pits or pinholes may mar the glaze.

When glazes are melted and are at or near their maturing temperature, they are viscous liquids, smoothly spread over the surface of the ware. One may reach in the spy-hole with an iron rod to touch the surface of the molten glaze on a pot, and it will be noted that the glaze is thick and sticky, much like honey or molasses. When the kiln is shut off and the temperature begins to fall, the glazes chill and gradually solidify.

3. Managing the Kiln and Gauging Temperature

The techniques used in firing will, of course, depend on the particular kind of kiln used. In the early stages of firing, an advance of 50° to 100°C per hour is usual, although thicker wares may need to be fired more slowly. The degree of fusion in glazes is a matter of time and temperature, not of temperature alone; and, if the firing is very rapid, more heat may be needed to mature the glazes. This is why fast-fired glaze tests often do not resemble the same glaze when fired slowly. In the early stages of firing, before the cones have started to melt, it is helpful to have a pyrometer on the kiln to indicate the temperature. The use of a pyrometer can help in saving fuel, since it permits firing to proceed as rapidly as is consistent with good final results.

As the temperature of the kiln nears the maturing temperature of the glaze, the firing is slowed down to allow the glaze to smooth out and all volatiles to escape. When the cones begin to bend, at least twenty minutes - preferably more - should be allowed to elapse between the bending of each cone. After the final cone is down, it is usual to maintain constant temperature in the kiln for about

thirty minutes. This "soaking period" helps to ensure the complete melting and smoothing out of the glaze.

After the kiln is shut off and cooling begins, the kiln should be tightly shut and the damper closed to prevent too rapid cooling. After the temperature has dropped about 100°C, the rate of cooling may be increased somewhat, since the glazes are stiffened by then. When the kiln is cooling from dull red heat to dark, there is danger of dunting or cracking the ware, and this stage must be passed slowly. The kiln may be safely opened at about 200°C, although the ware will still be too hot to handle with bare hands. In general, the period of cooling should be at least as long as the period of heating. For most efficient firing, the whole firing cycle should be as fast as is consistent with the desired results in the finished ware. However, it should be remembered that time is an important factor in the fusion of glazes. Overly fast firing may result in glaze flaws such as pitting and crawling, as well as loss of quality and color abnormalities. Shortening the firing time may result in underfired glazes. Conversely, a longer fire may bring about more complete fusion and better surface quality.

Pyrometric cones should always be used in glaze firing, even if the kiln is equipped with a pyrometer. While the pyrometer may accurately tell the temperature of the kiln, the cones are a more reliable indication of the state of the glazes, since their melting and deformation indicate the effect of both heat and time on the ceramic materials in the kiln.

An experienced potter can estimate the temperature of the kiln by its color. Being able to judge temperature by color is sometimes a help in noting unevenness in the kiln and in appraising the effects of burner adjustments on temperature. If a potter is used to always firing to the same temperature, the color at that temperature will be quite recognizable.

Draw trials are sometimes used as an aid in judging when a firing is complete. Small rings of clay may be set up in the kiln inside the spy-hole. These rings are made of the same clay and coated with the same glazes as the pots in the kiln. When the cones are bending, the rings are drawn out with an iron rod, dipped in water to cool, and examined for fusion and maturity of glaze. Sudden cooling prevents draw trials from giving much of an idea of what the final color of the glazes will be, but they do give a good indication of how far the melting has proceeded. Before the invention of the pyrometric cone, draw trials were the chief means of judging when a firing was finished.

Unless the ware in the kiln is intended for reduction firing, the glaze firing should be kept oxidizing; that is, the fire should be clean and free from smoke and show no sign of flame at the spyholes or damper. This is accomplished by adjusting the burners so that they have sufficient air and by opening the damper enough so that there is a flow of flame through the kiln. However, if too much air is allowed to pass through the kiln with the fuel, either from the burners or from the ports around the burners, the temperature will not advance because of the cooling effect of the air. In an electric kiln, of course, this is no problem, since no fuel is being burned. The atmosphere in an electric kiln is always neutral or oxidizing.

Kilns burning gas, oil, or wood all have their own peculiarities, and experience is necessary to work out the proper settings for burners and dampers to get the best results. When any new kiln is put into operation, it may be assumed that the first few firings will be less than satisfactory, and that good results can only follow the establishment of a routine of firing based on experience with that particular kiln. Almost every kiln, particularly those fired by gas, oil, or wood, has its own set of idiosyncrasies and character.

4. Uneven Temperatures

Uneven temperature inside the kiln is a problem which plagues most potters. Few kilns fire with perfectly even temperature throughout, and, at worst, some are really bad offenders, having a difference of several cones between top and bottom. In general, the downdraft type of kiln fires most evenly. Often the tendency of a kiln to fire unevenly can be corrected by simple changes in the way the ware is set, the height of bag walls, the size of the channels leading to the flue, the height of the chimney, the number and kind of burners, the rate of firing, or the adjustment of burners and dampers. But if the kiln fires unevenly after all possible corrections have been tried, the potter will simply have to learn to live with the uneven fire or pull the kiln down and rebuild with a better design. Most glazes have a range of three cones; that is, they do not have a radically different look if fired one cone hotter or one

cone cooler than normal. If the kiln does not fire evenly, glazes that are sensitive to slight overfiring or underfiring may have to be avoided. Effects which require exact temperatures may be placed in certain parts of the kiln where it is known that a particular temperature will be reached. Where the temperature variation in a kiln is large, different base glazes may be employed for the top and the bottom of the kiln, although this makes setting the kiln awkward.

5. Gas and Electric Firing Compared

Natural gas is probably the best fuel for firing pottery, although electricity is certainly the most convenient. Gas has the advantage of economy and also makes possible a variety of atmospheres in the kiln. However, gas kilns are bulky, need to be connected to chimneys, and require some skill and experience to manage.

For all these reasons, many situations call for electric kilns. Electric kilns are simple to operate and are practically foolproof. They are clean and compact. They require no chimney and, if properly installed, add no fire hazard to rooms or buildings. The cost of operating an electric kiln is low enough to be entirely practical.

Stoneware fired in an electric kiln is apt to be lacking in variety of surface, warmth of color, and texture, compared to that fired in a kiln burning gas, oil, or wood. This is no doubt due to the atmosphere in the electric kiln, which is static and neutral. It is difficult to account for the actual differences that do occur between gas and electric firing. Glazes tend to be more shiny and glossy in electric firing, and some glazes that are opaque in gas firing will be more transparent in electric firing. It is always well to make tests before changing from electricity to gas, or vice versa, to determine how much difference there will be in the appearance of the glazes. The electric kiln is ideal for most low-temperature work, and especially for pieces which have been treated with overglaze colors.

6. Firing with Bottled Gas, Oil, and Wood

Bottled gas (liquefied petroleum gas) gives results in pottery firing in every way identical with natural gas. It is more expensive and requires special equipment for storage and combustion. When bottled gas is burned rapidly, as in a kiln, large storage tanks are required to keep the gas from freezing in the tank because of rapid evaporation. Bottled gas and natural gas require slightly different types of burners with different sizes of orifice.

Results from oil firing are comparable to those obtained from gas. Oil burners, however, are more complex, more expensive, and more subject to mechanical failure than gas burners. Oil burners are usually dependent on electrically driven blowers, which means that one must be constantly on the alert against power failures during firings. Oil firing is inconvenient relative to gas firing: oil pumps and oil lines may become clogged; there is an unavoidable odor; and outside storage tanks must be provided for and kept full. In spite of all these difficulties, if no gas is available, oil may be the best fuel, and certainly beautiful ware can be made in oil-fired kilns.

Coal is seldom used today for firing kilns, since more convenient fuels are everywhere available. For the last twenty years or so, a resurgence of interest in wood firing has developed with consequent development of a particular aesthetic of the "natural surface." The masterpieces of pottery which have been made in the past in wood-burning kilns testify to the fact that wood as a fuel does not limit the kind or quality of ware that can be made. Many wood-firing kiln aficionados have designed a whole range of kilns from huge multi-chambered noborigamas and single-chambered anagamas requiring a firing crew and several days of firing, to small manageable kilns for the individual potter to fire alone. In an area where wood from sawmill scrap or other sources is cheap, the cost of wood firing may be about the same or even less than firing with gas. In firing a kiln with wood, very careful management of the fires is necessary, and the more or less constant attention of the fireman is required during the whole firing operation.

7. Failures in Firing

Firing glazed ware is the most exciting part of pottery making. There is an element of suspense and waiting, and the feeling of having committed all efforts to the fire, the results of which are, at best, somewhat uncertain. Once the pots are in the kiln, all that can be done is careful management of the fire. And there are a number of things that can go wrong.

Most bad firing is due to inattention to detail, and the prevention or cure of these difficulties is obvious. For instance, shelves may not rest securely and may totter; pots may touch each other and stick; refractory crumbs may fall into glazed pieces; the hastily made damp cone plaque may blow up in the early stages of firing and not be noticed until red heat is reached; cones may rest on nearby pots as they bend; or too rapid cooling may cause pots to dunt or craze. The most common firing difficulty, however, is overfiring or underfiring. Sometimes this may be out of the control of the potter, but more often it is caused by bad judgment as to when to shut off the kiln or by lack of attention during firing. A kiln requires very careful watching, and firing should be considered an important part of the creative process of pottery making. It is usually the final act of ceramic creation, and brings to fruition the visualizations that may have been months in the making.

8. Once-fired Ware

Glazes may be applied to either bisque or raw ware. Glazing raw ware and firing it only once has the advantage of eliminating the first firing, with the consequent saving of effort and expense. However, because of the increased hazards in glazing and the increased number of seconds and kiln wasters, once-firing seldom proves, in the long run, to be more efficient than twice-firing. Regardless, many potters prefer the once-firing method as they enjoy the spontaneity of making, surfacing, and glazing in a more fluid rhythm than that where the process is interrupted by the bisque firing normally done.

In glazing raw ware great care must be taken in handling to avoid breakage. The processes of dipping and pouring glaze are more difficult. Regardless of the glazing process, great care must be taken to prevent the water of the glaze from soaking into the clay and causing the pot to crack. Such cracks may not be detected until the ware comes from the glaze kiln. Most raw glazes have a high clay content, and use a deflocculant to eliminate some of the normal water requirements. Setting the kiln with glazed raw ware can be difficult because of the fragility of the pieces. Many glaze flaws occur with much more frequency in once-fired ware than in twice-fired ware, especially crawling and pinholing as sulfur and carbon gases escape through the sintering glaze. These difficulties are described in the next chapter.

23 GLAZE FLAWS

The various flaws that develop in glazes are not always easy to get under control, particularly in small-scale production where numerous glazes are used and there is not the opportunity for sustained laboratory experimentation and control work. Unfortunately, some of the most attractive glazes aesthetically are particularly subject to flaws, such as semi-opaque glazes and matte glazes. The "sure-fire" or "problem-free" glaze is apt to be a smooth, glassy, and rather uninteresting glaze.

The reasons for most of the defects that develop in glazes are well known, and careful compounding, application, and firing can ensure good results. But the beginner should not underestimate the difficulties of producing perfectly glazed pottery.

1. Crazing

Crazing is a common glaze flaw, but one rather easily corrected in most cases. Crazing is the development of a fine network of cracks in the finished glaze. These cracks may be present when the ware is first taken from the kiln, or they may develop days or months after the ware has been fired. Ware that is crazing when it comes from the kiln makes a tinkling sound each time a new crack appears. Crazed ware may be unsightly and unsanitary, and may permit leaking or seepage through ware which is used to contain liquids.

To understand the cause and cure for crazing, look for sources of tension between body and glaze. A glaze that crazes is actually under tension. It is too small for the area over which it is stretched, and

it therefore breaks like a splitting seam in a too-small pair of trousers.

During firing, when glazes are molten and are spread over the still red-hot ware in the kiln, they all fit perfectly. It is during the cooling of the ware that the tension develops in the glaze. In the case of crazing the difficulty arises from the fact that the clay body, when it cools, contracts less than the glaze coating. This contraction on cooling must not be confused with the firing shrinkage of clay bodies, all of which occurs during the heating of the ware. It is, rather, the contraction that occurs in any solid upon cooling. Most solids, notably metals, expand when they are hot and contract when they are cool. We are all familiar with the expansion joints on bridges that allow for this expansion on a hot day. Clay bodies and glazes are no exception to the general rule that things expand when hot, contract when cool.

Some materials expand more when heated, and therefore contract more when cooling, than do other materials. The value which expresses this relative tendency of solids to expand and contract when heated and cooled is called their coefficient of expansion. Fortunately, fired clay and glass have a coefficiency of expansion similar enough to make it possible for the glass to be melted onto the clay and to stick to it during cooling without undue strains developing between the glass and the clay. When such strains do occur, however, the glass cracks.

The cause of crazing, then, is always to be found in a high coefficient of expansion (and therefore contraction) in the glaze relative to the expansion of the body. The following list (from English and Turner) gives the expansion coefficients for the oxides that commonly make up ceramic glazes:

SiO_2	.05	x 10^{-7}, per °C, linear
Al_2O_3	.17	
B_2O_3	.66 (for small amounts)	
Na_2O	4.32	
K_2O	3.90	
PbO	1.06	
ZnO	.07	
CaO	1.63	
MgO	.45	
BaO	1.73	

From this list it can be seen that the oxides vary widely in their heat expansion; silica expands less than one-eightieth as much as sodium. Clay, being made up of alumina and silica, has a medium expansion; but some glazes, especially those high in soda, may have a high expansion, and therefore do not "fit" on the clay.

The mechanics of crazing are as follows: During the heating-up phase of firing the clay body is matured and made more or less vitreous, and the glaze is melted into a liquid silicate spread over the clay. At this stage, although the glaze must be completed by cooling and solidifying, the clay body is quite finished and, except for a loss of heat, it does not change much during the cooling of the kiln. After the glaze has solidified, both the glaze and the clay body begin to contract from cooling. As long as this contraction is similar in degree, no intolerable strain is set up between the clay and the glaze; but if the glaze contracts more than the clay, it is put in tension and must crack or craze. Actually, for maximum durability and fit, a glaze should be in slight compression over the body.

Crazing may be corrected by cutting down on the thermal expansion of the glaze and hence on its cooling contraction. This is accomplished by choosing oxides for the glaze which are lower in their coefficient of thermal expansion. Sometimes this is difficult to do without radically altering the maturing temperature or appearance of the glaze. In practice, the effective substitutions to correct crazing may include: (1) increasing the silica, (2) decreasing the feldspar, (3) decreasing any other material containing soda or potash, (4) increasing the boric oxide, (5) or increasing the alumina. Reference to

the list of expansion coefficients given above will show that all of these changes involve the decreasing of high-expansion oxides and the increasing of low-expansion oxides. Usually a modest increase in silica in the glaze will stop crazing. However, if a glaze contains a good deal of soda or potash in the form of feldspars, frits, or raw alkalies, it may be impossible to correct crazing without completely altering the character of the glaze. If a highly alkaline glaze is desired for some particular color effect, crazing may have to be accepted as inevitable.

Crazing may also be prevented by adjusting the composition of the clay body. Sometimes it is more convenient to change the clay than it is to change glaze formulas. One might think that in this case feldspar, frit, or other high-expansion material added to the body would increase the expansion of the body and therefore prevent crazing. However, fluxes such as feldspar, when added to high-fired bodies, tend to fuse and to combine with whatever free silica is available in the body. The reduction of this free silica will have the opposite effect and will cause crazing, as explained below. But in low-fired bodies the use of feldspar or frit incorporating high-expansion oxides such as soda or potash may have the effect of overcoming crazing.

Another and more practical way of correcting crazing by adjustments in the clay body is to add more silica to the clay. This may seem contradictory, since silica added to the glaze is also a remedy. However, silica added to a clay body acts quite differently from silica added to a glaze. When it is added to a glaze, it is melted into a liquid and cools as part of an amorphous or non-crystalline solid glass. When silica is added to a clay body, it remains a crystalline solid during the heating and cooling cycle. This is an important difference, since the crystalline silica in the body has quite different properties than the fused silica in the glaze. The property of the silica in the body which controls crazing is its inversion at 573°C from alpha to beta quartz. This change in crystalline arrangement is accompanied by a slight increase in volume, which is reversible; that is, silica that has expanded when heated to more than 573°C will, when cooled, contract to its original size. The crystalline changes in silica, although they produce minor changes in the size of the ware, are sufficient to affect the fit of glazes. When pottery is being cooled in the kiln and reaches the temperature of 573°C, the slight contraction in the body throws the glaze into compression and prevents it from crazing. This accounts for the fact that additions of silica to a clay body tend to correct crazing. If the amount of silica in a clay body is excessive, however, ware may break or crack during cooling, even if the cooling is accomplished quite gradually. This is due to an excessive volume change. Bodies that contain less than about 10% of silica may be expected to be difficult to fit with glazes. Bodies that contain more than about 25% of silica may be hard to fire without dunting or cracking.

Overfiring may also be a cause of crazing. If the firing has proceeded to a point where the free silica in the body has entered into glassy melts with the other materials, it does not go through any crystalline change upon cooling and so does not lose volume and put the glaze into compression.

Another type of crazing is the result of the usage of the ware or its exposure to the elements after firing. This is called moisture crazing. If a clay body is even slightly porous and moisture can enter it through exposed unglazed surfaces such as on the foot or base, it will, in the course of time, take on what humidity is available. Over a long period of time such moisture brings about a slight hydration of the fired clay, which is attended by a slight increase in volume. This may be sufficient to upset the fit of the glaze and to make it craze. To test for the likelihood of moisture crazing, ware may be subjected to steam pressure in an autoclave. This is the equivalent of extended time under normal conditions of humidity. If a sample can withstand one hundred pounds of steam pressure for a period of two hours without crazing, it is unlikely that it will ever craze in normal usage.

Crazing is often induced by heat shock, and if ware is taken from the kiln when it is still too hot, it may craze even though crazing might never develop if the same ware were properly cooled. Similarly, rough usage in the oven or on top of the stove may cause pottery to craze.

The use of crazed glazes for decorative effects is discussed in a later section. When done intentionally they are referred to as crackle or craquelure glazes.

2. Shivering

Shivering is the most dangerous of glaze faults because sharp slivers or flakes of glaze can loosen

from edges of objects and drop into food or drink. It is the reverse of crazing, and therefore the remedies are the opposite of the prescriptions for avoiding crazing. Shivering occurs when a glaze is under too great compression, which causes it to separate from the clay and peel or shiver. The effect might be compared to a sidewalk which buckles and rises from the ground in places as a result of expansion. Shivering is certainly a serious flaw, but it is usually easily corrected. The remedy is to increase the high expansion oxides in the glaze and thus make it contract more when it is cooling. This decreases the compression in the glaze, which causes the trouble. In practice, the silica in the glaze is decreased and the feldspar or other alkali-bearing materials are increased. If the cure is to be effected in the body, a decrease in the silica content of the clay usually takes care of the difficulty. In the case of high-fired bodies which are already low in silica, shivering can be corrected by adding small amounts of feldspar.

Glazes should be under a slight amount of compression if they are to remain in an unbroken film on the ware and never craze. Fitting glazes that are under compression may sometimes break the ware, especially if the walls of the pot are very thin and the glaze is thick. This kind of breaking usually occurs, if it is to occur, during the last part of the cooling of the ware, or after the ware has been out of the kiln for a few hours. Breaking of this sort is most likely to occur if the glaze is very thick on the inside of the piece and is applied thinly, or not at all, on the outside.

3. Crawling

In crawling, the glaze parts during melting and leaves bare spots of clay exposed. The crawl may expose only a few tiny places, or it may leave a reticulated pattern of exposed areas resembling the cracks in dried mud. In extreme cases the glaze may roll up into droplets or blobs, or it may crawl off most of the piece and be found in a melted puddle on the kiln shelf below the piece.

Crawling may result from glazes being applied over unclean bisque ware or from any other condition which causes the glaze to adhere imperfectly to the ware in the raw state. If a piece of bisqued pottery has a greasy spot on it, the raw glaze coating may be, at this point, in poor contact with the clay surface. Such a condition may go unnoticed, since the glaze coat on the surface may appear to be well applied. During the early stages of firing, however, when the glaze is beginning to sinter, the area not in good contact with the surface will loosen, crack, and perhaps fold back, leaving a bare spot. If the bare spot is of any considerable size, it will not heal over by the subsequent melting and flow of the glaze. To prevent crawling, bisque ware should be handled as little as possible and should be stored in a dust-free place. If bisque ware has become dirty, it should be carefully washed with water before glazing.

When glaze is applied by spraying, an excessively wet sprayed coat put on over a previously applied layer may cause the lower glaze coating to loosen, with the possibility of subsequent crawling in the fire.

Sometimes glazes will crawl on the inside of a piece but not on the outside, or vice versa. This may be caused by first glazing the inside and then applying a wet coat of glaze on the outside. Water may seep through the walls of the pot from the outside and loosen the glaze on the inside.

A frequent cause of crawling is the shrinkage and cracking of the raw glaze. Some glaze materials - notably clay, zinc oxide, light magnesium carbonate, white lead, and calcium borate - have a considerable shrinkage. Excessive grinding may increase the shrinkage of the glaze. If cracks appear in the dried surface of the glaze, crawling may result. Any cracks in the raw glaze should be rubbed over until filled with powdered dry glaze. Glazes which have a high raw shrinkage may be corrected by substitutions of raw materials. For example, calcined clay may be substituted for raw clay. Or gum may be added to the glaze slip to minimize cracking and to hold the glaze in closer contact with the clay during the early stages of heating in the kiln.

Certain types of glaze are much more subject to crawling than others. Fluid, transparent glazes seldom crawl, but the difficulty is common with very matte glazes, glazes that have a high viscosity when melted, and glazes that have a high clay or calcium borate content. In the case of the more fluid glazes, the cracks or breaks in glaze surface which occur in the early stages of firing tend to heal over when the glaze melts and flows.

Another frequent and annoying type of crawling is that which occurs over underglaze painting. Underglaze color, if it is applied too heavily, may remain on the ware as a dusty and refractory coat-ing under the glaze. The melted glaze may have difficulty spreading itself over such a surface, in much the same way that water will not spread evenly over a dusty road, but crawls up into little globules. The cure for this type of crawling is to apply the underglaze color more thinly. A small amount of gum or binder in the underglaze color may also help to prevent the glaze from crawling.

It must be admitted that even when all the possible causes of crawling are carefully avoided, crawls will sometimes still occur. If the trouble persists, it is better to change to another glaze, whatever the virtues of the offending glaze may be. At best, an occasional crawl will appear for no apparent reason.

4. Pitting and Pinholing

Pitting and pinholing are, by all odds, the most annoying and difficult glaze flaws to cure. The glaze may come from the kiln covered with minute pits or pinholes. These pinholes may be small, or they may be larger, resembling miniature volcano craters. Refiring may only serve to make the pinholes larger or more frequent.

Several conditions may be suspected as the cause for this trouble. A simple and easily cured source of the difficulty is the presence of air pockets or small "blebs" in the surface of the ware. This sometimes occurs in cast ware when the slip is not stirred sufficiently and remains full of air when it is cast. These little pockets of air under the glaze may pop through the molten glaze during firing, leaving a small break in the surface of the glaze.

Not many cases of pinholing are caused by the condition of the clay body. The composition of the glaze and the firing cycle are more often to blame. All glazes contain some volatile materials and normally go through a certain amount of agitation and boiling as these volatiles are released. Most pinholes and pits are the frozen craters of such boiling activity. It is as if a pan of simmering water could be suddenly frozen and the form of the myriad little bubbles rising and breaking on the surface could be fixed. The worst offenders for pitting are matte glazes and other glazes which are actually underfired and are used and valued for their underfired appearance. In such glazes the escape of volatiles may be very much in process when the kiln is shut off and the glaze begins to cool and to solidify. A longer firing cycle, which allows time for the volatiles to escape, will frequently cure the difficulty.

Glazes that are fluid when melted are much less apt to pinhole than are dry, matte, or underfired glazes. When the more fluid glaze reaches its lowest viscosity at the height of firing, there is a much greater chance for the pits and pinholes to heal and for the glaze to settle down to a smooth unbroken surface.

Sometimes a glaze that is not prone to pinholing will, if overfired by two or three cones, come from the kiln badly pitted. Such pits or blisters are caused by the boiling of the glaze as it nears the vapor phase. The boiling leaves craters, scars, or pits in the solidified glaze.

Even after the most careful adjustments in the firing cycle, some glazes will persist in pitting. It is, of course, difficult to fire a kiln exactly the same each time, and minor variations may cause a glaze which usually comes out well to be badly pitted. If pitting persists, it is wise to abandon the glaze rather than to attempt to follow an impossibly exact firing schedule.

Glazes that contain more than the normal amount of either zinc or rutile often have a tendency to pinhole.

Heavy reduction firing, especially in the early stages of firing, may deposit considerable amounts of carbon in the pores of the clay. Subsequent oxidation of this carbon may cause pitting as the carbon dioxide passes through the glaze.

The following remedies should be tried to cure pinholing and pitting: (1) lengthen the firing cycle, (2) apply the glaze more thinly, (3) add more flux to the glaze to make it more fluid, (4) cut down on the content of zinc oxide and rutile in the glaze, (5) increase the maturing temperature, (6) fire with a less heavily reducing atmosphere in the early stages of firing, (7) hold the temperature of the kiln at its highest heat for a soaking period, (8) allow a longer time for cooling between the top temperature and the temperature at which the glazes solidify.

5. Blistering and Blebbing

Lead glazes, if accidentally subjected to reducing atmospheres in the kiln, are apt to blister. The glaze is greyed and blackened and the surface may be covered with large blisters and craters. Lead oxide is sensitive to atmosphere and is easily reduced.

Care must be taken, therefore, when firing lead-glazed ware, to protect it from direct impingement of the flames from burners. Glazes which contain lead in fritted form only are less subject to blistering from reduction than are glazes which contain raw lead compounds.

If glazes are too thickly applied, blisters may result. This is frequently seen on the inside of bowls where the glaze has pooled in the bottom, or where the glaze coating has been too thickly applied. In such cases large blisters may be seen in the glaze, and those at the surface may be easily broken into. The cure for this difficulty is a thinner application of glaze.

Blebs are raised bumps which appear on the surface of glazed ware. They are caused by air pockets just below the surface of the clay. These air pockets, at the height of firing, may swell like small balloons, leaving a raised place or bump on the finished ware. Carefully made pieces with no entrapped air or pieces made from open bodies containing considerable grog will not be subject to this difficulty.

6. Underfiring and Overfiring

Perhaps the most common of all glaze flaws are overfiring or underfiring. Underfired pieces have a rough, scratchy, and sometimes unpleasantly harsh surface. Overfired ware, on the other hand, is usually shiny, and the glaze may run too thin on the upper parts of the ware, gather around the foot, or run off onto the kiln shelf. Either underfired or overfired glazes may have colors which are quite different from the color developed by normal firing.

Underfired ware may frequently be salvaged by a second glaze firing in which the glaze matures as desired. Overfired ware, if the flaws developed are serious, is lost. Overfiring may develop very beautiful qualities in the ware, even if they are not planned, while underfired pots are almost always unsatisfactory.

Usable glazes have a range of at least two or three cones, which greatly lessens the chance of losses from over- and underfiring.

7. Application Flaws

Poor application is a very frequent cause of glaze flaws. Too thin glazes may be rough and not the intended color. Too thick glazes may run, blister, crawl, or cause lids to be stuck to pots or pots to the kiln shelves. Unevenly applied glazes may cause unsightly and unwanted streaks or splotches. Glazing is one of the critical processes in pottery making and, until it is brought under control, satisfactory finished results cannot be expected.

8. Kiln Accidents

In spite of the most skillful compounding, application, and firing of glazes, accidents in the kiln may ruin otherwise good pottery. Shelves may break and fall on pieces. Pieces may lean and stick to each other. Bits of brick or mortar may fall from the crown of the kiln onto glazed surfaces. Volatile color, especially copper and chrome, may migrate from one piece to another, staining the glazes. Glaze may drip off one piece and down onto another. These are the accidents that try the soul of the potter, and the craft demands more than the usual amount of patience and the ability to take disappointments and to continue working in the sure knowledge that some of the best efforts will be lost.

To prevent kiln mishaps extreme care must be taken in setting the kiln. In handling shelves and ware, care must be taken not to allow crumbs of fire clay or brick to fall on the glazes. All shelves must be firmly supported, and those which are badly cracked should be discarded.

9. Refiring

There is no reason why pots may not be fired two or more times to bring about a satisfactory glazed surface. In fact, some refired pieces have a complexity and depth of color which would be hard to achieve in any other way. Granted that many pots coming from the glaze fire had best be given the hammer treatment, others are worth rescuing and should be given another chance in the kiln.

Applying more glaze to an already fired glazed surface is rather difficult because there is no absorption. One method is to use a glaze which is flocculated with magnesium sulfate, as described earlier. A thick coat can be made to adhere by dipping. If the pot is heated first, drying will be speeded up. Another method is to add a gum or acrylic medium to the glaze and apply it in several coats. Glaze that contains acrylic medium dries to a tough coat which will not be disturbed by subsequent coatings, and as much glaze as needed can be built up. Slow drying glue or acrylic medium can be painted on the surface and powdered glaze or color sifted over to achieve greater complexity or cover faults. This gives yet another layering process where a controlled pattern may be developed. Any excess or powdered glaze or color can be blown off once the glue has dried.

One objective of refiring may be to carry out the original plan or intent for the glaze, and this may be accomplished by adding more glaze to thin places, filling pinholes or blisters, adding more glaze to spots which have crawled, and the like. Another approach is to shift direction and try for a completely different effect. In this case another type of glaze altogether may be spread over the first one.

The potter should maintain an open mind as to what constitutes a glaze flaw. What might be considered a flaw on one type of pottery could be a virtue on another. The Japanese Shino ware, for example, which is valued for use in the tea ceremony, is crazed and usually has crawled places and pits in the glaze. Yet it is these very "flaws" that give the ware its character and beauty.

24 UNDERGLAZE COLORS AND DECORATION

1. Pigments Used in Underglaze Painting

One of the fascinations of pottery glazes is that colors and changes of color and texture may appear at different levels in the glaze coating, either on the surface or below the surface, and may be seen through a layer of glass. This makes for depth and variety of color and for a luminosity, which is quite unlike color in paint. Underglaze colors are seen beneath the coating of glaze, which may reveal them distinctly or may partially veil them with some other color. Underglaze colors may be applied by brushing or spraying over the body of the ware or over an engobe. The colors are then covered by a transparent or translucent glaze.

The pigments or colors used in underglaze painting are designed to (1) give the desired color when they are covered over with a transparent glaze, (2) resist the blurring, fusion, or running apt to occur when a glaze melts and flows over them, and (3) brush on easily, which requires that they be finely ground. The underglaze colors sold commercially are made to meet the exacting standards of the dinnerware manufacturers, and are compounded, calcined, and ground under carefully controlled conditions to ensure uniformity.

The coloring oxides, such as iron oxide, cobalt oxide, or copper oxide, may be used in underglaze painting, but they have the disadvantage of relatively coarse particle size, limited range of colors, and the tendency to run or smear under the glaze, as compared to underglaze colors which have been prepared especially for this purpose.

In order to get the full range of possible colors in underglaze pigments, combinations of oxides are used, such as chrome and tin, which gives various shades of pink to dark red, or chrome and zinc, which gives brown. All manner of greens and blues are made by combinations of copper, cobalt, and chrome. Naples yellow is made by combining antimony and lead. In making underglaze colors the metallic oxides are combined with enough flux to make them sinter and enough refractory material, such as silica, to keep them from running or blurring in use under the glaze. The combined materials are calcined until they sinter into a hard but unmelted mass. Many ceramic colors are crystals that have been formed by heat. The material is then ground in a ball mill to a very fine particle size. While it is possible for the studio potter to make underglaze colors in this manner, it is probably better to buy the prepared colors, which have the advantage of uniformity. Manufacturers of ceramic colors and stains do not, of course, publish the formulas used for their products, but the general proportioning of oxides used to get the various colors is well known. Out of print, older industrial ceramics reference books can be an invaluable source of recipes and information on underglazes and other stains. The following recipes indicate the typical ingredients in some underglaze stains:

Naples Yellow

Antimony oxide	24
Red lead	48
Tin oxide	16
Niter	2

Brown

Iron oxide	30
Green chrome oxide	28.5
Zinc oxide	72

Black

Red iron oxide	10
Chrome oxide	76
Black cobalt oxide	20
Manganese dioxide	12

Blue

Black cobalt oxide	26
Zinc oxide	104
Silica	70

Pink

Tin oxide	100
Calcium carbonate	40
Silica	40
Fluorspar	15
Chrome oxide	5

There are hundreds of different underglaze colors offered to the trade by various manufacturers. In spite of the confusing variety of names for these colors there are a limited number of types of colors, and the potter will usually settle on a few colors which work well with his particular glazes and processes to enhance the surfaces of his work. Although underglaze pigments are expensive compared to the coloring oxides, their great tinting strength makes them economical to use.

2. Application of Underglaze Pigments

The application of underglaze colors to the ware is simple. They are applied either directly on the raw or bisqued ware, or on the surface of the engobe. The color is mixed with water and sometimes with other additional media to improve the brushing consistency or to produce a tougher dry film of pigment. For better brushing, glycerine may be added, a few drops to each tablespoon of color and water. A small quantity of dextrine, gum arabic, or CMC gum helps to keep the color from dusting or smearing after it is on the ware. If the glaze has a tendency to crawl over the color, a small amount of flux, in the form of a low-melting frit, is added. The right amount of flux to add may be determined by testing, but it is usually added on the palette, more or less by eye rather than by weight.

The colors are applied very much in the manner of watercolors. In fact, a combination of underglaze color and gum arabic is essentially the same in working properties as the colors sold for watercolor painting. Acrylic binders of the type prepared for painting have been found to give excellent results. The most beautiful underglaze painting is usually made up of separate brush strokes not gone over or retouched. To paint in this manner requires great skill and confidence with the brush. Colors may overlap, but the resulting color in the fired product may not be what would be expected from the mixing of ordinary pigments.

The colors are strong and should be applied thinly. If they are applied too thickly, the glaze will reticulate or crawl off the color. If an underglaze decoration is not satisfactory, it is difficult to remove entirely from the bisque ware because, even though the ware is carefully washed, some of the color is likely to cling to it or impregnate the surface.

Underglaze color, thinned with considerable water, may also be sprayed on the ware with an airbrush. Solid colors may be laid on, or patterns developed by the use of stencils, masking tape, or sgraffito techniques.

Underglaze colors may be used for coloring the glaze itself in the same way that the coloring oxides are used. Coloring glazes in this way, however, may add excessively to their cost.

The kind of glaze used over underglaze pigments has an important influence on their color. Glazes containing zinc oxide, for example, will prevent the development of pink colors, and, in general, zinc should be avoided in any glaze intended for use over underglaze color. Lead glazes bring out a different range of color than alkaline glazes. The firing temperature also influences the color, and the higher glaze firing temperatures will dull the color of some underglaze colors or make them disappear altogether. Some colors, however, such as the blues resulting from cobalt oxide, are stable at all temperatures. Reducing atmospheres in the kiln also change many colors and prevent the development of others. In all cases the final color that develops is dependent on three things: (1) the materials in the glaze, (2) the temperature at which it is fired, and (3) the atmospheric conditions in the kiln.

3. Underglaze Prints

Underglaze prints are made from designs which are first engraved on copper or steel rolls. These designs are then printed (on a printing press) onto thin transfer paper. The medium used for printing is a mixture of underglaze color and a suitable oil, such as fat oil of turpentine. The transfer paper, with the fresh printing on it, is then placed face down on the ware and rubbed, which transfers the design to the surface of the ware. A similar transfer of the color to the ware may be made by decalcomania (decals), or by printing directly on the ware with rubber or sponge stamps or by silk screen printing. In all types of underglaze printing, the regular ceramic underglaze colors are used, mixed with media designed for the particular process employed. Most of the mechanical processes of printing on pottery require the use of an oily medium, and it is frequently necessary to run the ware through a hardening-on fire which burns off the oil and makes glazing over the colors possible.

Photographic images may be applied to ceramic surfaces in underglaze colors. This process requires specialized techniques in photography, silk screen printing, and decal transfer. A photograph is selected and a negative of it is prepared. This negative is projected onto sheet film of the desired size, using an acetate dotted sheet over the film to give the necessary halftone dots. The resulting positive is then projected onto a silk screen which has been prepared with an emulsion formula. After exposure to light, the screen is washed. Those parts of the emulsion that received light wash away, leaving permeable areas in the screen. The screen is now ready for printing. Up to this point the process is identical with the routines used for ordinary silk screen work involving halftone photographs, and can be carried out commercially for the potter by shops specializing in such work. Or he may choose to secure the necessary equipment and materials from a supply house and do it himself.

With an image fixed on the screen, printing may now be done directly on the ceramic surface or on a transfer. Ordinarily, the ceramic underglaze color or pigment is mixed with an oily medium. About four parts pigment to six parts varnish can be used, or a medium made up of equal parts varnish, turpentine, and boiled linseed oil can be mixed with the pigment until it is the consistency of tube paints. The image may be applied to the ceramic in underglaze color screened directly onto the body or onto a slip, or it may be in overglaze enamel placed on the finished glaze. In the case of underglaze there must be a hardening-on fire in which the oily medium is burned away before the glaze is applied. Printing directly on the pottery surface is limited to flat surfaces or surfaces that curve in one direction only; otherwise, the screen cannot be made to lie flat on the surface.

For transfer printing, the image is screened onto transfer paper consisting of a gelatinous film or cellophane backed up with a starched surface paper. The transfer to the ware is done the same way commercial decals are applied.

25 ON-GLAZE AND OVERGLAZE DECORATION

On-glaze and overglaze processes are two distinct decoration processes. On-glaze refers to applications of color or other glazes over the surface of an applied glaze that has not yet been fired. One can think of it as layering of unfired glazes and colorants, sometimes with separating layers of wax resist between them. This process is generally referred to as majolica, maiolica, tin-glazed earthenware, delft ware, or faience, depending on its origins.

Overglaze decoration, on the other hand, is decoration using specially compounded and colored low-temperature glazes applied to an already fired glazed surface of the ware, and fused on in a low-temperature firing as a third, and possibly more, firing. More firings may be required in relationship to the complexity of the design and the number of colors being used. The final firings are usually those using gold, silver, or platinum lusters. This process is generally referred to as overglaze enamel decoration or china painting. Historically, multiple firings were necessary because the colored overglazes fused at different temperatures. It was not uncommon for one piece to be fired eight or ten times. The lengthy process has been streamlined by formulating overglazes which will melt at the same temperatures so several colors may be fired at once. This helps with the inevitable loss encountered by refiring many times.

1. Majolica

Decoration on the raw glaze surface, usually called majolica, is actually a kind of color-on-glaze or glaze-on-glaze painting. The name "majolica" comes from Majorca, off the coast of Spain; it was apparently from this island that the technique was introduced into Italy. The ware is first covered with a background glaze to form the base or background for the decoration. This glaze is usually white or light in color and is ordinarily opaque or nearly so. Over this coating the decoration is applied with colored pigments or pigment-rich glazes. When the piece is fired, the decoration melts into and fuses with the background glaze. Majolica decorations are colorful in appearance and often have rather soft and blurry edges as a result of the tendency of the glazes to run together slightly.

A suitable background glaze for majolica is one which is opaque and does not run or flow much in the fire. Tin oxide is the preferred opacifier. Glazes in any temperature range may be used for majolica, but traditionally it was done on low-fired lead-based glazes. Sometimes a white slip was applied before the white glaze to give greater punch to the colors. The colored mixes to be used in decorations may be made from the same base glaze as the background. Or they may be made up from some other base glaze which has been tested and found not to crawl when applied over the background glaze. The colored glazes are made up by the addition of coloring oxides to give the desired shades of color. If the colored glazes are to be applied thinly, they may be made with a rather high concentration of coloring oxide, so as to have a high tinting strength, even though thin. If the colored glazes are to be applied thickly, by trailing with a rubber or plastic bulb or by applying brush strokes heavily, a smaller amount of coloring oxide may be more satisfactory.

The difficult thing about majolica decoration is that the raw background glaze is extremely dry, absorbent, and perhaps powdery, and it is difficult to do brushwork over it. To correct this, the background glaze may be made with additions of sugar or molasses, which, during drying, forms a slight crust on the surface of the glaze and hence gives a better surface on which to work. Or a thin spray of gum arabic solution or starch solution over the surface of the raw background glaze may serve the same purpose. Another technique is to apply the glaze, suitably flocculated, over bisque which is made nonabsorbent by soaking it in water, and then to paint the decoration on the still damp surface of the glaze. Because of the difficulty of glazing damp ware, this technique is rather awkward. The astonishingly detailed masterpieces of Italian Renaissance majolica painting may have been done on glaze surfaces which had been partially fired, or sintered into a background surface resembling watercolor paper in working properties.

Acrylic media added to the base glaze as a binder greatly facilitates majolica decoration. It gives a tough surface which is not disturbed when more glaze is applied over it, and its absorbency can be controlled by the amount of binder used. Such a surface makes an ideal background for painting, not unlike paper. Colors can be brushed over it freely to give effects like watercolor, or gouache-like effects can be done with colors that have been opacified.

In majolica decorating, glazes can be freely applied one over the other or overlapping. As a painting technique, all the processes usually used in painting may be employed. Colors may be brushed, stippled, scumbled, trailed, spattered, sprayed through stencils, dusted, or rubbed on. Many variations of application technique will occur to the inventive decorator. Different colored glazes applied one over the other by spraying or dipping may give interesting mottled or streaked textures in the finished glaze.

Underglaze colors also may be applied over the raw glaze. The regular commercial underglaze pigment can be thinned with water and painted directly on the glaze. In the fire the color fuses into the glaze and produces a somewhat blurred edge rather than the sharply defined edge characteristic of majolica decoration.

A variation of majolica decoration is the technique of scratching through the glaze with a pin. When fired, such scratches become thin lines of body color in the glaze. Beautiful patterns can be done with such lines, combined, if desired, with touches of color. A glaze must be selected which does not run enough to heal over the scratched lines.

Majolica ware must be carefully fired to prevent the glazes from running too much and thus making the decoration blurred. Crawling, running, and separating of the colors are the common difficulties. These can be overcome by the proper selection of glazes and by careful control over their application and firing.

2. Overglaze Enamels and China Painting

Overglaze enamels and china paints are applied on a finished fired glazed surface and are fused and made to adhere in a separate firing. They are actually low-fired colored glazes which, in fusing, attach themselves to the surface of the glaze on the ware. Overglaze colors are usually applied to the surface of whitewares or porcelain, the white background serving to give brilliance to the color much as the white surface of canvas or paper enhances the effect of oil or watercolor paints.

Overglazes are usually fired at a very low temperature in the range of cone 018 to 014. This low firing range permits a varied palette of brilliant colors. It also ensures that the ware itself, which has been fired originally to a higher temperature, will not be affected when the decoration is fired on. The overglazes are prepared with lead or alkaline frits, and a wide range of colors has been developed. The opaque colors are usually referred to as overglaze enamels and the more transparent ones as china paint. They are reasonably permanent after firing, but, of course, do not have the strength or toughness of glazes fired at higher temperatures. The use of strong detergents, cleaning with abrasives, or repeated cleaning in a dishwasher may gradually wear away the overglaze decoration.

Many formulas have been published for overglaze colors, and the potter who is equipped with a frit furnace could make his own by preparing suitable frits and adding coloring oxides. Careful grinding is necessary for good application characteristics. In almost every case, however, it may be best to rely on commercially prepared colors in spite of their relatively high cost. The highly technical procedures used in the industry to make overglaze colors results in a more reliable product than could possibly be achieved by the individual in a studio.

Many techniques can be used in the application of overglaze colors. Opaque enamels can be applied with a brush freehand or through stencils. The pigment is built up in a rather thick layer to give solid color, and may stand in some relief on the finished surface. An oily medium is used. Various oils give differing drying times and brushing consistencies. Linseed oil, fat oil of turpentine, lavender oil, and even mineral oil are used, the latter in cases where the painting is to be done over an extended period of time and where little or no drying is desired. Overglaze colors may be purchased from the manufacturer already mixed with a medium; these are similar in consistency and in brushing characteristics to oil paint. The more transparent colors may be applied by brushing, stippling, or spraying with an airbrush.

China painting technique usually involves the spreading of preliminary layers of very light tonalities; these are further developed by adding darker colors and accents. Highlights or "wipe-outs" can be achieved easily by rubbing off some of the color with solvent. Decorations are commonly fired several times, and after each firing more color is added. Usually the colors are allowed to dry or set before firing, but this is not absolutely necessary. In general, it is best not to mix colors indiscriminately unless the effect has been tested.

Firing may proceed on a rapid schedule. The oily medium with which the color is mixed burns off before the kiln reaches red heat. A total of about three hours to reach the desired cone is ample time. An electric kiln is ideal for firing overglaze decorations.

Overglaze colors may be applied on porcelain, stoneware or earthenware as well as on whitewares. Mixed techniques of slip decoration, underglaze painting, colored glazes, and, finally, overglaze colors are possible. Any low-temperature glaze can be used as an overglaze enamel on a piece that has been glazed at a higher temperature. Cadmium-selenium red or orange glazes, for example, can be applied and fired on glazed porcelain or stoneware.

Metallic overglazes, such as gold and platinum, are applied as a liquid and fired at very low temperatures. On a smooth glazed surface, metallic overglazes produce a highly reflectant, mirror-like effect. They are expensive. In using overglaze colors of any type, best results will be obtained by carefully following the directions given by the manufacturer.

3. Overglaze Prints

Overglaze prints are ordinarily applied as decalcomanias. In this process the overglaze enamels are printed, usually by lithography, in a design on paper faced with a gelatinous coating. To transfer this design to the ware, the surface of the ware is first coated with a varnish. Then the printed face of the decal paper is placed against the tacky varnish on the ware and rubbed from the back until good contact is achieved. The paper back of the decal is then washed off in water, which does not affect the print now firmly stuck to the ware with the varnish. After the print is transferred to the ware, the ware is put through a decorating fire to burn off the varnish and fuse the enamels to the surface of the glaze.

Overglaze enamels may also be printed directly onto the ware by the silk screen process. This is not extensively done in industry because of the difficulty of printing on curved surfaces and the lack of fine detail in silk screen printing relative to decal. Decals have the advantage of the numerous colors that can be applied to the ware in one operation.

The range of decorative processes available to the potter offers a dazzling array of possibilities for color and texture. Slip decoration and impressed decorations carried out directly in the clay can give surfaces which are integrally related to the body of the piece. Underglaze designs are seen as a part of the glaze color trapped and overlaid with glass, either clear or colored. The various overglaze processes are more like painting on a surface such as paper or canvas and are "applied" in the sense that the color is on the surface of the glaze, not under it.

26 REDUCTION FIRING AND REDUCTION GLAZES

1. Theory of Reduction Firing

Reduction firing and reduction glazes have come to be widely favored by the studio potter who has the opportunity to use a gas, oil, or other combustion-material-fired kiln. Reduction firing is impractical for industrial production since it is difficult to sufficiently control for the exact reproduction of colors. Perhaps partly for this reason it finds favor among those potters who place a value on the unique qualities of each piece they make, plus the different choices in color and surface not usually available with an electric kiln.

Whatever its limitations may be, there is no doubt that a reducing fire produces some of the richest and most satisfying glazes both as to color and as to tactile qualities. Moreover, the classic achievement of the ancient Chinese in ceramics consists almost entirely of pottery made by reduction firing. This gives the technique a prestige sanctioned by the best work of the past.

The theory of reduction firing is simple. When a fuel such as gas, oil, or wood is burned, the carbon contained in the fuel combines with the oxygen in the air to produce the chemical reaction of burning, and the products of this reaction are heat and carbon dioxide. The chemical equation for combustion is:

$$C + 2\,O \rightarrow CO_2$$
$$\text{(heat)}$$

If not enough oxygen is present during combustion, some free carbon is liberated (the familiar black smoke coming from the chimney), as well as carbon monoxide, CO. At the elevated temperatures in the kiln, carbon monoxide is chemically active and will seize oxygen from any available source, including some of the oxides in ceramic materials. The carbon may be thought of as being hungry for oxygen. When ceramic materials are deprived of some oxygen, they are said to be reduced. This reduction in the amount of oxygen in the material may affect its color and, to some extent, its surface.

Reduction is easily accomplished in kilns that burn fuel. The air supply is cut down and the draft in the kiln is diminished by closing the primary air ports and dampers. This causes the unburned fuel to remain in the kiln, and a smoky, dense atmosphere develops inside the kiln. Some smoke may be observed coming from the chimney or from the spyholes. The degree of reduction can be controlled by varying the amount of air allowed to mix with the fuel in the burners.

When kilns were more primitive in construction, and when potters relied entirely on wood or other solid fuels, reduction was a natural, if not an inevitable, occurrence, hard to prevent rather than hard to achieve. No doubt the Chinese developed their magnificent reduction effects because these effects were the natural result of the way they fired their kilns. Reduction should not be thought of as a difficult process resulting from some involved technique, but rather as the result of a smoky fire, as contrasted with the clean-burning, oxidizing fire normal in an efficiently operating kiln.

2. Effects of Reduction on Clay Bodies

Not many ceramic materials are much affected by reduction firing, and most of the effects characteristic of reduced ware are the result of the changes brought about in a few materials.

The main constituents of clay, alumina, and silica are not appreciably affected by reduction. These oxides are exceptionally stable and may be reduced only by the special techniques of metallurgy. However, the appearance of a clay body can be drastically affected by the atmosphere of the kiln. One effect in the appearance of a clay caused by reduction is the grey or black color resulting from carbon deposited in the pores of the ware during firing and remaining there in the finished product. For example, if the firing of porcelain is excessively reducing, the color may be a greyed or dirty white rather than pure white.

The major effect of reduction on clay bodies is the change brought about in the iron contained in the clay. In reduction the iron oxide present to some extent in all clays turns from brown or tan to grey or black. Iron oxide exists in several different combinations, and each proportion of iron to oxygen has a characteristic color as follows:

Fe_2O_3	–Ferric iron	–	red
Fe_3O_4	–Ferrous-ferric	–	yellow
FeO	–Ferrous iron	–	black
Fe	–Metallic iron		

The stable form of iron oxide is ferric iron, or red iron oxide, and most iron compounds in nature are in this form. In reduction fire the iron oxide tends toward the ferrous state, or black iron oxide, and this accounts for the characteristic black or grey color of clays which have been fired in reduction.

If a sample of clay that contains some iron is fired in reduction, it may come from the kiln a warm tan or brown on the surface, but inside, if the piece is broken open, the color of the body will be seen to be grey or black. This grey or black is the result of iron in the ferrous state. The tan or brown on the surface is caused by the reoxidation of the iron back to fer-

ric iron oxide. This reoxidation usually occurs during the cooling of the kiln. Often the surface of the clay will be reddish or orange in color. For reasons as yet not understood, this red or orange color of clay is warmer than the clay colors obtained from oxidation firing, although the color results from the oxidation of the extreme outer surface of the clay. In fact, one of the beauties of some reduced pottery is this exceptionally warm clay color, which is known to connoisseurs of old Chinese pottery as the "iron foot" effect. To obtain the richest tones of rust and brown in clay color, the ware must be fired in quite a reducing atmosphere, including some reduction in the early stages of firing before the clay becomes vitrified. In formulating a stoneware clay body that will fire in reduction to a warm tan or burnt-orange color, considerable fire clay should be used, and not too much ball clay. Feldspar should be kept to a minimum, and the body should not be too tight or vitreous.

In porcelain or whitewares, which contain only small amounts of iron oxide, the only noticeable effect of reduction is to change the character of the white to a blue-white as distinguished from the warm whites that result from oxidizing atmospheres. The cool white of reduced porcelain is produced by the presence of a small amount of ferrous iron in the clay.

When reduced stoneware is covered by a clear glaze, the body under the glaze shows as a cool grey. The glaze protects the iron in the body from reoxidizing, whereas the unglazed portions of the clay may be brown or rust.

Stoneware bodies intended for reduction firing may contain some iron or red clay, if a dark color is desired. However, if more than about 2% of iron is present in a clay, either in the form of a red clay or as added iron oxide, the fired ware may be very brittle and may crack during the volume adjustments of cooling. About 1% of iron in a body for reduction firing will give a warm rust to brown color.

In white bodies that are exceptionally iron-free, the blue-grey cast, which results from the reduction of the small amount of iron, has an effect similar to that of blueing in the laundry wash; it makes the clay seem even whiter than it is.

3. Reaction of Base Glazes to Reduction

The reaction of colored glazes to reduction involves several "transmutation" effects; that is, colors result that are the opposite of or are different from those obtained in an oxidizing fire. This is most noticeable with copper, which in oxidation is usually green but in reduction can be red. Before considering these, a word should be said about the effect of reduction upon the base glaze itself. Theoretically, a leadless glaze or glass is not much affected by reducing atmospheres. The oxides in glazes, such as alumina, silica, calcium, barium, and potassium, are stable oxides, not easily reduced to their metallic states, and no chemical change is made in them by reduction that does not occur in oxidation. Yet reduced glazes do seem to have a surface quality different from that of oxidized glazes, particularly in the case of matte glazes. In reduction, matte glazes seem to be smoother, more "buttery," more lustrous. Perhaps this quality is due to the longer firing cycle common in reduction firing, or perhaps it is due to longer soaking at top temperatures. In any case, the dense, smooth, opaque, satiny quality of some reduction glazes is irresistibly attractive and was prized by the ancient Chinese for its resemblance to jade. Such effects are difficult or impossible to achieve in an oxidizing fire.

4. The Color Range of Reduction Glazes

Although the range of color in reduction glazes is less than that of oxidation glazes, there are still a great variety of colors possible. Among the colors not generally possible are green, turquoise, and aqua colors from copper, although a high barium base glaze will often make the colors available even in reduction. However, these colors can be approximated by combinations of chrome and cobalt and titanium and cobalt, although the hues are not quite the same. Bright yellow is not possible in reduction except with the use of expensive inclusion stains or some stains containing praseodymium. With other yellow-giving colorants, uranium turns black and vanadium does not give color in reduction. Grape-purple is not possible either, since manganese in reduction will yield only brown. Cobalt, however, can be made to give a blue-violet, and red-violet can result from reduced copper, and combinations of copper and cobalt will give a wide range of purple to wine-red possibilities. So there are usually alternate ways to develop the colors of choice. With the current availability of inclusion stains and other stains, the range of possible color in reduction-fired glazes has widened considerably.

5. Colors from Iron Oxide in Reduction Glazes

In contrast to oxidation, iron oxide in reduction glazes usually gives cool colors of grey, grey-green, blue-green, or olive green, but may give reds, pinks, oranges, yellows, purples, and blacks, dependent on the glaze makeup and temperature as well as the degree of color saturation in the glaze, usually from 1% to 20%. Iron oxide is fairly easily reduced, and in glazes it changes from ferric iron, Fe_2O_3 to ferrous iron, FeO, which is characteristically black, grey, or green. The pale grey-green or blue-green color produced by adding a small amount of iron oxide to a glaze fired in reduction is called celadon. It is a subtle, slightly greyed, cool green and can be quite readily distinguished from the greens produced in oxidation glazes by additions of copper oxide or chrome oxide. Celadon glazes were a favorite of the ancient Chinese potters and aristocracy. A favorite technique was to use a celadon glaze over a pattern lightly incised in the clay. The pattern is beautifully shaded by the slightly pooled green glaze. The color has depth, character, and a changeability reminiscent of the color of a large body of water.

Celadons are typically clear or translucent glazes and are most colorful when used over a light body or engobe. Used over darker stoneware, celadon glaze will produce a dark greyed green.

The base glaze for celadon color should be high in feldspar and consequently fairly high in sodium or potassium. At least .4 equivalents of calcium should be present, and as much as .7 calcium may be used. Very simple celadon glazes can be made that contain only feldspar, calcium carbonate, and a small amount of clay. If too much feldspar is present, the glaze will craze over most bodies, but the celadon color will develop satisfactorily. A typical celadon base glaze might be as follows, for firing at cone 10:

KNaO	.25				
CaO	.45	Al_2O_3	.3	SiO_2	3.5
BaO	.2				
ZnO	.1				

In practice there is a considerable latitude in the formulation of celadon glazes, and the above composition is only typical of many possible formulas. Some barium oxide in the composition definitely favors a cool green color. If too much barium oxide, magnesia, or alumina is used, an opaque glaze will result and the color will be grey rather than green. A clear, fairly fluid glaze is the best for the development of the color. It is probable that the old Chinese celadons were made up of feldspar, limestone, wood ash, and some red clay which furnished the iron oxide for the color. Combinations of these simple materials will give very beautiful glazes if the firing is properly managed. In most clear glazes an increasing saturation of colorant from 1% to 10% will give a range of color from celadon to temmoku. If the glaze contains an amount of bone ash of over approximately 8%, saturations of iron up to 20% will give iron reds, oranges, and possibly microcrystalline surfaces.

Only a small amount of iron oxide is required in a glaze to produce celadon color. Half of 1% will give a light green, 1% gives a medium tint, and 2% will give a dark or "northern type" celadon. Amounts above 2% give a very dark and rather murky olive green, tending toward brown. Celadon glazes are best when thoroughly ground in a ball mill to prevent mottled color or iron spots in the finished glaze.

Celadons require a fairly heavy reducing fire. Care must be taken to keep all burners on the kiln reducing; otherwise, tan flashes may be noted on the ware where oxidation has occurred. Considerable variation in the color is usual from various firings, even though careful attention has been paid to keep the firing conditions uniform.

Opaque celadons are difficult to produce. If tin oxide or zirconium oxide is added, the color usually turns to a grey or grey-green rather than the cool green of the best celadon. Celadons can be made opaque by inducing opalescence. An opalescent glaze or glass is one which is clouded by the presence of innumerable small entrapped bubbles. Phosphorus added to a feldspathic glaze will produce this effect. About 4% to 8% of bone ash (calcium phosphate) is sufficient to opacify a glaze, and if the glaze also contains a small amount of iron oxide - 1% or less - and is fired in a heavily reducing atmosphere, a bluish, opalescent color may result. The "Chün blue" glaze of Song Dynasty stoneware is a glaze of this type. In the best examples the glaze is a deep, lavenderish blue, thick and unctuous. Chemical analyses of fragments of glaze from old Chün (or Jün) pots reveal the presence of phosphorus together with soda, potash, lime, alumina, and

silica in proportions which would indicate a very simple glaze recipe made up of feldspar, limestone, clay, and quartz. The phosphorus no doubt came from additions of ash to the glaze. Undoubtedly, the manner of firing had a great deal to do with the successful production of this beautiful glaze, because when a mixture is tried which has the same chemical makeup as the old glazes, and is fired in a gas kiln, it more often than not fails to yield the same color. The natural cycle of wood firing, with its frequent alternation between oxidizing and reducing conditions, may have been an important factor in producing the color. The Jün blue glaze is one of the few ancient Chinese glaze effects which cannot easily be reproduced, and for that reason it is a rather intriguing problem.

Some of the old Chinese Jün pots have copper red markings which appear as spots, splotches, or areas on the blue glaze. Many authorities have assumed that the whole piece was glazed with a copper-bearing glaze which turned red only at certain points where the reducing flame licked it. The discovery of old saggers with holes cut in them, apparently to let in flame, has been pointed to as evidence in support of this theory. However, chemical analysis of the blue areas of glaze proves that no copper is present in the blue glaze, which must, therefore, get its color from iron oxide. The red markings are no doubt caused by washes of copper slip under or on the glaze, or by the additions of a copper red glaze under or over the opalescent celadon glaze. The fact that some of the copper red markings are in obviously planned areas or patterns seems to indicate that their placement was deliberate rather than accidental.

When the iron oxide content of reduced glazes is 6% or more, a saturated iron effect results. In saturated iron glazes the iron, instead of yielding cool tones of grey or green, gives rich browns or red. This color results from the reoxidation of the iron on the surface of the glaze during cooling. When the iron oxide content of a glaze is high, the iron oxide has difficulty staying in the glassy solution during cooling. Some of the iron crystallizes out on the surface of the glaze. These crystals are subject to oxidation, especially if air is allowed to enter the cooling kiln, and they turn to a brown or red color. The mass of the glaze under the surface remains black in color.

Base glazes for saturated iron color should be fluid, fairly high in alkali, and should not contain a high amount of alumina, which inhibits the recrystallization necessary to the effect. A typical formula for an iron-red cone 9 reduction glaze might be:

KNaO	.25				
CaO	.55	Al_2O_3	.28	SiO_2	3.5
ZnO	.1	P_2O_5	.08		
MgO	.1				

Added to this formula is 10% of iron oxide and the glaze is applied rather thinly. Base glazes for celadon and for saturated iron are similar. If too much magnesia is present, the color will be mottled with opaque greenish patches. If the glaze is too refractory, because of too much alumina, barium, magnesia, or silica, rather dry, dirty browns will result instead of the brilliant crystalline red characteristic of the glaze at its best. When thickly applied, iron-red glazes may go black, and if the glaze pools into throwing marks and runs thin on high spots, spectacular combinations of red-brown and black may result on the same piece.

Saturated iron glazes require rather heavy reduction for the best color, and if the fire is too oxidizing, the glaze is apt to come out dull brown or black. For some unknown reason crystalline iron reds seldom develop in feldspathic glazes which are fired in oxidation.

When smaller amounts of iron are used in the glaze - up to about 7% - a khaki color may result. This glaze, a favorite of the Japanese potters, may be smooth, rich, and a rather autumnal, reddish brown in color.

6. Colors from Copper Oxide in Reduced Glazes

Copper oxide in reduction glazes may produce that unique color range known as copper red, oxblood, peach-bloom, or flambé. Like celadons, this range of glaze colors was made famous by the old Chinese potters.

Copper oxide, like iron oxide, is easily reduced. In a reducing fire it tends to change from CuO, cupric oxide, to Cu_2O, cuprous oxide, and to Cu, metallic copper, which is red in color. Dissolved in glaze, reduced copper oxide gives a variety of reddish tones, ranging from brownish red to bright blood red, to orange or light peach colors, to pur-

plish red. Since these red colors from copper are the complementary color of green, the color resulting from copper oxide in oxidation, the reduced glaze has been called a "transmutation" glaze.

Successful production of copper red glazes depends on the right kind of fire and kiln packing as well as on a suitable base glaze composition. The type of glaze composition which favors copper red colors is a rather highly alkaline glaze, fairly fluid at top temperature, and containing, in addition to the alkaline fluxes, some boron. Magnesia, barium, and alumina should be held to rather low amounts, but calcium oxide may be present in a fairly large quantity, provided it does not stiffen the glaze. A typical base for a cone 10 copper red glaze might be as follows:

ZnO	.1				
CaO	.5	Al_2O_3	.35	SiO_2	4.0
MgO	.05	B_2O_3	.15		
KNaO	.35				

About 3% of tin oxide added to the base helps to develop the color and to keep the glaze from becoming transparent over the clay. Also stannous oxide, SnO, is a good reagent for the formation of the red color.

For red colors, copper is added in small amounts, from .5% to 2%. Either copper carbonate or black copper oxide may be used. Cuprous oxide (red copper oxide), Cu_2O, is perhaps better yet, since it is already reduced. However it is often very difficult to mix well as it is usually such a fine powder.

Most stoneware glazes containing a small amount of copper will, when given a reducing fire, show some red color. However, the more matte and opaque types of glazes, such as those high in magnesia or clay, will develop only a rather muddy brownish red. Some glazes that are rather opaque will, if used for copper red, show a mottling of red, brown, and grey. For the full development of the color the glaze must be fluid and must contain considerable alkaline flux.

Analysis of fired copper red glazes have revealed that the red color results from cuprous oxide, with perhaps an influence also of some copper crystals of colloidal fineness. The presence of suboxides of copper produces muddy tones of brown or black.

Copper red glazes are very sensitive to the fire, and they are hard to duplicate exactly. A moderate amount of reduction seems most favorable to the color; if the reduction is too heavy, the glaze tends to become dark and murky in color. Moderately good copper reds can be produced by firing the kiln to maturity with an oxidizing atmosphere, then cooling it with a gas flame entering the kiln, which maintains a reducing atmosphere, down to dull red heat. Much work could yet be done in determining the amount of reduction that most favors the color and the timing of the reduction in the kiln cycle that would be most effective. In general, if a neutral fire is maintained all during the heating cycle, followed by a period of heavy reduction at maturity and a brief period of oxidation at the end of the firing, brilliant copper reds may result.

The addition of a small amount of iron oxide to the glaze - .5% or less - may make the red more brilliant in hue. Or the glaze may be applied over a very thin wash of iron oxide or yellow ocher put on the ware before glazing. Sometimes a clear glaze is put on over the glaze containing the copper to prevent reoxidation of the glaze during cooling. It is noticeable that when a copper red glaze has reoxidized to a green color during cooling, the glaze under the surface may still be red. Reducing the kiln at the latter end of cooling, from 750°C down, can develop lustrous red surfaces. A small amount (2% to 5%) of barium in the glaze will help to develop tomato red colors from reduced copper.

One problem encountered in firing copper red glazes at cone 10 or higher is that copper is quite volatile at that temperature, and if the firing is unduly prolonged for any reason, the copper may largely volatilize out of the glaze. A faster, more open packed firing is likely to produce the best reds.

The variety of copper reds, which have quite a range from rich deep red-purple to the faintest blush of pink, is due to different glaze composition, various firing schedules, and various amounts of copper in the glaze. It must be admitted that the production of uniform color from firing to firing is quite difficult. This waywardness of the color has made copper red an intriguing problem for the potter, and work has been done on this type of glaze all out of proportion to the inherent charm of the color.

7. Other Colors Obtained in Reduction Firing

Aside from the rather spectacular results obtained with iron and copper oxides, the color of reduced ware tends to be rather grey and not marked with brilliant hues. In selecting glazes for reduction firing it is well to avoid too many colors of a middle-value grey or brown, and to seek variety in whites, blacks, blues, and greens, in addition to those colors derived from iron, copper, and rutile. The beauty of reduction glazes is their warm, soft, subtle, and quiet colors - colors which suggest earthiness and the mellowing effect of high heat. These qualities, when overdone, may be just plain dull.

One of the most attractive types of high-fired reduction glazes is the high-magnesia glaze, which has already been described under the section on porcelain and stoneware glazes in Chapter 17. In reduction the high-magnesia glaze takes on a dense, smooth, opaque, and almost lustrous surface which is exceptionally attractive in its tactile appeal. A typical cone 9 base glaze of this type might be:

KNaO	.25				
CaO	.35	Al_2O_3	.38	SiO_2	3.5
MgO	.35	B_2O_3	.15		
ZnO	.05				

Magnesia glazes, if applied over dark stoneware clay, will take up some iron from the clay and fire to a soft grey color. If the clay contains granular impurities or has been colored with ilmenite or black iron oxide, the glaze will be flecked with black or reddish spots.

Magnesia glazes can give beautiful hues of blue, blue-grey, and blue-green. Cobalt oxide, being very little affected by reduction, gives a strong blue-violet color. The blue from cobalt oxide may be modified by small additions of chrome oxide, iron oxide, rutile, ilmenite, manganese, nickel oxide, or iron chromate. In reduction firing, the greyed blues made in this manner can be subtle and full of depth and variety of color and texture. Combinations of chrome oxide and cobalt oxide in high-fired reduction glazes high in magnesia give brilliant hues of turquoise and blue-green. About .5% to 2% of both chrome oxide and cobalt oxide are sufficient to give strong colors.

In reduction glazes manganese oxide gives brownish colors, and in combination with iron, rutile, or ilmenite it may yield rich, warm, and rather stony effects. Bright yellow glazes can now be developed in reduction through the use of inclusion stains. If rutile is washed onto the surface of a magnesia glaze in a thin coating or included in the glaze up to 10%, a creamy gold color can be produced.

High-barium glazes, described in a previous section, can be used to produce brilliant blues and greens from copper oxide in reduction. Iron in such glazes gives tan or yellow ochre rather than the grey or green that might be expected. The range of color in high barium glazes offers a good way of extending the palette in reduction firing, although they are not generally suitable for food-safe surfaces.

Black glazes are especially beautiful in reduction. Good blacks may be made by the addition of about 10% of dark coloring oxides - such as combinations of cobalt, iron, and manganese - to a fairly stiff magnesia base glaze. At their best, black colors in reduction can be soft, matte, and satiny in the touch. The difficulty usually encountered with black is that if an excess of coloring oxides is added, either the glaze becomes too fluid because of the additional flux or the metallic oxides devitrify too much on cooling and give a harsh, dry, and sometimes wrinkled surface. Fine blacks can be made from natural slip glazes, such as Albany slip or its substitutes, by adding up to 5% of cobalt, manganese, or iron oxides.

A beautiful range of greyed pastel colors can be obtained in reduction firing by adding small amounts of underglaze or glaze stains to the base glaze. Commercial stains made to produce grey, brown, black, or blue colors often yield tones when used as glaze colorants which are difficult to obtain with the usual coloring oxides. For example, .5% of a commercial black underglaze stain added to a stoneware glaze may give a dusty blue-green. Or 1% to 2% of a grey underglaze stain may give a deep grey-green.

8. Kiln Practice in Reduction Firing

Although a great deal of research needs to be done on reduction firing to make it more reliable and to find out the exact procedures necessary for certain effects, the rule-of-thumb methods now in use can be depended upon to produce good work. Better kilns and better reduction control through the use of carbon monoxide metering devices are giving more reliability to firing in reduction. However, there are so many variables that can add their particular part to the mix that there will always be

the probability of variation. If sameness is the goal, go for oxidation and electricity. It is like the difference between the sterility of an electric oven compared with the flavors from the barbecue.

The classic examples of reduced pottery are, of course, the stonewares and porcelains of the ancient Chinese. Since great quantities of pottery of high quality were produced in what were, actually, the first large factories in history, the firing obviously must have been under good control. The question arises as to why the Chinese, over a thousand years ago, were able to control reduction firing quite well, while we, with all our controls and technique, have difficulty. The answer is that, in firing kilns to elevated temperatures with wood or other solid fuels, a neutral or slightly reducing atmosphere is normal rather than exceptional. In wood firing the fuel is thrown into the fireboxes intermittently. With each stoking of wood, reducing conditions result in the kiln; that is, the wood, in the early stages of burning, gives off more or less smoke or carbon monoxide. As burning proceeds and air can combine with the fuel more completely, the smoke subsides, and essentially oxidizing conditions prevail in the kiln. Actually, in wood firing, if the most efficient advance of temperature is achieved, the atmospheric conditions in the kiln will be near to ideal for producing reduction glaze effects. Normal stoking, followed by complete burning, gives alternating reduction and oxidation in cycles of five to fifteen minutes. If more reduction is required at the end of the firing, the fireman need only put on a little more fuel and close the damper slightly, and if less reduction is required, he need only use smaller pieces of fuel and see to it that the draft is lively. In short, if wood is used as a fuel, the control and stabilization of the reduction fire is a relatively simple matter.

With gas or oil kilns the reduction is accomplished by starving the burners of air and cutting down on the draft through the kiln by partially closing off the damper in the flue. Any open-fired kiln which burns either gas or oil is easily reduced, and the question is, actually, when and how much to reduce. Reduction can be gauged in several ways. If the appearance of the inside of the kiln is somewhat murky or cloudy, rather than clear, reduction is taking place. Another indication is the presence of flame at the damper, which is usually at the bottom of the chimney. Flame here indicates that unburned fuel has traveled all the way through the setting. Another sign of reduction is the appearance of flame at the spy-holes. Usually, when the kiln is reducing, there is a very strong back pressure; that is, the damper is closed sufficiently to force some of the hot gas out the spy-holes or any other openings in the kiln.

A neutral fire is indicated by a moderate back pressure at the spy-hole, accompanied by a slight greenish flame and a small amount of flame visible at the damper. Reduction is indicated by strong back pressure, orange-yellow flame at the spy-holes, and heavy flame at the damper. Black smoke coming from the flue and spy-holes indicates an unnecessary excess of unburned fuel in the firing chamber. Since only carbon monoxide and not free carbon (smoke) enters into the reduction process, the presence of smoke means only that fuel is being wasted and the air polluted.

Since all kilns have their peculiar and individual characteristics, it is difficult to generalize on schedules for reduction firing. Much depends on the kiln, the kind of ware being fired, the glazes, and the effects aimed at. The following points are intended as a general guide which will be helpful in working out a schedule to suit particular needs:

1. The early part of the firing, up to at least 800°C, should be strictly oxidizing. Reduction before this point is unnecessary and may cause trouble by not allowing the carbon contained in the ware to burn out and by causing later bloating or blebbing, from too much carbon in the pores of the ware.

2. For the development of good reduced color in the clay, some reduction should begin at around 800°C. This permits the reduction of some of the iron in the clay while the clay body is still open enough to admit the carbonaceous vapors that affect the reduction. If the clay is vitrified when reduction begins, it will have, when firing is complete, the appearance of oxidized ware, no matter how heavy the reduction in later stages is. Objects such as casseroles, whose future use will be in the oven, should be oxidized to 1000°C, as body reduction inhibits the development of a strength-giving mullite crystal lattice within the clay.

3. A neutral or very slightly reducing atmosphere is usually sufficient from around 800°C up to the highest temperature. Heavy reduction during this period serves no purpose and may injure the ware by causing bloating and by increasing the possibility of pitting and pinholing.

4. It is important that the firing schedule not be too fast. Slow firing, especially toward the end of the cycle, permits the best development of glaze colors and surface quality.

5. Some increase in reduction is usual toward the end of the fire, when the last cones are bending. Celadon glazes may need a fairly heavy reduction at this point. In general, very heavy reduction, accompanied by clouds of smoke, serves no purpose at this period of the firing, and most effects can be secured by keeping the atmosphere only slightly smoky.

6. After the cones are down and the glazes are fully melted and matured, a final period of oxidation may favor the development of iron reds and may prevent brownish color in copper red. More important than oxidizing at this point is a long soaking period during which the temperature does not fluctuate. At least half an hour, and preferably longer, should be allowed between the bending of the last two cones.

7. The kiln should be well sealed during cooling.

The difficult thing about reduction firing is that it is hard to tell exactly how much the kiln is reducing. However, if, over a number of different fires, the potter carefully observes the condition of damper, burner, spy-hole, flue, and the appearance of the interior of the kiln, he should develop a feel for the proper conditions needed for his particular kiln and glazes. Carbon monoxide meters are now available at a reasonable price to determine and to record the amount of carbon monoxide in the kiln or flue. Potters who use CO meters often swear by their efficiency in controlling reliable reduction and saving fuel at the same time. Careful use of these meters often lowers the cost of firing, as most potters tend to reduce more than necessary. Heavy reduction amounts to inefficient heating and is wasteful of fuel.

Since many potters must use electric kilns only, the idea of achieving reduction in the electric kiln is a tempting one. This can be accomplished by introducing solid fuel of some sort into the kiln during firing. Various fuels have been tried, including charcoal, sugar cubes, oil-soaked bandages, twigs, and the like. Moth balls have also been used. This is a dangerous practice, since highly toxic fumes are released. The kind of fuel used is not critical so long as carbon is released. The quantity of fuel added must be determined by experiment for any particular kiln. Since the atmosphere in the electric kiln is static and inert, not very much carbonaceous matter need be added to achieve reducing conditions. The main disadvantage in reduction firing in electric kilns is that the reduction seems to be hard on the elements and makes more frequent replacement necessary.

Reduction colors have been approximated in an oxidizing fire by the addition of a local reducing agent to the glaze itself. Silicon carbide is usually used for this purpose. The silicon carbide must be very finely ground, otherwise the glaze will boil violently and craters will be left in the finished glaze. So-called "volcanic" glazes are made by adding the coarser ground silicon carbide to the glaze, or to a slip or engobe beneath the glaze. For reduction effects the silicon carbide should be 200-mesh or smaller. In a glaze or slip, 1% to 4% of silicon carbide is sufficient to bring about local reduction, and if an alkaline base glaze is used with about 1% of copper added, fairly good copper reds can be made. They are rather erratic, however, and for depth, brilliance, and beauty of glaze there is no substitute for reduction firing in producing copper red. A small amount of silicon carbide is sometimes added to copper red reduction glazes to make the development of the color more certain.

Reduction firing is usually done in the higher ranges of temperature, cone 8 to cone 14. One reason for this is that reduction glazes at their best are either of the highly feldspathic or magnesia types, and these glazes do not mature at lower temperatures. However, much variation is possible in glazes fired in reduction as low as cone 1. Some of the typical reduction glaze colors such as copper red and celadon can be made at lower temperatures by employing glazes fluxed with boron or alkaline frits. Firing procedures and colorants for glazes are, in general, the same for the lower temperature. One difficulty, however, is that below cone 4 pyrometric cones cannot be used in reduction firing because, when reduced, the iron-bearing cones of the lower temperature series do not give accurate indications of temperature. This difficulty can be overcome partially by the use of a pyrometer and draw trials. Since reduction firing at temperatures below cone 8 has no advantage other than a saving in fuel, most people hold to the higher temperatures where both body and glaze have a greater opportunity to fully mature. Potters don't want to be cut off in their prime!

HIGH-FIRE PIECES

Cone 8 to Cone 12 Approximately

Peter Callas, U.S.A., Exodus, 1999, wood-fired stoneware, anagama kiln, natural ash glazes, 38″ x 18″ x 20″. Photo by Craig Phillips.

Meira Mathison, Canada, Basket, thrown, altered, cone 10 reduction, lithium glaze, 12″. Photo by Janet Dwyer.

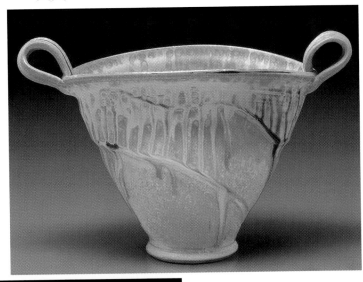

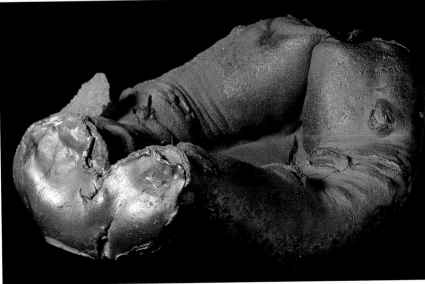

Torbjørn Kvasbø, Norway, Form, South Swedish stoneware "Fyle", slab built, one bottom, one top, then worked from the inside, anagama fired, natural ash glaze, 90cm x 60cm. (Faenza 1 prize, 1999). Photo by Morten Loberg, Norway.

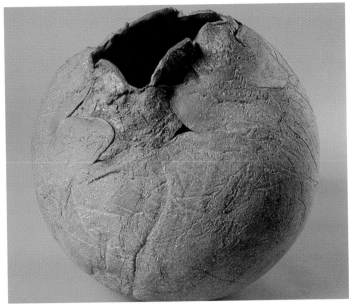

Judi Dyelle, Canada, Large Ball Form, hand-built stoneware and molochite, sprinkled ash on top, reduction fired to cone 9, 16″ x 15″.

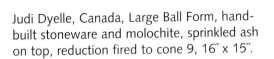

Val Cushing, U.S.A., Covered Jar (Acorn Series), stoneware, 26″ high.

Harris Deller, U.S.A., Blade Shape with Two Triangles (suppressed volume series), porcelain, 15″ x 12″ x 3″. Photo by Jeff Bruce.

Les Miley, U.S.A., Chün Jar, stoneware jar glazed with copper red glaze, placed in section of kiln to receive oxygen during firing results in flash of blue combined with copper red, 8-1/2″ x 7″.

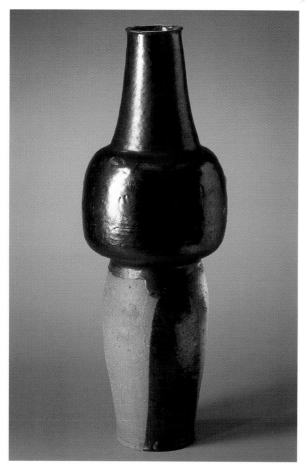

Frans Wildenhain, Tall Vase. Courtesy of the R.B. Johnson Collection, U.S.A. Photo by Geoff Tesch.

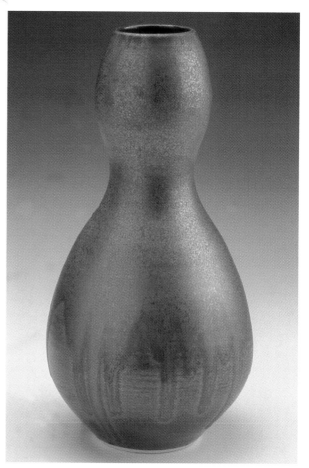

Angela Fina, U.S.A., untitled (container for flower arranging), porcelain, thrown, fired cone 10-11 reduction, high manganese glaze, 12″ high.

Robert Winokur, U.S.A., Hill Town (The Wedge Series), 1996, salt-glazed Pennsylvania Brick clay with slips and engobes, 40″ x 8″ x 16-1/2″ in two parts. Collection of the Los Angeles County Museum.

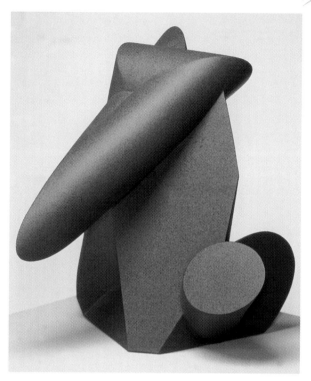

Anne Currier, U.S.A., Juncture, 1999, white stoneware, glazed, 22″ x 17″ x 17″. Courtesy of Helen Drutt, Philadelphia, and the artist. Photo by Brian Oglesbee.

Michael Cohen, U.S.A., Painted Mask, stoneware cone 9 reduction, 12″ x 8″. Photo by the artist.

Judi Dyelle, Canada, Kamloops Series Boat Form, hand-built porcelain, earthenware glaze with metallic oxides, reduction fired to cone 9, 5-3/4″ x 8-1/2″ x 20-3/4″. Photo by the artist.

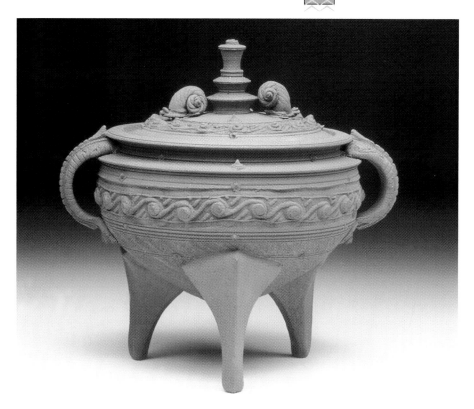

Susan D. Harris, U.S.A., Tripod Covered Ding with Gastropods, 1996, black
stoneware with gold luster, 8-1/2″ x 6-3/4″.

John Glick, U.S.A., Tea Bowl, 1998, wheel thrown and altered stoneware, reduction
to cone 10 with carbon trapping layered shino glazes, 6-1/2″ diameter. Photo by the
artist.

Malcolm Wright, U.S.A., Boat, 1992, stoneware, Chün glaze, ribbon, 5″ x 16″ x 6″. Private Collection.

Christopher Gustin, U.S.A., Vessel, 1999, stoneware, 21″ x 20″ x 30″. Photo by Dean Powell Photography, Newton, Massachusetts.

Harlan House, Canada, Vase a Vase a Vase and Tulips, flower vase, porcelain, celadon glaze over carved bas relief drawings, 33.5cm high. Photo by the artist.

Malcolm Davis, U.S.A., Shino Teapot, wheel thrown with grolleg porcelain, fired to cone 10, red shino-type carbon trap glaze developed by the artist, 8″ x 5-1/2″ x 4″.

Les Manning, Canada, Windswept, laminated stonewares and porcelain, thrown and altered, reduction fired cone 9, with post firing sandblasting and silver amalgam fillings to stress fractures, 21cm x 31cm. Photo by Howard Owen.

Robert K. Flynn, Canada, Covered Box, slab built stoneware, 24cm x 20cm x 10cm.

Richard Aerni, U.S.A., Platter, wheel thrown, cut and paddled with applied slips, single fired with eggshell semi-matte glazes sprayed underneath, various ash glazes sprayed over all, 20″ diameter. Photo by Walter Colley.

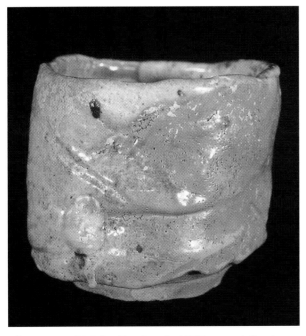

Al Tennant, U.S.A., Tea Bowl, 1998, wood-fired stoneware, shino glaze, 4″ x 4″.

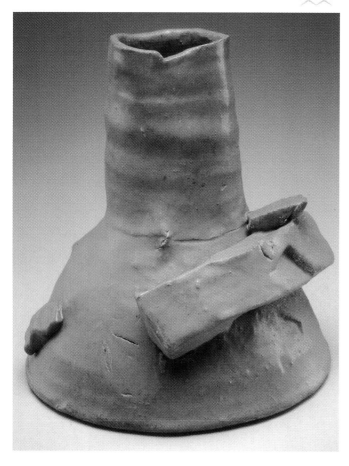

Robert Turner, U.S.A., Canyon III, 1997, stoneware, sandblasted after firing, feldspathic glaze, tin and iron, 10-1/2″ x 10″. Photo by Tim Thayer.

Robin Hopper, Canada, Axe Jar (Classical Series), 1994, porcelain with alkaline slip glazes colored with copper and rutile, brushwork in black/bronze pigment, fired at cone 9 in oxidation. Photo by Stan Funk.

Robin Hopper, Canada, Landscape Bottle (Canada Series), 1978, slab built and thrown porcelain, multiple glaze application, reduction fired at cone 10. Photo by Trevor Mills.

Rosette Gault, U.S.A., Paperclay Vessel, 1997, using formerly impossible wet porcelain over dry assembly, 36″ tall.

Peter Lane, U.K., Porcelain Bowl, thrown with carved rim, crackle glaze, 26cm diameter.

Valerie Metcalfe, Canada, Bowl, copper, cobalt, chrome and iron oxides, under a clear glaze, gold luster, 37cm x 13cm. Photo by Bruce Spielman.

Mary Roehm, U.S.A., Oval Punctuated Bowl, 2000, pale blue celadon glaze, 14″ x 8″ x 7″.

Les Lawrence, U.S.A., New Vision - Teapot, 1997, porcelain, slab, photo silk screen, mono print, stainless steel, 7-1/2″ x 13″ x 2-3/4″. Photo by John Dixon.

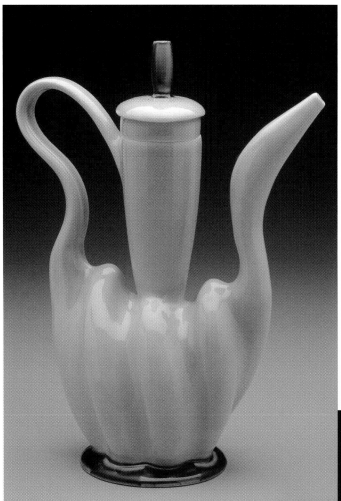

Peter Beasecker, U.S.A., Coffee Pot, 1998, porcelain, cone 10 reduction atmosphere with natural gas, latex and wax resist, 11-1/2″ x 7″. Photo by Harrison Evans.

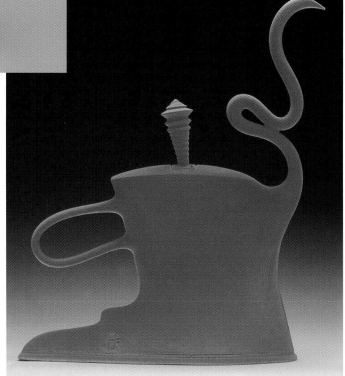

Patrick Horsley, U.S.A., T-Pot/Purple, stoneware thrown and altered with extruded parts, 22″ x 4″ x 21″. Photo by Bill Backhuber.

Curtis Benzle, U.S.A., Candle Sconce, 1998, colored porcelain, press molded, 12″ x 4″ x 4″. Photo by the artist.

Jim Robinson, U.S.A., lidded container, stoneware.

Robin Hopper, Canada, Trifoot Plate, Southwest Series, 1987, porcelain with white terra sigillata and bronze/black pigment, fired at cone 9 oxidation, chrome red glaze applied by brush and trailer and re-fired to cone 06 in oxidation. Photo by Trevor Mills.

Paula Winokur, U.S.A., Segments Erraticus, 1999, three segments of nine, slab constructed porcelain, each 22″ x 22″ x 5″. Photo by John Carlano.

Ron Roy, Canada, Lidded Jar, 2000, stoneware with shino glaze, 6-1/2″ high. Photo by Ron Roy.

Julie Brooke, U.S.A./Scotland, Porcelain Bowl, crystalline glaze with copper, oil drip reduction, cone 9. Photo by Julie Brooke.

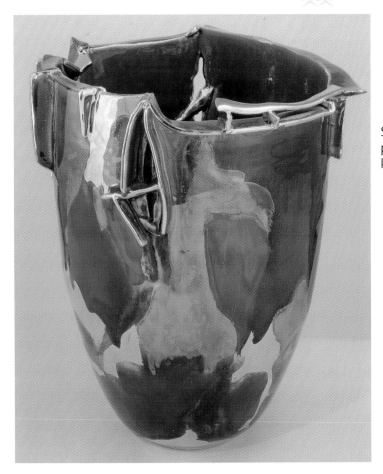

Sally Bowen Prange, U.S.A., Garden Walk, porcelain, glaze and lusters, fired in gas kiln, 8″ x 11-1/2″ x 10″.

Richard Burkett, U.S.A., Cups (for an industrial worker), 1997, soda-fired porcelain and found objects, each 4″ x 4″ x 2-1/2″.

Karen Newgard, U.S.A., Interior Scene Jar, salt-fired porcelain, carved, sgraffito process with terra sigillata, 18″ high.

Gail Nichols, Australia, Bowl, 2000, soda glaze, stoneware, 27cm diameter.

Wil Shynkaruk, U.S.A., Crackle Slip Jar,
1997, salt fired with silver lid, 5″ x 5-1/2″.

Jeff Oestreich, U.S.A., Beaked Pitcher, salt glazed, 9″ x 9″ x 4″.

Jeff Zamek, U.S.A., untitled, soda fired, 12″ high.

Peter Pinnell, U.S.A., Lidded Container, stoneware body augmented with spodumene and mica powder for color and texture, terra sigillata, soda fired.

Ruthanne Tudball, U.K., Teapot on 3 Feet. Photo by Robin Hopper.

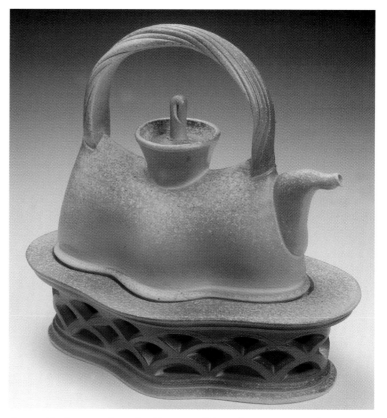

Bruce Cochrane, Canada, Ewer and Stand, 1998, porcelain, thrown and altered, wood fired at cone 10, 8″ x 5″ x 8″.

Jeff Oestreich, U.S.A., Oval Boat, with fiddle head designs, soda firing, thrown and altered, 6″ x 18″.

Suze Lindsay, U.S.A., Footed Bud Vase, 1999, salt-fired stoneware, hand-built, thrown and paddled elements, 6″ x 7″ x 1-1/2″.

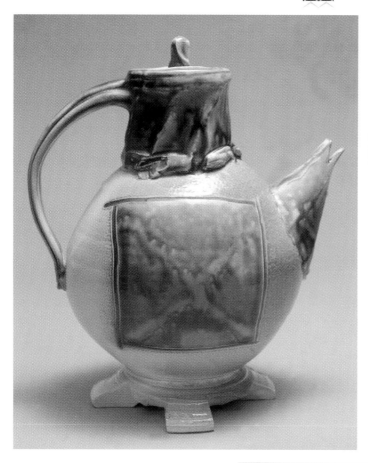

Jay Lacouture, U.S.A., Teapot, 1995, porcelain with soda vapor glazes, 10-1/2″ x 9″ x 6″.

Gail Nichols, Australia, untitled, 1999, soda glazed, stoneware, 40cm high.

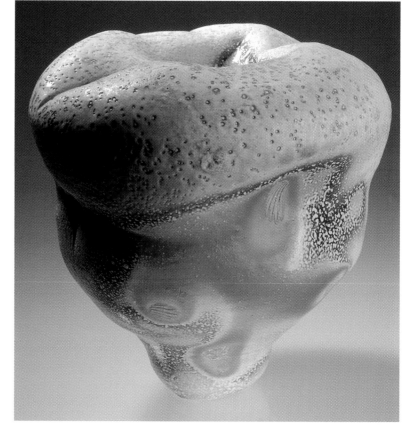

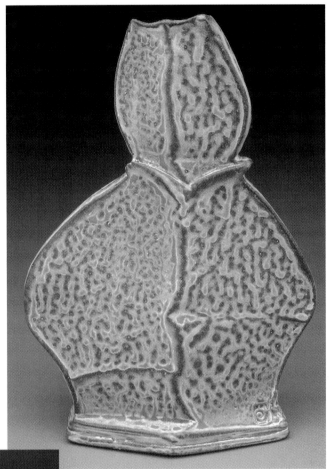

Brad Schwieger, U.S.A., Cut Vase, 1999, soda-fired stoneware, 12″ x 8″.

Jan McKeachie Johnston, U.S.A., Vase, wood fired.

Peter Voulkos, U.S.A., Untitled Tea Bowl, 1999, wood-fired stoneware, John Balistreri anagama kiln, Ohio, approximately 6″ high. Photo by Schopplein Studio.

Marc Lancet, U.S.A., Calling for Owls (JEFB Series), 1997, wood-fired ceramic, 9″ x 17″ x 12″. Photo by Hedi Desuyo.

Paul Chaleff, U.S.A., Covered Jar, 1987, wood fired, 11″ x 10″.

Randy J. Johnston, U.S.A., Footed Vase, wood
fired, 16″ x 9″ x 4-1/2″.

Don Reitz, U.S.A., untitled, 1997, wood fired, cone
10, 12″ x 6″.

Josh Deweese, U.S.A., Jar, 1999, wood-fired
stoneware, 22″ x 16″ x 15″.

John Neely, U.S.A., Cup, unglazed stoneware, wood fired.

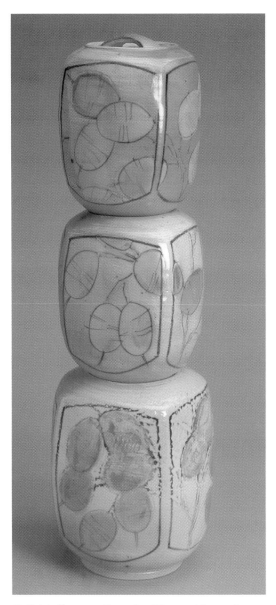

Cathi Jefferson, Canada, "Paper Money" Stacked Canister Set, wheel thrown and altered porcelaineous stoneware, salt/soda fired in gas kiln to cone 10, 15″ x 12″. Photo by Hans Sipma.

Daphne Roehr Hatcher, U.S.A., Two Curvy Spotted Bottles, wood fired at cone 12, ash and black glaze, 24″ high. Photo by Robert Bruce Langham III.

Steven Hill, U.S.A., Footed Jar, thrown and altered with extruded feet, slip trailing, multiple sprayed glazes, single fired stoneware, 7″ x 9″. Photo by Al Surratt.

Peter Callas, U.S.A., Vase (front view), 1998, wood-fired stoneware, anagama kiln, natural ash glazes, 10-1/2″ x 4-1/2″ x 4″. Courtesy The Gallery Dai Ichi Arts, Ltd., New York. Photo by Craig Phillips.

John Neely, U.S.A., Teapot, stoneware, reduction cooled, cane handle.

Peter Beasecker, U.S.A., Ewer, 1999,
porcelain, cone 10 reduction
atmosphere with natural gas, latex and
wax resist, 10″ x 10-1/2″. Photo by
Harrison Evans.

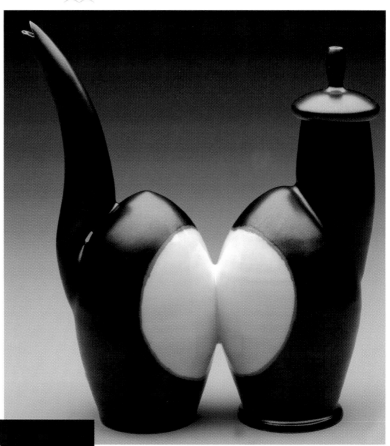

Karen T. Massaro, U.S.A., Moon Over Bananas,
1999, three parts, slip-cast porcelain elements,
underglaze, glaze and china paints, fired cone 10,
12″ x 10-1/2″ x 8″.

Torbjørn Kvasbø, Norway, Slab, stretched porcelain ornament, alumina rich stoneware, anagama fired to cone 12, natural ash surface, 100cm x 60cm x 2cm. Photo by Morten Loberg, Norway.

Jim Leedy, U.S.A., Stilted Vessel with Stripes and Loops, 1992, ceramic stoneware, 31-1/4″ x 15″ x 13″. Photo by Jim Walker.

Sarah Honeyman, Norway, Figure Vessel Form with Moon, Ivanhoe body, layers of porcelain slip, oxides, 11″ x 6″ x 7″.

David Shaner, U.S.A., Shaner's Canyon, 1998, Shaner's Red, 21″ x 24″ x 6″. Photo by Marshall Noice.

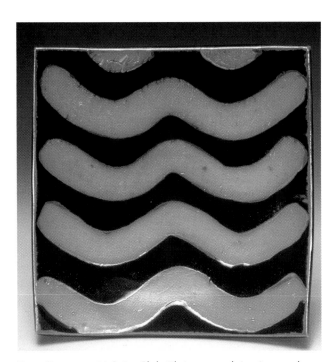

Don Sprague, U.S.A., Slab Plate, porcelain, temmoku glaze, 10″ x 10″.

Gary C. Hatcher, U.S.A., Indented Jar, wood fired at cone 12, purple glaze over khaki, wax resist, 20″ high. Photo by Robert Bruce Langham III.

Arne Åse, Norway, Plate, 1993, porcelain with washed shellac brushwork and soluble colorants. Photo by Glenn Hagebru.

Arne Åse, Norway, Bowl, 1995, porcelain with washed shellac brushwork and soluble colorants. Photo by Glenn Hagebru.

27 SPECIAL GLAZES AND SURFACE EFFECTS

1. Luster

Luster is a form of overglaze decoration in which a thin metallic film is developed on the surface of the glaze. There are two types. In one type the luster is achieved in an oxidizing fire with the aid of reducing agents. In the other type a reduction fire is used.

Lusters produced in oxidation are applied to the glaze in the form of metallic salts combined with resinates, plus an oily medium. Sodium resinate is prepared by boiling lye and rosin together. This material is then combined with metallic salt, either in the form of chlorides or nitrates. Oil of lavender is usually used as a medium. The luster is painted or sprayed onto the glazed surface and fired to red heat. The carbon formed by the resinate and oil reduces the metal, which is deposited in a very thin film on the glaze. The gold or silver banding and striping commonly used on tableware is fired on in an oxidizing decorating fire along with the other overglaze decoration in enamels. Prepared lusters of this type can be purchased ready for use from color manufacturers and are satisfactory in every way.

The other type of luster, which is developed in a reducing fire, was perfected by the Persian potters. In this process the metallic salts are applied to the ware without any local reducing agent, and the metallic luster film is formed by strong reduction in the decorating fire. Copper sulfate, silver nitrate, gold chloride, and bismuth subnitrate are used as sources of the metals. Copper carbonate and silver carbonate may be used instead of the soluble salts. In luster, copper gives red, salmon, or gold color; gold gives reddish purple; silver produces yellowish or ivory lusters; and bismuth lends a colorful iridescence to the surface.

Some vehicle must be used to apply these metallic salts or carbonates to the surface of the ware. Red or yellow ochre are usually used for this purpose, but any fine-grained red clay, such as Ohio Red Art, will usually work just as well. The ochres, which are nonplastic, iron-bearing clays, are the traditional vehicles, combined with some starch or gum to secure the luster film to the ware before firing. About three parts of either red or yellow ochre to one part of the metallic salt or carbonate by weight has been found to be a workable proportion. The ochre and color, plus the starch or gum, are ground to a smooth brushing consistency and are applied to the ware in a very thin film. If thinning the pigment is necessary, it is better to use a natural vinegar than water. The firing should reach the temperature at which the glaze just starts to melt and become tacky so the luster film will attach itself firmly.

Luster films of the Persian type may be fired in an oxidizing fire during the heating cycle. When the top temperature is attained, the kiln is heavily reduced for about half an hour. Strongly reducing conditions are maintained during the cooling cycle until the kiln darkens. Reduction during cooling may be accomplished by keeping a small flame burning in the kiln, with the damper kept almost shut. The reduction during cooling may result in the ware's being somewhat blackened by smoke when it is taken from the kiln, and the lusters may need to be polished or burnished with a mild abrasive to best show their color. The luster may be applied over almost any type of fired glaze surface, although if too much lead is present in the glaze, some darkening or greying may result from the reduction. Many of the most colorful of the old Persian pieces have a luster employed as a final touch over a transparent alkaline glaze which may appear over an engobe that has been both carved in sgraffito and touched with underglaze color. The combination of color under and in the glaze, plus the iridescence of the luster on the surface, results in color effects of great brilliance and depth.

Overall luster effects, or "flash lusters," are made by adding the metallic salt or carbonate directly to the glaze, which is fired in the usual way during the heating cycle but is reduced during cooling, which causes a thin metallic film to develop on the surface of the glaze. Either lead glazes or leadless glazes may be used. Lead glazes may favor the development of color from silver. Usually a low-fired glaze is used, but lusters have also been made successfully with high-fired glazes.

Glazes of the following type have been found to be successful for the development of luster in the temperature range of cone 06 to cone 04.

PbO	.5				
K_2O	.2	Al_2O_3	.18	SiO_2	1.5
CaO	.3				

K_2O	.1				
Na_2O	.6	Al_2O_3	.3	SiO_2	2.5
CaO	.2	B_2O_3	.25		
ZnO	.1				

To the base glaze mill batch is added 1% to 2% of silver nitrate, or 3% to 4% of bismuth subnitrate, or 1% to 2% of copper sulfate. Different amounts of metal will, of course, yield different concentration and character of color.

During the cooling cycle, reduction is begun at about 900° to 800°C. About half an hour of fairly heavy reduction, followed by reducing conditions maintained with a flame or by the introduction of carbon fuel into the kiln during the cooling until the kiln darkens, will be sufficient to develop the luster.

Luster glazes of the overall type may be used over fired glazed surfaces in majolica-like technique. If such a method is employed, the lustered part of the decoration will stand out somewhat from the surface of the ware in the manner of an overglaze enamel.

Iridescent or luster-like surfaces may be produced on glazes or glass by the fuming process. Fuming is done either during the cooling cycle or by reheating the glazed ware in a kiln. When the kiln is at 700°C, tin chloride (stannous chloride) is placed in the setting, where it volatilizes and comes to rest on the glazed surfaces. The tin chloride can be introduced in a small cast-iron cup through an opening in the kiln door. Better results are obtained if the metal cup used for the fuming salts is heated to red heat with a torch before it is filled and put into the kiln. The kiln must be sealed to prevent the fumes from escaping. About fifty grams of tin chloride is sufficient to produce effective fumes in a kiln of ten cubic feet. It may prove difficult to obtain an even distribution of fumes unless the material is moved about in the kiln to several locations. An even temperature distribution in the kiln is important; if the temperature is too high, scumming may result.

Tin chloride by itself gives a pearly iridescence on the surface of the glaze. The iridescent coating achieved by fuming is thin, and does not have the brilliance or reflective power of a luster glaze. It can, however, give a colorful sparkle to the surface. If heightened color is desired, strontium nitrate and barium chloride may be added to the tin chloride in amounts up to 20%. These salts cause red and blue coloration.

Fuming has been successfully used with salt glaze. When the kiln has cooled down to dull red heat or about 700°C, the fuming salts are placed among the pots in heated cast-iron cups. The thin, high-soda salt glaze iridizes well, and the process can extend the possible range of color in salt glazing.

A wide variety of glazes respond well to fuming, including stoneware glazes. Lead glazes may also be used. Fuming with tin chloride may greatly heighten the iridescence and color of commercial lusters.

Luster was used with magnificent effect by the Persian potters of the Middle Ages. The technique was the perfect ceramic vehicle for a culture which had developed a strong, rich, decorative tradition. Lusters can produce shimmering, highly reflective surfaces with color appearing as a somewhat changeable, elusive factor, adding subtle mystery to form. As with many other traditional techniques, luster still has a potential not yet fully exploited in contemporary work although many new directions in lustered surfaces are currently underway in the U.K., Australia, and France.

2. Salt Glazing

One of the attractive features of salt glazing is the fact that it is accomplished entirely in the firing process. The ware can be put in the kiln raw and taken out glazed. Bisque-firing and glaze application may be eliminated. Salt glazing was widely used in the 19th century for the production of utilitarian wares such as crocks, jugs, and churns, which were usually made in small potteries whose main equipment consisted of a mule-driven pug mill, a kick wheel, and a salt kiln. The process of salt glazing was discovered by German potters in the 12th or 13th century and since that time German potteries have continued to make salt-glazed ware of high technical quality. The German drinking stein is a familiar example of salt-glazed ware.

In salt glazing, the ware is placed raw in the kiln, and the temperature is advanced until the maturing temperature of the clay is reached. For successful salt glazing, the body of the ware must be mature. When a clay body reaches maturity, some of the silica in the body is in the vitreous state and is therefore much more reactive. When the maturing temperature of the body is reached, salt is thrown into the fireboxes of the kiln. The salt rapidly dissociates into a vapor, and the sodium in the salt combines with the silica of the ware to form a thin sodium-alumina-silicate glaze.

Water enters importantly into this reaction, as is illustrated by the equation below, which is a hypothesis for the chemical reaction involved in the salt-glazing process:

$$2NaCl + H_2O \rightarrow 2HCl + Na_2O$$
$$Na_2O + XSiO_2 \rightarrow Na_2O \cdot SiO_2$$

The water that provides the oxygen to form sodium oxide from salt is furnished by the moisture in the fuel, the atmosphere, or in the moisture added to the salt before it is put in the kiln. Hydrochloric acid escapes from the kiln as a fog. Repeated salting builds up the glaze coating to the desired thickness.

For successful salt glazing, a downdraft open-fired kiln is preferable. There should be ample space near the burners for combustion and for the salt to volatilize. The salt may be thrown in around the burner or through an opening above the burner. The kiln should fire with a reasonably even distribution of heat and should be vented into a chimney to prevent the fumes from escaping inside the building. Kiln furniture, such as shelves and props, should be coated with a paste of alumina hydrate, which prevents the glaze from forming on it. Or the shelves can be thickly dusted with powdered alumina hydrate. After repeated firings the kiln becomes glazed over on the inside, and the results are therefore better and less salt is required than when the kiln is new. Either gas or oil is a suitable fuel. Wood was formerly used, and undoubtedly some of the rich color and texture of the old salt-glazed pieces is due to the effect of ash flying through the kiln together with the salt vapors. Wood firing alone results in a kind of vapor glazing, although ordinarily only the parts of the ware exposed to the draft of the kiln will be glazed.

The temperature used in salt glazing depends on the maturing temperature of the clay bodies used. Salt firing can be successfully done as low as cone 04, providing the clay used hardens and approaches maturity at that point. For salting at the lower temperatures some borax can be added to the salt. Additions of borax tend to produce a smooth glaze and may prevent an "orange peel" surface. Stoneware temperatures of cone 6 to cone 10 are more usual, and the characteristic warm greys or grey-browns of salt glaze ware are more likely with stoneware clays fired to the higher temperatures. A temperature should be used which brings the clay to a hard, dense, impervious condition.

Most ordinary clays will salt glaze successfully. Some free silica in the body seems to favor a thicker coat of glaze. Clays that contain considerable iron oxide will salt glaze a dark, rather heavy brown color, such as is seen on salt-glazed drain tile. To obtain light greys or for light amber or tan effects, a clay body having very little iron in it must be used. A smooth, fairly grog-free body is usually preferred, since the thin salt glaze does not cover up the roughness or gritty surfaces caused by grog.

Color in salt-glazed ware is usually obtained by the use of engobes. Most engobe compositions work well, especially those containing considerable free silica. Since partially reducing conditions usually prevail during salt glazing, the color range is somewhat limited compared to the range of oxidized glazes. Cobalt oxide is used for blue, and iron oxide for various shades of tan, brown, or brownish black. Rutile in the engobe may result in beautiful ochre colors.

Instead of using an engobe, the potter may brush thin coloring oxides directly on the ware. Or the color may be brushed onto the ware in the form of soluble salts such as iron chloride or cobalt sulfate.

Salt glaze is perhaps at its best over carved, trailed slip or impressed textures in the clay or over sprigged designs. Texture may be beautifully revealed by the pooling of the glaze in the hollows and depressions of the design. The texture of salt glaze itself may be very rich or slightly rough. The orange peel surface is caused by the glaze gathering on the surface into slight beads or droplets.

The pots are placed in the kiln with some space between them to allow for the circulation of the vapor. It used to be the practice to make pots which could be piled one on top of another in bungs, thus eliminating the need for shelves and props. Jars were made so they could be placed one on another, lids were made so they would stack up, and smaller crocks were placed on larger ones.

One difficulty with salt glazing is that the salt vapors will not go down inside the pots; so the insides have to be covered with a glaze applied in the usual manner. Albany slip was commonly used for this because it was cheap, reliable, and easily applied. Now that Albany slip is not commercially available, substitutes such as Alberta slip may be used instead. However, unless it is protected from the salt vapor by being enclosed, slip glazes may not melt smoothly. Ordinary stoneware glazes work well in salt firing, but may be altered in color and texture.

When the kiln is being set, a series of draw trials are placed in front of the spy-hole. Draw trials are a necessity in salt glazing because they indicate the progress of the salting and the thickness of glaze coat. Cones are of little use to indicate the endpoint of the firing because they are affected by the salt vapors and subside before their normal deformation temperature is reached. Cones do help, however, in indicating the temperature at which the body is nearing maturity and at which salting should begin. Salt may be thrown into the fires by the use of a small shovel or scoop, or it may be moistened and packed into paper cups which are thrown into the fire. Sometimes a salt brine is dripped in front of the burner, since some moisture and steam is essential to the glazing reaction. In salting a kiln of about twelve cubic feet capacity, about one pound of salt may be thrown in at a time. When the vapor inside

the kiln begins to clear up, another batch is added. A total of about five to seven pounds of salt may be needed. The salt vaporizes quite rapidly, and dense clouds of vapor roll through the kiln. While salting is being done, it is necessary to close the damper somewhat to retain the vapors in the kiln until they can react with the ware.

After several saltings a red-hot draw trial is hooked out of the spy-hole, cooled in water, and examined. If it is insufficiently glazed, the firing is continued and more salt is thrown in. When a draw trial shows a substantial coating of glaze, the firing is stopped and the ware cooled in the usual way. However, if light grey colors are desired, rather than tan or brown, the kiln must be cooled very rapidly.

Because of the necessity of firing part of the time with the damper closed and using an open-fired kiln, salt-glazed ware is frequently flashed by the flame. This gives it an uneven color, sometimes darker on one side than on the other. For certain kinds of pottery such accidental flashings may be very pleasant and appropriate. In salt glazing, exact color is hard to control. Ware may vary considerably from one firing to another because of slightly differing atmospheric conditions.

Salt glazing has certain inherent disadvantages. It is very hard on kiln furniture. Because of the encrustations of glaze and the corrosive action of the salt vapors, the salt kiln has a relatively short life. If the cost of maintaining usable furniture and of replacing the kiln from time to time is reckoned in, it will be found that salt-glazed pottery is more expensive to produce than other glazed ware. The possible pollution of the air by poisonous chlorine vapors is another serious consideration to the process. Soda glazing (see following section) is a fairly recent development which produces similar results without the problems of straight salt. Many potters use combinations of both salt and soda. With combinations of salt and soda, the potential polluting gas emissions from the kiln would be reduced.

3. Soda Glazing

The person most often credited and acknowledged as being the first to develop soda firing as his 1973 M.F.A. two-part thesis is potter and ceramic consultant Jeff Zamek. He has written the following report on its initial development and methods of use:

"In the United States during the 1970s, several colleges started experimenting with varying the conventional salt-firing process. Mixtures of soda ash and salt were introduced into their kilns. Many urban centers were imposing restrictions on atmospheric pollution and it was thought at the time that soda ash would offer a cleaner alternative to salt firing. Soda ash when heated releases only sodium, water, and carbon dioxide while salt emits sodium, small amounts of chlorine gas, and hydrochloric acid as it combines with moisture in the atmosphere. Different ratios of salt and soda ash were thrown into pre-existing salt kilns, resulting in erratic degrees of orange-peel or pebble surfaces on the exposed clay. While some results did duplicate traditional salt firing, the true potential of substituting one sodium compound for another was not possible due to several factors.

"In the first series of tests the kilns were contaminated by their past use as salt kilns. Due to large amounts of previously fused sodium in the firebox, bag walls, and kiln walls, the kilns salted the ware when the pre-existing salt reached a temperature at which it turned into a vapor. Furthermore, the combination method of salt/soda didn't offer an accurate test of a pure sodium carbonate firing system. Salt was always present in the 'salting mixture' or in the existing interior or hot face of the kiln. As a further complicating factor the salt/soda mixture was not dispersed over a wide area when introduced into the firing kiln. Less surface area exposed to the heat created less sodium vapor reacting with the pots and greater amounts of ineffective fused sodium in the kiln firebox and bag walls.

"The past experiments were evaluated and while some promising results were indicated, a total salt substitute system was still not achieved. In the fall of 1972, the New York State College of Ceramics at Alfred University was the first institution to fully commit to the testing and development of a total sodium vapor firing system that was not dependent on salt. In evaluating approximately 240 different sodium compounds, two materials met the required conditions of duplicating salt-glazed effects on exposed clay surfaces while also offering an environmentally cleaner alternative to salt firing. Sodium carbonate and sodium bicarbonate (baking soda) showed the most promise as salt substitutes. At that time not much was known about sodium carbonate and its influence on clay bodies and

glazes. However, clay and glaze formulas used in salt firings worked in the new soda firing conditions.

"Soda firing, as in the traditional salt firing, is accomplished with the introduction of sodium carbonate (a white powder) into the kiln as the ceramic ware reaches maturity. When sodium carbonate is dropped into the kiln firebox it vaporizes, resulting in sodium vapor traveling throughout the kiln reacting with the exposed ceramic surfaces. In preparation, ware in the kiln is partially glazed, leaving bare clay, slipped, or terra sigillata coated surfaces to take advantage of the effect of vapor glazing. The exposed clay surface contains alumina and silica, which in the presence of sodium vapor, forms into a sodium-alumina-silica glaze. Chlorine gas and hydrochloric acid are not present in soda-fired kilns. Soda-fired glazed surfaces can range in color from grey to brown with an orange-peel pebble texture quality as found in conventional salt-glazed pottery.

"A primary objective of the soda-firing research was to exactly duplicate the salt-fired effects on clay and glaze surfaces. During the first year of tests, new kilns were built exclusively for soda firing. A complicated and ineffective method of spraying a sodium carbonate/water solution into the kiln was tested and eventually discarded. The spray method of vapor coverage on the pots was too cumbersome and time-consuming for practical application in a working pottery. During 1973 tests were begun on a system of placing dry sodium carbonate on an angle iron which would then be inserted into the kiln. It would be slowly turned over to discharge its contents into the firebox, producing a sodium vapor. The same simple procedure was also used with exceptional results in past salt firings. However, complete orange-peel coverage of the ware was not achieved until the construction of smaller kilns (twenty to forty cu/ft.) after 1974.

"Since the first series of soda firings began at Alfred University, several important characteristics of sodium carbonate have become apparent. The design and size of the kiln plays a significant part in the ability of sodium carbonate or sodium bicarbonate to duplicate uniform orange-peel effects similar to traditional salt kiln results. The same effects were achieved when using either sodium carbonate or sodium bicarbonate as the bicarbonate changes to the carbonate form when heated to 850°C. It was found that the method of inserting the sodium carbonate into the firing kiln determines, to a greater extent than salt, how uniformly the sodium vapor disperses on unglazed clay surfaces. If the size of the kiln and method of introducing the sodium carbonate are not carefully considered, the clay and glaze surfaces will closely resemble a wood/salt firing. Flashing patterns of glazed and unglazed orange-peel areas can be randomly deposited on the ware. Whether the potter wants traditional complete orange-peel coverage or an irregular pattern of soda vapor, the objective in both cases is to deposit only the sodium vapor on the ware, causing a sodium vapor glaze.

"The use of sodium carbonate vapor firing has become a widely accepted method for glazing ceramic objects. Many potters have found that brighter colors are possible with sodium vapor firing. As each new generation of potters experiments further with vapor firing, there will be countless variations on this resourceful glazing technique."

As Zamek states, new generations of potters are indeed experimenting with variations on a theme around the world. One gratifying thing with the development of a new, or variation of an old process, is that it is like a stone dropped in a pond, the ripples go on forever, changing and expanding as they move.

4. Slip Glazes

Slip glazes are glazes made wholly or largely from clays of low fusion point. Many common clays, when fired to cone 8 or higher, will fuse and become fluid enough to spread over the surface of pottery as a dark-colored glaze. Since a good deal of heat is required to melt any clay - even a clay loaded with iron and other fluxes - slip glazes are possible only in the stoneware range of firing and are commonly used over stoneware bodies. Since all clays with a low melting point contain iron and other mineral impurities, slip glazes have a color range limited to tan, browns, and black.

The best-known clay for slip glazing in North America is Albany slip. This clay, which was mined near Albany, New York, contains considerable iron and other impurities and melts by itself at about cone 8. Albany slip is no longer mined commercially, but it is similar to many fusible red clays or earths which are widely found around creeks, river beds, ponds, and lakes. Most surface red clays will

have similar responses to Albany slip and many other substitutes have been developed by ceramic supply companies. At cone 11, these fusible earths become bright, smooth brown or tan glazes. In reduction firing, they tend to become a reddish brown. Albany slip was widely used as a glaze on the utilitarian wares of the 19th century. It is the familiar brown or black that appears on the inside of salt-glazed pieces or on bean pots, crocks, and jugs. It has also been used extensively as a glaze on porcelain insulators.

Although Albany slip was perhaps the most widely used clay for slip glazing, many local clays will make interesting glazes for stoneware or for additions to glazes at all temperatures where a combination of both clay and iron is required. As a test, a small amount of clay can be put on a high temperature clay test tile and run through a glaze fire. If it melts completely and flattens itself out into a smooth puddle or glass, it may be usable as a glaze without further additions. Sometimes the clay is too refractory and needs the addition of some flux to make it melt satisfactorily as a glaze. Feldspar, nepheline syenite, or frit may be added for this purpose. Small additions of calcium and zinc may alter the color or texture of the glaze, and if darker colors of brown or black are desired, iron or iron and cobalt may be added.

Slip glazes are usually applied over raw, unfired ware. Since the glaze is largely made up of clay, it has a high shrinkage, and this may cause difficulties in application. If the ware is glazed while it is still leather-hard, the ware and the glaze shrink together, and the tendency of the glaze to crack may be avoided. Another possibility is to calcine the slip glaze lightly at red heat, which completes its shrinkage, and then to grind the material and apply it to bisqued ware in the usual way. One good thing about slip glazes is that they have a long firing range and may be good over a range of several cones' difference in heat. In general, they are free from the usual glaze flaws and do not craze or pit. Crawling may occur, however, because of the tendency of the glaze coat to crack during drying.

Some of the most famous and admired old Chinese glazes are slip glazes such as the temmoku or "hare's fur" glaze, the "oil spot" glaze, "mirror black," "partridge feather," and other dark iron glazes. All of these effects were secured by the use of natural slip clays of various kinds, with perhaps the addition of wood ash or other flux. These glazes are difficult to reproduce exactly because particular clays give certain colors and textures which are hard to match exactly with some other clay. The temmoku or hare's fur glaze is characterized by streaks of brown or black that run down the sides of the piece in a pattern suggestive of fur. The glaze is a fairly fluid one and tends to puddle in the center of bowls and to run and form a roll or heavy drop on the outside where the glaze ends near the foot. The glaze may run very thin at the edge of the piece. In the best examples of hare's fur from Song Dynasty wares the glaze has a warm lustrous brown color, streaked with a rich black, and gathers in a fat roll at the base of the pot. This glaze was greatly admired by early Japanese connoisseurs, who gave it the name temmoku (see the Glossary).

The so-called partridge feather glaze is marked by brown spots or mottling on a black field. The spots may be richly variegated and suggestive of the markings on feathers. This glaze can be made from a slip clay that goes through a boiling phase during its melting. The brown spots or marks are the remains of craters or bubbles which formed, broke, and with the advancing heat settled down to a smooth surface with only a change of color marking their position. The oil spot glazes result from the same phenomenon. Oil spot glazes are usually dark brown or black in general color, and are marked by small, rather evenly spaced spots, which may be lighter brown or silver colored. These spots are the remains of healed-over blisters that occurred during firing. To secure the mottled effects of hare's fur or oil spot glazes, a slip clay should be used that is high in iron and contains some sulfur, which induces boiling during firing. Some lime in the form of calcium carbonate or dolomite may be added. Firing should be oxidizing, and the higher temperatures of cone 10 to cone 12 give the best results. If the glaze is overfired, the spots or mottling will disappear, and for this reason close firing control is necessary. Some surface clays from along the Hudson River in New York have been found to produce perfect hare's fur glazes without the addition of any other material. The following combinations using Albany slip or Albany slip substitutes may produce mottled glazes or oil spots when fired to cone 11:

Albany slip		Albany slip	
substitute	80	substitute	75
Ochre	10	Iron oxide	5
Spodumene	10	Burnt sienna	10
		Feldspar	10

Slip glazes are perhaps of more interest to the potter than they are to the average collector or user of pottery. The almost uniformly brown or black color of such glazes must be used with great sensitivity if dull results are to be avoided. The best slip-glazed ware is very subtle in character. Slip glazes do have a fascination which comes from the directness of the process and from the fact that they are found on some of the best pottery of the past.

5. Ash Glazes

Wood or vegetable ashes have been used as glaze materials since antiquity, and they may lend a quality to glazes difficult to obtain with other materials. The discovery of ash as a glaze material undoubtedly came about when the early Chinese potters noted that the ware in their open-fired, wood-burning kilns was being partially glazed by the ashes which were carried through the kiln by the draft. Some of the old pre-Han Dynasty stoneware pots show a partial glaze on one side or on the shoulder where a film of ash from the fire landed on the ware and formed a thin coating of glaze. Some of the earliest glazes made in China were probably combinations of ash from the fires of the kilns together with some red clay, and very practical high-temperature glazes can be made from ash, feldspar, limestone, and clay.

The chemical analysis of wood and vegetable ashes shows that they contain 10% to 15% alumina, 30% to 70% silica, up to 15% potassium, up to 30% calcium, together with some iron oxide, phosphorus, magnesia, and other elements. These oxides are all useful in glazes, and potash is a valuable flux. Most ashes will melt to a fluid glass at around cone 10. When ash is used alone as a glaze, it will usually result in a rather thin, watery-looking glaze. Ashes vary rather widely in composition. The ash of a given variety of tree will vary, depending on the soil in which it grew as well as the time of year the tree was cut. The use of ash in glazes depends, therefore, on testing and experimentation with the material at hand. It may be difficult to locate a reliable source of ash that will be uniform in composition, but some potters have successfully used the ashes from the burning of waste in sawmills or furniture factories. The ashes from burned corncobs, rice hulls, or other agricultural wastes such as fruit pits offer possible sources. Inorganic volcanic ash has been successfully used as a glaze material giving results not unlike Albany slip.

To prepare ashes for use in glazes, they may first be mixed with a quantity of water and the resulting thin slurry passed through an 80-mesh screen. Rubber gloves should be used when working with ashes as they are caustic when wet. The material that does not pass the screen is discarded. The ash and water mixture is then allowed to settle, and the water is decanted off. The water will contain some of the soluble alkalies from the ash, and it may be advisable to give the ash a second washing and decanting to remove more of the soluble material. Too much washing, however, may remove too much of the potash and diminish the effectiveness of the ash as a flux. After decanting, the ash is allowed to dry and is then ready for use. An alternate method of preparation is to sift the dry ash through a screen to remove charcoal and coarse particles and to use the material without washing. Such unwashed ash will contain all the original soluble alkalies and may be caustic.

As a start in working out ash glazes, a simple combination of two parts of ash, two parts of feldspar, and one part of clay may be tried. If the glaze resulting from such a proportion is too fluid, more clay may be added, and if the glaze is too stiff, more ash or some other flux such as whiting may be added. Ash glazes will need high firing to fuse, and cone 8 to cone 11 is the usual temperature range, although ashes can be used as minor ingredients in lower temperature glazes, giving much textural variation. The following gives the probable limits of the various materials usual to cone 8 to 11 ash glazes:

Ash	20% to 70%
Calcium carbonate	5% to 20%
Silica	15% to 25%
Clay	5% to 20%

Other materials such as calcium borate, talc, dolomite, red clay, slip clay, or nepheline syenite may be used to make up the glaze. One way to incorporate ash into a glaze composition is to take any stiff stoneware glaze and add progressively larger amounts of ash to it until it shows the marked influence of the added material.

Ash glazes, particularly those fired in reduction, have a peculiarly broken surface texture which may be very attractive. High-fired reduction glazes which have some ash in their composition, together with rutile and a small amount of coloring oxide, can yield very soft, beautifully mottled and colored surfaces.

6. Dry or Unglazed Surfaces

In the potter's preoccupation with glazes, sometime the beauty and suitability of unglazed surfaces for many types of pottery and ceramics is overlooked. Some of the greatest pots of the past, including most Greek, Roman, and almost all pre-Columbian pottery, was unglazed, and these are certainly not lacking in color, variety, and decorative sophistication. Some pots are better left unglazed, allowing the bare clay to speak for itself, or treated in one of the many ways available to the ceramist for adding color and texture to the clay surface without glazing.

As has been discussed, fired clay has a very wide range of color and surface quality, ranging from the smooth, glass-like density of white porcelain to the rough, granular, earthy, and highly textural stuff of certain earthenware bodies. Even if the ceramist had only natural clay colors to work with, he would suffer from scarcely any limitation. There is the further possibility of inlaying or painting one color of clay on another, thus combining, say, a black clay with a light ochre one in the same piece.

The fire imparts a further range of color by its irregular effect on the surface. Where flames impinge directly on the clay, the surface is apt to become a darker color or even to fuse over, with a surface similar to that of a thin glaze. This effect is known as flashing. Of course, in electric kilns or in muffle kilns where flames are prevented from reaching the pots, no flashing will occur. But in oil- or gas-fired kilns with open settings, and especially in wood-burning kilns, flashing is common, if not unavoidable. Flashing is unpredictable and it is difficult or impossible to control, which is perhaps its charm. It is a mark of the fire, conferred without deference to the choices of the potter. Pottery fired in primitive pits or bonfires usually shows pronounced flashing or blackened areas where the clay was reduced or carbonized by the fire.

Flashing can be simulated by washing over the surface of the clay with a solution of salt and water. This technique works best at temperatures in excess of cone 6. The parts treated with saltwater fire to an earthy color or a darker brown than the untreated areas. Care must be taken not to get too much salt on the surface of the clay, however, or blistering will occur. If the potter uses saltwater, edges can be darkened or accented, or the high points in textured relief given a slightly different tone from the surrounding areas.

When dark-burning clays dry, a thin film of soluble salts is sometimes deposited on the surface. This film builds up over a period of months if the piece is kept on the shelf in a dry spot in the raw state. Some of this film can be scraped off with a tool just prior to firing, and the scraped areas will be clearly visible in the fired piece as lighter places. By scraping away part of this natural film on the dried clay surface, textures can easily be emphasized.

As was noted in the section in Chapter 8 on terra sigillata, clay can be polished in the raw state. If the firing temperature is kept very low, such a polish will survive on the fired piece. Polishing tends to align the plate-like particles of clay in a direction parallel to the surface, and it is the exposure of the flat surfaces of the particles which accounts for the smooth, glossy, waxy surface. Polishing can be done with the back of a spoon, with the traditional tool, a smooth pebble, or even the soft side of an old sweatshirt! After a pot is polished over its entire surface, a pattern of dull, unpolished areas can easily be achieved by painting over portions of the polished surface with a slip of clay and water; this technique has been much used by the Pueblo potters of New Mexico and Arizona. Their polished pieces are made either black or red, depending on the degree of oxidation or reduction in the fire. For oxidation they allow the fire to burn out normally with plenty of air getting to it. For reduction they cover the fire with sawdust, manure, buffalo chips, and sometimes green vegetation, and thus produce a concentration of smoke about the pots.

Engobes or slips for use under glazes such as those described at the end of the clay section can be used as the final surface. As has already been described, such engobes can be formulated to give a variety of colors and textures. If engobes are used as a surface without glaze, they tend to have a somewhat chalky appearance, but by proper formulation

of the engobe and sufficiently high firing, a dense, rock-like surface can be formed. Of course, surfaces achieved by the use of engobes alone will not be so impervious to moisture as a glazed surface and hence are not suitable on tableware. But for the outer sides of certain forms and for nonfunctional objects this may not be any disadvantage. Additions of some fusible frit to an engobe can bring it to a fired state which is somewhere between a clay slip and a glaze.

Another effective way of using engobes to achieve dry surface qualities is to cover the engobe with a matte glaze, keeping the glaze extremely thin. When fired, such a glaze, normally opaque, will reveal the color of the engobe below and will at the same time seal over the surface with a coating which gives a semi-glazed appearance. Such surfaces, formed by thinly glazed engobes, can be remarkably like the surface of certain rocks and minerals, and are useful for pieces where an earthy quality is desired or where the reflectant characteristic of glazes is not suitable.

Engobes can be applied as a wash over the surface of the clay and then partially rubbed or scraped off, which will emphasize surface relief. A light engobe, for example, brushed over a dark clay and then partially removed with a sponge will serve to emphasize texture; crevices and striations will be coated with engobe but high points and edges will be dark. If engobes are to be used as the final surface without a covering of glaze, their composition is not critical. For stoneware, for example, a coating may consist of kaolin with the addition of about 20% of feldspar for flux. Coloring oxides may be added to this, or such texturing agents as granular ilmenite, granular rutile, granular manganese, or iron or brass filings.

Pots fired in a wood-burning kiln, if they are not protected by saggers, may become partially glazed during the fire by a deposit of ash. Ashes in the form of fine dust travel through the kiln with the draft and settle irregularly on the ware. When the height of the firing is reached, if it is cone 8 or more, the ash fuses on the pots and forms a kind of glaze. The thickness and character of this glaze will depend on the fuel used and the length of the firing cycle; the glaze may vary from a kind of thin dark flashing to a thick layer of glaze. The thicker glaze tends to build up on the shoulders or rims of pots which naturally hold the accumulation of ash as it settles in the kiln. "Natural" ash glazing of this sort is an important feature of certain old Japanese wares, particularly those from Bizen and Tamba, and is also seen on Chinese stonewares of the Han or earlier dynasties. Such pots were, of course, fired in relatively primitive kilns in which irregular firing made kiln accidents the rule rather than the exception. The wayward and unexpected character of such partial glazing can sometimes give to a pot the quality of a natural event or happening wholly removed from the world of design or planned effect. The Japanese tended to accept and encourage such fortuitous surface modulations as a legitimate and integral part of pottery; they seemed to have a higher regard for the effects that came about as the result of natural forces and processes than for those achieved through conscious control. Certainly the varied surfaces that can result from firing in an open kiln which burns solid fuel are often interesting and seem to be integral to the form in a way that man-made decorations do not.

Another kind of surface modulation which does not involve glaze is the staining or coloration caused by organic matter fired with the clay. The most noteworthy example of this kind of surface treatment is the well-known Japanese Bizen pottery. In Bizen, the potters made an unglazed ware which they packed into the kiln with brine-soaked straw between pieces, presumably to prevent breakage losses. When the straw burned in the firing, it left traces of ash on the surfaces of the pots, and in the finished pieces this ash was fused to the clay, giving streaks of brown or red-brown on the rough exterior. These streaks were accidental in the sense that the potters had no exact control over the pattern they formed. It was precisely this accidental and unplanned quality in Bizen pottery that made it a favorite with the devotees of the tea ceremony.

It is rather surprising that small amounts of organic material fired on the surface of a plate or bowl will produce enough ash to cause discoloration. The effect is not noticeable below about cone 6, but in high firing, organic residues can produce very prominent mottling, spots, streaks, or flashings, especially on light-colored bodies. Besides straw, any other vegetable or organic matter may be tried. Fruits, fruit pits, banana peelings, grasses, eggshells and bones, weeds, sumac buds, and the like will, if fired on a flat unglazed plate, give more or less prominent spottings or flashings. There is no limit to the materials that may be tried. Plain wheat flour, for example, if painted or trailed over the clay, will give prominent brown markings. If straw or weeds are used, they may be dipped first in a light salt solution; the addition of salt increases the prominence of the resulting marks. Many possible experiments will occur to the potter. Various slips, especially those which burn to a light tonality, can be used in connection with added organic substances.

7. Crystalline Glazes

Ordinarily, when a glaze cools, it remains an amorphous, noncrystalline substance. Under special circumstances, however, the glaze can be made to crystallize partially as it cools, and various forms of crystalline glazes are the result. In ordinary glazes the presence of alumina largely prevents the glaze from crystallizing as it cools. Alumina also serves the valuable purpose of increasing viscosity, which prevents the glaze from running excessively. To make crystalline glazes, the amount of alumina in the composition must be drastically reduced, usually to less than .1 molecular equivalents, which in a high-fired glaze is one-third of normal. Many crystalline glaze compositions have no alumina at all. The absence of alumina usually makes the glaze very fluid, and, in producing ware with crystalline glazes, some provision must be made for the flow of glaze. Usually the pots are set in the kiln on a soft china clay pad, which is easily ground from the bottom of the piece, along with the glaze which has run down over it.

A high content of zinc oxide in the glaze favors the development of crystals. In crystalline glazes, about .3 equivalents of zinc are usual. The presence of some rutile or titania also favors crystalline development. The base glaze may contain lead as a flux, or it may be fluxed with alkalies or boron. Alkaline glazes are usually used.

Because of the presence of large amounts of zinc and rutile, crystalline glazes are typically somewhat opaque, and the absence of alumina makes them fluid and bright in surface. The crystals in the finished glaze may be either small and appear in clusters or groups, or the crystals may be large and spectacular in appearance. The presence of coloring oxides such as iron, copper, nickel, manganese, ilmenite, or cobalt may color the glaze and may also tint the crystals in an interesting fashion.

The firing cycle is a critical factor in producing crystals in glazes. The heating phase may be carried out at the usual speed, but cooling must be slowed down at the point where the materials in the glaze tend to crystallize. This is usually at a temperature somewhat below the top temperature but above the point where the glaze solidifies. The point of temperature at which crystallization occurs must be determined experimentally. Slow cooling through the right range of temperature will, if the glaze composition is right, produce large crystals. Typical crystalline glaze compositions might be as follows:

Ferro frit 3110	50	Ferro frit 3110	50
Zinc oxide	25	Zinc oxide	25
Silica	25	Silica	18
		Titanium dioxide	7

Matte crystalline glazes can be made which have little or no clay content and seldom run at cone 10. Developed primarily in Germany, they usually have soft frosty surfaces made with combinations of primarily feldspar, barium, and zinc. A typical barium matte crystalline glaze might have the following composition:

Feldspar	45	K_2O 0.13	Al_2O_3 0.20	SiO_2 1.96
Barium carbonate	30	Na_2O 0.06		
Zinc oxide	10	LiO_2 0.07		
Lithium carbonate	2	BaO 0.41		
Silica	13	ZnO 0.33		
Titanium dioxide	7	Add to basic glaze		

Added coloration would be similar to other crystallines.

Because of their abnormal composition and unusual firing cycle, crystalline glazes are rather hard to produce and perhaps should be classified as oddities among glazes. The presence of spectacular crystals on the sides of a pot, interesting though such crystals may be in themselves, has, in most cases, contributed as little to the aesthetic significance of the piece as it has to the function.

Aventurine glazes are crystalline glazes made with a considerable amount of iron oxide in the glaze. These glazes resemble the color and texture of the gemstone aventurine or gold-stone. In this type of glaze the alumina must either be absent or be present in very small quantity. The flux may be either lead, soda, or potash, but very high-lead glazes are usually favored. The iron oxide is usually present in amounts of from 5% to 9% of the glaze batch. The iron, which is taken into solution during melting, crystallizes out during the cooling cycle, which results in a surface marked by brilliant reddish or gold-colored crystals. Cooling must be slow to bring out the most brilliant crystals. Aventurine glazes can have other colorant additions in low percentages of saturation. Aventurine glazes are sometimes startlingly colorful, but, as in the case of other types of crystalline glazes, they tend to be technical curiosities.

8. Crackle and Pooled Glazes

Crackle glazes may be defined as glazes whose tendency to craze is used for decorative effect. The causes for crazing have already been discussed in a previous chapter. If a glaze is to be deliberately made to craze, alkalies or other high-expansion oxides are added to it. In practice this means, in the case of high-fired glazes, the adding of feldspar and, in the lower-fired glazes, the adding of some alkali such as potash or soda, preferably in the form of a frit. It is an easy matter to alter any glaze to make it craze.

The more serious the crazing, the closer together the network of cracks will be. In some badly crazed low-fired glazes, the cracks are so close together that it is rather hard to detect them. For a wide crackle the glaze should be adjusted so as to be poised between fitting and crazing. Some of the old Chinese stonewares, such as the Ru and Guan wares of the Song Dynasty, have craze lines which form beautiful large straight line patterns.

Craze lines may be emphasized by rubbing ink or other coloring matter into them after firing. One color may be rubbed in immediately after firing and another color may be applied after a few days, when another network of cracks will have developed, thus giving the appearance of a double network of craze lines. Another technique is to rub some soluble colorant, such as iron chloride, gold chloride, copper sulfate, or cobalt sulfate into the craze lines and then fire the piece again. The original craze lines will then appear as somewhat fuzzy lines of color, and the new craze lines, developed in the second firing, will be in a different position.

Pooled glazes are made by melting pools of glass into depressions in the clay or into the inside of bowls or trays. Glaze, frit, cullet, or pieces of broken glass are piled thickly on the part of the ware which is to have the pool, and the firing is then carried to a sufficiently high temperature to melt the glass. Glass melted into a thick mass in this manner, especially if the material is somewhat alkaline, will have a tendency to craze, and the fired result may resemble cracked ice. These effects are sometimes erroneously called crystalline. Some low-melting-point frits, such as Ferro frit 3110, are convenient materials to use. Such a frit may be colored by adding coloring oxides or stains. Broken glass of various colors may also be used. The technique, since it is restricted to flat surfaces, is of limited usefulness.

9. Egyptian Paste

Egyptian paste is an interesting technique because it is actually the earliest form of glaze and was developed prior to 5000 B.C. In Egyptian paste the glaze materials are added to the body in soluble form. When the clay dries, the glaze-forming materials migrate to the surface of the ware and are deposited there. When fired, a thin layer of glaze develops on the surface. The Egyptians used a body containing little or no clay, which they modeled or carved into simple forms or pressed into molds.

In formulating Egyptian paste, the potter must keep the clay content low to allow for sufficient glass-forming material to be present and to give an open, porous structure which will permit the migration of soluble ingredients to the surface. The material will contain about 60% of nonplastic ingredients such as silica, sand, and feldspar. Clay may be added in amounts up to about 20%. At least 10% of some soluble soda compound is necessary. Soda may be added as soda ash, bicarbonate of soda, borax, or combinations of these. Coloring oxides are added directly to the batch. Copper oxide or copper carbonate, which give a beautiful turquoise color, are the favorite colorants. About 3% will give strong blue. Cobalt oxide, manganese oxide, or many colored glaze stains may also be used. Coloring oxides may also be added as soluble sulfates or chlorides. Following is a typical recipe:

Feldspar	40
Silica	20
Kaolin	15
Ball clay	5
Sodium bicarbonate	6
Soda ash	6
Calcium carbonate	5
Fine white sand	8

At best, Egyptian paste is relatively nonplastic, and the forms made with it are, of necessity, simple. Bentonite or dextrine added to the material will partially overcome this difficulty. Objects made from Egyptian paste are fired to about cone 08. Jewelry or small sculptures made in this way may be very beautiful in surface and color. Beads may be fired strung on Kanthol wire in the kiln, which will prevent the slight scar that occurs if the bead is placed on a kiln shelf. (Such scars can be minimized, however, if the shelf is dusted lightly with alumina hydrate or calcium carbonate.) Different colors on the same piece may be achieved by inlaying pastes with various coloring oxides.

10. Black Glazes

Black glazes may be produced by an overcharge of coloring oxides. Oxides of cobalt, iron, copper, and manganese are usually used. About 2% of any three of these will yield a black color in most base glazes. The difficulty is that when a rich black has been obtained, it may be found that the glaze, because of the addition of considerable flux in the form of metallic oxides, has become too fluid. The base glaze may then have to be adjusted by additions of clay. Or, if too much coloring oxide is added to make a black, the metallic oxides may crystallize out in the cooling glaze and produce a dry or even wrinkled surface. A mirror-like black can be made by additions of copper oxide and iron oxide. The most attractive black glazes are those which are slightly matte or crystalline in surface. Such glazes are quite elusive and are perhaps best made with some natural slip glaze, such as Albany slip substitutes, darkened by additions of iron or cobalt oxide.

11. Red Glazes

Red, orange, and yellow are the colors that are most elusive for the potter. Although they can be achieved, to get some of the more vibrant colors, it's necessary to use chromium, cadmium, selenium, and uranium in high lead-based glazes at low fire. This makes them dangerous to use, and, if they are used, they should never be used on anything of a functional nature or for storing liquids in.

Listed below are all the possible sources of the color, some of which have already been described.

1. Chrome red. This color is achieved by adding about 2% of chrome oxide or soluble salts of chromium to a very high-lead glaze which is low in alumina and fires to a temperature not above cone 08. Little or no soda should be present in the glaze. The color is a brilliant orange-red. A typical cone 010 chrome red glaze might be:

White lead	68
Silica	20
Kaolin	10
Soda ash	2
Potassium bichromate	5

2. Uranium red. Uranium oxide may be used in the same type of base glaze as that described above for chrome red. The color is a brilliant orange-red, possibly mottled with black and occasionally with random cream markings.

3. Aventurines. This effect is produced by adding about 7% iron to a low-alumina base, as described above in the section on crystalline glazes. The color tends toward brown or reddish gold.

4. Cadmium-selenium glazes. Cadmium sulfide and selenium are fritted together to form a red glaze stain. This stain, when added to a low-melting-point frit containing some alkalies, will produce a brilliant opaque red color. The glaze must be cooled rapidly, as the color is fugitive. Manufacturers of cadmium-selenium stains will recommend a suitable frit composition for use with the stain to develop the best color. Firing with adequate ventilation in the kiln, as well as exact temperature control, is imperative for cadmium-selenium colors to develop.

5. Chrome-tin pinks. Chrome and tin together in a zinc-free glaze produce various shades of pink or mauve. A true dark red is not possible with this combination, but beautiful and subtle colors may result. Chrome must be present in small quantities - less than 1% of the batch.

6. Saturated iron reds. These colors are best done in a reducing fire. The color tends toward brown.

7. Copper red from reduction firing. Copper can give a range of generally darker, or crimson, or blood-like colors. Although visually and technically seductive, they tend to be quite difficult to control and much testing is usually required to master this group of glazes. Much has been written about copper reds, and probably the best information may be found in either *Copper Reds* by Robert Tichane or *Chinese Glazes* by Nigel Wood, both listed in the bibliography.

8. In recent years a number of inclusion stains have been developed, chemically encapsulating the toxic colorants of cadmium and selenium in a matrix of zirconium. These stains make possible a range of somewhat muted reds and oranges as well as bright yellows. They are chemically inert and will withstand high temperatures and reduction firing without burning out. Since they are complex to produce they are fairly costly to purchase, but do make possible some colors formerly difficult or impossible to achieve. The family of inclusion stains is in the process of development and glaze makers should make themselves aware of new developments through ceramic trade magazines or through the journals of the American Ceramic Society, 735 Ceramic Place, Westerville, OH 43086, U.S.A.

9. Lustered surfaces. Copper and gold used in overglaze lusters may give strong red and purple-red colors.

Of all of these types of red glazes, only those glazes colored with cadmium-selenium will be bright, spectrum red, or "fire-engine" red.

12. Raku Ware

Raku is an approach to pottery making that speeds up some of the processes and brings an immediacy and spontaneity into the work qualities often lost in the normal routine of making, bisquing, and glazing, sometimes with long time lapses in between. Raku, as it is practiced today, is derived from procedures developed by Japanese potters in the 16th century. Chojiro, who died in 1592, and his descendants, who became known as the Raku family, made earthenware utensils for the tea ceremony. The shapes were almost entirely confined to hand-modeled tea bowls of modest size and rather irregular form. These unpretentious bowls, undecorated and made of the most ordinary materials, came to have a masterwork status in Japan, where many people respond to the aesthetics governing the tea ceremony.

Japanese raku bowls were of two types. Red raku was made of a common red or buff clay and glazed with a thickly applied lead glaze which was sometimes used over a thin coat of ochre slip. The color, often somewhat milky or opalescent, was a warm, light red-brown or pinkish brown. Darkened places in the glaze and uneven glaze application gave variety, and the craze marks contributed to the soft mellow surface. The firing temperature was very low, perhaps cone 010 or lower. Black raku, which did not differ in form or function from the red, was glazed at a much higher temperature. The glaze, maturing at about cone 5, was made largely from a type of stone obtained from the bed of the Kamo River in Kyoto. This black glaze, rather leathery in texture, was usually somewhat pitted and had the quality of a wet river pebble. Both the black and the red raku were bisqued in the usual way. Glazing was done in a small, rather improvised wood-burning kiln. The Japanese raku kiln was a cylindrical structure, loaded and unloaded from the top; it had a single firebox for updraft circulation much like the larger bisque kilns widely used in Japan.

The pots were bisqued in the usual way. After glazing, they were carefully dried out on top of the kiln, then thrust directly into the preheated red-hot interior of the kiln. When the glazes had melted, the pots were lifted out with tongs and quickly cooled. In some cases the red raku was allowed to cool normally in the kiln, but the black raku was always taken out hot because this favored the development of the slightly rough surface. Bowls taken out of the kiln with tongs always have a scar in the glaze.

Japanese raku bowls are in perfect accord with the spirit of the tea ceremony; in fact, they might be said to be its most perfect embodiment in pottery. They are modest and intimate in scale, made directly with the hands with a minimum use of tools or wheel, quiet in form without any assertiveness in profile or in detail, and invariably show the unobtrusive marks of the process. The glazes are plain, simple to make, and in no way unusual or spectacular. The pieces have an ingratiating tactile quality; to be fully appreciated they must be handled and touched as well as viewed. They are made specifically for the tea ceremony and function best in the intimate surroundings of the tea room rather than on display in a museum case.

Raku, as it has developed in America, is so different from its Japanese prototype that even the use of the term raku seems inappropriate. Whereas Japanese raku is the ultimate expression of restraint, understatement, and quietism in pottery, raku as it is usually made in the West is apt to be flamboyant in color and flashing luster, assertive in form, and nonfunctional. But there is still much in common. The best of our raku sometimes has an intimacy and warmth, a close relationship to process, and a reliance on intuitive craftsmanship that make it the spiritual cousin, at least, of the Japanese raku.

Raku techniques are simple and make no special demands on either the skill of the potter or his equipment. A clay body must be selected which will withstand the shock of being placed directly into the hot kiln and of being cooled very rapidly. A coarse stoneware body is usually used, bisque-fired to about cone 04. Since the body is not carried to maturity in the bisque fire, it has an open, porous structure with enough flexibility to withstand the heat shock. The clay should contain at least 50% of fire clay or stoneware clay and about 20% of grog. Additional silica should not be included in the body formula. The following composition is typical:

Stoneware clay	30
Fire clay	25
Ball clay	15
Feldspar	5
Grog	25

Actually, a wide variety of bodies have been successfully used for raku, the only critical factor being resistance to heat shock and, of course, enough plasticity for easy working. The color of the clay can more or less be disregarded, since the rapid cooling usually results in a light buff or grey color in any case. If the bisque fire is too high, the body may become too tight and dense and thus be unable to withstand the shock of rapid heating and cooling; the structure of the bisqued clay must be open and porous, even if this means a somewhat soft and breakable finished piece. Engobe decorations may be applied to the raw clay before bisquing. The engobes should contain enough flux to make them adhere tightly to the bisque; otherwise they may peel off in the glaze fire. Underglaze colors may be used in the usual way. Up to the point of the glaze firing, raku making is essentially no different than ordinary pottery making.

Very high-lead glazes were the original form of glaze used on traditional Japanese raku. Lead glazes have been much used in raku because of their low fusion point and trouble-free melting. A typical lead glaze for raku might be:

White lead	55
Silica	25
Feldspar	10
Clay	5
Calcium carbonate	5

Such a glaze may be opacified, or colored with oxides or glaze stains. Glazes with an even higher raw lead content than the above example are sometimes used. These high-lead glazes have the serious disadvantage of toxicity in the raw state, and must be handled with care. Also, when fired, they will be slightly soluble in weak acids and therefore potentially dangerous to the health if used on containers in which acidic foods such as fruit juices are served. It might be argued that raku pots are seldom made specifically for functional use on the table, but the potter can never know what eventually will become of his pieces or how they will be used, and it is his responsibility to avoid making vessels which might become a hazard to health. Soft, lead-glazed raku pots fired at cone 08 or lower could be the source of serious lead poisoning. Used for tea, as in the original use of the tea bowl, there is no problem; but used for citrus juices or wine there may well be a cumulative problem. Raku ware, because it is fired for a relatively short time and is frequently underfired, is especially suspect, and a lead glaze which may be perfectly safe for use with food when fired with a normal cooling and heating cycle might be unsafe when fired with the raku rapid-fire technique.

Leadless glazes based on alkaline frits, boron frits, or calcium borate are good for raku ware, and in using them the potter does not have to worry about the toxicity of lead. The following glaze, for example, will fuse readily at cone 08 or lower:

Calcium borate	50
Nepheline syenite	20
Florida kaolin	10
Soda ash	10

After the potter has thrown, dried, and bisque-fired his pieces, he is ready for the glazing process. The pots are glazed in the usual way by dipping, pouring, or painting. The kiln is heated up to red heat. Any sort of small kiln may be used, provided there is an access door so that the pots may be lifted in and out with tongs. While the kiln is heating, the glazed pots may be dried out. It is essential that all the water that has been absorbed into the body from the glaze be evaporated; otherwise a piece may break in the kiln or the glaze may peel off. Several pieces may be placed in the kiln at once. Usually lifting the pots into the kiln results in some loss of heat, but after the door is closed heat builds up again; in ten or fifteen minutes the pots will be a glowing red and the glazes will be melting. When all bubbling in the glaze has subsided and the surfaces are smooth and shiny, the pots are lifted out one by one and placed on a brick or kiln shelf to cool. As each piece cools, red heat fades to a dark cherry red and then the color of the glaze slowly appears. Cooling may be hastened by quenching in a bucket of water, but this tends to weaken the body.

Reduction effects can be achieved in raku by placing the red-hot piece as it comes from the kiln in a closed container filled with straw, excelsior, sawdust, or dry leaves. Lacking air, the organic material surrounding the pot releases carbon gases which affect the body and glaze of the pot. Smoke penetrates the porous body, blackening it throughout. Craze lines in the glaze are made prominent by the deposit of carbon in them. The smoke treatment of raku pots produces a wayward complexity of surface which would be hard to achieve in any other way. The uneven development of dark areas on the clay, even when no glaze is used, can be all that a pot requires for decoration, as is well illustrated in some of Paul Soldner's raku pieces. The process of reducing raku pots by placing them in smoke-producing material was pioneered by Soldner.

If the technique of cooling raku in a smoke-filled container is used, glazes containing copper will develop some copper red or reflective lustered surfaces. Highly reflective surfaces or metallic lusters can be achieved by adding about 2% to 5% of silver nitrate to the glaze. The addition of 2% or 3% of tin chloride will also favor this effect. The irregularities which tend to result from the raku process often rescue lusters from gaudiness and give them a mellow, seemingly well-aged character. Many potters "get hooked" on probing in smoking straw with tongs to bring out gleaming, still hot, lustered pieces. Unfortunately, lusters made by smoke treatment are not so permanent as lusters made in a regular reducing fire, and they tend to fade and tarnish after a few months.

Raku can be degraded to a mere technical trick. But, at best, it can give the potter a sense of freedom and expectation in his craft and the experience of active collaboration with, rather than the rigid control of, process.

13. Multiprocess Ceramics

Multiprocess ceramics, for want of a better term, are pieces which are fired several times and are given surface treatments that make use of a complex range of colored glazes and decorative processes. Most of the decorative processes and the various possible glaze colors and effects have been discussed in previous sections. Suggestions for organizing and orchestrating some of these are given here.

If strong colors or overglaze elements are to be a feature of a ceramic piece, it is best to start with a light-colored body. The logic of this is obvious; if a dark-burning body is used, any transparent color placed over it will be darkened. To apply colorful glazes over a dark body is like trying to paint a watercolor over brown paper; only opaque colors would show any brilliance of hue. White or light-burning pottery bodies do present some difficulties, especially at the lower range of temperature where frit must be used as a flux. A body which matures at around cone 4 has many advantages. White bodies in this range have a wider firing latitude than those matured at lower temperatures, and are less expensive. An example of a white-burning cone 4 body is clay body D, as given in the table on page 109. Some bentonite could be added for increased plasticity, or, if larger pieces were planned, some addition of fine white grog would be helpful to prevent excessive shrinkage, warping, or cracking.

If a dark body is used, such as bodies A, B, or C in the chart on page 107, a white slip can be used over those parts of a piece which are later to be decorated with underglaze color. Middle-range engobes of the type given in the chart on page 118 will be suitable.

Various surface features can be carried out in engobes on the raw piece. The whole piece, for example, can be coated with a colored slip and designs cut into this in sgraffito style. Or figurative designs can be painted on the clay with various colored slips. If some acrylic media is added to the slips, they can be handled much in the manner of gouache paint. Or slips can be sprayed on with an airbrush, giving shadings from one color to another. At this point the whole range of slip-decorating technique can be employed.

Given the raw piece made out of white clay and coated to a greater or lesser degree with slips, the decision must be made as to whether to give it a high or a low bisque fire. This will depend on the nature of the glazes to be employed. If the glaze is to be a simple clear glaze, or is to incorporate colors which are easy to get at cone 4, then a low bisque fire at about cone 05 and a glaze fire at cone 4 is recommended. On the other hand, if certain colors are desired which are peculiar to a lower range of temperature, then it may be better to bisque at cone 4, maturing the body and slips, and to glaze at cone 05 or 04. For example, if brilliant alkaline glazes such as turquoise blue are desired, or highly colored lead glazes, then the lower glaze firing range should be used.

After bisquing and before the glaze is applied, underglaze colors may be used. These can be painted or sprayed with an airbrush on the white body or over any slip applied to the body. Underglaze pigments should be brushed on rather thinly. Flat areas of color can be laid on, or painting in the manner of watercolor can be done. The color range of commercially available underglaze colors is wide. Acrylic media may be added to the color to minimize the danger of fuzzing or blurring when the glaze is applied. If flowing, blurring, or streaked color is desired under the glaze, colored glazes can be used instead of underglaze pigments. The colored glazes will melt and become incorporated into the covering glaze spread over them. Another possibility is to paint, rub, or dust coloring oxides on the piece before glazing.

If transfer prints are to be used under the glaze, they are applied at this point. Photo transfer images are usually placed on the white body or on a light slip. They can be used in conjunction with colored slips and underglazed colors applied by brushing, stenciling, or spraying.

Applying glazes to the partially vitrified piece presents some problems. Since the piece will be relatively nonabsorbent, the usual techniques of dipping and pouring the glaze may not work unless the glaze is flocculated with magnesium sulfate. Or acrylic medium can be added to the glaze, which is then painted or sprayed on in several thin coats. If colorful lead or alkaline glazes are used, the piece should be fired in either an electric or muffle kiln to avoid the blistering or blackening that may result from direct contact with the flames of gas or oil burners.

This hypothetical piece is now fired to maturity and hardness and has been glazed, either with a cone 4 or a cone 04 glaze. Slip designs or areas appear under the glaze and also underglaze colors and perhaps transfer prints or photographic transfers. The remaining possibility is the addition of various overglaze elements. These must be fired on at a lower temperature in order to avoid further melting or movement in the already glazed surface. Opaque overglaze enamels can be painted or sprayed on over the glaze. These may be laid on in flat areas, or brushed on and partially wiped off, or broken into linear elements. It is best if overglaze enamels do not overlap; each color should be placed separately. The color range of enamels, which fire at about cone 010 to 015, is great, and various colors that are hard to get at higher temperatures are possible. If the overglaze painting is to assume something of the character of a watercolor painting, china paints can be used. Enamels and china paints are usually applied with an oily medium, but acrylic media have also been successfully used. The electric kiln is ideal for firing on the overglaze. Several firings may be required, particularly if china painting technique is used.

Commercial lusters and metallic overglazes are fired on at a still lower temperature, and thus require a separate firing at about cone 018. These are usually carefully painted on with the brush. The thickness of the luster pigment is critical. If metallic overglazes are to be highly reflectant and mirror-like, the clay surface over which they are spread must be very smooth. If the ceramist wishes to exploit lustered surfaces to the full, he should employ reduction techniques, as described in a previous section, to produce a true Persian-type luster. The reduction lusters are much more iridescent than the commercial lusters, and are incomparably more colorful and reflectant. Producing them is, however, not simple, and requires a gas kiln that can be held under heavy reduction during the cooling cycle.

Descending still farther in the temperature range, the potter comes to the possibility of fuming, as described in an earlier section. Some of the commercial lusters have been found to develop greatly increased iridescence when subjected to fuming. Fuming will give greater iridescence to most glazes.

It is unlikely that all of the processes, as briefly outlined above, would be used on any one piece, although this would be possible. It will be seen that the possibilities for color, depth, and reflectance in the ceramic surface are virtually unlimited. If a complex surface is desired, one which requires several firings at different temperatures, the ceramist must organize the work carefully and carry out each operation with much attention to the details of application and firing.

In making ceramics in which low-fired colorful glazes and overglazes are a prominent feature, it is wise to purchase at least some of the materials prepared and ready for use. In spite of the relatively higher cost, purchase of certain colors and glazes will be worthwhile for the savings in time and for the more uniform results that can be expected. Red and orange glazes are hard to make and are best purchased. Commercial lusters, china paints, and most enamel colors, especially reds, pinks, purples, and yellows, are difficult for the individual to prepare and should almost always be obtained from a supply house.

Persian potters of the medieval period achieved a color expression in ceramics that has not been surpassed and which remains an inspiration to those who feel drawn toward surface color and modulation. Although most Persian pieces are quite straightforward in technique, in many cases they do have color placed not only under the glaze but in it and over it. This reflectance from different levels gives the surface its subtle optical quality. Designs were sometimes carried out in sgraffito through a white slip. Underglaze colors elaborate or amplify the design. The glaze itself may be a rich turquoise blue. Over it appear areas of luster in a white gold or coppery tone.

Another approach to the full use of color is the elaborate decoration used by the Chinese on their porcelain in the Ming and later dynasties. These pieces were almost always painted with blue underglaze beneath a clear high-fired glaze as the first step. The enamel colors were then fused on in final low-temperature firings. An astonishing range of color was developed in the enamels, including bright persimmon-orange, yellow, green, and purple, often in a succession of firings.

Beginning in the 18th century, overglaze enamels were perfected in France and Germany. Incredibly elaborate and often highly realistic decorations were carried out on porcelain, sometimes executed by well-known artists. Figurines were finished in naturalistic colors. The individual ceramist working today could hardly hope to equal the technical virtuosity of these old pieces. They were made by teams of specialists, often working under royal patronage. No expense or pains were spared in the search for refinement, elegance, and elaboration.

A full palette of overglaze colors makes possible the production of realistic facsimiles, or ceramic pieces which, though made of clay, masquerade as objects common to other materials. The French potter Bernard Palissy, working in the 16th century, was a pioneer in the making of naturalistic objects from clay. He made casts of lizards, turtles, vegetables, and the like and glazed them in polychrome glazes.

Pottery may be given finishes which are not ceramic, that is, not fired on. There are historical precedents for painting on pots, rather than using fired slips and glazes. In the Chinese Han Dynasty certain pots, made to be placed with the dead in tombs, were painted with opaque, rather chalky colors. Minoan pots were painted in white and red pigments. As a last resort, and one with considerable aesthetic considerations, pottery can be painted with acrylic paints, as is often done in Mexico. These have the advantage of durability and strong color. Plastic varnishes, which are available either in bright or matte surfaces, can be used to cover clay surfaces. Such varnishes are, in fact, very similar in appearance to transparent glazes, and can be used effectively over slip decorations. They are durable, but will not withstand heat and therefore cannot be used on cooking or baking wares. Printed illustrations may be applied to the surface of glazed pots with acrylic. In this process an acrylic medium is used to make a printed picture (from a magazine, for example) adhere to a glazed surface, face down. After the medium has thoroughly set, the paper is washed off with water, leaving the image in printer's ink stuck firmly to the glaze. Such transferred pictures are very durable, especially if covered with one or more coats of acrylic varnish.

The ceramic medium has a bewildering array of possibilities through various layering, ware types, firing and cooling processes. Almost anything is possible in surface, color, and texture. Probably the greatest difficulty for the potter is in limiting the options and finding out who he really is and what he wants to say or do.

28 CONCLUSION

1. Choices in the Use of Ceramic Materials

The selection and use of ceramic bodies, slips, glazes, colors, and textures present problems which ultimately involve aesthetic rather than practical considerations. Any discussion of ceramic techniques which fails to recognize such problems is less than complete.

Ceramics as a medium for artistic expression actually suffers from a plethora of means. There seem to be too many colors, too many textural and tactile possibilities to choose from. Our present-day technical skill has placed any known ceramic color or texture within fairly easy reach of anyone who wants to avail himself of the means. While the achievement of any desired color or texture may involve some testing and work, probable success is assured.

The real problem, then, is not a technical one of how to obtain any given effect, but of how to use it. The choices of colors, textures, and designs which the potter makes when he plans and executes his ware are, of course, a reflection of the true purposes and meanings of his work. In former times the potter had only a limited number of effects available to him, and his expression was contrived in terms of these means. This limited choice undoubtedly contributed greatly to the quality of relaxation and ease which is so characteristic of the best folk art. Secure and untroubled in his work, the traditional craftsman was able to convey serenity and a certain neutrality and timelessness in the forms he created. In the past, craftsmen have been the voice of a collective feeling; they produced works of great aesthetic merit without even being conscious that they were doing more than fulfilling everyday needs to the best of their ability. Not faced with a thousand different possibilities for color and texture, and only using the one clay available to him, the traditional potter made the most of what he knew. From long apprenticeship and from daily repetitious work he became skilled to the point where technique was an unconscious part of him and the making of a pot no more difficult than tying a shoelace. We sense the strength in certain pieces from the past and admire the way in which ends and means are merged and techniques are carried out with a simple, straightforward vigor. These qualities are rarely seen in pottery today. When they do appear, it is usually in the work of some potter who has settled, after a long period of trial, error, and experimentation, on a technique which is congenial to his temperament. From this narrowing down of the possibilities, from this concentration, comes strength.

Much as we may admire the simple, direct, unselfconscious craft of the past, the fact must be faced that our own time has a different task for the artist. Lacking an underpinning of any coherent tradition, the artist's work is characterized by search, and the search itself, rather than any finding, may confer meaning. In this search the limitless availability of technical means, confusing as it is, should be a source of joy. Since fixed values have lost their authority, the distinction between what is experimental and what has been found through experimentation has become blurred or nonexistent.

In ceramics the availability of innumerable colors, glazes, textures, and processes is bewildering, especially to the beginner. With experience the potter gradually learns to thread his way through this complexity of means, and eventually he will find himself able to give up willingly certain areas of technique not congenial to him. To reach this point, it is necessary to try many things and to experience failure as well as success. From the wide range of possibilities some ceramists have been able to work certain veins, to concentrate on and master certain ways of working, and they have eventually succeeded in creating works which are truly reflections of themselves. The failures, false starts, blind alleys, and periods of confusion in their work then appear in retrospect as way stations along the road to a goal which was not at first sensed. Strength and commu-

nicability come from the full, committed unfolding of the idea.

If the potter works in the spirit of open-minded search, he may achieve clarity and a harmony between means and end. If his search is in the area of functional pottery for daily use, he will be led to fitting glazes, pitchers which pour, and tactile surfaces which are pleasant to the touch. On the other hand, ceramics conceived as sculptural form, fantasy, or objects governed only by their own internal logic will assume forms, colors, and surfaces true to that logic. It is obvious that conventional ideals rooted in the craft of functional pottery can no longer serve as criteria for all ceramic expression.

Work in ceramics should be a natural unfolding of the spirit, a concretizing of feeling through the easy and playful intermeshing of the whole person with the beautiful medium we have inherited.

GLOSSARY

Aeolian. Wind-borne.

Air-floated. Sorted as to particle size by air separation.

Amorphous. Without crystalline structure.

Amphoteric. Chemically neutral; neither acid nor base.

Bag wall. A fire wall in a kiln which channels the course of the flame.

Bat. A slab of plaster or fired clay used for drying out clay or as a platform for work in clay.

Bisque. Ware which has had one firing unglazed.

Blowhole. An opening at the top of a kiln to let out heat and facilitate cooling, or to let out steam during the early part of firing.

Blunge. To mix a slip.

Bone china. English soft porcelain made with calcined bones or bone ash as a flux.

B.T.U. British thermal unit. The amount of heat necessary to raise one pound of water 1° Fahrenheit.

Bung. A stack of saggers or pots in the kiln.

Calcine. To heat to red heat or more.

Calorie. Metric unit of heat. The amount of heat necessary to raise one gram of water 1° Centigrade.

Catalyst. An agent which promotes chemical change.

Chamotte. The European name for grog.

Clam. To mud-in the door of a kiln.

Coil. To make clay objects by building with ropes or coils of clay.

Colloidal. Jelly-like, without grain structure.

Crackle. Decorative craze lines in the glaze.

Crazing. The formation of a network of cracks in a glaze.

Damper. A device for adjusting or for closing the opening from the kiln to the chimney.

De-air. To remove the air from clay, as in a de-airing pug mill, which removes the air from the clay by passing it through a vacuum chamber.

Decant. To remove the water that has collected at the top when a material settles in a liquid.

Deflocculate. To disperse the particles in a slip so that less water is required for fluidity.

Dehydration. The loss of water from a clay during firing.

Devitrify. To recrystallize on cooling.

Disc grinder. A grinder composed of two discs, one stationary and one moving, which grind the material between them.

Dissociation point. The degree of temperature at which a substance breaks down into its constituent parts.

Draw. To remove fired ware from the kiln.

Draw trial. A piece drawn from the firing kiln to gauge the progress of the firing.

Dry foot. The foot of a pot which has been cleared of glaze.

Dry pan. A mixer for dry materials in which a pan revolves under heavy wheels or mullers.

Dunt. To break from strains in cooling.

Earthenware. Pottery or other objects made from fired clay which is porous and permeable. Earthenware may be glazed or unglazed, and is usually but not always buff, red, or brown in color.

Effervesce. To give off gas, as in the form of bubbles rising in liquid.

Effloresce. To dry or crystallize into white powder.

Electrolyte. An agent which causes deflocculation. A substance in solution, conducting electricity.

Engobe. A layer of slip applied to ware to change the color of the body.

Eutectic. (1) The lowest-melting mixture of two or more substances. (2) *adj.* Describing the temperature of lowest melting.

Extrusion. The process of making shapes such as drain tile by forcing the clay through dies.

Faience. Glazed earthenware. Originally, the tin-glazed earthenware made at Faenza, Italy.

Fat clay. Highly plastic clay.

Fettle. To finish or smooth the surface of leather-hard clay. To trim off the spare from cast or jiggered pieces.

Filler. A material of little or no plasticity which helps to promote drying and control shrinkage in clay bodies or engobes.

Filter press. A device which removes the excess water from clay slip to make it into plastic clay.

Fit. The adjustment of a glaze to a clay.

Flashing. The impingement of flame on a pot in the kiln. Flashing often causes discoloration of the body or glaze.

Flocculate. To thicken.

Flux. A substance which causes or promotes melting.

Frit. A material used in glazes and enamels consisting of a glass which has been melted, cooled, then ground to a powder for use.

Fuse. To melt.

Gel. To turn to a thick jelly-like consistency.

Glassification. Turning to glass; melting into a glass.

Greenware. Unfired pottery.

Grog. Clay which has been fired and then ground into granules of more or less fineness.

Hakeme. A Korean and Japanese technique of applying slip with a coarse brush.

Hard paste. A hard, white, translucent body; a true porcelain.

Hare's fur. A streaked brown slip glaze. Also known as temmoku (Japanese).

Heat. A form of physical energy generated by combustion, chemical action, or friction, and measured by calories or B.T.U.s.

Igneous. Formed by cooling from a molten state.

Jaw crusher. A machine for crushing composed of one stationary and one movable jaw.

Jiggering. Forming a pot between a revolving mold which shapes the inside and a template which shapes the outside and foot.

Jollying. Forming a pot between a revolving mold which shapes the outside and a template which shapes the inside.

Kaolinization. The formation in nature of kaolin from feldspar.

Kiln wash. A refractory mixture, usually kaolin or flint, which is painted on kiln shelves and saggers to prevent glaze from adhering.

Lagging. The material used for insulating the outside of kilns, such as asbestos.

Lawn. To pass through a screen.

Leather-hard. Clay dried sufficiently to be stiff, but still damp enough to be joined to other pieces with slip.

Levigation. Refining clay by water floatation.

Loss on ignition (L.O.I.). The burning off of carbonates and sulfates etc. during the process of firing.

Luting. Joining leather-hard clay by slip.

Mature. Fired to a tight, hard, serviceable structure.

Mealy. Crumbly, nonplastic.

Mishima. Inlaid slip decoration.

Muffle. The inner lining of a kiln which protects the ware from the direct impingement of the flame.

Neutral atmosphere. An atmosphere in a kiln between reducing and oxidizing.

Open. To make a clay more open or porous in structure by adding fillers or grog.

Open firing. Firing in which the flame may impinge on the ware.

Oxide. Any element combined with oxygen.

Paste. A white clay body.

pH. The relative alkalinity or acidity of a solution.

Pins. Refractory supports used in placing ware in racks or saggers.

Pitchers. Fired pottery ground to a powder.

Plasticity. The property of a material enabling it to be shaped and to hold its shape.

Porcelain. Pottery or other objects made from a white, vitrified, and translucent body.

Pottery. Objects, and especially vessels, which are made from fired clay. The term "pottery" includes earthenware, stoneware, and porcelain.

Pug. To mix.

Pyrometer. A mechanical device for measuring the temperature in the kiln.

Pyrometric cone. A device for measuring heat treatment in the kiln.

Raw glaze. A glaze which contains no fritted material.

Reduction. Firing with reduced oxygen in the kiln.

Refractory. Resistant to heat.

Roll crusher. A machine for crushing, composed of two rollers that break the material to be crushed as it passes through.

Sagger. A fire clay box which protects ware from the flame during firing.

Salt glaze. Glazing by the vapors from salt in the kiln.

Sang de boeuf. A copper red glaze.

Sedimentary. Formed in layers or strata by sedimentation.

Sgraffito. The decorative process which employs a scratched line through a layer of slip to expose the clay body beneath.

Shards. Pieces of broken pottery.

Short. Nonplastic; poor in working properties.

Siccative. A medium which promotes the drying of oils used in underglaze or overglaze colors.

Sinter. To fire to the point where cohesion of the materials begins.

Slake. To moisten dry clay with water.

Slip. A fluid suspension of clay or other materials and water.

Slip glaze. A glaze made mostly from clay.

Slurry. A mixture of plastic clay and water.

Soak. To hold the kiln at one temperature for a period of time.

Soluble. Capable of being dissolved in water.

Spare. The scrap clay which is trimmed off during casting pottery.

Sprig. A relief decoration added to a clay surface. Sprigs are usually thin slabs formed in a mold.

Spurs. Triangular refractory supports which hold glazed ware up and away from contact with kiln shelves or saggers.

Stack. To set a kiln with pottery.

Stilliards. Ware racks for pottery.

Stoneware. Pottery or other objects made from fired clay which is dense and vitrified. Stoneware is fired at temperatures above 1200°C. It may be dark or light in color, but is not translucent.

Strata. Layers, as of rock formations or clays in nature.

Strip mining. Mining from open pits from which the overburden of unwanted material has been stripped away.

Temmoku. The name temmoku comes from Tien-mu-Shan, "Mountain of the Eye of Heaven," a mountain in Chechiang province, China. It was from a monastery on this mountain that Dogen, a Japanese Zen priest, was said to have brought the first temmoku bowl to Japan in 1228. *See also hare's fur.*

Temperature. The intensity of heat as measured in degrees Fahrenheit or degrees Centigrade.

Throw. To make pottery by hand on a wheel.

Tin enamel. A lead glaze opacified by tin oxide.

Tooth. Roughness in a clay; coarse grain structure.

Viscosity. The relative resistance of a liquid to stirring or movement.

Vitrify. To fire to the point of glassification.

Wad. Bits of clay used to level shelves or sagger lids in the kiln.

Water glass. Sodium silicate.

Water-smoking. The early stage of firing during which water is driven from the clay by the advancing heat.

Wedge. To knead or mix plastic clay by cutting or rolling.

Wet pan. A mixer for damp materials in which wheels or mullers revolve in a pan.

Wicket. The door of a kiln.

Win. To dig or mine clay.

APPENDICES

Appendix 1

Laboratory Tests on Clay

1. Test for the Water of Plasticity

This test determines the amount of water required to make a clay plastic and workable. The more water a clay requires to become plastic, the finer its grain structure is apt to be, and therefore the more it is apt to shrink on drying.

1. Thoroughly dry the clay sample and pulverize it so it will pass a 30-mesh screen.
2. Weigh out 500 grams of the clay onto a glass slab.
3. Fill a 500-c.c. graduate with water and add the water to the clay a little at a time, mixing well after each addition.
4. Knead the clay, adding more water from the graduate if necessary, until it is a smooth mass of about the right consistency for modeling.
5. Note the amount of water which has been added to the clay.
6. Calculate the amount of water of plasticity by the following formula:

Percent water of plasticity =

$$\frac{\text{Weight of water}}{\text{Weight of dry clay}} \times 100$$

2. Test for Drying Shrinkage

The amount of shrinkage is a highly important characteristic of any clay. In this test the linear shrinkage is determined.

1. From a well-kneaded mass of clay of average modeling consistency make a number of bars of the following dimensions: 14 cm. long, 4 cm. wide, and about 1 cm. thick.
2. On the face of each bar make a sharp scratch exactly 10 cm. long.
3. Allow the tiles to dry, turning frequently to avoid warping.
4. Determine drying shrinkage by the following calculation:

Percent linear shrinkage =

$$\frac{\text{Plastic length—Dry length}}{\text{Plastic length}} \times 100$$

3. Test for Firing Shrinkage

Firing shrinkage is usually determined on samples which are fired to several different temperatures. This gives an idea of the progressive tightening of the clay with advancing temperature.

1. Fire the dried bars made in the previous test.
2. Measure the length of the scratch on the fired bar.
3. Calculate the firing shrinkage by the following formula:

Percent linear shrinkage =

$$\frac{\text{Dry length—Fired length}}{\text{Dry length}} \times 100$$

4. Total shrinkage may be calculated as follows:

Percent linear shrinkage =

$$\frac{\text{Plastic length—Fired length}}{\text{Plastic length}} \times 100$$

4. Test for Water Absorption of Fired Clay

The degree of water absorption is a measure of the maturity of a fired clay body. As a clay body approaches vitrification, its absorbency nears zero.

1. Make bars of the clay about 5 cm x 5 cm x 10 cm. At least three bars should be made for each temperature at which the clay is to be fired and tested.
2. Fire the bars.
3. Carefully weigh the fired pieces to the nearest centigram.
4. Boil the fired pieces in water for two hours.
5. Dry the surface of the bars with a towel and weigh them again.
6. Calculate the absorption, using the following formula:

Percent absorption =

$$\frac{\text{Saturated weight—Dry weight}}{\text{Dry weight}} \times 100$$

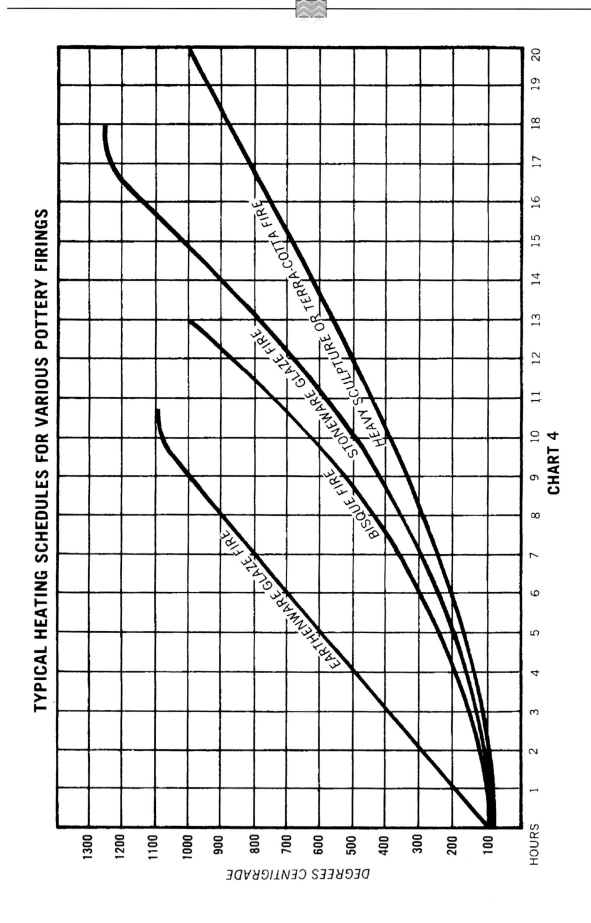

TYPICAL HEATING SCHEDULES FOR VARIOUS POTTERY FIRINGS

STONEWARE GLAZE FIRE

HEAVY SCULPTURE OR TERRA-COTTA FIRE

BISQUE FIRE

EARTHENWARE GLAZE FIRE

DEGREES CENTIGRADE

HOURS

CHART 4

Appendix 2

Chemical Analyses of Various Clays

	English china clay	Georgia kaolin	Tennessee ball clay	Fire clay	Jordan stoneware*	Barnard black-burning clay*	Dalton red clay*
SiO_2	48.3	45.8	53.9	58.1	69.4	41.4	63.2
Al_2O_3	37.6	38.5	29.3	23.1	17.7	6.7	18.3
$Fe_2O_3 + FeO$	.05	.7	.98	2.41	1.6	29.9	6.4
KNaO	1.6		.4	1.56	2.89	1.5	2.8
MgO			.3		.5	.6	.5
CaO	.1				.1	.5	.3
H_2O	12.0	13.6	12.8	13.26	6.4	8.4	6.4
TiO_2		1.4	1.64	1.79	1.3	.2	1.3

* United Clay Mines Analysis.

Water of Plasticity, Shrinkage, and Absorption of a Group of Pottery Clays

	Water of Plasticity	% Shrinkage	% Absorption	% Shrinkage	% Absorption	% Shrinkage	% Absorption
		Fired to Cone 04		Fired to Cone 4		Fired to Cone 9	
Ohio red clay	30.4	11.5	3.9	12.5	0	Bloated	
Red clay	30.5	11.0	9.7	15.0	3.4	15.0	0
Stoneware clay	30.0	9.0	12.2	10.5	8.4	12.0	3.2
Stoneware clay	33.0	6.5	16.8	8.5	11.6	10.5	5.3
Common surface clay	26.0	10.0	1.5	Bloated		Fused	
Sagger clay	40.0	10.0	9.5	13.0	16.0	16.0	5.0
English ball clay	42.6	14.0	16.0	18.0	15.0	18.0	2.0
Fire clay	18.0	8.0	11.7	10.0	8.9	11.0	6.3
Florida kaolin	40.0	12.5	25.2	16.5	12.7	18.5	6.5
Georgia kaolin	35.0	8.0	29.6	9.0	26.9	12.0	22.9

Appendix 3

Atomic and Molecular Weights of the Elements and Oxides Commonly Used in Ceramics:

Element or Oxide	Symbol	Weight
Aluminum	Al	26.9
Antimony	Sb	121.7
Barium	Ba	137.3
Bismuth	Bi	209.
Boron	B	10.8
Cadmium	Cd	112.4
Calcium	Ca	40.
Carbon	C	12.
Chromium	Cr	52..
Cobalt	Co	58.9
Copper	Cu	63.5
Hydrogen	H	1.
Iron	Fe	55.8
Lead	Pb	207.
Lithium	Li	6.9
Magnesium	Mg	24.3
Nickel	Ni	58.6
Oxygen	O	16.
Phosphorus	P	31.
Potassium	K	39.
Selenium	Se	79.2
Silicon	Si	28.
Silver	Ag	107.8
Sodium	Na	22.9
Strontium	Sr	87.6

Tin	Sn	118.7
Titanium	Ti	48.1
Uranium	U	238.1
Vanadium	V	50.9
Zinc	Zn	65.3
Zirconium	Zr	91.
Aluminum oxide	Al_2O_3	101.9
Antimony oxide	Sb_2O_3	291.
Barium oxide	BaO	153.4
Boric oxide	B_2O_3	69.6
Calcium oxide	CaO	56.1
Chromium oxide	Cr_2O_3	152.
Cobalt oxide	Co_2O_3	165.9
Copper oxide	CuO	79.6
Iron oxide	Fe_2O_3	159.7
Silicon dioxide	SiO_2	60.
Lead oxide	PbO	223.2
Lithium oxide	Li_2O	29.8
Magnesium oxide	MgO	40.3
Magnesium dioxide	MnO_2	86.9
Nickel oxide	NiO	74.7
Potassium oxide	K_2O	94.2
Sodium oxide	Na_2O	62.
Strontium oxide	SrO	103.6
Tin oxide	SnO	150.7
Zinc oxide	ZnO	81.4
Zirconium oxide	ZrO_2	123.

Raw Materials Added to Glazes for Color and Texture

Material	Formula	Molecular Weight	Equiv. Weight	Fired Formula	Fired Weight
Antimony	Sb_2O_3	288	288	Sb_2O_3	288
Chromium oxide	Cr_2O_3	152	152	Cr_2O_3	152
Cobalt oxide, black	Co_3O_4	241	80	CoO	75
Cobalt carbonate	$CoCO_3$	119	119	CoO	75
Copper oxide	CuO	80	80	CuO	80
Copper carbonate	$CuCO_3$	124	124	CuO	80
Iron oxide	Fe_2O_3	160	160	Fe_2O_3	160
Manganese carbonate	$MnCO_3$	115	115	MnO	71
Manganese dioxide	MnO_2	87	87	MnO	71
Nickel oxide	NiO_2	75	75	NiO_2	75
Potassium bichromate	$K_2Cr_2O_7$	294	294	$K_2O \cdot Cr_2O_3$	294
Tin oxide	SnO_2	151	151	SnO_2	151
Zircon (zircopax)	$ZrSiO_4$	183	183	$ZrO \cdot SiO_2$	183
Zirconium oxide	ZrO_2	123	123	ZrO_2	123

Appendix 4

End Points of Pyrometric Cones When Heated at 20 Degrees Centigrade per Hour

Cone Number	End Point	Cone Number	End Point
012	840°C	1	1125°C
011	875°C	2	1135°C
010	890°C	3	1145°C
09	930°C	4	1165°C
08	945°C	5	1180°C
07	975°C	6	1190°C
06	1005°C	7	1210°C
05	1030°C	8	1225°C
04	1050°C	9	1250°C
03	1080°C	10	1260°C
02	1095°C	11	1285°C
01	1110°C	12	1310°C
		13	1350°C
		14	1390°C

This list represents the cones and temperatures most used by ceramic artists in North America. Orton pyrometric cones range from cone 022 to cone 42.

Appendix 5

Weights and Measures

The metric system of weights and measures

Weight

1000	grams	=	1	kilogram	(kg.)
100	grams	=	1	hektogram	(hg.)
10	grams	=	1	dekagram	(dkg.)
1	gram	=	1	gram	(gm.)
0.1	gram	=	1	decigram	(dg.)
0.01	gram	=	1	centigram	(cg.)
0.001	gram	=	1	milligram	(mg.)

Length

1000	meters	=	1	kilometer	(km.)
100	meters	=	1	hektometer	(hm.)
10	meters	=	1	dekameter	(dkm.)
1	meter	=	1	meter	(m.)
0.1	meter	=	1	decimeter	(dm.)
0.01	meter	=	1	centimeter	(cm.)
0.001	meter	=	1	millimeter	(mm.)

Capacity or Liquid Measure

1000	liters	=	1	kiloliter	(kl.)
100	liters	=	1	hektoliter	(hl.)
10	liters	=	1	dekaliter	(dkl.)
1	liter	=	1	liter	(l.)
0.1	liter	=	1	deciliter	(dl.)
0.01	liter	=	1	centiliter	(cl.)
0.001	liter	=	1	cubic centimeter	(cc.)

Comparisons of Metric and U.S. System of Weights and Measures

1 gram = .35274 ounce
1 kilogram = 2.2046 pounds
1 ounce = 28.3495 grams
1 pound = 453.5924 grams
1 millimeter = 0.03937 inches
1 centimeter = 0.3937 inches
1 meter = 39.37 inches
1 inch = 2.54 centimeters
1 foot = 30.480 centimeters

Appendix 6

Temperature Conversion Chart

(after Albert Sauveur)

Any centigrade temperature, in column °C, is expressed by the number of degrees Fahrenheit, read from the center column, same line. Similarly, any Fahrenheit temperature, under column °F, is expressed in Centigrade degrees by the adjacent number at the left in the center column. The center column can be used as meaning, originally, either Centigrade or Fahrenheit; and its equivalent in Fahrenheit or Centigrade, respectively, will be found by the number at the right or left.

°C		°F
-18	0	32
-7	20	68
+4	40	104
16	60	140
27	80	176
38	100	212
49	120	248
60	140	284
71	160	320
82	180	356
93	200	392
104	220	428
116	240	464
127	260	500
138	280	536
149	300	572
160	320	608
171	340	644
182	360	680
193	380	716
204	400	752
216	420	788

°C		°F
227	440	824
238	460	860
249	480	896
260	500	932
271	520	968
282	540	1004
293	560	1040
304	580	1076
316	600	1112
327	620	1148
338	640	1184
349	660	1220
360	680	1256
371	700	1292
383	720	1328
393	740	1364
404	760	1400
416	780	1436
427	800	1472
438	820	1508
449	840	1544
460	860	1580
471	880	1616
482	900	1652
493	920	1688
504	940	1724
516	960	1760
527	980	1796
538	1000	1832
549	1020	1868
560	1040	1904
571	1060	1940
582	1080	1976
593	1100	2012

°C		°F	°C		°F
604	1120	2048	949	1740	3164
616	1140	2084	960	1760	3200
627	1160	2120	971	1780	3236
638	1180	2156	982	1800	3272
649	1200	2192	993	1820	3308
660	1220	2228	1005	1840	3344
671	1240	2264	1016	1860	3380
682	1260	2300	1027	1880	3416
693	1280	2336	1038	1900	3452
704	1300	2372	1049	1920	3488
716	1320	2408	1060	1940	3524
727	1340	2444	1071	1960	3560
738	1360	2480	1082	1980	3596
749	1380	2516	1093	2000	3632
760	1400	2552	1104	2020	3668
771	1420	2588	1116	2040	3704
782	1440	2624	1127	2060	3740
793	1460	2660	1138	2080	3776
804	1480	2696	1149	2100	3812
816	1500	2732	1160	2120	3848
827	1520	2768	1171	2140	3884
838	1540	2804	1182	2160	3920
849	1560	2840	1193	2180	3956
860	1580	2876	1204	2200	3992
871	1600	2912	1216	2220	4028
882	1620	2948	1227	2240	4064
893	1640	2984	1238	2260	4100
904	1660	3020	1249	2280	4136
916	1680	3056	1260	2300	4172
927	1700	3092	1271	2320	4208
938	1720	3128	1282	2340	4244

Appendix 7

Suggested Additions of Coloring Oxides to Oxidation Glazes

Cobalt carbonate	1/2 %	medium blue	Cobalt carbonate	1/2%	}	grey-blue
Cobalt carbonate	1%	strong blue	Iron oxide	2%		
Copper carbonate	2%	light green	Cobalt carbonate	1/2%	}	purple-blue
Copper carbonate	4%	strong green	Manganese carbonate	5%		
Iron oxide	2%	tan	Cobalt carbonate	1/2%	}	blue-green
Iron oxide	4%	medium brown	Copper carbonate	2%		
Iron oxide	6%	dark brown	Copper carbonate	2%	}	warm-green
Manganese carbonate	4%	medium purple	Iron oxide	2%		
Manganese carbonate	6%	dark purple	Copper carbonate	3%	}	yellow-green
Chrome oxide	2%	green	Vanadium stain	3%		
Rutile	5%	tan	Copper carbonate	3%	}	warm-green
Nickel oxide	2%	grey or brown	Rutile	3%		
Iron chromate	2%	grey	Cobalt carbonate	1/2%	}	warm-green
Vanadium stain	6%	medium yellow	Rutile	3%		
			Vanadium stain	5%	}	warm-ochre
			Rutile	4%		

Suggested Additions of Coloring Oxides to Reduction Glazes

Cobalt carbonate	1/2%	medium blue	Ilmenite	2%	}	textured yellow-brown
Cobalt carbonate	1/4%	light blue	Rutile	2%		
Cobalt carbonate	1/2%	} turquoise	Iron	1%		celadon
Chrome oxide	1%		Iron	2%		dark olive celadon
Cobalt carbonate	1/2%	} warm textured blue	Iron	4%		mottled green or brown
Rutile	3%					
Cobalt carbonate	1/2%	} grey-blue	Iron	10%		saturated iron red
Nickel oxide	1%		Copper	1/2%		copper red
Nickel oxide	1%	grey or grey-brown	Copper	1%		deep copper red
Manganese carbonate	4%	brown	Copper	3%		red to black
Manganese carbonate	4%	} textured brown	Cobalt	1%	}	black
Rutile	4%		Iron	8%		
Ilmenite	3%	spotty brown	Manganese	3%		

Appendix 8

Base Glazes and Formulas

This selection of glaze bases and formulas are given for four temperature ranges in most popular use at the time of this edition: raku - cone 012 to cone 06; earthenware - cone 04 to cone 1; low temperature stoneware and porcelain - cone 6; and high temperature stoneware and porcelain - cone 8 to cone 10. Except for cones 8 and 11, which contain coloration material as part of the glaze, all the formulas given are for colorless base glazes. In the case of clear or transparent bases, tin oxide, zirconium oxide, and titanium dioxide may be added for opacity and to give possibilities for color change with added coloxrants. All base glazes may be colored by the addition of a wide range of coloring oxides, carbonates, and stains. Adding 2% titanium dioxide to cone 6 to cone 10 oxidation glazes will increase both surface and color interest.

Unless otherwise indicated the basic materials used in these glazes are Custer feldspar, EPK kaolin, OM4 ball clay, and Cadycal 100 for calcium borate. In low-temperature glazes any feldspar may be substituted without much difference showing in the fired glaze. In high-fired glazes the choice of feldspar may have a noticeable effect on the appearance of the fired glaze. However, since particular brands of feldspar come and go on the market, and since the composition of these may change from year to year, it is thought best not to specify a particular kind. In using these formulas the glaze maker is encouraged to experiment with different kinds of feldspars, kaolins, ball clays, and frits to both observe the variables and to create more varied glazes.

These glazes have mainly been developed and tested at the Metchosin International Summer School of the Arts, Victoria, B.C., Canada, over the period 1984 to 2000. They have proven very reliable under our firing conditions. However, glaze formulas may need to be altered and adjusted to work well with particular firing conditions and differing clay bodies. The appearance of a glaze may be different, depending on application, firing temperature, clay body, kiln atmosphere, and the purity of the raw materials.

None of the following glazes contain **lead** in any form. Those that contain **barium** should not be used as glazes intended for storage of foods or liquids for consumption, for cooking in or serving from.

Raku Glazes: Cone 012 to 06

1. Alkaline Frit Base Glaze - Cone 012 to 06

Ferro frit 3110	85	K_2O	.06	Al_2O_3	.18	SiO_2	2.80
Calcium carbonate	5	Na_2O	.56	B_2O_3	.08		
Kaolin	10	CaO	.39				

This is a glossy, clear glaze which is likely to form crackle patterns in cooling. It is a very good base for additions of copper, manganese, cobalt, and many stains which may be greatly affected by highly alkaline glazes.

2. White Raku Crackle Base Glaze - Cone 012 to 06

Ferro frit 3195	75	K_2O	.10	Al_2O_3	.50	SiO_2	3.43
Custer feldspar	25	Na_2O	.31	B_2O_3	.93		
		CaO	.59				

This glaze is a dense, white, smooth satin matte. Its color potential is very diverse. It tends to have a wide format of crackle lines.

3. Smooth White Raku Base Glaze - Cone 012 to 06

Ferro frit 3195	70	K_2O	.03	Al_2O_3	.35	SiO_2	2.15
Lithium carbonate	10	Na_2O	.19	B_2O_3	.63		
Custer feldspar	10	CaO	.39				
OM4 ball clay	10	Li_2O	.38				

This glaze works very well to give lustrous results from added copper or brushed on copper. When oxidized with copper additions up to 5%, beautiful turquoise blues will result.

4. Calcium Borate Raku Base Glaze - Cone 012 to 06

Cadycal 100	80	K_2O	.03	Al_2O_3	.10	SiO_2	.50
Custer feldspar	10	Na_2O	.02	B_2O_3	1.29		
OM4 ball clay	10	CaO	.94				
		MgO	.01				

A glossy, milky, opalescent glaze which will take color very well.

5. Textured Gloss Raku Base Glaze - Cone 012 to 06

Cadycal 100	70	K_2O	.01	Al_2O_3	.11	SiO_2	.42
Nepheline syenite	10	Na_2O	.04	B_2O_3	1.00		
Bone ash	10	CaO	.94	P_2O_5	.07		
OM4 ball clay	10	MgO	.01				

A textured, white, opalescent glaze giving lustrous qualities to the surface and capable of a wide range of color from oxides, carbonates, and stains.

6. Alkaline Fritted Raku Base Glaze - Cone 012 to 06

Ferro frit 3195	70	K_2O	.02	Al_2O_3	.40	SiO_2	2.85
Ferro frit 3110	15	Na_2O	.35	B_2O_3	.91		
Cadycal 100	5	CaO	.63				
OM4 ball clay	10	MgO	.01				

This glaze has a smooth white surface, capable of taking colorants in wide variety.

7. Barium Matte Raku Base Glaze - Cone 012 to 06

Nepheline syenite	12	K_2O	.02	Al_2O_3	.17	SiO_2	.87
Barium carbonate	50	Na_2O	.05	B_2O_3	.36		
Cadycal 100	20	CaO	.27				
EPK kaolin	10	BaO	.66				
Silica	8						

A beautiful satin matte glaze which gives jewel-like colors from copper, cobalt, iron, and many stains. Plum purples from manganese dioxide.

8. Flash Copper Luster Raku Base Glaze - Cone 012 to 06

Ferro frit 3110	20	Na_2O	.06	Al_2O_3	.01	SiO_2	.29
Copper carbonate	80	CaO	.03	B_2O_3	.01		
		CuO	.90				

This is more of a patina than a glaze, giving a wide variation in color to a ceramic surface. Varying the copper and frit content will help to stabilize the surface which may change color from oxidation over time.

Earthenware Glazes: Cones 04 to 01

9. Glossy Opalescent Base Glaze - Cone 04 to 01

Ferro frit 3134	25	Na_2O	.18	Al_2O_3	.33	SiO_2	2.28
Ferro frit 3269	35	CaO	.51	B_2O_3	.52		
Lithium carbonate	5	Li_2O	.3				
Cadycal 100	5						
EPK kaolin	20						
Silica	10						

A smooth, serviceable glaze which will take a wide range of colorants and stains.

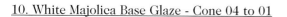

10. White Majolica Base Glaze - Cone 04 to 01

Ferro frit 3124	80	K_2O	.02	Al_2O_3	.40	SiO_2	3.39
EPK kaolin	10	Na_2O	.28	B_2O_3	.55		
Silica	10	CaO	.70				

With an added 8% to 10% tin oxide, this glaze makes a good base for color painting with colorants and stains.

11. Honey Colored Base Glaze - Cone 04 to 01

Ferro frit 3124	40	K_2O	.03	Al_2O_3	.30	SiO_2	2.35
Cadycal 100	30	Na_2O	.14	B_2O_3	.93		
EPK kaolin	10	CaO	.82	Fe_2O_3	.02		
Silica	10	MgO	.02				
Ohio red art clay	10						

A warm-toned, creamy base glaze for use with colorants and stains.

12. Translucent White Base Glaze - Cone 04 to 01

Cadycal 100	40	K_2O	.06	Al_2O_3	.21	SiO_2	1.87
Custer feldspar	20	Na_2O	.03	B_2O_3	.79		
EPK kaolin	10	CaO	.74				
Silica	20	MgO	.17				
Dolomite	10						

Good for use with most colorants and stains.

13. Satin Matte Base Glaze - Cone 04 to 01

Cornwall stone	30	K_2O	.06	Al_2O_3	.56	SiO_2	4.00
Spodumene	30	Na_2O	.08	B_2O_3	.27		
Wollastonite	10	CaO	.59	Fe_2O_3	.01		
Cadycal 100	10	Li_2O	.27				
OM4 ball clay	10						
Silica	10						

A satin-matte creamy white glaze particularly good for coloration with iron oxide to 10%, mixed iron and tin oxide to a total of 10% and up to 5% copper.

14. Dry Matte White Base Glaze - Cone 04 to 01

Ferro frit 3134	50	Na_2O	.16	Al_2O_3	.10	SiO_2	1.49
EPK kaolin	15	CaO	.73	B_2O_3	.33		
Dolomite	10	MgO	.11				
Wollastonite	10						
Calcium carbonate	5						
Silica	10						

A dry matte surface suitable for on-glaze painting with a variety of colorants, including iron chromate.

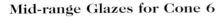

Mid-range Glazes for Cone 6

15. Smooth Opalescent Cone 6 Base Glaze

Ferro frit 3124	25	K_2O	.19	Al_2O_3	.52	SiO_2	2.12
Custer feldspar	45	Na_2O	.18	B_2O_3	.70		
Cadycal 100	20	CaO	.62				
EPK kaolin	10						

A smooth, glossy glaze which when colored with 5% rutile has a very active effect when trailed, brushed, and poured over other colored glazes.

16. Stony Matte Cone 6 Base Glaze

Nepheline syenite	40	K_2O	.04	Al_2O_3	.20	SiO_2	1.00
Calcium carbonate	5	Na_2O	.11				
Dolomite	40	CaO	.47				
OM4 ball clay	10	MgO	.38				
Silica	5						

A dry, stony, matte base which takes color very well, and is particularly good with cobalt, rutile, and copper additions.

17. Shiny Transparent Cone 6 Base Glaze

Custer feldspar	40	K_2O	.13	Al_2O_3	.36	SiO_2	2.43
Silica	15	Na_2O	.06	B_2O_3	.20		
EPK kaolin	15	CaO	.45				
Cadycal 100	10	ZnO	.36				
Calcium carbonate	10						
Zinc oxide	10						

A good base for added colorants and stains.

18. Satin Matte Cone 6 Base Glaze

Custer feldspar	45	K_2O	.13	Al_2O_3	.46	SiO_2	2.25
Ferro frit 3134	15	Na_2O	.13	B_2O_3	.23		
EPK kaolin	25	CaO	.45				
Dolomite	15	MgO	.22				
Cadycal 100	5	BaO	.07				
Barium carbonate	5						

A good satin matte base for use with a variety of colorants, particularly cobalt to 5% and varying mixtures of copper and rutile. Very good with glaze base #15 used over the top.

19. Reticulating Cone 6 Base Glaze 1 - Lichen or Cracked Mud Surfaces

Kona F4 feldspar	30	K_2O	.03	Al_2O_3	.24	SiO_2	1.09
Magnesium carbonate	30	Na_2O	.06	B_2O_3	.04		
Ferro frit 3195	6	CaO	.04				
Talc	8	MgO	.74				
Zinc oxide	6	ZnO	.13				
EPK kaolin	19						

This is a highly textured glaze that forms networks of varied width cracks as it dries. It is best used over a colored or black slip to show the reticulation to full benefit. It can be colored with any colorants or stains and fired over a wide firing range, from very dry at cone 4 to a smooth matte at cone 9.

20. Reticulating Cone 6 Base Glaze 2 - Lichen or Cracked Mud Surfaces

Kona F4 feldspar	35	K_2O	.04	Al_2O_3	.23	SiO_2	1.26
Magnesium carbonate	25	Na_2O	.07	B_2O_3	.13		
Cadycal 100	10	CaO	.11				
Talc	15	MgO	.78				
EPK kaolin	15						

This is similar to glaze #19 but develops smaller cracks and fires to a more shiny surface. It is best used over a colored or black slip to show the reticulation to full benefit. A wide range of colorants can be used either in the glaze or sprayed on top.

21. Glossy Food-safe Cone 6 Base Glaze

Nepheline syenite	36	K_2O	.06	Al_2O_3	.45	SiO_2	2.45
Dolomite	18	Na_2O	.17	B_2O_3	.20		
Cadycal 100	10	CaO	.47				
EPK kaolin	18	MgO	.30				
Silica	18						

A smooth shiny glaze suitable for tableware, and very responsive to color additions, particularly iron, cobalt, and copper.

22. Velvet Barium Cone 6 to 9 Base Glaze

Barium carbonate	25	K_2O	.07	Al_2O_3	.35	SiO_2	1.75
Nepheline syenite	60	Na_2O	.24				
Lithium carbonate	10	CaO	.02				
Silica	5	Li_2O	.34				
		BaO	.32				

This base is not for functional ware use. It is a beautiful frosty matte surface that works well with all colorants, particularly copper to 5%, cobalt to 5%, manganese to 10%, and chromium to 2%.

23. High Gloss Smooth Cone 6 Base Glaze

Nepheline syenite	25	K_2O	.05	Al_2O_3	.38	SiO_2	2.16
Ferro frit 3124	25	Na_2O	.21	B_2O_3	.60		
Cadycal 100	20	CaO	.54				
EPK kaolin	10	ZnO	.20				
Silica	15						
Zinc oxide	5						

A smooth food-safe glaze which has a good response to most colorants.

24. Stony Matte 2 Cone 6 Base Glaze

Custer feldspar	60	K_2O	.17	Al_2O_3	.35	SiO_2	2.24
Calcium carbonate	15	Na_2O	.07				
Zinc oxide	5	CaO	.40				
Talc	10	MgO	.20				
EPK kaolin	10	ZnO	.16				

A good surface for sculpture that takes most colorants very well.

Glazes for Cone 8 to Cone 10 - Oxidation or Reduction

25. Calcium-Alumina Matte Base Glaze - Cone 8 to 10

Custer feldspar	30	K_2O .11	Al_2O_3 .53	SiO_2 2.94
EPK kaolin	30	Na_2O .05		
Calcium carbonate	16	CaO .53		
Talc	12	MgO .31		
Silica	12			

This is a good basic high-temperature glaze for functional ware. It has a lightly frosted surface that takes color well.

26. Smooth Calcium Borate Glaze Base - Cone 8 to 10

Kona F4 feldspar	30	K_2O .05	Al_2O_3 .37	SiO_2 2.01
Cadycal 100	40	Na_2O .10	B_2O_3 .88	
Calcium carbonate	5	CaO .84		
EPK kaolin	15	MgO .01		
Silica	10			

A smooth, translucent glaze which can be opacified with tin oxide for more density. It is good with all colorants and stains, particularly iron, copper, and cobalt.

27. Waxy Matte White Base Glaze - Cone 8 to 10

Custer feldspar	35	K_2O .10	Al_2O_3 .20	SiO_2 2.39
Cadycal 100	17	Na_2O .05	B_2O_3 .31	
Dolomite	10	CaO .37		
Talc	16	MgO .48		
EPK kaolin	4			
Silica	18			

This glaze is an opaque white with a waxy feeling surface. It is good with most colorants and is particularly useful for developing mauve to purple glazes from cobalt additions to 5%.

28. Transparent Shiny Base Glaze - Cone 8 to 10

Custer feldspar	60	K_2O .32	Al_2O_3 .58	SiO_2 5.42
Cornwall stone	10	Na_2O .17		
Calcium carbonate	10	CaO .51		
Silica	20			

This base glaze is good for the development of celadon to temmoku glazes with yellow iron oxide from .5% to 10% and also copper red glazes with copper to 2% and tin oxide to 5% in the base glaze.

29. Matte Barium Base Glaze - Cone 8 to 10

Kona F4 feldspar	35	K_2O .05	Al_2O_3 .31	SiO_2 1.93
Petalite	5	Na_2O .10		
Dolomite	15	CaO .25		
Barium carbonate	25	MgO .23		
EPK kaolin	10	Li_2O .02		
Silica	10	BaO .35		

This glaze is not suitable for functional pottery. With iron it produces a range of yellows to yellow-browns, and with copper it may produce tomato red colors in reduction. It responds to other colorants as a typical barium fluxed glaze.

30. Translucent White Base Glaze - Cone 8 to 10

Material	Amount	Oxide	Value	Oxide	Value	Oxide	Value
Custer feldspar	50	K_2O	.17	Al_2O_3	.32	SiO_2	2.87
Cadycal 100	10	Na_2O	.08	B_2O_3	.22		
Calcium carbonate	8	CaO	.53				
Silica	17	MgO	.11				
Dolomite	6	BaO	.07				
Zinc oxide	1	ZnO	.04				
Barium carbonate	4						
EPK kaolin	4						

This white base is primarily designed to develop copper red glazes by the addition of 5% tin oxide and up to 5% copper carbonate. It is also very good with other colorants, particularly replacing the tin with titanium to develop a range of opalescent red to purple to blues from copper.

31. Oriental Iron Base Glaze - Cone 8 to 10

Material	Amount	Oxide	Value	Oxide	Value	Oxide	Value
Custer feldspar	30	K_2O	.10	Al_2O_3	.29	SiO_2	2.38
Dolomite	15	Na_2O	.04	P_2O_5	.13		
OM4 ball clay	20	CaO	.63				
Bone ash	15	MgO	.23				
Silica	20						

This base glaze is good with a variety of colorants and stains. It is particularly good for developing iron colored glazes from pale green celadons at 1% to 5% to black/brown temmoku at 10% and iron red at 15%. Using yellow iron oxide removes the likelihood of staining.

32. Satin White Glaze Base - Cone 8 to 10

Material	Amount	Oxide	Value	Oxide	Value	Oxide	Value
Custer feldspar	35	K_2O	.12	Al_2O_3	.32	SiO_2	3.00
OM4 ball clay	17	Na_2O	.05				
Calcium carbonate	19	CaO	.58				
Talc	10	MgO	.25				
Silica	19						

This base is good with most colorants and stains, particularly iron, mixed iron and rutile, copper and mixed cobalt, and rutile.

33. High Alumina Matte Glaze Base - Cone 8 to 10

Material	Amount	Oxide	Value	Oxide	Value	Oxide	Value
Custer feldspar	50	K_2O	.17	Al_2O_3	.54	SiO_2	2.36
Dolomite	20	Na_2O	.07	B_2O_3	.11		
Cadycal 100	5	CaO	.42				
EPK kaolin	25	MgO	.34				

This glaze is a slight variation on the High Alumina Matte from the original edition of this book. It has a soft matte surface which gives beautiful pastel or opacified colors. It is good with most colorants and stains, particularly iron, cobalt, copper, and manganese.

Bibliography

Books on Pottery and Ceramics

Andrews, Andrew I. *Ceramic Tests and Calculations*. New York, J. Wiley and Sons, 1928.

Binns, Charles F. *The Potter's Craft, 4th ed*. Princeton, Van Nostrand, 1967.

Cardew, Michael. *Pioneer Pottery*. London, Longmans, 1969.

Clinton, Margery. *Lustres*. Australia, Kangaroo Press, 1991.

Conrad, John. *Advanced Ceramic Manual*. San Diego, California, Falcon Co., 1987.

Cooper, Emmanuel and Derek Royle. *Glazes for the Potter*. New York, Scribners, 1978.

Creber, Diane. *Crystalline Glazes*. London, A & C Black, 1997.

Currie, Ian. *Stoneware Glazes*. Australia, Bootstrap Press, 1985.

Cushing, Val M. *Cushing's Handbook*. Alfred, New York, self published, 1994.

Fraser, Harry. *Glazes for the Craft Potter*. New York, Watson-Guptill, 1973.

Green, David. *A Handbook of Pottery Glazes*. London and Boston, Faber and Faber, 1978.

— *Experimenting with Pottery*. London, Faber and Faber, 1971.

— *Pottery Glazes*. New York, Watson-Guptill, 1973.

— *Understanding Pottery Glazes*. London, Faber and Faber, 1963.

Hamer, Frank. *The Potter's Dictionary of Materials and Techniques*. New York, Watson-Guptill, 1975.

Hetherington, Arthur L. *Chinese Ceramic Glazes, 2nd ed*. South Pasadena, P.D. and I. Perkins, 1948.

Honey, William B. *The Art of the Potter*. London, Faber and Faber, 1946.

Hopper, Robin. *Functional Pottery*. Philadelphia, Chilton Book Co., 1986. New edition, Iola, Wisconsin, Krause Publications, 2000.

Hopper, Robin. *The Ceramic Spectrum*. Philadelphia, Chilton Book Co., 1984.

Koenig, John H. *Literature Abstracts of Ceramic Glazes*. Philadelphia, College Offset Press, 1951.

Lawrence, W.G. *Ceramic Science for the Potter*. Chilton Book Co., 1972.

Leach, Bernard H. *A Potter's Book, 2nd ed*. London, Faber and Faber, 1945.

— *A Potter's Portfolio*. London, Lund, Humphries, 1951.

McKee, Charles. *Ceramics Handbook*. Belmont, California, Star Publishing, 1984.

Mowry, Robert D. *Hare's Fur, Tortoiseshell, and Partridge Feather*. Boston, Harvard University Art Museums, 1996.

Nelson, Glenn C. *Ceramics, 3rd ed*. New York, Holt, Rinehart and Winston, 1971.

Norton, Frederick H. *Ceramics for the Artist Potter*. Cambridge, Addison-Wesley, 1956.

— *Elements of Ceramics*. Cambridge, Addison-Wesley, 1952.

— *Fine Ceramics*. New York, McGraw-Hill, 1970.

Obstler, Mimi. *Out of the Earth, Into the Fire*. Ohio, The American Ceramic Society, 1996.

Parmelee, Cullen W. *Ceramic Glazes, 2nd ed*. Chicago, Industrial Publications, 1951.

Poor, Henry V. *A Book of Pottery; from Mud to Immortality*. Englewood Cliffs, Prentice-Hall, 1958.

Reigger, Hal. *Raku: Art & Technique*. New York, Van Nostrand Reinhold, 1970.

Rhodes, Daniel. *Kilns*. Philadelphia, Chilton Book Co., 1968.

— *Stoneware and Porcelain*. Philadelphia, Chilton Book Co., 1959.

— *Tamba Pottery*. Tokyo, Kodansha International, 1970.

Ruscoe, William. *A Manual for the Potter*. London, Tiranti, 1963.

Sanders, Herbert H. *Glazes for Special Effects*. New York, Watson-Guptill, 1974.

— *The World of Japanese Ceramics*. Tokyo, Kodansha International, 1967.

Tichane, Robert. *Ash Glazes*. Iola, Wisconsin, Krause Publications, 1998.

— *Celadon Blues*. Iola, Wisconsin, Krause Publications, 1998.

— *Clay Bodies*. The New York Glaze Institute, 1990.

— *Copper Red Glazes*. Iola, Wisconsin, Krause Publications, 1998.

Tudball, Ruthanne. *Soda Glazing*. London, A & C Black, 1997.

Wood, Nigel. *Chinese Glazes*. London, A & C Black. Philadelphia, University of Pennsylvania, 1999.

Zamek, Jeff. *What Every Potter Should Know*. Iola, Wisconsin, Krause Publications, 1999.

Magazines and Periodicals

American Ceramics, 9 East 45th St., New York, NY 10017.

American Craft Magazine, 72 Spring St., New York, NY 10012.

Ceramic Review, 21 Carnaby St., London, England W1V 1PH.

Ceramics Art and Perception, 35 William St., Paddington, Sydney, NSW, Australia 2021.

Ceramics Monthly, 735 Ceramic Place, PO Box 6102, Westerville, OH 43086.

Ceramics Technical, 35 William St., Paddington, Sydney, NSW, Australia 2021.

Clay Times, PO Box 365, Waterford, VA 20197.

Crafts, Crafts Council, 44a Pentonville Rd., London, England N1 9BY.

keprameiki techni, International Ceramic Art Review, PO Box 80653, Piraeus 185 10, Greece.

Pottery In Australia, PO Box 937, Crows Nest, Sydney, NSW, Australia 2065.

Studio Potter, PO Box 70, Goffstown, NH 03045.

INDEX

mining of, 72-73
plasticity of, 68, 95
in porcelain, 110
typical composition of, 27
whiteness of, 68
Kaolinite, 28
chemical composition of, 67-68
Kiln
accidents with, 259
gauging temperature, 251-52
managing, 251-52
melting of glazes in, 135
in reduction firing, 272-74
setting glazed ware in, 250
Kneading, 76
Kyanite in raku, 110
Laboratory porcelain, 112-13
Laboratory tests on clay
for drying shrinkage, 331
for firing shrinkage, 331
for water absorption of fired clay, 331
for water of plasticity, 331
Laguna borate, 140, 206
Lead, in making glass, 128
Lead boro-silicate glazes, 140
Lead glazes, 21, 204-5
calculation of batch from formula of simple, 187-88
color range of, 205
early, 130-31
over engobes, 119
Lead oxide (PbO)
as flux, 197
in glazes, 134, 137-39
melting point of, 197
poisonous nature of, 212
Lead poisoning, 137-39, 145, 205
Lead sulfide, adding to glaze, 130-31
Lepidolite as source of lithium for glazes, 113
Lichen glazes, 211
Lignite, 61
Lime
as impurity in clay, 72
in making glass, 128
in porcelain bodies, 111
Limit formulas, 201-2, 210
Limonite, color and, 72
Line blends, 239-40
Litharge, in glazes, 144
Lithium
in flameproof ware, 113
sources of, for glazes, 113
Lithium carbonate in glazes, 145-46
Lithium oxide in glazes, 134, 140
Lizard-skin glazes, 211
Low-fired glazes, 135
Low-temperature alkaline glazes, 203-4
Luster, 308-9
Lustered surfaces, 320
Macaloid, workability and, 99
Magnesia glazes, 271-72
Magnesium
as flux, 197
in igneous rocks, 25
Magnesium carbonate in glazes, 143
Magnesium oxide in glazes, 134, 139
melting point of, 197
opacity and, 216
Magnetic filters in removing iron, 75
Maiolica, 263
Majolica, 263-64
Majolica-like technique, 309
Manganese
in coloring clay, 105
color of clay and, 103
color resulting from, 136
glaze color and, 203
in reduction glazes, 268
Manganese dioxide
in adding color to glass, 128
in coloring clay bodies, 103-4
Manganese oxide
color of glaze and, 223
in Egyptian paste, 319
Marbled ware in coloring clay, 105
Masks, wearing, 20

Mason, 242
Matte crystalline glazes, 318
Matte glazes, 139, 217-18
in reduction, 268
Mechanical mixers for clay slips, 73-74
Metamorphic rock, 26
Methodical blending, 239
Micron, 59
Mid-range glazes for cone 6, 343-46
Mineral, defined, 26
Mixing clays, 73-75
Modeling, 76
Modeling clays, 99
Moisture crazing, 256
Molds, 20
Molecular formula in originating glazes, 209
Molecular weight, 178-79
Molecules, 178
Molochite, and silica and texture of clay, 104
Molochite in achieving white specks, 105
Mullite, 65, 112
ovenproof and flameproof bodies in, 112
Multiprocess ceramics, 323-25
Naples yellow, 134, 140, 260
Natural clay bodies, 94
Nepheline syenite, 98, 143
formula of, 210
in porcelain, 110
Nickel, 25
Nickel oxide, glaze color and, 223-24
Niter, 186
as glaze material, 146
Obsidian, 128
Oemco 54, 206
Oil firing, 253
Oil spot glazes, 314
Once-fired ware, 253
On-glaze process, 263
Opacifier, antimony as, 140
Opacity in glazes, 216
Opalescence, 269
Open-strip mining, 72
Originating glazes, 208-11
based on properties of particular mater-
ial, 210-11
molecular formula in, 209
as percentage recipes, 208-9
Orthoclase
formula for, 28
in glazes, 142
Ovenproof bodies, 111-13
Overfiring, 256, 258
danger of, 203
Overglaze decoration, 263
Overglaze enamels
decoration, 263
painting and, 264-65
Overglaze prints, 265
Oxidation, 133-34
of clays, 64-65
Oxidation glazes, suggested additions of col-
oring oxides to, 339
Oxides, 133-34
addition of single to glazes, 238-39
defined, 133
fluxing action of various, 197-201
in glaze forming, 133-40
grouping, according to function in
glazes, 177-78
Oxygen, 178
Painting, glazing by, 247
Palissy, Bernard, 208
Paperclay, 115-16
Partridge feather glaze, 314
P'Clay¨, 115, 116
Pearl ash as glaze material, 146
Pearlite in modeling clays, 99
Pemco, 242
Pemco frit 54, 140
Percentage analysis, 125
Perlite in modeling clays, 99
Petalite
in flameproof ware, 113
in ovenproof bodies, 112
as source of lithium for glazes, 113
Pigments in underglaze painting, 260-61

Pinholing, 257-58
Pink clays, 104
Pitted shino, 211
Pitting, 257-58
Plants as force in geologic change, 26
Plaster molds, corrosive effects of deflocculants on, 102
Plasticity, 94
of ball clays, 68
bentonite and, 70
in casting clay, 102
of clays, 59-60
development of, in clay over period of
time, 75-76
of earthenware clays, 69, 106
engobe decoration and, 120
in formulating stoneware body, 96
jiggering and, 102
of kaolin, 68, 95, 104
pressing and, 102
testing for degree of, 72
throwing clays and, 98
Plastics, adding, to clay bodies, 96
Poisoning, lead, 137-39, 145, 205
Polymer, 99
Pooled glazes, 319
Porcelain, 110-11
effect of reduction on, 267
as example of clay body, 95
Porcelain body
composition of, 95, 104
formulating, 95-96
Porcelain glazes, 206-7
Porcelain grog in achieving white specks, 105
Porcelain slip, preparation of, 75
Potassium
as flux, 197
in glaze, 203
in igneous rocks, 25
in making glass, 128
Potassium carbonate in glazes, 146
Potassium nitrate in glazes, 146
Potassium oxide in glazes, 134, 136-37
Pottery clays, water of plasticity, shrinkage,
and absorption of, 333
Pottery firing, 252-53
Pouring, glazing by, 247
Powdered quartz and texture of clay, 104
Praseodymium in reduction glazes, 268
Precipitation, 141
Pressing, 102
Primary clays, 60-61, 65
Propeller mixer, 74
Prospecting, 71-73
P'Slip®, 116
Pug mill, 76
Pyrometric cones
end points of, when heated at 20
degrees centigrade per hour, 335
in glaze firing, 251
Pyrophyllite in engobes, 118
Pyroplastic deformation, 23
Quartz, percentages in earth's crust, 26
Quartz inversions of clays, 65
Quartz in glazes, 142
Raku ware, 110, 320-23
glazes for, 340-41
lead glaze used in, 138
method of rapid firing, 209
Recording tests, 243
Recrystallization, prevention of, during cooling
of glaze, 136
Red glazes, 319-20
Red iron oxide, 220
color and, 72
in coloring clay, 103
reduction and, 267
Red lead, 138, 185
in glaze materials, 144-45
Red raku, 321
Reduced glazes, colors from copper oxide in,
270-71
Reduction
colors obtained in firing, 271-72
effects in raku, 322
effects of, on clay bodies, 267

reaction of base glazes to, 267-68
Reduction firing, 252, 258
color of clay and, 220
kiln practice in, 272-74
theory of, 266-67
Reduction glazes
color range of, 268
colors from iron oxide in, 268-70
suggested additions of coloring oxides
to, 339
Refiring, 259
Refractoriness
of fire clays, 68
of kaolin, 68
Reinforced clay bodies, 113-15
Residual clays, 60-61
Resistance to heat of fire clays, 68
Rocks
igneous, 25
metamorphic, 26
Roy, Ron, 123
Rusting, 134
Rutile, glaze color and, 224
Sagger clays, 69
Salt glazes, 132, 310-11
fuming with, 309
Sand
shrinkage and, 63
in stoneware, 109
Saturated iron, 221
Saturated iron reds, 320
Scrap, reuse of, 101
Scum, 72
Secondary clays, 61, 65
Selenium, glaze color and, 225
Semi-opaque glazes, 217
over engobes, 119
Shale, 70
Shivering, 20, 256
Shrinkage
cracking and, 105
drying of clay and, 62-63
in formulating stoneware body, 96
of kaolin, 68
as problem with ball clays, 68
testing for earthenware, 106
vitrification and, 65
Silica
in correcting crazing, 255-56
in earthenware, 107
in engobes, 118
in formulating stoneware body, 96-97
in glass, 127-28
in glazes, 134-36, 142, 201
as oxide of glass, 135-36
in porcelain, 110
in porcelain body, 104
shrinkage and, 63
in throwing clays, 98
in white porcelain, 95
Silicon dioxide, 178
in glazes, 134
Silicosis, 141
Silver, glaze color and, 225
Simpson type mixer, 75
Slimes, 99
Slip. See Engobes
Slip glazes, 131, 142, 313-14
Smectites, plasticity and, 99
Soda ash
in casting clays, 100
as glaze material, 145
Soda glazing, 311-13
Soda in glass making, 128
Sodium
as flux, 197
in igneous rocks, 25
presence of, in glaze, 203
Sodium aluminum fluoride in glazes, 145
Sodium carbonate in glazes, 145
Sodium hydroxide as deflocculant, 100
Sodium oxide in glazes, 134
Sodium poly acralates, 100
Sodium pyrophosphate as deflocculant, 100
Sodium silicate in casting clays, 100

Photo Index

Historical

Contemporary

Other Books by Robin Hopper

The Ceramic Spectrum
Second Edition

As a former painter frustrated by the lack of solid information on ceramic color development, Robin Hopper has researched the processes of color development until he gained mastery over the technical side of this art form. His personal journey of discovery is the core of *The Ceramic Spectrum*. Since publication of the first edition in 1984, Hopper has done further extensive research into glaze, color, texture, and surface enrichment.

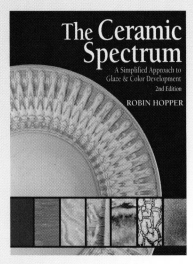

In addition to the material in the first edition, the second edition features several new or expanded chapters including:

- Egyptian Pastes
- Terra Sigillatas
- Flux Variation Triaxial
- Calculation - what it does and doesn't do
- Improved Frit Listings
- Patination
- High Texture Glazes, Raku Glazes, Oriental Iron Glazes and Copper Reds/Purples
- Reduced Lusters

The Ceramic Spectrum is the perfect text for the creative ceramic artist. It explores glaze and color making in a hands-on way that follows the empirical understanding used for thousands of years. It is also the perfect practical complement to any glaze theory, or processes of calculation from slide-rules to software.

CESP2 $44.95
Published August 2001

Functional Pottery
Second Edition

Functional Pottery, the best-selling pottery reference first published in 1986, has been extensively revised and updated to include more than 250 color photos as well as hundreds of black and white photos and illustrations. Covering historical as well as contemporary pottery, this acclaimed and inspirational book presents both philosophical and practical experiences from the 43-year pottery-making career of Robin Hopper, one of North America's most recognized ceramic artists.

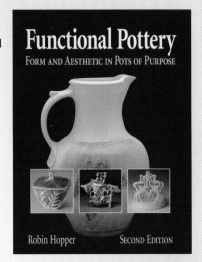

Perusing this book is like having a ceramic museum, art gallery, encyclopedia, and master potter at hand, teaching and inspiring at the same time. Beginning with a view of the historical development of pottery, the book presents a wide discussion on the aesthetics of form and design. Also addressed are the mechanics of making and the practical solutions to functional design in pots for eating, drinking, storage, pouring, cooking, serving, and pots for rituals and contemplation. The recent work and short biographies of 16 internationally recognized ceramic artists are showcased in the Portfolio section.

- Practical and philosophical discussions on pots of purpose
- Portfolio section includes work of 16 leading ceramists

FPOT2 $44.95
Published January 2000